HISTORY OF THE DELHI CORONATION DURBAR

HISTORY OF THE DELHI CORONATION DURBAR

HELD ON THE FIRST OF JANUARY 1903 TO CELEBRATE THE CORONATION OF HIS MAJESTY KING EDWARD VII EMPEROR OF INDIA

BY STEPHEN WHEELER

GYAN

Published by

Gyan Publishing House
5, Ansari Road
Daryaganj, New Delhi-110002
Phone: 011-47034999, 9811692060
E-mail: books@gyanbooks.com

Distribution Network
gyanbooks.com
India, USA, Canada, UK, Australia

ISBN: 978-93-6208-557-3 (PB)
First Published, 1904

2nd Impression 2024

Printed at: Gyan Press, Delhi.

HISTORY OF THE DELHI CORONATION DURBAR
Author: STEPHEN WHEELER

HISTORY OF THE DELHI CORONATION DURBAR

HISTORY OF THE DELHI CORONATION DURBAR

HELD ON THE FIRST OF JANUARY 1903
TO CELEBRATE THE CORONATION OF
HIS MAJESTY KING EDWARD VII
EMPEROR OF INDIA

COMPILED FROM OFFICIAL PAPERS BY ORDER OF
THE VICEROY AND GOVERNOR-GENERAL OF INDIA

BY STEPHEN WHEELER

WITH PORTRAITS
AND ILLUSTRATIONS

1904

PREFACE

THE task of writing an authoritative account of the great celebrations held at Delhi in December and January, 1902–3, in honour of the Coronation of Edward VII., King and Emperor, was entrusted to Mr. Stephen Wheeler, whose father had voluntarily charged himself with a somewhat similar undertaking in the case of Lord Lytton's Assemblage for the Proclamation of the Imperial title twenty-six years before. There are material differences, however, between the narratives, as there were between the occasions. The much greater scale of the proceedings in 1903, the amount of preparation devoted to them, the attention that they excited throughout the world, and the success by which they were crowned, seem to demand a more exhaustive and authoritative record than was attempted in 1877. If the Delhi Durbar be ever repeated, such an account will be invaluable to those who are responsible for its organisation. If, as seems more likely, it remains without imitator or rival, it is all the more desirable that its history should be written as that of a series of solemnities and pageants that closed the page of the India of the past—the India of ancient chivalry and romance, of barbaric finery and mediæval pomp—and appropriately opened the new chapter, more prosaic, but also more progressive, of the Twentieth Century. In either case it is thought that there will be but few among those who took a prominent part, whether as actors or guests, in the principal scenes, who will not welcome an authentic account of them. Accordingly, the Government of India placed at the disposal of Mr. Stephen Wheeler the whole of the papers and official information in their possession, and the proofs of the various chapters, as successively written, have been despatched to India for final revision. While this process may have somewhat delayed the production of the volume, it will, it is thought, be more than justified by the greater accuracy that may now be predicated of the entire work, and that is especially desirable in the case of a narrative involving so much detail and so dependent upon precise reference to persons and facts. At the same time it is hoped that this book will be found to contain much more than an official record in the narrower sense of the term ; for an attempt has been made to give information not easily obtainable elsewhere, to portray the broader impressions and to grasp the wider aspects of the Delhi ceremonial, and not merely to expand or illustrate the dry pages of official Gazettes.

It was, indeed, these larger aspects that lent its chief importance to the Delhi Durbar. Those who went there thinking that they were merely to witness a show realised that they were assisting in a great ceremonial. People either in India or outside it who only regarded India as a portion of the burden of empire which Great Britain has, whether consciously or unconsciously, assumed, realised, perhaps for the first time, the magnitude and splendour of the responsibility, and the dynamic force that it must exercise in the future history of the world. Above all, those who talk lightly of an alien yoke, as though this could be easily imposed upon three hundred millions of human beings, learned, in the demonstrations that attended the Coronation of the first English Emperor of India, how profoundly the blessings of that rule are recognised by this vast collection of humanity, how genuine is the loyalty towards the British throne that is felt by all its classes, from the Prince of ancient lineage to the humble peasant, and how deeply the proceedings were affected by the personality of the late Queen-Empress Victoria, everywhere known in India as the mother of her people, and scarcely less by that of her son, the reigning Sovereign, King Edward VII., to commemorate whose happy succession these imposing celebrations were designed. The Delhi Durbar did much to bring the Princes and peoples of India together. But it perhaps did even more to bring both of them home to the knowledge of the world, and to the sympathy and regard of the British race.

CONTENTS

CHAPTER I

INTRODUCTION

CHAPTER II

THE STATE ENTRY INTO DELHI

CHAPTER III

THE GOVERNMENT IN CAMP

CHAPTER IV

THE PRINCES AND NOBLES OF INDIA

CHAPTER V

THE EXHIBITION OF INDIAN ARTS

CHAPTER VI

THE IMPERIAL DURBAR

CHAPTER VII

TWO STATE CEREMONIES

CHAPTER VIII

IN THE PALACE OF THE GREAT MOGHUL

CHAPTER IX

THE ARMY AT DELHI

CHAPTER X

SPECTACLES, INTERLUDES, ASSEMBLIES

CHAPTER XI

LOCAL CELEBRATIONS

CHAPTER XII

CONCLUSION

OFFICIAL PAPERS

APPENDIX I

APPENDIX II

APPENDIX III

CONTENTS

APPENDIX IV

APPENDIX V

APPENDIX VI

APPENDIX VII

APPENDIX VIII

APPENDIX IX

ILLUSTRATIONS

PORTRAITS

PHOTOGRAVURES BY MESSRS. WALKER & COCKERELL

HALF-TONE ENGRAVINGS

MAPS, PLANS, ETC.

His Excellency Lord Curzon of Kedleston, P.C., G.M.S.I., G.M.I.E.,
Viceroy and Governor General of India

CHAPTER I

INTRODUCTION

THE accession of His Most Gracious Majesty, King Edward VII., Emperor of India, was proclaimed at St. James's Palace on Thursday, January 24th, 1901, two days after the death of Queen Victoria. The news of this mournful event had already been borne by the telegraph to the utmost limits of the Empire; and nowhere had it aroused deeper regret or evoked a sincerer outburst of public sorrow, than at the Courts of Indian Princes, and in the territories under the British Indian administration. His Excellency the Viceroy, Lord Curzon, who had sent a telegram to the King-Emperor, expressing the unaffected grief of all classes in India at the death of a Sovereign, "who was revered as a mother," received from His Majesty the following reply:

> I recognise the affection and loyalty inspired by Queen Victoria in all classes of Her subjects in India by the wisdom and justice of Her long reign and Her earnest personal solicitude for their welfare. I am deeply touched by the universal sorrow evoked by Her death, and desire that My acknowledgments of the homage tendered to Me on My accession may be made known to the Chiefs and people, whose country I have seen, in whose attachment to the Throne I have full confidence, and whose prosperity and happiness will always be to Me of the highest interest and concern.

But if the death of the Queen-Empress Victoria had nowhere been more deeply lamented, it is not less true that nowhere was the accession of His Majesty the King-Emperor, Edward VII., hailed with more fervent loyalty than throughout his Indian dominions. To many of the ruling Chiefs, and to no inconsiderable part of the population, both in the Native States and in the British provinces, the King-Emperor was a personage whom they had seen with their own eyes when, as Prince of Wales, he had made a prolonged tour through the country twenty-five years before. Several of the Chiefs and leading men had also paid their respects to him in England, and some of them had been the privileged recipients of his hospitality. Moreover, it was felt, on all sides, that the accession of the first Emperor of India whose right was undisputed throughout the length and breadth of the Indian continent, whose title was acknowledged by Hindu and Muhammadan, by Rajput and Mahratta, by Sikh and Pathan, was properly an occasion for national rejoicing, full as it was of happy promise for the land and the people.

The memory of the Queen-Empress Victoria, and of the blessings enjoyed during her long reign, will not quickly be obliterated; but the knowledge that her place was taken by a son and successor who had elected to follow the same high paths of duty as a ruler, and who possessed the advantages, unshared by any of his predecessors on the British throne, of acquaintance with India and the Indian people, was a source of universal thankfulness and consolation. With such feelings was the news of the King-Emperor's accession received in India, where the Royal Proclamation, identical in terms with that already promulgated in London, was formally read in all the principal cities and towns, on Saturday, January 26th, 1901. On February 4th, the King-Emperor was graciously pleased to send through the Viceroy the following special Message to the Indian Princes and people:

Windsor Castle, February 4th, 1901.

Through the lamented death of My beloved and dearly mourned Mother, I have inherited the Throne, which has descended to Me through a long and ancient lineage.

I now desire to send My greeting to the ruling Chiefs of the Native States, and to the inhabitants of My Indian dominions, to assure them of My sincere good will and affection, and of My heartfelt wishes for their welfare.

My illustrious and lamented Predecessor was the first Sovereign of this country who took upon Herself the direct administration of the affairs of India, and assumed the title of Empress in token of Her closer association with the Government of that vast country.

In all matters connected with India, the Queen-Empress displayed an unvarying deep personal interest, and I am well aware of the feeling of loyalty and affection evinced by the millions of its peoples towards Her Throne and Person. This feeling was conspicuously shown during the last year of Her long and glorious reign by the noble and patriotic assistance offered Her by the ruling Princes in the South African War, and by the gallant services rendered by the Native Army beyond the limits of their own country.

It was by Her wish and with Her sanction that I visited India and made Myself personally acquainted with the ruling Chiefs, the people, and the cities of that ancient and famous Empire.

I shall never forget the deep impression which I then received, and I shall endeavour to follow the great example of the first Queen-Empress to work for the general well-being of My Indian subjects of all ranks, and to merit, as She did, their unfailing loyalty and affection.

EDWARD, R. ET I.

On November 1st, 1858, the Government of India had been directly assumed by the Crown; and in her Proclamation upon that occasion, partly written, as we know, by Her Majesty's own hand, Queen Victoria had stated in ever memorable language the principles upon which she proposed to conduct the government of India and the ties of mutual obligation that unite the Crown with the Indian Princes and people. Seventeen years later the brilliant conception of Lord Beaconsfield was responsible for a further advance in the direction of Imperial consolidation; and the Act of Parliament commonly known as the Royal Titles Bill (39 and 40 Vict. c. 10) was passed, by which the Sovereign of the United Kingdom of Great Britain and Ireland also became the first Empress of India.

The Imperial Title was assumed by Queen Victoria in a Royal Proclamation given at the Court of Windsor on April 28th, 1876. This Proclamation was published in India by Lord Lytton, Viceroy and Governor-General, on August 18th, 1876; His Excellency at the same time announcing that it was his intention, on the first day of the new year, to hold at Delhi an Imperial Assemblage, "for the purpose of proclaiming to the Queen's subjects throughout India the gracious sentiments which have induced Her Majesty to make to Her Sovereign Style and Titles an addition specially intended to mark Her Majesty's interest in this great Dependency of Her Crown, and Her Royal confidence in the loyalty and affection of the Princes and people of India." To this Assemblage were invited the Governors, Lieutenant-Governors and heads of administrations from all parts of India, as well as those Chiefs and nobles in whose persons, as Lord Lytton declared, "the antiquity of the past is associated with the prosperity of the present, and who so worthily contribute to the splendour and stability of this great Empire." The Imperial Assemblage held at Delhi on January 1st, 1877, if it was eclipsed in magnificence by the Durbar which is described in the present volume, must nevertheless be remembered as an event of deep political significance, marking, as it did, the commencement of a new chapter in the history of British India, and the final ratification of a definite theory of constitutional relationship between the Crown and its greatest dependency. It was the logical and historical corollary of Lord Beaconsfield's statesmanlike though much criticised measure of the previous year; and it brought home to the Indian public, in a way which no mere written pronouncement could have done, the nature and reality of the process by which India had become incorporated in the British dominions, and which in the course of the reign of a single Sovereign had converted the Native States from isolated and quasi-independent Powers into powerful and contented feudatories of a common Sovereign.

A further addition to the Royal Style and Titles was made by King Edward VII. during the first year of his reign; which addition, since it holds good throughout the Indian Empire, as well as elsewhere in His Majesty's dominions, must also be recorded here. In a Royal

Proclamation issued on November 4th, 1901, it was declared that, in accordance with the Royal Titles Act passed in the previous session, the Royal Style and Titles would in future run as follows, in the Latin tongue:—"Edwardus VII. Dei Gratia Britanniarum et terrarum transmarinarum quæ in ditione sunt Britannica, Rex, Fidei Defensor, Indiæ Imperator;" and, in the English tongue:—"Edward VII. by the Grace of God of the United Kingdom of Great Britain and Ireland, and of the British Dominions beyond the Seas, King, Defender of the Faith, Emperor of India."

The history of the Coronation of His Majesty the King-Emperor at Westminster on August 9th, 1902, of the grave and, for many days, alarming illness which had delayed the ceremony, of the hopes and fears that preceded, and the rejoicings that attended its ultimate celebration, does not come within the scope of the present narrative. Nine months earlier, however, *viz.*, in November 1901, the first announcement of the intention to hold a Coronation Durbar had been made in India, at a time when invitations were being issued to some of the ruling Indian Chiefs to attend the forthcoming Coronation in England. Early in 1902 the following viceregal Proclamation was published in the *Gazette of India:*

PROCLAMATION

Whereas by His Royal Proclamations bearing date the twenty-sixth day of June and the tenth day of December 1901, His Imperial Majesty King Edward VII., Emperor of India, has declared His Royal intention to celebrate the Solemnity of His Royal Coronation and that of His dearly beloved Consort the Queen upon the twenty-sixth day of June 1902, I now hereby publicly notify under this my hand and seal, as Viceroy and Governor-General of India, that it is my intention to hold at Delhi, on the first day of January 1903, an Imperial Durbar for the purpose of celebrating in His Majesty's Indian dominions this solemn and auspicious event.

To this Durbar I propose to invite the Governors, Lieutenant-Governors, and Heads of Administrations, from all parts of His Majesty's Indian dominions; the Princes, Chiefs, and Nobles of the Native States under His Majesty's protection; and representatives, both European and Native, of all the Provinces of this great Empire.

I also hereby notify that I shall forthwith issue such orders in Council as may be suitable to the occasion, and in conformity with the desire that will be felt by all classes of His Majesty's subjects to demonstrate their loyalty by appropriate public ceremonies and rejoicings.

Dated at Calcutta this fourteenth day of February 1902.

CURZON,

Viceroy and Governor-General of India.

It had been the Viceroy's hope that the King-Emperor might himself hold an Imperial Durbar at Delhi, and, in the presence of the Chiefs, nobles and people, crown himself Emperor of India. His Excellency explained the circumstances which had led to the suggestion being put forward, and the reason for its abandonment, in a speech addressed to the Legislative Council on September 5th, 1902:

"Of course the occasion would be made both more solemn and more historic if the King-Emperor were able to be present in person and could place the Crown of all the Indias upon his own brow. Long ago, when we were first formulating our plans, I ventured to present this aspect of the case to His Majesty. The idea was most agreeable to him, and he would have greatly rejoiced to be able to carry it out. His love for this country has always been great, and I venture to affirm that he is as proud to be the first Emperor of all India as the late Queen Victoria was to be its first Empress. But the duties of State are too absorbing to permit His Majesty to be absent from England for so many weeks as would have been required, and he was compelled to desist from gratifying a wish that would otherwise have had for him the greatest attractions."

Lord Curzon subsequently again alluded to the idea when proposing His Majesty's health at the state banquet on the night of the Durbar:

"Your Royal Highnesses, Your Excellencies, and Gentlemen, I venture to say that but one regret has filled all our minds here to-day. It is that His Majesty the King-Emperor has not been able to be present here in person to receive the homage of his loyal Feudatories and the acclamations of his Indian people. There is, indeed, no necessity for an Emperor of India to come out here to be crowned. His Majesty was our acknowledged and Sovereign Lord as soon as the Throne was vacant nearly two years ago. But India would dearly have loved to see the face of her Emperor and to listen to his voice; and some day we may hope that, as time and distance continue to dwindle under the magic finger of science, it may be found possible for the Viceroy on some future occasion like the present to be eliminated as a superfluous phantom, and for the real figure to appear upon the scene."

It may be that some day the prediction of the Viceroy will be realised, and that India will witness the Coronation of her own Emperor. Should such an event ever take place, it may confidently be anticipated that it will be attended by such an outburst of loyalty and enthusiasm as has never before been known in the country.

On the present occasion, for the reasons already stated, the idea was incapable of fulfilment; but in the course of the autumn of 1902 all India was delighted by the news that His Majesty had specially deputed his brother, His Royal Highness the Duke of Connaught, and the Duchess of Connaught, to represent the Royal family at the forthcoming Durbar. This intention was a proof of the keen personal interest taken by His Majesty in the ceremony; and it was also a source of widespread gratification throughout the country, where Their Royal Highnesses, who had spent many years in India, were already widely known and universally beloved. His Majesty's nephew, the Grand Duke of Hesse, was also present at Delhi during the Durbar celebrations, as the Viceroy's guest.

From an early date it was clear that the Imperial Durbar of January, 1903, would be on a vastly larger scale than the Imperial Assemblage held by Lord Lytton. The bounds of the Empire had been considerably enlarged since 1877; there had been a great spread of railway communications, rendering travelling at once easier and less costly; above all, in strict fulfilment of Lord Lytton's forecast, there had been a wonderful growth and diffusion of the Imperial spirit. Only sixty-three ruling Chiefs attended the Imperial Assemblage of 1877; while it was anticipated that as many as a hundred would accept the invitations to the Coronation Durbar. The number of retainers accompanying the Chiefs would, of course, increase in the same proportion. Durbaris ranking below the rulers of Native States, titular and subordinate Chiefs, noblemen and native gentlemen of distinction, were also certain to come in far greater numbers. Similar reasons were likely to produce a much larger influx of the English community in India, while the increased facilities of communication with Europe and with foreign countries, and the ever-widening interest excited by India and its problems throughout the civilised world, warned the organisers of the Durbar to be prepared for that which was the most striking omission in 1877, namely, the presence of outside visitors in great and unusual force. As will presently be seen, these expectations, in the case of all the classes to whom reference has been made, were more than fulfilled; and it was to the conception of the Durbar from its first initiation as a ceremony destined to be on an unparalleled scale, both of numbers and importance, that the absence of subsequent failures or disappointments was mainly due.

The appearance of the Viceroy's Proclamation was immediately followed by the issue of invitations to the forthcoming ceremony to all the leading officials of the British Government in India. Those to the Governors of Madras and Bombay were couched in the following terms:

Fort William, the 15th February, 1902.

YOUR EXCELLENCY,

The accompanying Proclamation published in the *Gazette of India*, dated 15th February 1902, will inform you that it is my intention to hold at Delhi, on the 1st of January 1903, an Imperial Durbar in order to celebrate the Coronation of His Imperial Majesty the King-Emperor.

To this assemblage I invite your attendance.

It is my hope that you may be able to provide for the carrying on of your administration during your brief absence from the Presidency.

I am anxious that you should bring with you to the Durbar a limited number of the Members of your Administration, officials of high rank, native noblemen and gentlemen, and heads of representative bodies in Madras (or Bombay), so that by their presence the dignity of the occasion may be enhanced.

Of the persons whom you will bring with you, it will doubtless be convenient that

Field-Marshal H.R.H. the Duke of Connaught.
K.G., K.T., K.P., G.C.B., G.C.S.I., G.C.I.E., etc.

some should be treated as your personal guests. These will be accommodated in a camp set apart for your own convenience. Other officials and gentlemen will receive accommodation in a separate but neighbouring provincial camp. The entire camp equipage, including tents, for both camps, should be sent under your orders to Delhi. I shall be glad to receive as early as possible a list of the persons of either category whom you would propose to invite, with an approximate estimate of the total number of persons who may be expected to attend.

You will shortly receive from the Foreign Department of my Government a copy of the Orders in Council that will be issued, containing full information and instructions as to the details of the arrangements that are to be made, and as to the question of the provision and allocation of the requisite funds.

You will receive a separate communication regarding the invitations that will be addressed to the ruling Chiefs in your province.

I have, &c. &c.,

CURZON,

Viceroy and Governor-General of India.

Similar letters, *mutatis mutandis*, were addressed to Their Honours the Lieutenant-Governors of Bengal, the North-West Provinces and Oudh (since designated the United Provinces of Agra and Oudh), the Punjab, and Burma, to the Chief Commissioners of Assam and the Central Provinces, the Residents in Hyderabad and Mysore, and the Agents to the Governor-General in Central India, Rajputana, Baluchistan and the North-West Frontier Province.

Of the invitations to ruling Chiefs in India, upwards of fifty were issued by the Viceroy himself, being addressed to Chiefs whose position entitles them to this privilege. The remainder were sent through the various Local Governments. To the Imperial Assemblage at Delhi in 1877, forty-two ruling Chiefs had been summoned by Lord Lytton; the Local Governments inviting twenty-one. All the principal Indian Feudatories then bidden to meet the Viceroy were included in the invitations issued in 1902; but in addition to these, Lord Curzon invited the attendance of a number of rulers on the outskirts of the Empire, who, in 1877, were either beyond the sphere of British influence or were not considered important enough to merit the honour. Among these may be mentioned the Shan Chiefs from the borderlands of Burma and Siam; the chieftains from the North and North-West Frontiers such as the Mehtar of Chitral, the Mirs of Hunza and Nagar, the Khan of Nawagai, and the Nawab of Dir; the potentates of the Aden Protectorate, namely, the Sultans of Shehr and Mokalla and of Lahej, and the Amir of D'thali.

In issuing the invitations to the Imperial Durbar it seems desirable to point out, in view of misrepresentations that found currency in some quarters at the time, that the utmost care was taken to avoid even the semblance of compulsion. Every Chief clearly understood that it was open to him for any good reason to decline the invitation; while to the poorer Chiefs, whose territories had been seriously affected by the famines and scarcity of the three preceding years, intimation was privately conveyed that the summons was in no sense an order. In other cases, the invitation was purposely withheld; either because the Chief was a minor—though certain minors were asked to attend—or because there were independent circumstances rendering his presence undesirable or inconvenient. Of ruling Chiefs entitled to a salute, seventeen were not invited at all; while as many more, after having been asked, were excused from attending, mainly on the ground that they could not well afford the expense. Of minor Chiefs not entitled to a salute, only a few were asked or expected to come to Delhi, since in most cases it was felt that an undue strain might thereby be placed on their finances. For the benefit of all the Chiefs, the Government, as in 1877, imposed a salutary restriction on the number of retainers whom they might bring with them. Chiefs of the first class were allowed to have retinues of 500 men, exclusive of menials; Chiefs of the second class, 400 men, and so on. In 1877, 25,000 retainers came under these conditions; but in 1903, the number, of course, was very much greater.

The following letter was addressed by His Excellency the Viceroy to the Nizam of Hyderabad, the Maharaja of Mysore, the Gaekwar of Baroda, the Maharaja of Jammu and Kashmir, the Khan of Kalat, the Maharajas of Gwalior, Indore, Jaipur and Jodhpur, the Maharana of Udaipur, and the Maharaja of Travancore:

Calcutta, the 19th March 1902.

MY HONOURED AND VALUED FRIEND,

I have the pleasure to inform Your Highness that it is my intention to hold an Imperial Durbar at Delhi on the 1st January, 1903, for the purpose of celebrating, in a befitting manner, the solemn event of the Coronation of His Imperial Majesty King Edward VII., Emperor of India, and of his dearly beloved Consort the Queen.

In instructing me to hold this Durbar, His Majesty has desired it to be made known that he is anxious to afford to all the Princes and Chiefs of India the opportunity of testifying their loyalty to his throne and person, and that attendance thereat will be regarded by His Majesty as equivalent to presence at his Coronation in England.

I enclose, for Your Highness's information, a copy of the announcement which I have caused to be published in the *Gazette of India* and I request the honour of Your Highness's presence on this auspicious occasion.

Due notice will be given through the usual channel of the particular date at which Your Highness will be expected at Delhi.

I desire to express the high consideration which I entertain for
Your Highness, and to subscribe myself
Your Highness's sincere Friend,
CURZON,
Viceroy and Governor-General of India.

The replies of the Nizam of Hyderabad and the Maharaja of Mysore were as follows:

YOUR EXCELLENCY,

I have the pleasure to acknowledge the receipt of Your Excellency's kind letter, dated March 19th, 1902, with enclosure, regarding the Imperial Durbar proposed to be held at Delhi on the 1st January, 1903, for the purpose of celebrating, in a befitting manner, the solemn event of the Coronation of His Imperial Majesty King Edward VII., Emperor of India, and of his dearly beloved Consort the Queen.

I have the honour to accept the kind invitation Your Excellency has extended to me on behalf of His Majesty, and I hope to have the pleasure of meeting Your Excellency on the date which may eventually be fixed.

I remain,
Your Excellency's sincere Friend,
MIR MAHBUB ALI KHAN,
Nizam of Hyderabad.

PURANI HAWAILI, HYDERABAD, DECCAN,
April 10th, 1902.

MY HONOURED AND VALUED FRIEND,

I have been honoured with Your Excellency's kind invitation to be present at the Imperial Durbar to be held at Delhi on the 1st of January next. The Coronation of His Majesty King Edward VII. is looked forward to with the greatest interest throughout India, and the Proclamation at that famous place of His Majesty's accession as Emperor of India cannot but recall to mind those great historical Assemblies which have met there in the past for similar celebrations. The occasion will be one of great rejoicing in the Native States, and will afford to the Princes of India a welcome opportunity of paying their homage to His Majesty the Emperor so worthily represented by Your Excellency.

To me personally it will be a duty as pleasing as honourable to take part in this glorious and memorable function. I rejoice that I have been thus afforded another opportunity of following the example of my forefathers and testifying once more personally my devotion and attachment to the British Throne.

With feelings of high consideration and respect,

I beg to subscribe myself,
Your Excellency's sincere Friend,
KRISHNA RAJA WADIYAR,
Maharaja of Mysore.

OOTACAMUND,
May 7th, 1902.

His Highness the Gaekwar of Baroda had replied, even more promptly, with a formal acceptance of the invitation. The Maharaja of Jammu and Kashmir, in a letter dated April 4th, 1902, wrote that he would be highly pleased to attend the Durbar, adding:

I need hardly say that for us Indians it will be an occasion of great rejoicing as well as of a happy realisation while we, expressing in public our innermost sentiments of loyalty and devotion to the British Crown, shall feel the kind and fatherly attachment which His Imperial Majesty, like his august mother, Her late Majesty the Queen-Empress of blessed memory, holds to his Indian subjects, protectorates and allies, and the kind interest he takes in their welfare and prosperity. It may not be out of place to add that a meeting together of the Princes and Chiefs of India on so noble an occasion cannot but remind them of the days when it was the custom with the Emperors and Overlords of the land to gather together all the Rajas and Maharajas round their loving yet awe-inspiring persons as they celebrated an Ashwamedha or a Rajasuya—occasions which decidedly did more than aught else to win the hearts and affections of the rulers who had the privilege of being under their protection.

A formal acceptance of the invitation was received from His Highness Beglar Begi Mir Sir Mahmud Khan, Khan of Kalat. The *kharita* in which the Maharaja of Gwalior responded to the Viceroy's letter was typical of the writer's outspoken loyalty. The following is an abstract translation:—

May the portals of happiness and joy, and the means of pleasure and felicity, remain open to His kind and gracious Excellency, the store of boundless good qualities.

In these happy days when numerous gates of pleasure and success are open to the well-wishers of the British Government, and thousands of means are available for the realisation of objects of their desire, I have received your very kind letter, through my esteemed friend Major C. Pritchard, Resident at Gwalior, containing gladdening and soul-inspiring news. I am informed of your intention to hold an Imperial Durbar at Delhi on the 1st January, 1903, for the purpose of celebrating the Coronation of His Imperial Majesty, Emperor Edward VII., and his Consort the Queen (may their prosperity be perpetual).

Your letter further intimates that in instructing Your Excellency to hold this Durbar His Imperial Majesty the Emperor has desired it to be made known to all the Princes and Chiefs of India that this is an opportunity for them to demonstrate their loyalty to his throne and person, and that attendance at the Durbar will be regarded by His Majesty as equivalent to presence at his Coronation in England.

A copy of the announcement published in the *Gazette of India* has accompanied your letter. This letter also contains an invitation to me to attend the Durbar on this auspicious occasion, and adds that the particular date at which I shall be expected at Delhi will be communicated to me in the usual way. This letter has revived and strengthened our friendship and union; my heart has felt immense pleasure.

As the Imperial Durbar at Delhi will be held for the purpose of celebrating the Coronation of His Imperial Majesty the Emperor and his Consort the Queen (may their prosperity and glory be perpetual), it will be an occasion of the greatest happiness, and it is the bounden duty of all the well-wishers of Government to attend so magnificent a Durbar, attendance at which will confer distinction and honour. God willing, I shall, in compliance with the wishes contained in Your Excellency's kind letter, attend the Durbar, and shall have the very great pleasure of meeting you.

What more could I write?

MADHO RAO SCINDIA,

April 23rd, 1902. *Maharaja of Gwalior.*

The Maharaja of Indore, writing on May 28th, signified his loyal acceptance of the Viceroy's invitation.

The Maharaja of Jaipur, writing on May 2nd, assured His Excellency that he himself and, he hoped, all the Princes and Chiefs of India, fully appreciated "the opportunity which His Majesty the Emperor of India has so graciously accorded to testify our loyalty to his throne and person, and to express our gratitude and joy at the special mark of favour thus shown to us."

The Maharaja of Jodhpur wrote:

MY MOST VALUED AND HONOURED FRIEND,

I beg to acknowledge with many thanks the receipt of Your Excellency's kind letter inviting me to the Imperial Durbar to be held at Delhi to celebrate the solemnity of the Royal Coronation of Their Imperial Majesties the Emperor and Empress of India.

It is needless for me to add that nothing could give me greater pleasure than to cordially respond to such a kind invitation on an auspicious occasion, which is calculated to celebrate the grand and solemn event in His Majesty's Indian dominions and thereby to afford the people and Princes of India a golden opportunity of demonstrating their deep sentiments of loyalty and devotion to the august person and throne of their gracious Sovereign.

I hail this opportunity the more, as my ancestors' guiding principle has always been staunch fealty and unswerving allegiance to the British throne and which I ever hold to be my priceless heritage.

With sentiments of highest esteem and regard which I entertain for Your Excellency,

I beg to remain,
Your Excellency's sincere friend,
SARDAR SINGH,
Maharaja of Jodhpur.

MUSSOORIE,
April 23rd, 1902.

The Maharana of Udaipur (Mewar), writing on August 21st, expressed his pleasure in accepting the Viceroy's invitation, but added that, if the health of his son Kunwar Bhopal Singhji showed no visible improvement before the date of the Durbar, he hoped he might be excused from leaving him.

The Maharaja of Travancore most cordially and gratefully accepted the Viceroy's invitation to Delhi, assuring His Excellency that he valued highly the privilege of testifying his attachment and loyalty to His Imperial Majesty's throne and person.

The letter of invitation addressed by the Viceroy to ruling Chiefs of the second rank was in the same terms as that sent to the Nizam of Hyderabad, save that it began, "My esteemed Friend" and ended with "I remain, with much consideration, Your Highness's sincere friend." Eighteen ruling Chiefs were thus addressed, as well as the Maharaja of Benares, who occupies a status between that of a ruling Chief and of the great zamindars of Bengal. The list comprised the Begum of Bhopal, the Maharajas of Rewa, Alwar, and Bikaner, the Maharao Raja of Bundi, the Maharaj Rana of Dholpur, the Maharawal of Jaisalmer, the Maharajas of Karauli and Kishangarh, the Maharao of Kota, the Nawab of Tonk, the Raja of Cochin, the Rao of Cutch, the Mir of Khairpur, the Maharaja of Kolhapur, the Nawabs of Rampur and Bahawalpur, and the Maharaja of Patiala. The reply of the Begum of Bhopal, dated the 11th Moharrum, 1320, anno Hegiræ (April 20th, 1902), was to the following effect:

His Excellency of high dignity, kind and gracious, bestower of favours on the supplicants, may God keep His Excellency safe and sound!

After expressing sentiments of sincerity and loyalty, I beg to state that I had the honour of receiving Your Excellency's *kharita*, dated the 19th March, 1902, together with the Proclamation issued by the Foreign Department, and that it caused me great pleasure and honour.

I have learnt that a Durbar to celebrate the Coronation of His Imperial Majesty King Edward VII., Emperor of India and England, and Her Majesty the Queen-Empress, will be held at Delhi.

I will, please God, in accordance with Your Excellency's wishes, and His Majesty the Emperor's desire, willingly, gladly, and with a sincere heart do myself the honour of attending the Durbar on the date which Your Excellency has promised to communicate to me, so that I may express and prove the well-known loyalty of my house and family towards the British Crown.

May the days of tranquillity and success attend Your Excellency!

SULTAN JAHAN,
Begum of Bhopal.

The Maharaja of Alwar, in a *kharita* dated April 30th, 1902, wrote:

His Excellency the bestower of favours and the fountain of liberality and beneficence; may His Excellency's favour continue for ever!

In these auspicious days when the tidings of joy and pleasure pour in from all quarters and shouts of felicity and happiness echo in all directions, I am highly honoured by Your Excellency's most welcome and esteemed favour conveying the happy news of the celebration, at Delhi, of the Coronation of His Imperial Majesty King Edward VII., Emperor of India, and of Her Gracious Majesty the Queen-Empress, on January 1st, 1903, and desiring me to be present on that auspicious occasion.

The happiness which this most welcome news has afforded me is beyond the range of written and verbal expressions.

May the Almighty Creator ordain that the two brilliant stars of British Sovereignty shine for ever to further enhance the prosperity and glory of the British Throne.

In compliance with Your Excellency's kind invitation, I shall be most happy to do myself, together with other well-wishers residing in my State, the honour of attending the grand Durbar.

Trusting Your Excellency will always consider me a true friend and well-wisher of Your Excellency and the Supreme Government, and will continue to honour me with kind letters.

May joyful and happy days attend Your Excellency!

JEY SINGH,

Maharaja of Alwar.

The Maharawal of Jaisalmer, whose letter of acceptance was dated May 13th, 1902, said:

It gives me the greatest pleasure to most cordially respond to such a kind invitation as Your Excellency has been pleased to extend to me, more especially as this happy and auspicious occasion of unprecedented grandeur affords a unique and a glorious opportunity to all the Princes and the people of this vast continent of India to demonstrate their deep-seated feelings of unswerving loyalty and devotion to the august person and the throne of their beloved and exalted Sovereign, the never-setting sun in whose empire is symbolical of its glory and greatness.

Allow me to add that this ancient house of Bhatis has always been foremost in its unalterable attachment and allegiance to the British Throne, and it is my guiding principle to be ever true to this sacred and glorious heritage.

The *kharita* in which the Maharaja of Kishangarh signified his grateful acceptance of the Viceroy's invitation ended with the flattering appeal, "O God, may the whole universe, from the zenith to the nadir, remain under His Excellency's control and command."

The Maharao of Kota said:

I am one of those Chiefs and Princes of India who have not had the honour and privilege of attendin g the Coronation of His Imperial Majesty King Edward VII. and of his dearly beloved Consort the Queen, and it is, therefore, most cheerfully that I avail myself of this favourable opportunity of testifying, in some measure, my loyalty to the throne and person of His Majesty the Emperor, who has graciously been pleased to express his desire that attendance at this Durbar will be regarded by him as equivalent to presence at his Coronation in England.

The other replies from the Chiefs of this class conveyed a brief but cordial acceptance of His Excellency's invitation.

The letter of invitation addressed to twenty-five ruling Chiefs of the third order of dignity began, in accordance with the traditions of official etiquette, "My friend," and ended "I remain, Your Highness's sincere friend." The Chiefs thus addressed were the Maharajas of Charkhari, Chhatarpur and Datia, the Rajas of Dhar and Dewas (senior and junior Branch), the Nawab of Jaora, the Maharaja of Orchha, the Rajas of Rajgarh and Rutlam, the Maharaja of Samthar, the Maharawals of Dungarpur and Partabgarh, the Raj Rana of Jhalawar, the Maharao of Sirohi, the Maharajas of Kuch Behar and Sikkim, and the Rajas of Hill Tippera, Jind, Nabha, Kapurthala, Mandi, Sirmur, Faridkot, and Manipur.

From these Chiefs, likewise, came letters in which the writers expressed their great gratification at being asked to the Durbar, and, with one or two exceptions, they cordially accepted the invitation. The Raja of Rajgarh wrote:

> To take part in this happy and auspicious ceremony, I consider, is a source of worldly prosperity for the well-wishers of the Crown and Throne and a cause of gratification to the Master of the Empire, who, being the Sovereign of the time, is owed homage and allegiance by his people.
>
> I, the humble one, shall, therefore, enjoy the distinction of attending this Durbar, which is an origin of blessings.
>
> Further, may the pearl of wealth and good fortune, and the star of magnificence and bounty, continue with the aid of the Almighty always bright and luminous.

"I esteem it," the Raja of Rutlam wrote, "both a great honour and a privilege to be allowed to pay my homage to our august Sovereign, the King-Emperor, on this auspicious occasion, and to show the feelings of loyalty and of profound affection and devotion which I cherish towards His Majesty's person and throne."

The Maharao of Sirohi, in accepting the Viceroy's invitation, wrote:

> I may be permitted to add that I would lose no opportunity in my power of showing my loyalty and devotion to the British Crown, and my esteem and regard for Their Imperial Majesties' august persons at the sacrifice of all that I possess and even of my life, humble though I am.

The reply received from the Maharaja of Sikkim was elegantly addressed, "To the lotus feet of my noble friend, His Excellency the Viceroy and Governor-General of India," and was as follows:

The humble Thutob Namgyal, Maharaja of Sikkim, most respectfully begs to state that he very gratefully rejoices at the receipt of an invitation to be present at the Coronation ceremony of Their Most Gracious Majesties the King-Emperor and Queen-Empress to be held at Delhi, which Your Excellency has so graciously sent him. He from the fulness of his heart welcomes the opportunity so graciously offered him to do himself that great honour of attending the Coronation ceremony.

With a silk scarf as enclosure, he presents this letter on an auspicious day (dated the 1st of the third month of Water-Tiger year) from his residence Gangtok Phodang.

THUTOB NAMGYAL,

Maharaja of Sikkim.

The Raja of Nabha, in a *murasila*, dated June 14th, 1902, said:

I do myself the honour of addressing His Excellency the gracious and of exalted position, whose stirrup is the vault of Heaven, the benefactor of the people of the world; may His Excellency's good fortune continue for ever.

I have the honour to very gladly acknowledge the receipt of Your Excellency's letter, dated 19th March, 1902, together with a copy of the Proclamation expressive of Your Excellency's intention to hold an Imperial Durbar at Delhi on the 1st of January, 1903, for the purpose of announcing to the people of India the performance of the ceremony of the Coronation of His Majesty King Edward VII. and of Her Majesty the Queen of Great Britain and India, and inviting me to that Great Durbar. I am heartily thankful for the kindness shown towards me on this occasion, and cannot refrain from expressing regret at my inability from weakness to attend the Coronation Durbar in London. My prayer now is that I may keep health in order that I may be able to acquire the honour of attending the Durbar at Delhi.

I hope that Your Excellency will be pleased to consider me as one of the hearty well-wishers and dependants of the illustrious and magnificent Government and will do me the honour of writing letters of kindness and favour.

HIRA SINGH,

Raja of Nabha.

The rulers of two States which are in close political connection with India, also received invitations, namely, the Amir of Afghanistan and the Maharaja Dhiraj of Nepal, to whom, on May 20th, 1902, the Viceroy

H. E. Maharaja Chandra Shamsher Jang, Rana Bahadur.

Prime Minister of Nepal.

wrote, announcing his intention of holding an Imperial Durbar in honour of the Coronation, and inviting them to come to Delhi as guests of the Indian Government. The Amir of Afghanistan was unable to leave his country so soon after his accession, but nominated his cousin, Colonel Muhammad Ismail Khan, the Afghan Envoy with the Government of India, to represent him. The reply received from Sri Maharaja Dhiraj Prithvi Bir Bikram Jang Bahadur, Shah Bahadur, Shamsher Jang, the Ruler of Nepal, dated June 11th, 1902, was as follows:

His Excellency the most gracious of the times, and the refuge of his followers; may his favours continue for ever!

I have received with great pleasure Your Excellency's letter, dated the 20th May, 1902, inviting me to the Imperial Durbar which Your Excellency will hold at Delhi on 1st January, 1903 in connection with the Coronation of His Most Gracious Majesty King Edward VII. Emperor of India; but I regret to say that for certain reasons I am unable to avail myself of the invitation. During the sixteen generations the throne of Nepal has been occupied by my dynasty, it has been enjoined (by an edict) on every occupant not to go out of his country into that of another, and whoever has transgressed this has not prospered. When my great-grandfather, Sri (5) Maharaja Dhiraj Rajendra Bikram Shah, went to Benares, all his officers, nobles and subjects were greatly displeased with him and dethroned him.

Although I am unable to attend the Imperial Durbar, which I regret very much, I hope Your Excellency will continue your kindness and favour towards me and excuse me.

As I cannot come, my Prime Minister and Marshal, Maharaja Chandra Shamsher Jang, Rana Bahadur, Thong, Lui Pim Ma Ko Kang Wang Sian, whom I consider my other self, will wait upon Your Excellency at the Durbar. I hope that, with your usual kindness and favour, and considering the firm friendship which exists between the two Governments, Your Excellency will show him the honour and consideration due to his high position. I trust Your Excellency will always consider me as desirous of Your Excellency's good health and will gratify me by keeping me informed of the same.

I hope His Excellency will be pleased to consider me always engaged in prayers for His Excellency's good health, and will gladden my heart by writing and communicating to me the good tidings of the same.

What more can I write?

PRITHVI BIR BIKRAM,
Maharaja Dhiraj of Nepal.

Thus the *de facto* head of the Nepalese Government was present with the other Princes of India at Delhi.

The Sultan of Maskat, Seyyid Feisal bin Turki, whose relations with the Government of India are of a peculiarly intimate character, was also invited. He also was unable to leave his dominions; but in a letter dated September 2nd, 1902, he begged that he might be allowed to send his son Timur, with one or two high officials. His Highness added:

> It has given me great pleasure to hear of the recovery of His Majesty, the great King, and of the Coronation of Their Majesties, the King and the Queen in London. I pray God to grant them a long life, and to keep permanent the British Government, and grant prosperity to it.
>
> I express my extreme gratitude for Your Excellency's friendship and help to me. Please God, my friendship to the British Government will ever increase as the years roll on.

Invitations were also sent to the Courts of Persia, Siam, and Japan, the Indian Empire having friendly intercourse with each of these independent States, and being actually contiguous with two of them. His Majesty the Shah of Persia was asked to depute a representative to attend the celebrations at Delhi, as the guest of the Indian Government; and it was thought probable that he would desire to appoint a special envoy. Persia and India, as the Viceroy pointed out, when writing to the English Minister at Teheran, have a common frontier for several hundreds of miles, and the ancient friendship between the British and Persian Governments renders it desirable that the two nations should lose no opportunity of extending their respective knowledge of each other's circumstances and interests. In view, however, of the fact that a special envoy from Persia had already attended the Coronation in London, the Shah was not directly represented at Delhi.

His Majesty the King of Siam, to whom the Viceroy sent a personal invitation, likewise considered, as Prince Devawongse Varoprakar, the Foreign Minister, told Mr. Archer, His Majesty's Chargé d'Affaires at Bangkok, that Siam had been duly and properly represented at the Coronation in London by His Royal Highness the Crown Prince; and His Majesty was unable therefore to accept the invitation for himself, but he had great pleasure in deputing General Chow Phya Surawongse, his principal Aide-de-Camp, to represent him at the Durbar.

The invitation to a Japanese envoy was a new departure, to which no small importance was attached by the Viceroy. The alliance into which the two nations had recently entered for the defence of their common interests in the Far East had evoked the liveliest satisfaction in India; and the Viceroy drew attention to the existence of this feeling when inviting the Japanese Government to depute a representative to attend the celebrations at Delhi. The Government of His Imperial Majesty the Emperor of Japan, gladly reciprocating these feelings, selected General Baron Oku, one of their most distinguished commanders, for the mission; and the General, accompanied by Major Jui, Captain Ito and Lieutenant Udaka, not only attended the Durbar, but also availed himself of an invitation to witness the military manœuvres which preceded it.

In another way, also, the Viceroy desired to furnish a novel and important demonstration of the increasing unity of the Empire and of India's position within it. The South African Colonies and the Commonwealth of Australia were for the first time invited to send representatives to an Indian celebration. Writing in July 1902, to Lord Milner, High Commissioner of South Africa, and Administrator of the Transvaal and Orange River Colony, the Viceroy said:

> The occasion will be one that will primarily interest the inhabitants of this country. At the same time the connection between all parts of the British Empire is now so close, and their future is so intimately interwoven, that what affects the one cannot be ignored by the other. Particularly is this the case with regard to India and South Africa. In the future they cannot fail to be brought into more direct relations of politics, strategy, and trade; and it will be of common advantage that the statesmen of South Africa should know something at first hand of the greatest Eastern dependency of the British Crown.

In view of these considerations, the Viceroy hoped that the High Commissioner would depute some one to represent South Africa at the Durbar; and eventually, Sir Richard Solomon, Advocate-General for the Transvaal, was charged with the mission.

In his letter to Lord Hopetoun, the Governor-General of the Commonwealth of Australia, the Viceroy, after extending a similar invitation, alluded to the fact that the Government of India had despatched an Indian military contingent to take part in the inauguration ceremonies of the Australian Commonwealth in 1900, and added that it would give the Government of India great pleasure to return this act of hospitality, and to welcome the brave representatives of the sister part of the Empire who have recently rendered such splendid service to the Crown. The Federal Ministers replied that, as the Commonwealth had already been represented at the Coronation in London by a military contingent, and as any such force that might be sent to India would be of comparative insignificance in so great an army as would be assembled at Delhi, they felt bound, though with reluctance, to decline the invitation in so far as it concerned the military forces of the Commonwealth. They gladly availed themselves, however, of the invitation to send a representative, and this important duty was entrusted to Sir Richard Baker, President of the Federal Senate.

The Governor-General of Portuguese India and the Governor of the French Establishments in India cordially accepted the invitations addressed to them by the Viceroy. His Excellency Colonel Sir Eduardo Augusto Rodrigues Galhardo, K.C.I.E., Governor-General of Portuguese India, intimated in his reply that, in addition to the gratification it would afford him to be present at the Coronation Durbar, he would be most happy to return the visit which the Viceroy had paid to him at Goa in 1901. His Excellency M. Victor Lanrezac, the Governor of the French Establishments in India, likewise expressed his pleasure in accepting the invitation. With the successors of Almeida and Albuquerque, Bussy and Dupleix, the Government of British India has for long maintained the most friendly relations; and the presence of the representatives of these two important foreign Powers at Delhi showed that in India as in Europe their interests are identical and their friendship sincere.

Invitations to attend the Durbar were also sent to the members of the consular body in India, and the following Consuls-General and Consuls attended and were accommodated as the guests of the Government of India in a special camp with the Indian Foreign Office staff:

Don Rafael Acquaroniy de Solis . . .	Consul for Spain at Bombay.
Mofakhames Sultan Mirza Ali Mahmud Khan	Consul-General for Persia at Bombay.
Mr. A. A. Apcar	Consul for Siam at Calcutta.
Monsieur A. de Koster	Consul for the Netherlands at Calcutta.
Viscount de Wrem	Consul-General for Portugal at Bombay.
Monsieur M. Gerard	Consul-General for Belgium at Bombay.
Mr. S. Hayashi	Consul for Japan at Bombay.
Mr. C. C. Kilburn	Consul-General for Denmark at Calcutta.
Count A. R. Massiglia	Consul-General for Italy at Calcutta.
Emin Bey Mehemed	Consul-General for Turkey at Bombay.
Mr. F. C. Pallachi	Consul for Greece at Calcutta.
General R. E. Patterson	Consul-General for the United States of America at Calcutta.
Herr E. R. Maurig von Sarnfeld .	Consul-General for the Austro-Hungarian Empire at Calcutta.
Mr. E. Voigt	Consul-General for Sweden and Norway at Calcutta.
Dr. E. A. Voretzsch	Acting Consul-General for Germany at Calcutta.

The following were prevented by illness from being present:

Monsieur Pilinski de Belty	Consul-General for France at Calcutta.
Monsieur W. de Klemme	Consul for Russia at Bombay.

Throughout the summer of 1902 the preparations continued apace. At Simla the majority of these devolved upon the Foreign Department, the Secretary of which, Mr. Hugh Barnes, was appointed by the Viceroy to be President of the Central Committee, the remaining members being Major-General G. Henry, Quarter-Master-General in India; Mr. T. Gordon Walker, Commissioner of Delhi; Lieutenant-Colonel the Hon. E. Baring, Military Secretary to the Viceroy; Mr. J. M. Campion, Chief Engineer, Punjab (who was succeeded on his retirement from the service in August 1902, by Colonel J. W. Thurburn, R.E.); Lieutenant-Colonel C. J. Bamber, I.M.S., Sanitary Commissioner of the Punjab; and Mr. F. S. Cowie, Assistant Secretary in the Foreign Department, who was Secretary to the Committee. Mr. Barnes was in daily consultation with the Viceroy, who laid down the entire plan of operations. Other Departments interested themselves in so much of the programme as fell within their sphere. At Delhi an Executive Committee was formed consisting of Colonel H. F. Lyons Montgomery, Supply and Transport Corps; Major M. W. Douglas, Deputy Commissioner of Delhi; Major H. Hudson, Assistant Quarter-Master-General; and Captain A. d'A. G. Bannerman of the Political Department, who was Secretary to the Committee; and undoubtedly the heaviest labour devolved upon these officers in carrying out the instructions that came down to them from head-quarters. By the time the summer was over, and before the Government of India had left Simla upon its annual autumn migration in October, not only had all the main arrangements been completed, but almost every detail had been provided for. Intense anxiety had been caused by the sudden illness of His Majesty the King-Emperor immediately before the date fixed for his Coronation in London on June 26th. But the Indian preparations were not for one moment relaxed; and as the news of His Majesty's rapid recovery and restoration to health arrived, they were pushed forward with renewed vigour. Arrangements were at the same time made and published, both in the English and Indian papers, for the accommodation at Delhi of the hundreds of foreign or unofficial visitors who were expected to be present, and for the entertainment of the representatives of the Press from all parts of the world, who were to be the guests of Government. Simultaneously the Supply and Transport Department concerned themselves with the gigantic organisation that fell to their sphere of duty; while the military authorities made preparations for the stationary camps at Delhi, and for the manœuvres in the neighbourhood of Delhi that were to precede the Durbar, and that were expected to engage a force of more than 37,000 men. An additional but temporary cause of anxiety was the sudden cessation of the monsoon rains at the end of July and in the beginning of August. But this was followed by a resumption of rainfall so opportune and abundant that by the commencement of September all cause for apprehension had been removed, and the Government of India could look forward with confidence to a celebration which, humanly speaking, was certain of being carried out by a happy and prosperous as well as a loyal people.

H.H. the Nizam of Hyderabad,
G.C.B. G.C.S.I.

CHAPTER II

THE STATE ENTRY INTO DELHI

"THE city and its vicinity rejoiced and were decorated like the garden of Iram, and the gates and walls were adorned with the gold tissues of Chín and the brocades of Rúm. Triumphal arches were raised, the tops whereof a strong-winged bird could not surmount; and the gleam of the lightning of the swords and the splendour of the arms suspended on all sides of them struck terror into the spirit of the beholder." Such is the account given, by a contemporary historian, of Kutb-ud-Dín Aibak's entry into Delhi, after receiving, at Ghuzni, from the hands of his suzerain, towards the end of the twelfth century, a patent conferring on him the government of Hindustan. Similar language might not inaptly be used to describe the state entry into Delhi on December 29th, 1902. The ancient city had, for months, been preparing for the reception of the Viceroy and his royal guests. While the executive committee and its army of workmen had been laying out the big encampment, the district and municipal authorities, liberally aided by the enterprise and enthusiasm of private citizens, were busily engaged in the various tasks on which depends the success of a great civic ceremonial such as the celebration of the King-Emperor's Coronation. Road making and mending, the decoration of streets and public buildings, the erection of stands and archways, police arrangements, regulations for the control of public traffic, and a hundred other details, were carefully elaborated beforehand. The thoroughness with which all this had been done was fully demonstrated on the day of the state procession from the railway station through the heart of the city.

Their Excellencies the Viceroy and Lady Curzon and Their Royal Highnesses the Duke and Duchess of Connaught reached Delhi on the morning of Monday, December 29th. The state entry was a splendid and fitting prelude to the dazzling succession of brilliant spectacles that were to give lustre to the record of the ensuing fortnight. Indeed to many it seemed, at the time, that, as a pageant, the royal and viceregal progress from the railway station in Queen's Road, along old and new streets of the Moghul capital, thronged with admiring crowds, past the red walls of Shah Jehan's palace fortress, still scarred with memories of a momentous siege, round the great cathedral mosque, and through the wealthy Chandni Chauk, could not be equalled, and still less surpassed, in the wonderful opulence and picturesque variety of its grandeur. A long troop of tramping elephants is, of course, a customary and time-honoured feature in an Indian triumph; but it may be doubted if ever before such an array of these majestic beasts, so gorgeously caparisoned, and bearing in their howdahs of gold and silver so exalted a company, had traversed the highways of an Eastern city. When Lord Lytton entered Delhi in December 1876, and, after receiving the Chiefs, mounted his state elephant to ride to his camp, the procession that followed was composed only of English officials, also on elephants — Governors, Lieutenant-Governors, and other heads of administrations, members of Council, secretaries to Government, etc. At the head and rear of the elephant procession were the troops of the viceregal Escort; but the ruling Chiefs did not accompany His Excellency. Only the elephants of native nobles below the rank of ruling Chief, which had been waiting at various points along the line of route, were allowed to fall in behind the procession as it passed.

The procession on December 29th, 1902, was on a far more imposing scale, and, at the same time, was more Asiatic in character. It is true that the viceregal establishment, in these days of special trains and state carriages and teams, no longer includes a stud of elephants for use on occasions of ceremony. His Excellency's *howdah-khana* has long since been broken up, and the animals dispersed. The army, indeed, keeps up a limited number of elephants; yet few, if any, of these can boast of tusks, or of dimensions that would lend dignity to a state pageant. Their Excellencies and Their Royal Highnesses the Duke and Duchess, with their staffs, rode accordingly upon animals which had been courteously placed at their disposal by certain of the ruling Chiefs; and though Governors, Lieutenant-Governors, members of Council and other high officials followed in carriages or on horseback, the splendour and length of the elephant progress were enhanced by the presence of the principal ruling Chiefs of India, mounted on their own animals; while the numerous elephants of their retinues joined the procession later on.

A distinguished gathering had assembled at the railway station to await the arrival of Lord and Lady Curzon and the Duke and Duchess of Connaught. The Grand Duke of Hesse, who had reached Delhi on the preceding day, was present with his staff. All the ruling Chiefs who afterwards took part in the procession were there, as well as the following:—the Jam of Las Bela, the Maharawal of Dungarpur, the Rana of Barwani, the Rao of Cutch, the Raja of Cochin, the Mir of Khairpur, the Nawab of Junagadh, the Thakur Sahib of Bhavnagar, the Rana of Porbandar, the Nawab of Cambay, the Thakur Sahib of Morvi, the Thakur Sahib of Gondal, the Sultan of Lahej, the Raja of Bariya, the Thakur Sahib of Palitana, the Amir of D'thali, the Pant Sachiv of Bhor, the Chief of Miraj (Senior), the Rajas of Nalagarh and Keonthal, the Thakur of Piploda, the Sardar of Kalsia, the Nawabs of Loharu and Dujana, Maharaja Sriram Chandra Bhanj Deo of Moharbhanj, the Shan Chiefs of Yawng Hwe, South Hsenwi, Möng Pawn and Gantarawadi; the Rajas of Sonpur, Rehrakhol, Raigarh and Khairagarh; the Mir of Hunza, Raja Sikandar Khan, son of the Mir of Nagar, and Raja Baldeo Singh of Poonch. His Excellency Maharaja Chandra Shamsher Jang, Rana Bahadur, Prime Minister of Nepal, was also present.

Her Highness the Begum of Bhopal was present, secluded from public gaze in a small coloured silk *shamiana* or pavilion, with a gold embroidered curtain, through which she could see without being seen. This had been erected on the platform the night before, on the extreme right of the line of Chiefs. Among the ladies on the platform were the Thakurani of Gondal and her daughter.

The high officials in attendance at the railway station included the Governors of Bombay and Madras with their staffs; the Lieutenant-Governors of the Punjab, Burma, Bengal and the United Provinces of Agra and Oudh, with their staffs; the Commander-in-Chief, and the Lieutenant-Generals Commanding in Bengal, the Punjab, Madras and Bombay, with their staffs; the ordinary members of the Council of the Governor-General, the Residents at Hyderabad and in Mysore; the Agents to the Governor-General in Rajputana, Baluchistan and Central India; the Chief Commissioner and Agent to the Governor-General in the North-West Frontier Province; the Chief Commissioners of Assam and the Central Provinces; the president of the Durbar central committee, the officiating Foreign Secretary, and the Commissioner of Delhi.

The band of the first battalion, Bedfordshire Regiment, was drawn up on the railway station platform; while, outside the station, west of the porch, was posted a guard of honour furnished by the first battalion, Northamptonshire Regiment (one of the corps forming the Viceroy's Escort), with the band of the regiment.

Just before half-past eleven, a flourish of trumpets from a party of trumpeters on the station bridge signalled the approach of the Viceroy's train, which steamed in, a few seconds later, in charge of Mr. Burt, manager of the Oudh and Rohilkhand Railway. As Lord and Lady Curzon stepped on the platform, the band of the Bedfordshire Regiment played the national anthem, and a royal salute of thirty-one guns was fired from a battery posted near. His Excellency was wearing a Privy Councillor's uniform, with the riband of the Star of India. Lady Curzon was attired in a costume of white and violet. After greeting the Grand Duke of Hesse and the high officials assembled on the platform, the Viceroy shook hands and exchanged salutations with the native Chiefs, the large majority of whom he already knew well. A quarter of an hour had been spent in this manner when a second flourish of trumpets from the railway bridge gave notice of the approach of the special train in which the Duke and Duchess of Connaught had come from Bombay. Travelling in the same train, which was in charge of Mr. G. Huddleston, general traffic manager, and Mr. T. R. Browne, locomotive superintendent of the East Indian Railway, were Sir Maurice FitzGerald and Colonel Weston Jarvis, equerries to His Royal Highness; Colonel the Hon. Cecil Bingham, A.D.C., and the Hon. Mrs. Bingham; Colonel J. Leslie, A.D.C., and Mrs. Leslie; Colonel Beevor, R.A.M.C., Captain the Hon. J. R. L. Yarde-Buller, A.D.C. to the Viceroy; the Hon. Mr. Edgerley, Chief Secretary to the Government of Bombay; and Colonel Lionel Herbert, 1st Central India Horse, who was attached to the staff of His Royal Highness during his tour in India, Captain A. M. Farquhar, R.N. (H.M.S. *Renown*), and Commander F. D. Gilpin-Brown, R.N. (H.M.S. *Renown*).

Their Royal Highnesses, on alighting, were received by Their Excellencies the Viceroy and Lady Curzon, the band on the platform playing the national anthem, and the guns of the battery firing a royal salute of thirty-one guns. The Duke of Connaught was in field marshal's uniform; the Duchess wore a dress of Star of India blue. The principal officials and Chiefs were then presented to Their Royal Highnesses by the Viceroy; and Lord Kitchener, the Commander-in-Chief, introduced a number of military officers to the Duke; after which the Chiefs left the station to mount their elephants. These had been drawn up, in two lines, along either side of Queen's Road, extending about 234 yards eastward from the station gate. Nearest to the gate were the elephants of the Nizam of Hyderabad and the Maharaja of Mysore, standing to the right and the left of the road as one looked eastward. Ranged beyond them were the elephants of the other Chiefs who, two by two, were to fall in after the leading pair, till the whole array, advancing eastward, should be in motion. In attendance on each elephant were parties of spearmen and mace-bearers (*chobdars*); ten such foot attendants accompanying a Chief entitled to a salute of nineteen or more guns; eight a fifteen-gun Chief, and six a Chief for whose salute only thirteen or fewer guns are fired. The elephants with their henchmen were marshalled in four sections, each in charge of a mounted attaché;

the whole of the arrangements in connection with the elephant procession being directed by Mr. P. Bramley, a district superintendent of police in the United Provinces.

His Highness the Maharana of Udaipur, owing to the illness of his son and heir, did not reach Delhi till two days after the Viceroy's arrival. His Highness the Gaekwar of Baroda, who was to have ridden in the elephant procession alongside the Nizam of Hyderabad, was prevented from being present at the Viceroy's entry, in consequence of the death of the Maharani Rudabhai, widow of the late Gaekwar, Maharaja Gunpat Rao; and he also did not arrive till December 31st. The Rao of Cutch, who was among the ruling Chiefs at the railway station, was unable to join the procession as his elephant—headstrong, an oriental chronicler might say, as Satan—had gone astray. Those of the ruling Chiefs who were not to appear in the procession were conducted by the officiating Foreign Secretary to a special stand in front of the Town Hall in the Chandni Chauk.

While the Chiefs were mounting their elephants, the Viceroy, accompanied by his royal guests and followed by the high officials, went outside the station, where His Excellency and the Duke of Connaught inspected the guard of honour of the Northamptonshire Regiment, under Major Weallens and Lieutenants Hughes and Giffard, which had presented arms as His Excellency and Their Royal Highnesses came out of the station. On the other, or east side, of the porch, their elephants were waiting. The Viceroy and Lady Curzon were to ride a lordly tusker, named "Luchman Prasad," lent by the Maharaja of Benares.

The howdah on its back was of burnished silver, with the royal arms, in gold resplendent on the side panels, and figures of Wisdom and Plenty in front, with a crown above them, while an umbrella, woven of silk and gold, overshadowed the crimson velvet seats. This stately howdah is the property of the Governor-General, and was made for the use of Lord Lytton in 1877. A scarlet velvet housing (*jhúl*), heavy and stiff with gold embroidery, hung almost to the ground. For the Duke and Duchess of Connaught, "Maula Bakhsh," an elephant belonging to the Maharaja of Jaipur, was waiting, a no less lordly animal and as

Lawrie & Co.

THE STATE ENTRY. APPROACHING THE JAMA MUSJID

richly caparisoned. The howdah for their Royal Highnesses, which was lent by the Maharaja of Bulrampur, was likewise of silver, with golden decorations in high relief; the arm at either side of the front seat being formed by a tiger springing upon a doomed antelope.

Mounting these elephants, Their Excellencies and Their Royal Highnesses, preceded by six elephants carrying their staffs, rode out of the station gate, and turning eastward along Queen's Road, passed slowly between the lines of elephants on which the ruling Chiefs were now sitting, in their state howdahs. Each pair of elephants, on opposite sides of the road, as Their Excellencies and Their Royal Highnesses came up, saluted by raising their trunks, and then fell into the line of the procession, following behind the Duke and Duchess of Connaught in double file. As the Viceroy and Their Royal Highnesses reached the end of the lines of elephants, the portion of the Escort preceding His Excellency, which had been drawn up along the road beyond, also began to move forward; while, behind the last of the ruling Chiefs, the remainder of the procession, beginning with the Grand Duke of Hesse, fell in. The order of the procession was as follows:

C. Brown, Esq., Inspector-General of Police, Punjab.

Captain G. B. H. Rice, Deputy Assistant Quarter-Master-General, Viceroy's Escort.

One squadron, 4th (Royal Irish) Dragoon Guards,
Commanded by Captain B. L. Carew.

H Battery, Royal Horse Artillery,
Commanded by Major Lecky.

Three squadrons, 4th Dragoon Guards,
Commanded by Major Woodright.

Lieutenant G. W. S. Sherlock,
Orderly Officer, Viceroy's Escort.

Major A. G. Peyton,
Deputy Assistant Adjutant-General.

Brigadier-General J. S. Collins, commanding Viceroy's Escort.

Major A. G. Maxwell, Herald.

Drummer and twelve Trumpeters.

The Viceroy's Body-guard, Major R. E. Grimston commanding.

Major-General His Highness the Maharaja of Idar, Honorary Commandant
and
Major W. A. Watson, Commandant, Imperial Cadet Corps.

The Imperial Cadets.

ON ELEPHANTS.

1st Elephant.

Aides-de-Camp to the Viceroy.

Captain R. G. T. Baker-Carr
Captain C. Wigram

2nd Elephant.

Aides-de-Camp to the Viceroy.

Captain the Hon. J. Yarde-Buller
Captain the Hon. R. Lindsay

3rd Elephant.

Aides-de-Camp to the Duke of Connaught.

Colonel J. Leslie
Colonel the Hon. C. Bingham

4th Elephant.

Aides-de-Camp to the Duke of Connaught.

Sir M. FitzGerald
Colonel L. Herbert

5th Elephant.

Walter Lawrence, Esq., Private Secretary to the Viceroy.
Colonel E. H. Fenn, Surgeon to the Viceroy.

6th Elephant.

H. S. Barnes, Esq., President of the Durbar Central Committee.
Lieutenant-Colonel the Hon. E. Baring, Military Secretary to the Viceroy.

THEIR EXCELLENCIES THE VICEROY AND GOVERNOR-GENERAL
and
LADY CURZON.

THEIR ROYAL HIGHNESSES THE DUKE
and
DUCHESS OF CONNAUGHT.

The procession of ruling Chiefs riding on elephants was marshalled in the following order:

On the Left.	On the Right.
H.H. the Maharaja of Mysore.	H.H. the Nizam of Hyderabad.
H.H. the Maharaja of Kashmir.	H.H. the Maharaja of Travancore.
Central India Chiefs.	*Rajputana Chiefs.*
H.H. the Maharaja of Gwalior.	H.H. the Maharaja of Jaipur.
H.H. the Maharaja of Indore.	H.H. the Maharao Raja of Bundi.
H.H. the Maharaja of Rewa.	H.H. the Maharaja of Bikaner.
H.H. the Maharaja of Orchha.	H.H. the Maharao of Kota.
H.H. the Maharaja of Datia.	H.H. the Maharaja of Karauli.
H.H. the Raja of Dhar.	H.H. the Maharawal of Jaisalmer.
H.H. the Raja of Dewas (Senior).	H.H. the Maharaja of Alwar.
H.H. the Raja of Dewas (Junior).	H.H. the Nawab of Tonk.
H.H. the Maharaja of Samthar.	H.H. the Maharao of Sirohi.
H.H. the Maharaja of Charkhari.	H.H. the Raj Rana of Jhalawar.
	Bombay Chiefs.
H.H. the Raja of Rajgarh.	H.H. the Maharaja of Kolhapur.
H.H. the Raja of Narsingarh.	H.H. the Sultan of Shehr and Mokalla.
Punjab Chiefs.	*Bengal Chiefs.*
H.H. the Maharaja of Patiala.	H.H. the Maharaja of Sikkim (represented by his son).
H.H. the Nawab of Bahawalpur.	H.H. the Maharaja of Kuch Behar.
H.H. the Raja of Nabha.	H.H. the Raja of Hill Tippera.
	United Provinces Chiefs.
H.H. the Raja of Jind.	H.H. the Nawab of Rampur.
H.H. the Raja of Kapurthala.	H.H. the Maharaja of Benares.
H.H. the Raja of Sirmur.	H.H. the Raja of Tehri.
	Bombay Chiefs.
H.H. the Nawab of Maler Kotla (represented by his son).	The Raja of Bansda.
H.H. the Raja of Faridkot.	The Thakur Sahib of Limri.
Assam Chief.	
H.H. the Raja of Manipur.	The Nawab of Janjira.
Burma Chief.	*Burma Chief.*
The Sawbwa of Möng Nai.	The Sawbwa of Keng Tung.

IN CARRIAGES DRAWN BY TEAMS.

His Royal Highness the Grand Duke of Hesse and staff, accompanied by a Captain's Escort of the 15th King's Hussars.

His Excellency Lord Northcote, Governor of Bombay, with Lady Northcote, and staff, escorted by his Body-guard.

His Excellency Lord Ampthill, Governor of Madras, with Lady Ampthill, and staff, escorted by his Body-guard.

IN A CARRIAGE AND PAIR.

His Honour Sir C. Rivaz, Lieutenant-Governor of the Punjab, with Lady Rivaz, and staff, accompanied by his Escort.

ON HORSEBACK.

His Excellency Viscount Kitchener, Commander-in-Chief, and staff, escorted by a squadron of mounted volunteers.

IN CARRIAGES AND PAIRS.

His Honour Sir Frederic Fryer, Lieutenant-Governor of Burma, and staff, accompanied by his Escort.

His Honour Mr. J. A. Bourdillon, Lieutenant-Governor of Bengal, and staff, accompanied by his Escort.

His Honour Sir J. D. La Touche, Lieutenant-Governor of the United Provinces of Agra and Oudh, and staff, accompanied by his Escort.

IN THREE CARRIAGES.

The Honbles. the Ordinary Members of the Council of the Governor-General.

ON HORSEBACK.

The Lieutenant-General Commanding, Bengal, and staff.

H. H. The Khan of Kalat.

The Hon. Colonel C. E. Yate, Agent to the Governor-General in Baluchistan.

Bourne & Shepherd, photo. Walker & Cockerell, ph. sc.

H. H. the Khan of Kalat, G.C.I.E.
the Jam of Las Bela, and other Baluch chiefs

Followed by Baluchi Chiefs:

Mir Kamal Khan, Jam of Las Bela.
Sardar Ghaus Bakhsh, Raisani.
Sardar Bakhtiyar Khan, Rustamzai.
Sardar Pasand Khan, Zarakzai.
Khan Bahadur Ghulam Haidar Khan, Achakzai.
Khan Sahib Baha-ud-din, Bozai.
Khan Bahadur Mir Khair Bakhsh, Marri.
Khan Bahadur Nawab Khan, Luni.
Sardar Bahadur Muhammad Akbar Khan, Jogizai.
Khan Sahib Miran Khan, Kibzai.
Sir Naoroz Khan, of Kharan.
Sardar Abdul Rashid, Shahwani.
Wadera Nur Muhammad, Bungalzai.
Khan Bahadur Yusuf Khan, Kurd.
Khan Bahadur Arbab Khudadad Khan.
Malik Sultan Muhammad Khan, Sargari.
Nawab Sir Shahbaz Khan, Bugti.
Mir Mehrab Khan, Khetran.
Zarghun Khan, Jogizai.
Malik Dewa Khan, Hamzazai.
Sardar Muhammad Ali Khan, of Chageh, etc.

The Hon. Lieutenant-Colonel H. A. Deane, Chief Commissioner and Agent to the Governor-General in the North-West Frontier Province.

Followed by Chiefs of the North-West Frontier:

The Mehtar of Chitral.
The Nawab of Dir.
The Khan of Nawagai.
Raja Jehandad Khan, of Hazara.
Raja Sher Ahmad Khan, of Hazara.
Sultan Barakat Khan, of Boi.
Khan Bahadur Arbab Muhammad Hussain Khan, of Peshawar.
Khan Bahadur Arbab Muhammad Azim Khan, of Peshawar.
Khan Bahadur Arbab Dost Muhammad Khan, of Peshawar.
Aminulla Khan, Orakzai.
Khan Bahadur Muhabbat Khan, of Toru.
Khan Bahadur Abdul Ghafur Khan, of Zaida.
Khan Bahadur Muhammad Ibrahim Khan, of Mardan.
Nawab Allahdad Khan, Saddozai, of Dera Ismail Khan.
Nawab Hafiz Abdulla Khan, Alizai, of Dera Ismail Khan.
Nawab Ghulam Qasim Khan, Alizai, of Dera Ismail Khan.
Nawab Muhammad Afzal Khan, of Kulachi.
Khan Bahadur Haq Nawaz Khan, C.I.E., of Dera Ismail Khan.

IN CARRIAGES AND PAIRS.

The Hon. Mr. J. B. Fuller, Chief Commissioner of Assam, and staff, accompanied by his Escort.

The Hon. Mr. J. P. Hewett, Chief Commissioner of the Central Provinces, and staff accompanied by his Escort.

The 11th (Prince of Wales' Own) Bengal Lancers.

From the railway station to the viceregal camp, a distance of about six miles, the roads by which the Viceroy and Their Royal Highnesses had to pass were lined with troops, disposed as follows:

First Infantry Brigade, including the 1st battalion, South Wales Borderers, 2nd battalion, Welsh Regiment, the 4th Rajputs and 32nd Punjab Pioneers—from a point one hundred yards west of the railway station, along Queen's Road to its junction with Elgin Road. At the Kauriapul Gate, nearly opposite the railway station, were posted the massed bands of the 4th and 13th Rajputs; while five hundred yards further on, at the junction of Queen and Elgin Roads, was the band of the 28th Madras Infantry.

Second Infantry Brigade, including the 2nd battalions of the Gordon and the Argyll and Sutherland Highlanders, the 23rd Punjab Pioneers and 27th Baluch Light Infantry—along the Elgin Road to a point opposite the Delhi Gate of the Fort, where the procession was to turn westward into Khas Road. The massed bands of the 2nd battalion, Yorkshire Regiment, and 1st battalion, Norfolk Regiment, were posted on the Fort Glacis near the Lahore Bastion.

Third Infantry Brigade, including the 1st battalions, of the Royal Irish Rifles and 3rd Gurkha Rifles, and the 13th Rajput Infantry—along Khas Road, round the Jama Musjid, and up Esplanade Road to a point opposite the civil hospital. The massed bands of the 2nd battalion, Welsh Regiment, and 1st battalion, South Wales Borderers, were placed north of the Khas Road, near the imperial entrance to the Jama Musjid.

A divisional battalion from the first Infantry division lined Esplanade Road from the civil hospital for a distance of about 250 yards northward.

Fourth Infantry Brigade, including the 1st battalions of the Bedfordshire and Norfolk Regiments, the 20th Punjab Infantry and 38th Dogra Infantry from the northern end of Esplanade Road to its junction with the Chandni Chauk, along the Chauk itself, to its western end, and the first 250 yards of Ahmad Pai Road. Two of the battalions lined the Chandni Chauk, the most densely crowded part of the route, the men standing not more than three yards apart, and closer still at the entrances to the side streets. Near the junction of Esplanade Road and the Chandni Chauk was posted the band of the 6th Jats; in Kauria-pul Road, near where it enters the Chandni Chauk, the massed bands of the 23rd, 32nd, and 34th Pioneers; at the clock tower opposite the Town Hall, the massed bands of the 2nd battalion, King's Royal Rifles, and the 1st battalion, Royal Irish Rifles; and at the western end of Chandni Chauk, near the Fathipuri Musjid, the massed bands of the 20th Punjab Infantry and 27th Baluch Light Infantry.

Fifth Infantry Brigade, including the 3rd battalion, Rifle Brigade, the 2nd battalion, King's Royal Rifle Corps, and the first battalions of the 2nd Gurkha Rifles and 39th Garhwal Rifles—along the northern end of Ahmad Pai Road, along Queen's Road to the entrance to the Dufferin Bridge, over that bridge and onwards to the Mori Gate. The bands of the 15th Sikhs and the 1st battalion, North Staffordshire Regiment were posted, the former at the junction of Ahmad Pai and Queen's Roads, and the latter outside the Mori Gate.

The Infantry Volunteers lined the road from the Mori Gate to Circular Road; the band of the 1st battalion, North Staffordshire Regiment being posted outside the Mori Gate.

A divisional battalion from the second Infantry division lined the route from the last-named point, along a portion of the Boulevard Road to an open space where Lord and Lady Curzon and the Duke and Duchess of Connaught were to alight from their elephants and enter the carriages here waiting for them. The massed bands of the second battalions of the Gordon and the Argyll and Sutherland Highlanders were posted to the south-west of this open space; the massed bands of the 4th Dragoon Guards, 9th Lancers, and 15th Hussars to the north-west.

Sixth Infantry Brigade, including the 2nd battalion, Yorkshire Regiment, 1st battalion, North Staffordshire Regiment, 4th Infantry, Hyderabad Contingent, and 28th Madras Infantry, along the carriage route up the Rajpur Road to the Flag-staff station on the camp railway. The band of the 4th Infantry, Hyderabad Contingent, was posted on the left of the Rajpur Road; and the massed bands of the first battalions of the 2nd and 3rd Gurkha Rifles and 39th Garhwal Rifles near the station.

The road up the Ridge to the Flag-staff tower and onwards to the viceregal camp was lined by troops from the Viceroy's Escort. At the Flag-staff tower were posted the massed bands of the 2nd battalion, Royal Munster Fusiliers and the Bengal Sappers and Miners.

The troops lining the route stood with fixed bayonets, and everywhere as the Viceroy approached, presented arms by companies, remaining at the present till Their Royal Highnesses the Duke and Duchess of Connaught had passed, and with rifles sloped till the whole of the procession had gone by. Each of the bands, also, which had been playing various programmes during the long interval of waiting, struck up the national anthem on the approach of His Excellency and Their Royal Highnesses, and again when the Grand Duke of Hesse drove past. As the procession neared the junction of the Elgin Road and the approach to the Lahore Gate of the Fort, flourishes were sounded by trumpeters on the battlements, the viceregal flag was hoisted on the Fort, and the batteries fired a royal salute of 31 guns. The flourishes, which were the same as those previously sounded from the railway station bridge, and on all subsequent occasions, to announce the arrivals of the Viceroy or His Royal Highness, were specially composed by Captain Sanford, Director of Music at the Durbar.

As the procession came to the Champ de Mars, a wide space of open ground between the Fort and the Jama Musjid, which was cleared after the Mutiny, another and striking feature of the day's celebration was carried out.

Here were drawn up the elephants ridden by the Sardars and attendants of the Indian Chiefs. Marshalled in two ranks, sixteen yards apart, to the west of Elgin Road, they faced the Fort. The front rank stood eighty yards behind the troops lining the road; but the intervening space was broken by a single line of one thousand men of the Imperial Service Troops. An interval of eight yards separated each elephant from his nearest neighbour, and the rear rank was so ordered that each gap in the front rank was covered by an animal in the rear. The order of the retinue elephants was as follows:

Rajputana.		*Central India.*	
Jaipur	4	Gwalior	15
Bundi	4	Indore	5
Kota	1	Bhopal	2
Karauli	4	Rewa	11
Bharatpur	2	Orchha	8
Jaisalmer	1	Datia	7
Alwar	9	Dhar	1
Tonk	3	Samthar	6
Sirohi	1	Charkhari	5
Jhalawar	2	Rajgarh	1
Shahpura	2	Narsingarh	1
Kashmir	6	Hyderabad	16

Punjab.

Patiala	6	Sirmur	4
Bahawalpur	2	Kapurthala	1
Nabha	6	Maler Kotla	2
Jind	5	Faridkot	2
Kalsia	2		

United Provinces.

Benares	6
Bulrampur	8
Rampur	5

Total number of retinue elephants . 166

As the elephants of the Viceroy and the Duke and Duchess of Connaught passed, the retinue elephants, whose howdahs were occupied by Sardars and attendants, saluted with their trunks; and when the whole of the main procession had gone by, and the last files of the 11th Bengal Lancers had turned into Khas Road, they started in its wake; the Rajputana elephants, in charge of Major Minchin, leading. The Central India elephants, led by Captain E. Barnes, followed, and the remainder in the order appointed, Captain Wood bringing up the rear. The marshalling of the retinue elephants, a somewhat onerous duty, was successfully superintended by Major Dunlop Smith, Political Agent for the Phulkian States and Bahawulpur.

But long before the last of the retinue elephants had begun to move, the Viceroy and the Duke of Connaught, followed by the ruling Chiefs and high officials, had reached the Jama Musjid round which the procession wound itself, in a glittering coil, its head stretching into Esplanade Road, and pointing toward the Chandni Chauk. It was from the galleries of the Jama Musjid, that its progress was viewed by the Viceroy's guests, the foreign representatives and a large number of other visitors to Delhi, who were admitted to the arcades.

A capacious stand for English spectators had also been erected in Khas Road, hard by the western entrance to the mosque. On the opposite side of Khas Road were seated rows of Indian students, from the various schools and colleges in Delhi; each group distinguished by the colour of the boys' turbans. The great staircases and gateways of the mosque were crowded with native spectators. To those assembled on the open arcades of the Jama Musjid, the approach of the procession presented a scene of unparalleled brilliance; nor could there be found in all Asia a better position whence to observe a grand and historic spectacle. Built by the Moghul Emperor Shah Jehan, the architect of the famed Taj Mahal at Agra, at a cost of ten lakhs of rupees, the spacious cathedral mosque of Delhi is a noble adjunct to his palace fortress. With its three swelling domes of white and black marble, its towering minarets of white marble and red sand-stone, its fine portals, and the elevated arcades surrounding a court-yard where, a few days before the Viceroy's entry, on the last Friday of Ramazan, thousands of the faithful had assembled for their devotions, it may justly be described, in the words of Bishop Heber, as the largest and handsomest place of Mussulman worship in India. Its galleries had been placed at the Viceroy's disposal, for the accommodation of English and other European guests, by the courtesy of the managing committee, who afterwards received from His Excellency an expression of his thanks, with a donation to the funds of the mosque.

Herzog & Higgins

THE STATE ENTRY. SCENE AT THE JAMA MUSJID

The Viceroy's personal guests, including the Duke and Duchess of Portland, the Duke and Duchess of Marlborough, the Earl and Countess of Crewe, the Earl and Countess of Lonsdale, the Earl of Durham and Lady Anne Lambton, Lord and Lady Wolverton, and many others were provided with seats in the north-eastern cupola. Other privileged spectators were admitted to the covered arcades, to the north and east of the court-yard, and to the roofs above. Among those present were General Baron Yasukata Oku, the Japanese Envoy; Sir Richard Baker, President of the Senate of the Australian Commonwealth; Sir Richard Solomon, Advocate-General of the Transvaal; His Highness the Aga Khan, etc.

The spectators who had tickets of admission to the Musjid were requested to take their places some time before the arrival of the Viceroy's train; and more than an hour had been spent in watching the crowds below, when the first boom of cannon from the saluting battery near the railway station gave the welcome signal that the interval of expectancy was about to be terminated. The second salute, for the Duke of Connaught, again broke the stillness; and, a little later, in the direction of the Fort ramparts, across the Champ de Mars, beyond the still stationary retinue elephants, cavalry were seen slowly advancing, on the far left, between the two lines of troops. Minutes went by, and the leading horsemen wheeled into nearer view, when yet another salute and the hoisting of the flag on the Fort gave notice that the elephants of His Excellency and the Duke of Connaught were abreast of the Lahore Gate. And now, moving along Khas Road, and heading straight for the imperial entrance to the Jama Musjid, by the same way that the Emperor Aurungzeb, as Tavernier records, used to come in state to the Friday service, the various sections of the procession, troops of the Escort, Viceroy and Royal Duke, ruling Chiefs, high officials, troops again, and the retinue elephants in rear, appeared, in long succession, a stately and glittering panorama of Asiatic pomp. When within a few yards of the gateway, the procession turned to the spectator's right to pass round the mosque, coming into view again on the left; and so, for the space of nearly two hours, might be watched the column advancing from the direction of the

Fort, on the one hand, and winding away towards the heart of the city on the other.

From the order of the procession already given some idea may have been obtained of the extraordinary contrasts that it presented. Dragoons and Royal Horse Artillery swept past with the finished smartness of British mounted troops. Following the Commandant of the Escort, the Herald, Major Maxwell, mace in hand, ornate in gold broidered, emblazoned tabard, and accompanied by drummer and trumpeters, recalled for a moment the chivalrous traditions of mediæval Europe. The Governor-General's Body-guard, swarthy men of great stature, in scarlet and gold uniforms, are the best mounted corps in the Indian army.

Next the Imperial Cadets, young princes and scions of the noblest families in Asia, rode proudly by, on black Australians with white leopard skin saddle-cloths; the gallant knight and Maharaja Sir Pertab Singh of Idar at their head, alongside the Commandant, Major W. A. Watson. In their elegant uniform, a cream-white coat, set off with collar, cuffs, and *cummerbund* of turquoise blue, embroidered with gold, a golden aigrette surmounting a blue turban, on which is bound with triple chain of gold the corps' cypher—"For the King"—these high-born cavaliers, in whose ranks rode five of the ruling Chiefs of India, were watched throughout the celebrations at Delhi with approving eyes and the heartiest good wishes. It was the first occasion since the institution of the corps a year before by Lord Curzon, on which they had been seen in public; and worthily they sustained the trial.

Then came, on elephants, the aides-de-camp and staff of the Viceroy and the Duke of Connaught; then the Viceroy and Lady Curzon, on "Luchman Prasad," acknowledging with lifted hand and gracious smile the salutes of the soldiery and the plaudits of the spectators; the Duke and Duchess of Connaught, whose appearance was everywhere greeted with renewed cheers that betokened not only loyalty to the brother of the King-Emperor, but affectionate regard for the soldier prince and his royal consort, both of whom India remembered so well; and then the ruling Chiefs, all glorious in apparel, and radiant with gems and marvellous tints of every

Lowrie & Co.

THE IMPERIAL CADET CORPS

orient dye. Pride was in their port, for as one Maharaja, a Rajput of the bluest blood and highest rank, avowed, the Princes of India deemed it no small honour to escort their Sovereign's representative, since what more envied privilege could be assigned to them? In their demeanour was reflected the dignity of illustrious lineage, exalted rank, and, what counts not least, of tried and proven fidelity to the paramount Power that has given peace to the land, and confidence to its people.

First after the Viceroy and their Royal Highnesses came the elephants of the Nizam of Hyderabad and the Maharaja of Mysore. The Nizam, attired in sober black, but with a diamond aigrette sparkling from his yellow turban, occupied a howdah, also yellow, of somewhat severe but elegant design, the canopy fringed with gold. His Highness's elephant was clothed in a housing of yellow velvet. The young Maharaja of Mysore wore a coat of gold brocade, diamonds in his turban, a necklace of big pearls and ruby pendant. The howdah in which the Maharaja of Travancore rode was ornamented with figures of Hindu gods and mythological monsters, curiously carved and lavishly gilt. The double dome was supported on gilt pillars. The *jhúl* was gold embroidered velvet; the saddle-cloth, purple and gold. The Maharaja himself might be distinguished by the drooping plume that nodded from his turban. Beside the Maharaja of Kashmir sat his soldier brother, Raja Sir Amar Singh, in uniform. Fantastic painting adorned the forehead and trunk of the noble beast they rode. But to note down the caparisons of each elephant in the *cortège*, the shape of its howdah, the garb of its master, would hardly be possible; nor, perhaps, would such details convey a proper idea of the ever-moving panorama. For slowly as the huge animals advanced, and although a second view was obtained when the procession, after circling the mosque, reappeared on the left, it seemed to the spectator that what he beheld must be, not so much a series of Indian Chiefs, mounted in their pride, to be scanned, as each went by, like the portraits in a picture gallery; but rather a resplendent vision of Asiatic pomp, interminably changing, in colour and arrangement, like the tints in a kaleidoscope, yet, in its general aspect, ever the same presentation of gilt and jewelled splendour, a glittering demonstration of the fabled wealth of Ind, to be viewed, not with sober discrimination, but with sheer bewilderment. The eye might rest for a moment on the figure of the Maharaja Scindia or the diamonds gleaming on his dark red coat, richly broidered in gold; on the golden furniture of the elephant that carried the Maharaja of Rewa; on the silver howdah in which the Maharaja of Bikaner rode; on the silver crocodile and peacock that adorned the forehead of the Maharaja of Karauli's elephant; or the leopards painted on the Raja of Charkhari's animal. The Nawab of Tonk was seen in a black velvet coat with the Star of the Order of G.C.I.E.; the Nawab of Bahawalpur, with huge twisted turban and long curling locks, in raiment of crimson, purple and green; the white-bearded Raja of Nabha, in a howdah of silver and crimson; the Raja of Kapurthala in a silver howdah on an elephant caparisoned in blue and white; the Maharaja of Benares, in gold embroidered coat, with a diamond necklace and pendant of emeralds worth a king's ransom; the Maharaja of Kuch Behar, riding in a howdah of gold and silver, and clad in pink brocade. But the blaze of jewels, the sheen of gold and silver embroidery, the rich tints of silk and satin, the gorgeous trappings of majestic elephants, inlaid with patines of bright gold, the variegated costumes of their riders, contrived to produce an effect that defies description.

Onward the procession swayed and surged, embracing the great mosque, with its thousands of spectators on the steps and arcades, in an immense, moving, coruscating curve. Last in the long array of Chiefs come the two Sawbwas of Keng Tung and Möng Nai from the remote Shan States of Eastern Burma, in their quaint costumes of purple velvet overlaid with gold plates, with ruffles of red gold round their necks, and head-dresses that looked like miniature pagodas. The Sawbwa of Keng Tung was accompanied by his sister the Princess Tip Atila. The two Shan Sawbwas, who had never before appeared among the ruling Chiefs of India, had bought elephants specially for the occasion.

These Asian elephants and their riders might have marched in the train of the Great Moghul; but the *cortège* of carriages and horsemen that followed was symbolic of the West and of the European Power which now holds India. The Grand Duke of Hesse, to whom an honourable position was due as the King-Emperor's nephew and the reigning sovereign of a European State, drove in a carriage and four, with postilions, escorted by Hussars. The Governors of Bombay and Madras, with their Body-guards, and the Lieutenant-Governor of the Punjab, who in his own province takes precedence of the Commander-in-Chief, followed. Lord Kitchener, mounted on his thoroughbred charger, *Democrat*, and followed by a brilliant staff, was a striking figure in the procession. Other Lieutenant-Governors, Members of Council, Chief Commissioners, and Agents to the Governor-General in the frontier Provinces followed. Side by side with Colonel Yate, Agent to the Governor-General in Baluchistan, rode the Khan of Kalat, and after them a company of wild-looking Baluch chiefs. Colonel Deane, Chief Commissioner and Agent to the Governor-General in the newly constituted North-West Frontier Province, was in like manner followed by a cavalcade of frontier chiefs.

Passing down Esplanade Row, the viceregal procession turned into the Chandni Chauk, at a point nearly opposite the Delhi Bank, once the residence of the celebrated Begum Somru; a place which has its memories, also, of the Mutiny, for on the roof of an outhouse, the manager of the Bank, Mr. Beresford, on May 11th, 1857, desperately defended himself and his family till he was overpowered. The march of the procession through the Chandni Chauk, the Silver Street of Delhi, which was thronged with Indian spectators, who also filled every window on either side, and crowded the flat roofs, was watched with intense and eager interest. The street was gaily decorated with flags and streamers; and with coloured cloths, patterned carpets and even costly shawls, hung from carved balconies, of which some were veiled with muslin curtains, that the ladies of a rich man's household might view the procession unobserved. Outside many of the shops were hung pictures of the Royal family; others displayed mottoes appropriate to the occasion. The Viceroy and the Duke of Connaught were received in this portion of the procession with cheering such as is rarely heard from an Asiatic crowd; and a buzz of sound, breaking at times into a roar, swept from one end of the crowded avenue to the other.

The tall pinnacle of the gothic clock tower, half way down the street, was the centre of a scheme of decorative festoons, and thereby lost its usual air of being entirely out of place in an Eastern city. The pillars of the Town Hall were swathed in foliage. Hardly a building along the whole length of the street lacked outward signs of loyal rejoicing. As for the people, no one who studied the earnest faces and keen glances of those who looked on, or who heard the ceaseless chatter that prevailed, could doubt that the spectacle was enjoyed to the full, and that to the thousands who had gathered in the Chandni Chauk it was the most admirable thing they had ever beheld in their lives. Every available point of observation was occupied. A number of Muhammadans were collected outside the Sonari Musjid, the little mosque with three gilt domes, in front of which, it is said, Nadir Shah, the Turkoman conqueror, sat, from morning till evening, whilst his troops wreaked a fearful vengeance on the helpless citizens. A large stand, in front of the Town Hall, was reserved for those of the ruling Chiefs who did not ride in the elephant procession. Other stands had been erected in the Chandni Chauk; and so, throughout its progress along the crowded street, the stately *cortège* was welcomed by high and low, till it turned northward, near the Fathipuri Musjid, a building erected by one of Shah Jehan's wives, on its way to the Mori Gate.

A short distance outside the walls of the city, near the intersection of the Rajpur and Kudsia Roads, the Viceroy and the Duke of Connaught halted their elephants, while the ruling Chiefs, with whom they exchanged salutations, filed past them and proceeded to their respective camps. Lord and Lady Curzon and the Duke and Duchess of Connaught then dismounted from their elephants and, entering their carriages, drove to the viceregal camp, crossing the Ridge by the road leading past the well-known Flag-staff tower. The military Escort, with the exception of the Body-guard and the Imperial Cadets, which accompanied the carriages to the Circuit House, was dismissed at the foot of the Ridge. On the arrival of the procession at the Circuit House, a royal salute of thirty-one guns was fired by a battery of Royal Artillery, and the viceregal standard was displayed from the flag-staff. A guard of honour, furnished by the 3rd battalion, Rifle Brigade, was drawn up in front of

Bourne & Shepherd

THE STATE ENTRY. SCENE IN CHANDNI CHAUK

the viceregal residence, and presented arms when His Excellency arrived. Similar compliments were paid by other guards of honour when Their Royal Highnesses the Duke and Duchess of Connaught and His Royal Highness the Grand Duke of Hesse, attended by the Viceroy, reached their camps. The procession, from the time at which it left the station, had lasted a little short of two hours.

CHAPTER III

THE GOVERNMENT IN CAMP

Its history and geographical position alike point to Delhi as the most fitting site in India for great ceremonies of State, such as attended the proclamation, by Lord Lytton, of Queen Victoria's assumption of the Imperial Title, and, twenty-six years later, the Durbar held by Lord Curzon in honour of the Coronation of the King-Emperor, Edward VII. A seat of empire from the earliest ages, Delhi, more than "Agra and Lahore of Great Mogul," may lay claim to the distinction of being the hereditary political capital of India. It was described by a Persian chronicler of the fourteenth century as, in honour and position, like the heart within the body, its provinces placed around like limbs. "Delly," says an Elizabethan traveller, "is the name of a city and province of late belonging to the great Potan [Pathan] Kings; but at this day is under the imperial crown of Industan: the city now in being is antient, large and pretty beautiful; such appearing in that variety of antick monuments and tombes of above twenty Kings and great ones there inhumed; admired by travellers, and adored by infinite troopes of superstitious Indians. Not a little famous also is that pyramid three miles distant (in old Delly, where lies buried King Homayon, grandfather to Iangheer), by fame and inscription speaking Alexander; at what tyme (as now) Delly was the mausoleum of many Potentates; now Delly is wald about but with small security; is watered by part of Ieminy [Jumna], over which we enter by a twelfve archt bridge."

An iron pillar, driven deep into the earth till it rested, the legend says, on the back of the monstrous serpent which supports the world,

Her Excellency, Lady Curzon.

commemorates in mystic inscriptions that long defied interpretation, the dominion of Hindu and Scythian dynasties. The magnificent remains of the unfinished mosque of the Kutub, the stupendous ruins of Tughlukabad, the tomb of the poet, Amir Khusru, the Kotila of Firoz Shah, and other buildings in the vicinity, still reflect the splendours of the earlier Muhammadan invaders of Hindustan. Better preserved monuments recall the deeds of conquerors and sovereigns of the same faith, but of other blood, who came after them. The mausoleum of Humayun, son and successor of the first of the Moghul Emperors, and father of the greatest of them, stands four miles south of modern Delhi, a striking example, according to Fergusson, of their skill as master builders before the vigorous originality of Akbar had been toned down into the more effeminate elegance of the Taj Mahal at Agra. Within the walls of this modern Delhi, the golden prime of the Moghuls has left its yet uneffaced record in the Jama Musjid and the Palace. Memories of the inroad of Nadir Shah, of Mahratta aggression, and the first intervention of the English, cling to streets in the city, and overshadow the plains outside; while the very stones that lie scattered about the Ridge to the north tell the story of the most eventful episode in the military annals of British India. Many and memorable are the historic associations connected with Delhi; and, if it is no longer the central seat of government, the locality is rightly selected as the meeting-place where Princes and Governors, and the people committed to their charge, assemble, at the summons of the Sovereign's representative, for the performance of a great state ceremony.

A glance at the map will indicate the locations of the various encampments in which the majority of the Indian Princes, Government officials, troops and visitors resided during the Durbar celebrations. The main or central camp, which comprised the camps of His Excellency the Viceroy, the Governors of Presidencies and Lieutenant-Governors and Chief Commissioners of Provinces, the Commander-in-Chief, etc. was pitched, as in 1877, to the west of the Ridge, on the site of the old English cantonment, thus occupying the space between the Ridge and the Najafgarh Canal. Lord Lytton's camp, however, looked toward the Ridge; whereas Lord Curzon turned the face of his camp in the opposite direction, the Ridge being at the back, and the avenues of tents opening out below it, until they were closed by the trees on the bank of the canal. Their Excellencies the Viceroy and Lady Curzon themselves resided in a new building, erected on the slope below the Ridge, and intended, after the notable house-warming which it thus received, to provide a Circuit House for the accommodation of the Lieutenant-Governor of the Punjab when on tour. The Viceroy prepared the plans for this residence, and caused it to be furnished with Indian art works and fittings which were either duplicates of those contained in the Arts Exhibition, or could not find space within the latter. After the Durbar all these objects, like so many of the contents of the main Exhibition, found willing purchasers. The exterior of the house was in a plain but dignified style; and the building, being on a rather higher elevation, furnished a very effective background to the sea of white tents below it, being itself backed by the eminence of the Ridge. A lawn and fountain occupied the space in front of the Circuit House, and the main road from the Ridge swept past it at a slight distance, and presently merged in the central avenue of the camp.

At the upper end of this, in the centre of a well turfed lawn, stood the viceregal flag-staff, over forty feet high. To the east of the flag-staff were three immense tents, one behind the other; a reception *shamiana*, 130 feet by 60 feet, a drawing-room tent, 88 feet by 36 feet, and a dining-tent, 180 feet by 40 feet, in which the Viceroy gave a series of state banquets throughout the fortnight. A little to the north were the tents of Their Royal Highnesses the Duke and Duchess of Connaught, occupying an area of 300 feet by 400 feet, and including a fine *shamiana*, and a suite of tents each for the Duke and Duchess. Another set of tents, occupying a corresponding position on the other or southern side of the main road, was reserved for the Grand Duke of Hesse and his staff. From the flag-staff circus, the road, fifty feet wide, ran due west to the Najafgarh Canal, which it crossed almost at right angles. On either side of the broad thoroughfare, separated from it by a hundred feet of grassy lawn, and likewise along other parallel and cross roads, were pitched the tents for the Viceroy's personal and official guests and His Excellency's staff. All of these were furnished with a completeness and comfort that suggested an English country-house rather than life under canvas. Each tent was warmed with a fireplace and lit by electric light. Half-way towards the canal the road encircled another grass plot, on which were mounted some interesting pieces of ordnance. One or two of these bore inscriptions showing that in the middle of the eighteenth century they belonged to the Compagnie des Indes de France. Another, a brass gun, was cast in 1799, by "his noble Highness Safdar Jang." Near to this spot, on the right-hand side of the road, were the reception tents reserved for the Viceroy's guests and staff, including a spacious drawing-room, 110 feet by 40 feet, and a dining-room of even greater size, where over 100 guests sat down to every meal, exclusive of those who were being entertained in the state *shamiana* at the head of the camp. Altogether, the Viceroy's camp comprised about 1400 tents and covered an area of upwards of 93 acres. With its wide, well-gravelled roads, green lawns, and parterres of flowering plants and shrubs, the white lines of tents, pitched with a precision only attainable in India, the rocky mass of the Ridge rising behind, and a dark avenue of trees running across the foreground, the city of canvas, in which Lord Curzon's guests resided, was probably as picturesque an encampment as had ever been seen in the East.

The total number of Europeans in the Viceroy's camp was 250; and the entire number of persons who resided in it throughout the fortnight was 3250. Besides Their Royal Highnesses the Duke and Duchess of Connaught and the Grand Duke of Hesse, the Viceroy entertained the following guests:—

Private.

The Duke and Duchess of Marlborough.
The Duke and Duchess of Portland.
The Earl and Countess of Lonsdale.
The Earl of Durham and Lady Anne Lambton.
The Earl and Countess of Crewe.
Lord Elcho.
Viscount Errington.
Lord and Lady Wolverton.
Lord Lamington.
Lady Ulrica Duncombe.
Lieutenant-Colonel the Hon. C. and Mrs. Harbord.
The Hon. Dudley and Mrs. Marjoribanks.
The Hon. George Peel.
The Hon. Spencer Lyttelton.
The Hon. F. Curzon.
The Hon. Lady Miller.
The Right Hon. Sir George Taubman Goldie.
Miss Grenfell.

Sir John Dickson Poynder, M.P., and Lady Poynder.

Sir Robert Mowbray, M.P.

Sir Edgar Vincent, M.P.

Mr. Hicks-Beach.

Sir E. Ruggles Brise.

Sir Richard Baker and Miss Baker.

Mr. and Mrs. W. James.

Major and Mrs. L. Drummond.

Major and Lady Eleanor Byng.

Mrs. and Miss Leiter.

Mr. and Mrs. E. Tennant.

Miss Mure.

Mr. and the Hon. Mrs. Rochfort Maguire.

Captain and Mrs. H. Lindsay.

Mrs. Craigie.

Mr. E. T. Reed.

Mr. Owen Seaman.

Official.

The Most Rev. the Bishop of Calcutta, Mrs. and the Misses Copleston.

The Hon. Mr. T. Raleigh, Member of Council.

The Hon. Sir E. FitzG. Law, Member of Council, and Lady Law.

The Hon. Major-General Sir E. Elles, Member of Council, Lady Elles and Miss Teague.

The Hon. Mr. A. T. Arundel, Member of Council, Mrs. and Miss Arundel.

The Hon. Sir Denzil Ibbetson, Member of Council, Lady and Miss Ibbetson.

His Excellency Rear-Admiral Sir Charles Drury, Commander-in-Chief of His Majesty's Naval Forces in the East Indies.

The Hon. Sir A. H. L. Fraser, President of the Police Commission, and Lady Fraser.

Sir Colin Scott-Moncrieff, President, of the Irrigation Commission, and Lady Scott-Moncrieff.

Sir Hugh Barnes, Secretary, Foreign Department, and Lady Barnes.

Mr. J. M. Macpherson, Secretary, Legislative Department, and Mrs. Macpherson.

Major-General Sir E. Barrow, Secretary, Military Department, and Lady Barrow.

Mr. E. N. Baker, Secretary, Finance Department, and Mrs. Baker.

Mr. J. O. Miller, Secretary, Revenue Department, and Mrs. Miller.

Mr. H. H. Risley, Secretary, Home Department.

Mr. S. Preston, Secretary, Public Works Department, and Mrs. Preston.

Sir Walter Lawrence, Private Secretary to the Viceroy, and Lady Lawrence.

Lieutenant-Colonel the Hon. E. Baring, Military Secretary to the Viceroy.

Lieutenant-Colonel E. H. Fenn, Surgeon to the Viceroy, and Mrs. Fenn.

Captain W. E. A. Armstrong, I.M.S., in medical charge of the Camp.

Mr. F. S. Cowie, Secretary, Durbar Central Committee.

Colonel H. Goad, A.D.G., Director, Army Remount Department.

Captain F. G. Smallwood, R.A., in executive charge of the Camp, and Mrs. Smallwood.

Major C. F. T. Murray, Supply and Transport Officer.

Lieutenant-Colonel the Hon. C. Harbord, A.D.C.

Captain R. G. T. Baker-Carr, Rifle Brigade, A.D.C.

Captain C. Wigram, 18th Bengal Lancers, A.D.C.

Captain the Hon. J. R. L. Yarde-Buller, Scots Guards, A.D.C.

Captain the Hon. R. Lindsay, late 2nd Dragoons, A.D.C.

Captain the Earl of Suffolk, A.D.C.

H.R.H. The Duchess of Connaught and Strathearn, V.A., C.I., R.R.C.

Lieutenant G. A. Akers-Douglas, Argyll and Sutherland Highlanders, A.D.C.

Captain A. W. F. Knox, 5th Punjab Infantry, A.D.C.

Lieutenant V. A. S. Keighley, 18th Bengal Lancers, A.D.C.

Lieutenant L. A. Jones Mortimer, Somersetshire Light Infantry, A.D.C.

Lieutenant R. H. S. Dashwood, Royal Irish Rifles, A.D.C.

Major F. Lee, 4th Hussars, A.D.C.

Lieutenant K. Wigram, 2nd Gurkha Rifles, A.D.C.

Major A. V. Poynter, Scots Guards, A.D.C.

Lieutenant the Hon. F. W. Stanley, 10th Hussars, A.D.C.

Captain F. L. Adam, Scots Guards, A.D.C.

Major E. L. C. Berger, 30th Baluch Infantry, A.D.C.

Mr. F. W. Latimer, Assistant Private Secretary to the Viceroy, and Mrs. Latimer.

Major R. E. Grimston, Commandant, Viceroy's Body-guard.

Captain H. N. Holden, Adjutant, Viceroy's Body-guard.

In charge of the Police arrangements at the Camp:—Captain H. T. Dennys, Mr. F. X. J. Cassera, and Mr. F. C. Isemonger.

Other official guests of the Viceroy, including Sir B. Franklin, Director-General of the Indian Medical Service, and Lady Franklin, Sir T. Higham, member of the Irrigation Commission, and Mr. L. W. Dane, officiating Foreign Secretary, and Mrs. Dane, were entertained in the Foreign Department camp.

His Royal Highness the Duke of Connaught was accompanied by the following officers of his staff:—Lieutenant-Colonel the Hon. Cecil Bingham, 1st Life Guards, A.D.C., and Mrs. Bingham, Colonel Leslie and Mrs. Leslie, Lieutenant-Colonel Weston Jarvis, Major W. Beevor, R.A.M.C., and Sir Maurice FitzGerald, Colonel Lionel Herbert, Central India Horse, and Mrs. Herbert, and Captain A. M. Farquhar, R.N., commanding H.M.S. *Renown*. All of these resided in the Viceregal camp.

His Royal Highness the Grand Duke of Hesse's staff included Baron Massenbach, Hessian Light Dragoons, Major-General Von Wachter, Captain Kraemer, and Major A. R. Dick of the 2nd Punjab Cavalry.

The Durbar of 1877 had attracted so few visitors from the outside that only four guests from England partook of the Viceroy's hospitality in Lord Lytton's camp. In fact the great influx of European visitors from all parts of India, and still more from abroad, was one of the most striking features of the Delhi gathering of 1902–3.

To the south of the viceregal encampment were the camps of the Governor of Bombay, the Commander-in-Chief, and the Chiefs of the four military commands; to the north, stretching beyond the Alipur Road, were the camps of the Governor of Madras, and of Lieutenant-Governors, Chief Commissioners, and Agents to the Governor-General. The Commander-in-Chief, General Lord Kitchener of Khartoum and the Vaal, was lodged, with his staff and a number of distinguished guests, in a well-appointed camp; his quarters including an elegantly furnished reception tent, 58 feet long by 40 feet wide, and a large dining-room tent, hung in red and white, where as many as sixty covers might be laid on a table resplendent with the gold and silver plate presented by grateful citizens. The sides and roof of the reception tent were lined with pale blue cloth, stamped with a Kashmir shawl pattern in silver; and, on entering, the visitor could hardly fail to see, standing on an easel, a portrait of Lord Clive, whose descendant, the Earl of Powis, was among Lord Kitchener's guests. In addition to the officers of his staff, the following visitors to Delhi also stayed with His Excellency:—Lord Stanley and Lady Alice Stanley, the Countess of Powis, Sir George Dashwood and Miss Dashwood, Lieutenant-Colonel Sir Henry Rawlinson, Sir Richard Solomon, Advocate-General of the Transvaal, and Miss Solomon (now Lady Girouard), Mrs. Adair, Captain T. Y. Allen, Mr. and Mrs. Walter Long, Mr. Pandeli Ralli, Mr. A. and Lady Winifred Renshaw, Colonel Frank Rhodes, and Miss Thesiger.

The camp of His Excellency Lord Northcote, Governor of Bombay (since appointed to be Governor-General of the Australian Commonwealth), was pitched next to the Commander-in-Chief's camp, and south of the Viceroy's. The Governor's tents included a reception-room, 76 by 57 feet, draped with Indian art fabrics, a dining-room, in which two hundred guests could be entertained, and drawing-, smoking-, and billiard-rooms. In the dwelling tents, particular care had been taken to provide an adequate defence against the chills of a Delhi winter; and with fireplaces which never suffocated them with smoke, and the luxury even of wooden doorways, the guests of the Governor congratulated themselves on being able to enjoy all the advantages of camp life, without any of its discomforts,

In addition to the officers of the Governor's staff, the following distinguished visitors were Lord and Lady Northcote's guests:

The Earl and Countess of Pembroke and Lady Beatrix Herbert (now Lady Beatrix Wilkinson), the Earl and Countess of Jersey with the Hon. Arthur and Lady Beatrix Villiers, Lord William and Miss Seymour, the Earl and Countess of Dartrey with Lady Edith Dawson, Sir Michael, Lady and Miss Hicks-Beach, and His Highness Aga Khan, the spiritual head of the Khoja community. His Excellency's official guests included the Hon. Sir James Monteith and the Hon. Mr. E. M. H. Fulton, Members of Council, and Miss Fulton, the Hon. Messrs. Basil Scott (Advocate-General), F. S. P. Lely, Commissioner of the Northern Division, and Mrs. Lely, John Tate and Mrs. Tate, W. C. Hughes and Mrs. Hughes, S. M. Moses and Mrs. Moses, S. Rebsch and Mrs. Rebsch, D. McIver, and W. Greaves, additional Members of the Legislative Council, the Hon. Sir Lawrence Jenkins, Chief Justice of Bombay and Lady Jenkins, and the Hon. Mr. E. T. Candy, Judge of the High Court; the Hon. Mr. J. Muir-Mackenzie, Chief Secretary to Government; Messrs. S. W. Edgerley, W. T. Morison and Mrs. Morison, G. A. Anderson and Mrs. Anderson, and A. M. T. Jackson and Mrs. Jackson, Secretaries to Government; the Venerable Archdeacon and Mrs. W. E. Scott; Mr. A. D. Younghusband, Commissioner of the Central Division, and Mrs. Younghusband; Mr. R. M. Kennedy, Commissioner of the Southern Division; Brigadier-General Maitland, Resident at Aden, and Mrs. Maitland; Surgeon-General and Mrs. W. McConaghy; Mr. J. E. Down, Inspector-General of Police; Mr. H. Wenden, Agent, Great Indian Peninsula Railway Company, and Mrs. Wenden.

The camp of His Excellency the Governor of Madras was situated between the viceregal camp and Alipur Road. The flag-staff, in the centre of the square, stood on a large, oval mound, ornamented with rockery work and elevated several feet above the carriage drive running round it. In this way the appearance of flatness, which marked several of the encampments, was happily avoided; while pains had been taken in other matters to give to the Madras camp a distinction of its own. Roads ran to the flag-staff oval from points near the centre of each side, thus dividing the remainder of the square into four equal portions. One of these was laid out as a garden, while that on the other side of the flag-staff oval was set apart for Lord and Lady Ampthill's tents, including dining- and drawing-rooms, and a large entrance hall. In the two blocks on either side of the Governor's residence were the tents allotted to his guests. The decorations of the Madras camp were much admired, especially the

Governor's reception tent, with its crimson lining; the dining-room tent in yellow and red; and the drawing-room effectively decorated in yellow, and green.

His Excellency's guests included, besides his staff:

The Hon. Sir C. A. White, Chief Justice of Madras, the Hon. Messrs. R. S. Benson, Judge of the High Court, and Mrs. Benson, H. M. Winterbotham, senior Member of Council, Mrs. and Miss Winterbotham, J. Thomson, Member of Council, Mrs. and Miss Thomson, J. N. Atkinson, and H. A. Sim, Members of the Board of Revenue, and Mrs. Atkinson, G. Stokes, F. Spring, and G. S. Forbes, Secretaries to Government; Mr. G. H. Stuart, Director of Public Instruction, and Mrs. Stuart, the Bishop of Madras, Sir George, Lady and Miss Arbuthnot, Colonel R. G. Gordon-Gilmour, Grenadier Guards, and Lady Susan Gilmour, the Ladies Agnes and Mary Lygon, Major the Hon. Alick Russell, Grenadier Guards, the Hons. Constance, Romola and Theo Russell, Lieutenant-Colonel the Hon. Sir George Moore, president of the Madras Municipality, Sir J. F. Price, Major A. D. G. Shelly, chairman of the South Indian Railway Company, and Mr. E. Thurston, superintendent of the Madras Central Museum.

The camp of Sir Charles Rivaz, Lieutenant-Governor of the Punjab, who, being in his own province, took precedence over other Lieutenant-Governors, was pitched next to the Viceroy's. The heads of other provinces, the Residents in Hyderabad, Baroda, and Mysore, the Agents to the Governor-General in Rajputana and Central India, and the Chief Commissioners of British Baluchistan and the North-West Frontier Province, were encamped on the other side of the Alipur Road. As in the case of the Governors of Bombay and Madras, each head of a Local Government or administration was accompanied by a number of English officials and other visitors, including representatives of various public bodies, who were treated as their personal or official guests.

The central camp also included the camps pitched for the consular representatives of foreign Powers, for the special correspondents of English and Indian newspapers, and for the accommodation of various heads of departments, including the Directors-General of Military Works, Ordnance, Post Office, and Telegraphs. Among the occupants of the European Press camp, which was under the charge of Mr. O. V. Bosanquet, I.C.S., were the representatives of the *Times*, *Daily Telegraph*, *Daily Mail*, *Manchester Guardian*, *Illustrated London News*, *Graphic*, *Sketch*, and of all the principal English papers published in India. In an

Wiele & Klein

THE VICEROY'S CAMP FROM THE CIRCUIT HOUSE

adjacent camp, the correspondents of forty-five Indian journals were lodged, every possible provision for their comfort being made by their compatriot, Mr. J. N. Gupta, I.C.S., who had been placed in charge of this camp. Both English and Indian journalists were treated as the guests of the Government.

A census of the main or central camps showed a population of 12,983 persons, including 1222 Europeans, 159 native and other Asiatic guests, and 11,202 followers. Seven and a half miles of twelve-foot road, and three and a quarter miles of sixteen-foot road, were made in the central camp at a cost of Rs. 28,000 and Rs. 15,000 respectively. It was also connected with the city and the Durbar Amphitheatre by means of a two and a half feet gauge light railway, seven miles in length. The whole of the central camp was lighted by electricity, more than one hundred arc lamps being placed along the principal thoroughfares, and 9300 incandescent lights elsewhere and in the tents; the electrical plant, which had been ordered by the Military Department for the lighting and ventilation of soldiers' barracks, was utilised for the purpose. The lighting was arranged on the three-wire system, with a pressure of 220 volts on the lamps. Fifty-four tons of bare copper wire and over twelve miles of insulated wire were used. The plant worked well; and, from December 7th to January 22nd, the current was never once interrupted. The scheme was devised and the installation most successfully supervised by Major Stuart, R.E., and Captain Halliday, R.E., of the Military Works Services, and the contract for the camp lighting was given to Messrs. Kilburn and Co., of Calcutta, whose staff was assisted by twenty-one non-commissioned officers of the Indian Submarine Mining Corps. The attention paid to the lighting of the camps contributed in no small degree to the comfort and security of their inhabitants; nor could anything have been finer in its way than the view of the illuminated canvas city, seen at night from the neighbouring eminence of the Ridge. The white of the tents lay like snow on the foreground, mapped out in symmetrical partitions by twinkling points of fire. An unlimited supply of drinking water, drawn from the Jumna above Delhi, carefully filtered and distributed by pipes, was also provided for the central camps. Water for the gardens was laid on in specially constructed ducts from the Najafgarh canal.

The medical and sanitary arrangements were under the control of Lieutenant-Colonel C. J. Bamber, I.M.S., with Major F. Wyville-Thomson, I.M.S., as special health officer, and Captain C. H. James, I.M.S., as special plague officer. Ample provision, as will be shown later, was made for the postal and telegraph service of the camp, for supplies, for police, for conservancy, and, generally, for the material welfare of the encampment. At the particular request of the Bishop of Lahore, a chapel was built in the central camp at a cost of Rs. 2,800, of which the greater part was provided by the Bishop and the balance by the Durbar committee. Services were held daily, and when the camp had dispersed the materials and furniture of the chapel were presented to the Universities Mission at Delhi.

For the convenience of the many visitors to the Durbar who were not guests of the Viceroy, or of Native Chiefs, or Government officials, and who might have found difficulty in procuring accommodation in the Delhi hotels, two camps, with furnished tents, were formed by the Military Secretary to the Viceroy, who received applications from all parts of the globe, and himself allotted quarters. No. 1 Visitors' camp was pitched in the compound of Maiden's Hotel, the whole of which was also rented by Government, as an annexe to the camp. No. 2 Visitors' camp was situated near the Mori Gate. Three hundred and seventy-one Europeans, with 606 servants, were accommodated in these two camps. For others who wished to bring their own tents and make their own arrangements for messing, &c., a camping-ground was set apart to the north of the central camp, and was occupied by 355 Europeans with 888 servants. All of these quarters were rapidly taken up, and long before the end of December there was hardly an empty space of ground between the Kashmir Gate and the Ridge, or rentable accommodation anywhere, that had not found an occupant. The aspect of the roads between the city and the camps recalled some great fair. They were crowded with every variety of vehicles and by crowds of pedestrians of diverse nationality and hue. Clouds of Delhi dust were the only feature that marred the complete enjoyment of the scene. But this drawback did not extend to the camps, where the smooth and well-watered roads would have done credit to a London park.

H. H. The Gaekwar of Baroda, G.C.S.I.

CHAPTER IV

THE PRINCES AND NOBLES OF INDIA

WHILE the camps occupied by the Viceroy, the various Local Governments and administrations, the Commander-in-Chief and the provincial commands covered a compact area below the Ridge, considerations of space and public health necessitated the location elsewhere, and often at great distances, of the encampments in which the ruling Chiefs and Indian noblemen, officials, and gentry were to reside. These, as will be seen from the map, formed, so to speak, the outworks of the main camp on the side away from the River Jumna.

The camps of the Maharaja of Kashmir and of the Punjab Chiefs lay between three and four miles to the north-west of the viceregal residence. To the south of these and a little further away from the same centre were those of Baroda and Mysore, while those of the Central India Chiefs were some seven miles distant by road in the same direction. The Rajputana camps, south-west of the Circuit House, were about three miles away; while the Bombay Chiefs, more to the south, were a mile or two further distant, their tents being only a few minutes' walk from the famous observatory built early in the eighteenth century by the astronomer Raja Jai Singh, who also founded and gave his name to the spacious city of Jaipur in Rajputana which is still ruled over by his descendants.

In the British Indian provincial camps all arrangements were made by the Local Governments concerned, who provided tents and everything necessary for the entertainment of the native guests invited. The ruling Chiefs, however, came to Delhi with large followings befitting their dignity, and it would have been impossible to accommodate them in the same way. Each of them was, therefore, allotted a piece of land, the size of which was regulated by the salute of guns that he was entitled to receive, and within his own plot he was allowed to make what arrangements he pleased. The result provided one of the most interesting features of Delhi during the Durbar fortnight, for each of these encampments, with its little military force, its durbar hall, its quarters for the residence of different classes of retainers, and its bazar, became in itself a miniature town transplanted from the territory of the Chief to which it belonged. It was thus possible, in the course of a couple of days' driving round Delhi, to get a good idea of the most prominent characteristics of almost every important Native State in India. Nothing could have been more interesting than to be able to compare at a glance the manners and customs, and the state of advancement or backwardness, of the representatives of peoples of every race and religion, more diverse than those of Europe itself and drawn from an area of more than a million square miles and a population of nearly seventy-three millions, all living very much as they would in their own countries. Most of the ruling Chiefs resided in these camps of their own devising, but a few of them, unused to the rigours of a Punjab climate, preferred to live in houses in the city or its environs, and only made occasional visits to the canvas dwellings which they had provided, and which in such cases were occupied by their nobles and retainers.

Very elaborate arrangements were made for the accommodation of the Nizam of Hyderabad, the premier ruling Chief in India, at Ludlow Castle, a well known building, famous for its association with the siege in 1857, and employed at a later date as an official residence, until it passed into the hands of the Delhi Club, who rented it to the Nizam for the occasion. The exterior of this usually somewhat sombre-looking building was completely transformed by the setting of bright yellow—the Hyderabad State colour—which now framed it: there were yellow flowers in the garden, yellow flags and banners, and everywhere men in the same brilliant yellow livery. A miniature replica of the Char Minar at Hyderabad was erected at the entrance to the grounds, which were covered with the tents of His Highness's personal suite and those of his eldest son, the Shahzada Osman Ali Khan. There was also erected near the castle a portable canvas mosque, with minarets and every detail complete, which it is understood the Nizam always takes with him when travelling.

His Highness was accompanied at Delhi by over thirty high officials and nobles, among whom were the chief Minister, Maharaja Peshkar Sir Kishen Pershad Bahadur, and Colonel Nawab Afsur-ud-daula, who figured as a member of Lord Roberts' staff at the Coronation ceremonies in London. All of these pitched their camps or hired houses as near as possible to Ludlow Castle. There were also 180 horses, 20 carriages, 18 elephants, and some 970 of the Nizam's soldiery, including the 50 Arabs of His Highness's body-guard, whose dashing appearance made them always the most noticeable among the many brilliant cortèges that at this time crowded the streets of Delhi.

This was not the Nizam's first public visit to Delhi, for he had been present at Lord Lytton's Imperial Assemblage in 1877, as a boy of 11, who had succeeded his father eight years before. His appearance on that occasion as a great feudatory of the Empire was a new departure in the annals of Hyderabad, and gave rise to a good deal of discussion among the Muhammadan population of India. It was even rumoured that the Nizam himself did not attend, but that another boy had been sent to personate him. During his stay at Delhi on the present occasion His Highness visited all the Muhammadan shrines in and around the city, and even took the ladies of his zenana so far as the Kutub Minar, some eleven miles distant from Delhi. After leaving the imperial city he made a prolonged tour in Northern and Western India, staying five days at Agra and as many weeks at Bombay; and finally, on his return to his own capital, His Highness met with a great popular reception, in the course of which he made a speech referring to his visit to Delhi in the following terms :—

"It was a source of great pleasure to me that I was enabled to take my part in the Coronation Durbar of His Majesty the Emperor of India (may his generosity live for ever), and after the custom of my ancestors to show, in a simple, straightforward and soldierly manner, by word and deed, my historical friendship and loyalty. . . . I also count this journey fortunate in that it enabled me to meet at Delhi my contemporary Chiefs and high officers."

The Nizam, His Highness Asaf Jah Muzaffar-ul-Mamalik Nizam-ul-Mulk Nizam-ud-Daula Nawab Mir Mahbub Ali Khan Bahadur Fateh Jung, is a direct descendant of the famous Nizam-ul-Mulk Asaf Jah, Viceroy of the Deccan, who between 1713 and 1748 made himself independent of the Moghul Emperors. The State has a revenue of 135 lakhs of rupees and an area of some 80,000 square miles. These figures are exclusive of the territory of Berar, which in 1853 was assigned to the British by the Nizam to pay for the maintenance of the Hyderabad Contingent, but which has been leased to the British Government in perpetuity for an annual rent of 25 lakhs, by an agreement concluded between Lord Curzon and the Nizam, and made public just before the Durbar. This agreement, which put an end to a long and at one time embittered controversy, was equally beneficial to both parties, for it provided an assured instead of a precarious source of revenue to the Nizam, while it enabled the Government of India to carry out a number of important military and administrative reforms. It was in recognition of the conclusion of this agreement that His Highness was subsequently invested with the Grand Cross of the Order of the Bath by the Duke of Connaught while at Delhi.

The camp of His Highness Maharaja Sir Sayaji Rao Gaekwar of Baroda covered an area of over 100,000 square yards, on the plain near the village of Shakarpur, four or five miles to the west of the city. Its smart appearance, replete with every modern luxury, at once suggested that the Chief who presided over it must be a man of great enlightenment. Such is indeed the case. His Highness, who has made several visits to Europe and is now about forty years of age, is one of the most cultured and progressive rulers in India. Baroda is another State which was carved out of the Moghul empire by a successful military leader—in this case the Mahratta Damaji Gaekwar, who lived about the middle of the eighteenth century. It is situated in the fertile province of Guzerat in the north of the Bombay Presidency, and is one of the few Native States which have a seaboard and ports of their own.

The Gaekwar lived in his camp in a remarkable palace ingeniously constructed at Baroda and fitted together at Delhi. The wooden framework was covered on the outside with stucco and richly decorated with carved panels within. The central dome, fifty feet high, could be seen, rising above the tents, for miles round. At the entrance to the camp stood a triumphal arch, fifty-six feet high, brilliantly illuminated after dark by the electric light, of which lavish use was made throughout the encampment.

Mounted near this arch, so that all passers-by could see them, were the Gaekwar's two famous gold and silver guns. These expensive pieces of ordnance were the work of a native founder, the silver one being made in the time of the Maharaja Khandi Rao Gaekwar and the golden one for his brother and successor, the late Maharaja Mulhar Rao. They were scanned with as much interest, by native sight-seers, as if they had been the mangonels from which Ala-ud-din, the Khilji Sultan, threw bags of gold into the fortress of Delhi, to induce the garrison to surrender.

The Gaekwar was accompanied, on his visit to Delhi, by his son, the Maharaj Kumar Fatteh Sing Rao Gaekwar, also by two of his cousins, by the Diwan and the Chief Justice of Baroda, a number of nobles and of Europeans and Indian officials, as well as by 150 military retainers and about 400 servants and menials.

An even more modern camp, almost severe in its simplicity, was that of the Maharaja of Mysore, which was situated close to the Gaekwar's. The Maharaja himself occupied a temporary iron bungalow in the centre: on the right were the tents of his twenty-six European guests, and on the left those of twenty-seven Sardars and native officers and guests. His Highness was attended by 200 retainers and 370 servants, and 150 men of his troops were also quartered in the camp. A fine durbar tent served for state receptions; and ample provision, in the way of mess tents, *et cetera*, was made for the comfort of his guests. Two houses in the city, the old Bengal Bank house and an adjoining bungalow, were rented for the accommodation of Their Highnesses the Maharanis and their attendants, some seventy in number.

His Highness the Maharaja was accompanied by his father-in-law,

Rana Singhji of Wana, his brother the Yuvaraja, his brothers-in-law, Lieutenant-Colonel J. Desraj Urs, Mr. Kantaraj Urs, and Mr. Lakhshmi Kantaraja Urs, Sir P. N. Krishnamurti, Diwan of Mysore, and a number of European and Indian guests.

Area for area, Mysore is perhaps the most prosperous Native State in India. Situated on a healthy plateau, the province receives the benefit of both the south-west and north-east monsoons, a natural advantage which, in conjunction with the ancient system of irrigation tanks distributed in hundreds throughout the districts, has brought to Mysore a larger degree of immunity from famine than almost any other internal tract of India. Ivory, coffee, sandal-wood, and gold are amongst the products of this highly-favoured region, and the famous Kolar gold-fields in the State are worked by electric power, which is conveyed for a distance of over ninety miles from the Cauvery Falls, the first electric power scheme of such a magnitude in Asia. A long period of administration by British officers led to the introduction of a system based on British models, which has been maintained under a series of exceptionally able native Ministers, and the State can boast of public works, hospitals, and research laboratories second to none in India.

From time immemorial Mysore has been ruled by a Hindu dynasty, the ancestors of the present Maharaja claiming to be descended from an offshoot of the Yadav Rajput line. In the middle of the eighteenth century it was usurped by the famous Hyder Ali, whose successor, the still more notorious Tippu Sultan, fell in arms against the British at the capture of Seringapatam in 1799. The old Hindu dynasty was restored in the person of a child whom a romantic fate had spared to survive as almost the sole representative of the ancient Rajas; but in 1831 the people of the State broke into open rebellion as a result of misrule, and for the preservation of law and order the British Government then assumed the direct management of Mysore. In 1881, however, it was restored to native rule, and now ranks as one of the best administered feudatory States of the Empire.

The present Maharaja, Krishnaraja Wadiyar Bahadur, is now in his twentieth year, and succeeded his father in 1895. He received his powers as a ruling Chief in August 1902, when the Viceroy, Lord Curzon,

H. H. The Maharaja of Mysore

as a special mark of his interest in the young Chief and his State, made a journey from Simla to Mysore for the purpose of investing him. During the six preceding years he owed much to the friendly supervision of Lieutenant-Colonel Sir Donald Robertson, British Resident in the State, and received a careful general education and special training in his administrative duties at the hands of Mr. S. M. Fraser, of the Indian Civil Service, who was selected by the Government of India to act as the Maharaja's tutor and governor during his minority.

From the sunny clime of Mysore to the snows of Kashmir is a long cry—nearly as far as from London to Astrakhan—but here on the Lawrence Road at Delhi, where the Burma and Baluchistan camps were also placed, the transition was an easy one, and was accomplished in less than two miles. The Maharaja of Kashmir's camp, in its picturesqueness and in the luxury and profusion of its appointments, was characteristic of the beautiful valley from which it had come. The main feature of the camp was the magnificent durbar tents that were made in the time of the late Maharaja, and used at the Delhi Assemblage of 1877. The two reception tents were 72 feet by 46 feet and 66 feet by 54 feet respectively, supported on eighty silver poles each surmounted by a golden ball. The tents were made of the finest pashmina, spun like a Kashmir shawl, and were draped inside with old Kashmir shawls of a kind that are very rarely, if ever, seen outside Kashmir itself, while under foot there were carpets of the finest gold embroidery. Some of the tents were hung entirely with very rare furs.

The present Maharaja, who is a descendant of the famous Dogra Rajput soldier, Gulab Singh, was born in 1850, and succeeded in 1885. He was present with his father, the late Maharaja Ranbir Singh, at the 1877 Durbar, and now holds the honorary rank of Major-General in the British Army. His State in point of area is as large as Hyderabad; and besides possessing one of the most delightful climates in the world, contains vast stores of wealth in its valuable mineral deposits, which every effort is now being made to develop. It is also of great importance in another way, for it runs right up to the confines of that mysterious country where three Empires meet, and for this reason maintains a large and efficient force of Imperial Service Troops, to which the custody of the longest stretch of external land frontier of any province or State in India is entrusted. The Maharaja, therefore, well deserves his title of Shield of the Empire.

His Highness was accompanied at Delhi by his brother, Raja Sir Amar Singh, Vice-President of the State Council and Commander-in-Chief of the Kashmir forces, who was one of Lord Lytton's pages at the Imperial Assemblage of 1877; Mian Hari Singh, Sir Amar Singh's son, who was one of the Viceroy's pages at the Chapter of the Indian Orders on the present occasion; the Governors of Jammu and Kashmir; and Raja Kedar Chand of Chineni, the Maharaja's son-in-law. The Raja of Poonch, the Mir of Hunza, Raja Sikandar Khan, *de facto* Mir of Nagar, Raja Alidad Khan of Gilgit, the Governor of Yasin, Raja Shah Sultan of Astor, Raja Mir Baz Khan of Punial, and the headmen from Chilas also resided in the camp as the Maharaja's guests.

Including retainers and menials, His Highness's following numbered some 1400 persons. The transport brought to Delhi comprised eight camels, eight elephants, and over 330 horses and 100 carriages.

The Rajputana, Central India, Bombay, and Punjab Chiefs each had a separate camp, but those of each territorial group were pitched in close proximity, so as to form a series of separate small towns, the first three of which contained some 10,000 inhabitants each, and which required regular municipal organisations of their own for water-supply, lighting, and conservancy. There was for every group a separate officer in political charge of the whole encampment, a special medical officer, an inquiry officer whose business it was to supply any information that might be required regarding the arrangements for the various state ceremonies and public events, and a camp magistrate, whose office was happily a sinecure. Each camp had also its own special post offices, telegraph office, and police station.

The Rajputana encampment was situated on a level plain about a couple of miles to the west of the suburb of Sabzi Mandi, not far from the station of Rohilla Serai on the Rajputana-Malwa Railway. The various camps of which it was composed were grouped so as to

H.H. The Maharaja of Jammu and Kashmir, G.C.S.I.

form a large cross, at the centre of which was a small circular garden, where a band played. The four nearest camps were the large enclosures of Udaipur, Jodhpur, Jaipur, and Bundi, separated from each other by broad roads leading to the other camps.

The first in rank of all the Chiefs in Rajputana is the Maharana of Udaipur, who is considered by Hindus to be the representative of the mythical Rama, King of Ajodhya, by one of whose descendants, Kunak Sen, the present family was founded in A.D. 144. It is the proud boast of the family that they never, like the other great princely houses in Rajputana, gave a daughter in marriage to any of the Muhammadan Emperors. No State in India has had a more interesting or romantic history, and its great nobles are still very much in the same position as the feudal barons of the eleventh century in England. It has been the scene of some of the greatest exploits of Indian chivalry; and its old capital, Chitor, was besieged and captured with great slaughter by the Muhammadans on no less than three occasions, in 1290, in 1533, and in 1568. It was after the last sack that the Chief, Udai Singh, retired to the Aravalli Hills and founded the picturesque city of Udaipur, famous for its beautiful lakes and island palaces and temples.

His Highness the Maharana came to Delhi, but his dignified figure was missed from all the celebrations, as he was unfortunately prevented by illness from taking part in them. His spacious camp and the number and distinction of the retinue, which included forty Sardars, many of whom were the great feudal chieftains of the State, twenty-four State officials, 230 troops, and over 360 servants, were worthy of the position that belongs to his house.

The Maharaja of Jaipur's camp accommodated nearly 1200 guests, officials, troops, and retainers. It was essentially Indian in style, and was arranged in the characteristic form of an old Rajput encampment, which has been handed down from more troublous times when it was necessary for the tents of the Chiefs to be surrounded by concentric circles of those of his retainers arranged according to their rank. But the refinement and elegance of this camp, with its carefully-planned Italian garden in front, indicated that its principal occupant, while preserving his traditions intact, was ready to make the fullest use of what he had learnt by contact with Europeans, where there was no conflict between the two forms of civilisation.

The name and personality of the Maharaja are well known from his visit to England in 1902 as one of the Coronation guests of His Majesty the King, and for his princely benefactions. It was he who started and endowed, with a donation of 15 lakhs, since increased to 21 lakhs of rupees, the "Indian People's Famine Fund." Donations of a quarter of a lakh to the Lady Curzon Scholarship branch of the Countess of Dufferin's Fund, and of £5000 to the King's Hospital Fund, and the offer of five lakhs of rupees to the Queen Victoria Memorial Fund are further instances of his liberality. His Highness, who succeeded to the *gadi* in 1888, is the head of the Kachhwaha clan of Rajputs, and traces his descent from Kush, one of the sons of Rama. In wealth, prosperity, trade, manufactures, and general advancement, Jaipur is unquestionably the leading State of Rajputana. Its capital city, named after the great Maharaja Jai Singh, has a world-wide reputation for its boulevards, its school of art, and its beautiful public gardens and palaces.

The Maharaja of Jodhpur, the head of the great Rahtor clan of Rajputs, came to Delhi as a member of the Imperial Cadet Corps, and consequently did not live in the Jodhpur camp, which, however, accommodated some 460 of his nobles, officials, and retainers. The Rahtors have always been a great fighting race, and their reputation has in no way suffered with time. Only in 1901 a regiment of the Jodhpur Imperial Service Lancers acquitted itself with credit in China, under the command of the veteran Sir Pratap Singh, now Maharaja of Idar, who was for many years *Musahib Ala*, or chief Minister, of Marwar (Jodhpur) in the time of the Maharaja Jaswant Singh, who died in 1895.

One of the most interesting old-world camps was that of the Maharao Raja of Bundi, which was surrounded, like all other purely Indian encampments, by a high canvas wall, guarded by sentries in a uniform that has probably undergone no modification for centuries.

The Maharao took with him to Delhi a retinue of twenty nobles and high officials, 100 officers of his personal staff, and a military escort of 185 horse and foot. His Highness was a conspicuous figure on state

Henry G. Higgins, Mhow, photo. | Walker & Boutall Ph. Sc.

H.H. the Maharaja of Jaipur.
G.C.S.I. G.C.I.E. G.C.V.O.

occasions at Delhi, clad in the picturesque full-dress costume of his forefathers, consisting of a full-pleated white skirt, with a tight-fitting coat and chain mail armour. His slight figure, pale complexion, and Rajput manner of wearing the hair rendered him a typical specimen of a Rajput prince of high lineage and pure descent. One of the Chiefs of Bundi earned the gratitude of Government at the beginning of the last century by giving assistance to Colonel Monson's expedition against Holkar, while his son co-operated in the campaign against the Pindaris.

The Maharaja of Bikaner's camp was chiefly noticeable for the handsome arch erected at its entrance. It held altogether 700 persons, including fourteen guests from England and fifteen Sardars of the State. On January 6 His Highness entertained the Grand Duke of Hesse at luncheon in this camp, which was the scene of many festivities during the fortnight. The Maharaja, though quite a young man, having been born in 1880, has already given evidence that he inherits the martial spirit of his Rahtor ancestors, for he went to China in 1901 in command of the Bikaner Imperial Service Camel Corps, which has since done good work in Somaliland; he bears the rank of honorary Major in the British Army, and was appointed an A.-D.-C. to H.R.H. the Prince of Wales at the Coronation in London. The Maharaja is a vigorous and careful ruler of his State, which he has done much to develop by opening up new railways across the great desert that was formerly passable only by camels, and by tapping the valuable coal deposits that occur in his territory.

The Maharao of Kota is another of the younger generation of Rajput Chiefs who takes a very keen interest in the administration of his State, which he has now ruled with conspicuous success for nine years. He has been granted the honorary commission of Major in the British Army, and, like the Maharajas of Bikaner and Alwar, he received his education at the Mayo College at Ajmer. The Maharao came to Delhi with fourteen Sardars and officials, and 780 troops and retainers. His camp was a plain and simple one, distinguished only by the great state flag, which, as in all the other camps, was flown in front of the durbar tent.

The Maharaja of Alwar, who is just 21, and who has since been invested with full ruling powers by the Viceroy at his capital, was conspicuous at Delhi for his prowess on the polo ground. His camp was remarkable for the curious mosaic garden which it contained, and for the great arch of a pattern peculiar to Alwar erected at its entrance. The State of Alwar was formerly a part of Jaipur, from which it was separated by an ancestor of the present Chief in the eighteenth century.

The Maharaja of Kishangarh and the Maharaj Rana of Dholpur both came to Delhi as members of the Imperial Cadet Corps, but the camps where their Sardars and retainers lived were among those of the other Chiefs. That of the former was marked by the elaborate archway at its entrance, and the neat Dholpur camp might have belonged to an English officer.

The camps of the Maharaja of Karauli and the Nawab of Tonk were characteristically old-fashioned with their walled enclosures, coloured tents, and servitors in chain armour. The Maharaja of Karauli is, according to tradition, descended from the deified hero Sri Krishna, and his ancestors have ruled the State since the tenth century. His predecessor, the Maharaja Madan Pal, rendered valuable assistance to the British Government during the Mutiny.

The Nawab of Tonk, whose State consists of two detached portions, one in Central India and one in Rajputana, is a descendant of the famous Pathan soldier of fortune, Amir Khan, and is the only Muhammadan ruler in Rajputana. The Nawab succeeded to the *masnad* of the State in 1867, and is one of the few Chiefs now living who attended Lord Lytton's Durbar in 1877 as rulers of their States.

The remaining Rajputana Chiefs who had camps at Delhi were the Maharawal of Jaisalmer, the lord of a very old State dating back to the ninth century, which, though once very large and prosperous, had, by the time when British rule was established in India, been reduced to the vast desert, over 16,000 square miles in area, which is all that it comprises now, and in the centre of which is situated its ancient capital, ninety miles from the nearest railway; the Maharao of Sirohi, another old State, dating from the thirteenth century, in which is situated Mount Abu, the political head-quarters of Rajputana; the Maharawal of Dungarpur, of the same high lineage as the Udaipur family, who is being educated at the Mayo College at Ajmer, and whose State is mainly inhabited by Bhils and other aboriginal tribes; the Raj Rana of Jhalawar; and the infant Maharaja of Bharatpur, who was taken to the Durbar in the arms of his mother, Her Highness the Maji Guraj Kuar. There was also a small encampment for the notables from Ajmer-Merwara, the only piece of British territory in Rajputana.

Three miles to the west of the Rajputana camps, and ranged picturesquely along both sides of the shady Rohtak Road for about a mile, were the nineteen camps of the Central India Chiefs, which formed a collection even more diverse than those of Rajputana. Here on the road, the common ground of all the camps, were to be seen Bundelas and Baghels from Bundelkhand and Baghelkhand, Pathans from Bhopal or Jaora, Rajputs from Malwa, and Mahrattas from Gwalior, Indore, Dhar, and Dewas.

One of the most noticeable camps was that of His Highness the Maharaja Scindia, which, like the beautiful Jai Belas Palace at Gwalior itself, was enclosed in an elaborate and well laid-out garden. It was difficult to believe that, only a few weeks before, this trim and well-cultivated plot, with its fountains and palm trees, had been nothing more than a field of wheat. The camp was most sumptuously furnished; each dwelling tent had hot and cold water laid on, and contained a special form of heating apparatus, invented by a Mahratta engineer who was in charge of the camp, with a view to avoiding all risk of fire. There was also a cleverly designed enclosed winter garden attached to the quarters of Her Highness the Maharani. The camp contained, besides the Maharaja's Sardars and high officials, a following of over 900 retainers, 22 elephants, and 270 horses.

The Maharaja Scindia of Gwalior was a notable guest at the Coronation of the King-Emperor at Westminster Abbey; and his person and services to the Crown are well known in England. Born in 1877 he succeeded the late Maharaja Jaiaji Scindia, in 1886. Like the famous Mahadaji Scindia, who fought at Panipat in 1791 and many others of his race, His Highness is devoted to the profession of arms, and has, on several occasions, been eager to place the military resources of his State at the disposal of the British authorities. His Imperial

Service troops took part with those of several other States in the operations on the North-West frontier during the Tirah campaign. He himself served on Sir Alfred Gaselee's staff in China in 1901, and furnished a fully equipped hospital ship, the *Gwalior*, for the use of the troops engaged in the campaign. He is an honorary Aide-de-Camp to the King-Emperor, and an honorary Colonel in the British Army.

Opposite the Gwalior camp was that of another great Mahratta Chief, the Maharaja Holkar of Indore, decorated in blue and yellow, the colours worn also by all His Highness's liverymen. The camp was divided into sections for the separate suites of the Maharaja, the two Maharanis who accompanied him to Delhi, and the Maharaja's eldest son, the Bala Sahib. It was the largest one of the group, and the colour effect was very striking.

His Highness the Maharaja Shivaji Rao Holkar, with his commanding presence, was one of the most conspicuous figures at the various state ceremonies at Delhi, all of which he attended in spite of the fact that he was suffering from ill-health at the time. Very soon after the Durbar, on January 31st, His Highness abdicated in favour of his son the Bala Sahib, a boy of fourteen, and has now retired into private life, at his beautiful country seat of Barwaha on the river Nerbudda.

Close to the Gwalior camp also was that of Her Highness the Begum of Bhopal, which the great green flag, surmounted by a crescent, and the numerous Persian and Arabic inscriptions, at once betokened to be that of a Muhammadan. Bhopal is the principal Mussulman State in Central India, and ranks next in importance to Hyderabad among the Muhammadan States in India. The ruling family was founded by Dost Muhammad, an Afghan in the service of the Emperor Aurungzeb. The most noticeable feature of this camp was the great walled enclosure in the centre, which screened the apartments of Her Highness from the public gaze. The gardens attached to this camp were tastefully laid out, and bands were kept playing there almost continuously from sunrise to sunset. The Begum, who succeeded her mother in 1901, is the only female ruler in India, and, curiously enough, is the third who has been Chief of Bhopal in succession. All three Begums have taken a very

Bourne & Shepherd

THE DURBAR CAMPS

great interest in the work of governing their State, which they have carried on with marked success. Her Highness was accompanied at Delhi by her three sons and a large retinue, including a detachment of her Imperial Service Lancers. She never appeared in public unveiled, and on the occasions of the Viceroy's arrival and departure, a special enclosed *shamiana* was erected for her at the railway station. Nevertheless, it was in person that the Begum offered her congratulations at the Durbar, determined that no disability attaching to her sex should prevent her from testifying the well-proved loyalty of Bhopal in the same public manner as her brother Chiefs.

Her Highness's camp adjoined those of her neighbours in Central India—the Rajas of Narsingarh and Rajgarh, two Rajput States which were formerly united, but separated in 1681. The former is a boy of sixteen, who succeeded to the State in 1896, and is now being educated at the Mayo College at Ajmer. The latter is an older man, who succeeded his nephew only in 1902.

The Maharaja of Rewa, premier Chief of Baghelkhand, whose father earned the gratitude of the British Government by his loyal services during the Mutiny, came to Delhi with a large retinue, including 360 troops, 16 elephants, 24 camels, and a motor car. The Maharaja's camp was one of the most elaborate in the whole of Delhi. It was lavishly equipped, and so profusely decorated with bunting, and modern in style, that a visitor might have imagined himself in a corner of the Paris Exhibition. The camp contained the whole of the large retinue which the Maharaja brought with him to Delhi, consisting of about 800 men, 18 elephants, and a large number of horses. The Maharaja is, according to native history, the 33rd of his line, and is 25 years of age. He succeeded his father in 1880, when he was only three years and six months old. His Highness is a keen administrator and a great sportsman.

To a student of local manners and customs, the camps of the Bundela Chiefs of Orchha, Datia, Charkhari, and Samthar could not fail to have been the most interesting, with their curious high-walled enclosures, painted all over on the outside with the figures of soldiers and animals, pierced at intervals by small guard-houses and watch towers, and surmounted at the entrance by a lofty *naubat khana* or musician's gallery, from which proceeded an incessant din of tom-toms and drums.

The Maharaja of Orchha, the oldest of the Bundela States, and the only one which successfully defied the Mahratta Peshwa, took a prominent place among the Central India Chiefs at the Durbar. His Highness, who was born in 1854 and succeeded his brother in 1874, is descended from Raja Bar Singh Deo, a man of mark in the reigns of Akbar and Jehangir. The Bundelas always held high positions under the Moghul Emperors by reason of their military genius, to which the great fortresses in their own country are still a witness. The Maharaja of Orchha is a strong ruler, and takes a great personal interest in the development of his State. He has himself designed most of the engineering and irrigation works that have been executed there within recent years. He bears the hereditary title of *Saramad-i-Rajaha-i-Bundelkhand*—"First of the Princes of Bundelkhand."

Next to Orchha was the camp of the Maharaja of Datia, a State which was originally an offshoot of Orchha. The Chief is now 57 years of age, and succeeded to the *gadi* in 1857. He was present at Lord Lytton's assemblage in 1877, when the title of *Lokendra*—"Lord of the World"—which he now bears, was conferred on him.

The camp of the Maharaja of Samthar, a small State which was separated from Datia in the eighteenth century, bore a curious family likeness, with its high walls and lofty red tents, to the fort at Samthar itself, where the Maharaja resides. That of the Maharaja of Charkhari, which adjoined it, was very similar.

Another interesting camp was that of the two Rajas of Dewas, a State which was founded in the first half of the eighteenth century by two Mahratta brothers, who at first administered jointly, but subsequently divided, their lands. Their descendants are known as the senior and junior branches of the family, and since 1841 each has ruled his own portion as a separate State, though the lands belonging to each are so intimately entangled, that even in the capital town it happens that the two sides of a street are under different administrations and have different arrangements for water-supply and lighting.

There remain to be mentioned the camps of the young Puar Mahratta Raja of Dhar, of the Rajput Rana of Barwani, whose territories, situated in the heart of the Satpura hills, are inhabited largely by aboriginal Bhils, and of the Nawab of Jaora and the Raja of Rutlam. The two last named Chiefs were at Delhi in the Imperial Cadet Corps, and so did not, as a rule, live in their trim and tastefully decorated little camps. The Rao of Alipura, who had been to Delhi in 1877, and the Thakur of Piploda, two petty Rajput chieftains in Central India, also set up their tents in this encampment. The Maharaja of Chatarpur, who attended the 1877 Assemblage, had made all preparations to attend the Durbar, and had laid out a camp for his reception, but at the last moment he was forbidden by his medical adviser to undertake the journey.

The visitors from Rajputana and Central India were more or less at home at Delhi, but those from Madras, who were located some two miles to the north of the Central India encampment, were complete strangers in the land, knowing neither the language nor the climate of the Punjab. The three ruling Chiefs among them, the Maharaja of Travancore and the Rajas of Cochin and Pudukota, had their camps with the rest, but preferred themselves to live in rented houses in the city.

The Maharaja of Travancore rules over one of the most picturesque regions in India, which extends more than 150 miles along the west coast as far as Cape Comorin, the southernmost point of the peninsula. The State is remarkably prosperous, and is administered on lines resembling those of British India. The ruling family follows the ancient *marumakkatayam* law of inheritance through females, and dates from the time of one of the three legendary kings of Southern India, Cheraman Perumal, who, about the middle of the ninth century, became a Muhammadan and sailed for Arabia, leaving his dominions to be divided among his principal vassals.

The present Maharaja was born in 1857, and succeeded his uncle in 1885. In 1892, in accordance with the national custom which is still kept up, he was weighed against gold, which was afterwards distributed in charity to Brahmins. The Chief suffered severely from the cold of

Northern India, but gallantly remained at Delhi until the celebrations were concluded. Two years before, Lord Curzon had been the Maharaja's guest at his two capitals, Quilon and Trevandrum, the first Viceroy of India who had ever been to Travancore.

The Raja of Cochin, whose State borders Travancore on the north, and contains some of the most fertile tracts in the whole of India, traces his descent directly from Cheraman Perumal. He was born in 1852, and conducts his administration with considerable energy and on enlightened principles.

The Raja of Pudukota rules over a small State of 1380 square miles area, entirely surrounded by the British districts of Trichinopoly, Tanjore, and Madura; he is the representative of a line of Chiefs formerly known as the Tondimans, one of whom rendered signal assistance to the English Commander, Stringer Lawrence, during the siege of Trichinopoly in 1752. The present Raja was born in 1875, and succeeded his grandfather in 1886.

Profound regret was caused by the death at Delhi of one of the Madras notables, Sir Muhammad Munawar Khan, titular Prince of Arcot and lineal descendant of the Nawabs of the Carnatic. The Prince, who was forty years of age, succumbed to an illness brought on by cold and exposure, his death occurring suddenly at the Delhi railway station on January 4th, 1903, as he was entering the train to return to Madras.

The Bombay Chiefs were encamped about three miles to the south-west of the modern city of Delhi, their tents extending for two miles along both sides of the Gurgaon Road.

The Maharaja of Kolhapur, Sir Shahu Chatrapati Maharaj, who is descended from Shivaji, the founder of the Mahratta empire, claims the first rank among the ruling Chiefs of the Bombay Presidency, and is one of the quartet of great Mahratta Chiefs in India, the others being the Maharajas of Baroda, Gwalior, and Indore. His Highness was born in 1874 and installed as Raja in 1894, the title of Maharaja being conferred on him six years later as an hereditary distinction. He was present at the Coronation of the King in London in 1902. The Kolhapur camp, which accommodated also His Highness's brother, the

Chief of Kagal, and the other feudatory Jagirdars of the State, was a large one of a very modern type, enclosed in a well-laid-out garden.

The "red camp" pitched for the Rao of Cutch took its name from the dull red colour of its tents, matched by the red gravel scattered over the ground. The reception tents were made of purple velvet supported on silver poles, and are said to be a hundred years old. The ruling family of Cutch, who belong to the tribe of Jareja Rajputs, are the descendants of Lakka, the son of Gara, whose ancestors ruled in Sind, and who entered Cutch about the middle of the fifteenth century. The Maharao is thirty-seven years of age, and succeeded his father in 1876. In 1887 he visited England to take part in the celebration of the Jubilee of the late Queen-Empress Victoria. He is a capable and progressive ruler; and his capital, Bhuj, where a British force is stationed under an old treaty, is an interesting mixture of mediæval architecture and modern institutions.

The camp of the Mir of Khairpur, a State in Northern Sind between the river Indus and the great Rajputana desert, was conspicuous for its large durbar tent with stained-glass windows. Situated between the warlike Rajputs on the one hand and the uncivilised Baluchis on the other, Khairpur was bound to have an interesting history. It was at first ruled by a Rajput dynasty that was conquered by Muhammadans from Arabia in A.D. 711. Subsequently, along with the rest of Sind, Akbar incorporated it in the Moghul empire, from which it was dissevered in 1740 by Nadir Shah. After his assassination the State became subject to the Durani rulers of Kandahar; and when it first came into contact with the British Government, it was in the hands of the despotic Kalhoras. These in their turn were overthrown in 1786 by a Baluch tribe, the Talpurs, to which the present Mir belongs. The late Chief rendered valuable services to the British Government on several occasions during the Sind war and during the Mutiny. The present Mir is sixty-eight years of age, and succeeded his father in 1894. He is greatly addicted to sport.

The Nawab of Junagadh, the only important Muhammadan State in the Kathiawar peninsula, traces his family and power to Sher Khan Bali, a Pathan soldier of fortune who, in the first half of the eighteenth century, expelled the Great Moghul's deputy governor, and set himself up as ruler. Sir Rasul Khanji, the present Nawab, is forty-five years of age, and succeeded his brother in 1892. His camp at Delhi was gay with flags, and contained a fine display of garden flowers that had all been brought from Junagadh. His State is remarkable as containing the sacred hill of Girnar, with its ancient Jain temples, and one of the most famous of the inscriptions of Asoka; and also the forest of Gir, the only place in India where the Indian lion, that up to half a century ago still roamed the jungles of northern and central India, still survives.

The most elaborate camp among those of the Kathiawar Chiefs was that of the Thakur Sahib of Bhavnagar, a maritime State with a considerable shipping trade of its own. The camp, which was of an Indian design, was lit throughout by electricity, and contained a picturesque garden. The approach to it was through a great gateway profusely decorated in gold and silver, and ornamented with native paintings.

The Maharaja of Idar, Sir Pratap Singh, one of the best known of the Indian Princes, also had his camp here. His Highness, who is fifty-seven years of age, is a brother of the late Maharaja of Jodhpur, a State with which Idar has close historical associations. He is an honorary Major-General in the British Army, an Aide-de-Camp to the King-Emperor, a Knight Commander of the Bath, and an honorary LL.D. of Cambridge University, distinctions which have been well earned by valuable service to the Empire. His Highness has seen active service in the Tirah, Mohmand, and China campaigns, and he visited England on the occasion of Her late Majesty's Jubilees in 1887 and 1897, and of the King-Emperor's Coronation in 1902.

The other Kathiawar Chiefs residing in the Bombay camp were the Rana of Porbandar, whose tribe, the Jelhwa Rajput, claims descent from Hanuman, the monkey god; the Thakur Sahib of Morvi, a well-travelled and capable ruler; and the Thakur Sahib of Limri. Here, too, were encamped the Raja of Bariya, the Nawab of Janjira, a descendant of the Abyssinian Admirals of the Moghul Emperor Aurungzeb, and the Chief of Miraj of the Patwardhan Brahmin family

Wiele & Klein

THE IMPERIAL CADETS

from the southern Mahratta country, whose ancestors rendered notable military service to Sir Arthur Wellesley in his Deccan campaigns. The Thakur Sahib of Gondal, who received his education in Edinburgh, and his fellow Chief of Palitana, rented houses in the Civil Lines. The Nawab of Cambay, whose ancestor, a Shiah Moghul of Persian origin, was for some time Viceroy of Ahmedabad, and was appointed Nawab of Cambay by the Moghul Emperor in the eighteenth century, rented a house at Paharganj, as did also the Pant Sachiv of Bhor and the Raja of Bansda.

The Sultan of Lahej and the Amir of D'thali, Arab chieftains from the Aden Protectorate, resided in the Bombay camp, and, adding yet another picturesque type to the gathering, helped to recall the fact that the political boundaries of the Indian Empire extend across the seas beyond the confines of the great peninsula. The Sultan of Shehr and Mokalla, who rules over a portion of the Hadramaut in the same political charge, rented a house in the Civil Lines.

The encampment of the Punjab Chiefs, situated not very far from the Kashmir camp on the Lawrence Road, had the advantage of a plentiful water-supply, and was thus able to bring its groves and gardens to a greater state of perfection than those of any other camp. Nearly every camp possessed some characteristic features, and was even more Indian in style than many of those already described. The most conspicuous was that of the young Maharaja of Patiala, who takes the first place among the Chiefs of the three Sikh Phulkian States, Patiala, Nabha, and Jind. It was surrounded by a hedge of orange and rose bushes, and over six hundred palm-trees had been planted in the gardens, in which a dozen fountains were continually playing. Two colossal statues of knights in armour, bearing electric lights, guarded the entrance to the camp, which at night was illuminated by a profusion of lamps, arranged to form legends expressive of devotion to the Sovereign, while Urdu and Persian mottoes, written in letters of gold, and breathing the same sentiments, were visible by day. On one side of the garden stood the small silver pavilion which was constructed for, though never occupied by, the present King-Emperor when he visited the Punjab in 1876, and which contains some very curious old historic paintings by native artists.

The Maharaja is eleven years of age, and succeeded to the *gadi* in 1900 on the death of his father, who was well known for his skill as a horseman and polo-player. He was accompanied at Delhi by his uncle, Kunwar Sir Ranbir Singh, by the members of the Council of Regency, between thirty and forty European and Indian guests, and by 1340 officials and servants.

The Bahawalpur camp was pitched next to that of the Raja of Jind and, with its great arch and decorations of Muhammadan design, formed a curious contrast with its Sikh surroundings. The Nawab ranks second in order of precedence among the Punjab Chiefs, and his camp was on a scale corresponding to his dignity. The large durbar tent, 46 yards long, and 36 yards wide, supported on silver poles, was especially noticeable. His Highness was accompanied on his visit to Delhi by the Superintendent of the State, by the Wazir and five members of the Council, and by thirty-seven civil officials and officers of his private staff, who all resided in the camp, in addition to his body-guard, military police, and camel corps detachment.

The State of Bahawalpur dates from the first half of the eighteenth century, when the present ruling family, which claims descent from Abbas, uncle of the Prophet, and had originally emigrated into Sind from Khorasan, was driven across the Indus by Nadir Shah's governor into the tract which now forms the State. By Khorasan is probably meant the country west of the Sulaiman Range,

The Nawab, who is now twenty years of age and was educated at the Aitchison College at Lahore, had already taken a large share in the government of his State, and had been at pains to make himself an expert in all matters connected with the land revenue administration, before he was invested with full powers by the Viceroy at Bahawalpur in November 1903.

The coloured tents of the Raja of Jind's camp were particularly striking; they were reached through a three-storied wooden gateway, constructed on the model of a mediæval fortification and guarded by Akalis, members of a Sikh religious order. In the middle storey was kept the Granth—the holy scripture of the Sikhs. Like those of Patiala and Nabha, the rulers of Jind are descended from Phul, who held the office of revenue collector under the Emperor Shah Jehan in the early part of the seventeenth century. The three territories ruled by his descendants are now known as the Phulkian States. Jind rendered valuable assistance during the Mutiny, and the Raja was the only Chief who joined his forces with the British army and took part in the siege of Delhi. The present Raja is twenty-three years of age, and succeeded his grandfather when a minor.

Close at hand was the simple but dignified camp of the veteran Raja of Nabha, who came to Delhi and was a prominent figure on all state occasions, notwithstanding the risks to which his infirm health exposed him. This camp was entered through a tent fashioned like a miniature castle. Inside was a neat garden decorated with thousands of small coloured lamps, and beyond this again was another enclosure leading to the durbar tent, and finally to an inner garden in which the Raja dwelt in a small brick bungalow. This, after the Durbar, was made over, free of all encumbrances, to the owner of the land in perpetuity, to commemorate the fact that it had been used by a Raja of Nabha and in honour of the Coronation. The Granth was kept in a small room on the roof of this bungalow. The camp accommodated altogether some 860 officials, troops, retainers and servants. His Highness is now sixty years of age, and succeeded to the *gadi* in 1871.

The Raja of Kapurthala himself resided in a house in the Civil Lines, but had a camp near that of the Raja of Nabha, where most of his retainers and troops lived. The latter were conspicuous at Delhi for their soldierly appearance and smart uniforms of white and dark blue. The Kapurthala family is descended from Jassa Singh, a contemporary of Nadir Shah and Ahmad Shah, who by his intelligence and bravery made himself the leading Sikh of his day. The Raja is thirty years of age and has made several visits to Europe.

Among the nobles and gentlemen residing in the Punjab provincial camp, which was pitched a short distance from the tents of the ruling Chiefs, were the Nawab Fatheh Ali Khan, Kizilbash, the descendant of a family, formerly settled in Afghanistan, which earned the lasting gratitude of Englishmen by succouring the officers and ladies who were held captive by Akbar Khan, during the first Afghan War; the

Hon. Kunwar Sir Harnam Singh Ahluwalia, uncle of the Raja of Kapurthala, and member of the Punjab Legislative Council; the veteran Baba Sir Khem Singh, Bedi, who, like the Nawab Fatheh Ali Khan and Sir Harnam Singh, attended the Coronation of the King in London in 1902, and who traces his descent from Baba Nanak, the great Guru of the Sikhs, and is himself the most noted spiritual guide of the Sikh people at the present day; the Nawab Sir Imam Bakhsh Khan, Mazari, the head of an important Baluch tribe on the border; Makhdum Hassan Bakhsh, hereditary guardian of the famous Muhammadan shrine at Multan; Mirza Suliman Shikoh, the chief surviving representative of the old royal house of Delhi; and Khan Bahadur Dhanjibhai Commodore, a Parsee gentleman, who, at the time of the frontier disturbances in 1897–98, and more recently, during the war in South Africa, organised ambulances for the troops at his own expense.

The Chiefs and notables invited to the Durbar by the Bengal Government had a camping-ground assigned to them five miles west of the Lieutenant-Governor's tents and close to those of the Indian guests from Assam, Burma, and Madras.

The ruling Chiefs in this camp were His Highness the Maharaja of Kuch Behar, His Highness the Raja of Hill Tippera, and the Raja of Moharbhanj, the largest of the tributary States of Orissa.

The Maharaja of Kuch Behar is descended from a Tibetan or Dravidian family that once held sway over the whole of what is now known as Northern Bengal. During the seventeenth century, however, the State was encroached on by the Moghul armies, and about the beginning of the last century was reduced to its present dimensions. His Highness, who succeeded his father in 1863, and is married to a daughter of the celebrated Bengali reformer, Babu Keshub Chandra Sen, served in the Tirah campaign of 1897–98, and is now an honorary Colonel in the British Army and an Aide-de-Camp to the King-Emperor, in which capacity he attended His Majesty at the Coronation in 1902.

The Raja of Hill Tippera is the ruler of a State of great antiquity and many vicissitudes in Eastern Bengal on the confines of Assam, and belongs to an Indo-Chinese stock, with an admixture of Aryan blood.

The Maharaj Kumar Sidkyong Tulku, son and heir of the Maharaja of Sikkim, who was prevented from coming to Delhi, also pitched his quaint and picturesque tents near those of the Bengal Chiefs. The young prince himself traced the plans of his camp, which was arranged in the usual circular fashion of a Buddhist encampment, surrounded by curious-looking banners inscribed with texts. Inside a large four-sided tent, the roof of which was covered with strange decorations, including the head and hands of the demon who protects Sikkim, was a Lama altar, with all its proper appointments of gold and silver vessels, the eight emblems of happiness and the seven aids to good government. These curious and valuable specimens of Buddhist ecclesiastical art were brought from the Maharaja's ancestral treasure house at Salong. On the walls also were displayed some ancient priestly robes, richly embroidered, and aprons of carved human bones. Scattered about were strangely-fashioned swords, beautiful rugs, and huge brazen trumpets.

The premier nobleman among the zamindars of Bengal—the Nawab of Murshidabad—was unable to attend the Durbar on account of failing health, but he was represented by his son, Asif Kadr Saiyid Wasif Ali Mirza. The Nawab is the eldest son of the last Nawab Nazim of Bengal, Behar and Orissa.

Two other absentees owing to illness were Maharaja Sir Jotindro Mohun Tagore, a large landed proprietor and a well-known citizen of Calcutta, and Prince Kamr Kadr Mirza, the eldest son of the last King of Oudh.

Among the great zamindars of Bengal who attended the Durbar and resided in the Bengal provincial camp were Maharaja Dhiraj Bijay Chand Mahtab Bahadur of Burdwan, the owner of a very large estate, on whose ancestor the title of Raja was conferred by the Emperor Aurungzeb; Maharaja Sir Ravaneshwar Prasad Singh Bahadur of Gidhaur, a member of the Lieutenant-Governor of Bengal's Legislative Council, and the heir of a Rajput family which obtained possession of their estates in Bengal some seven centuries ago; Maharaja Sir Rameshwar Singh Bahadur of Darbhanga, on whose ancestor the title of Maharaja was bestowed by the British Government in recognition of good service rendered during the Nepal War of 1814–15; and Maharaja Girija Nath Roy of Dinajpur, the adopted son and successor of a lady, still living, on whom the title of Maharani was conferred in recognition of the services rendered by her during the famine of 1873–74.

The adjacent Assam camp contained a number of notables from that province, and one ruling Chief, the Maharaja of Manipur, who brought with him an establishment including thirty military police and fifty-six retainers, polo-players, and servants. His Highness, who is still under tutelage, being only eighteen years of age, was accompanied by his tutor and by the Political Agent in Manipur.

In the United Provinces camp were the tents of His Highness the Nawab of Rampur, His Highness the Raja of Tehri, and the Maharaja of Benares. Rampur is the sole surviving representative of what were once termed the Rohilla States, and the ruling family claims descent from Shah Alam and Hussein Khan, two Afghan brothers, who came to India in the latter part of the seventeenth century to seek service under the Moghul emperors. The great-grandfather of the present Chief alone among the leading men of Rohilkhand remained loyal during the Mutiny, and his conspicuous services were rewarded not only with titles and decorations, but also by a substantial strip of territory.

The Raja of Tehri (Garhwal), a Rajput of the solar race, is also the great-grandson of a Chief who rendered valuable assistance to the British in 1857. His Highness was born in 1874, and succeeded his father in 1887. He has travelled in Europe. The title of "Sah," which is borne by the Rajas of Tehri, was bestowed on them by the Moghul emperors.

The Maharaja of Benares, though only a territorial magnate, receives a salute, and was given on this occasion the honours of a ruling Chief.

The leading Talukdars of Oudh, including the Maharajas of Bulrampur and Ajudhya, Raja Jagmohan Singh of Atra, Raja Tasadduk Rasul Khan of Jehangirabad, and Raja Bhup Indra Bikram Singh of Piyagpur, resided in the United Provinces camp, as well as several Nawabs and Rajas from the province of Agra, among whom were Raja Jai Krishen Das Bahadur, Raja Balwant Singh of Awa, Raja Ram Singh of Bansi, Nawab Faiyaz Ali Khan of Pahasu, who attended the King-Emperor's Coronation as the representative of his province, and is the son of the well-known minister of Jaipur of the same name, and Nawab Saiyid Ahmad Shah of Sardhana, whose family was expelled from Kabul on account of the services rendered by them to Sir Alexander Barnes and to the English during the disastrous retreat in 1842.

The seven Shan Chiefs, who came from the region of the Salween and the Mekong to attend the Imperial Durbar, shared with the Burmese guests of Government a quaintly-decorated camp of Burmese design, the tents of which, roofs and walls, were painted over with brightly-coloured figures of dragons and other Burmese devices. It was their first journey to India, and having no friends among the Indian princes and nobles, they lived very quietly in the intervals between the various ceremonies, spending their time in visiting places of interest in the neighbourhood. They were accompanied by five ladies of their families and by 160 ministers, clerks, body-guards, and retainers.

The Chiefs of four feudatory States in the Central Provinces, the Rajas of Sonpur, Khairagarh, Rehrakhol, and Raigarh, came to Delhi to attend the Durbar, and resided in a small camp near that of the United Provinces notables.

The Khan of Kalat and the Jam of Las Bela, with a number of Baluch headmen and notables, resided in the Baluchistan provincial camp, adjoining that of the Punjab Chiefs. His Highness Beglar Begi Mir Sir Mahmud Khan, Khan of Kalat, who succeeded his father in 1893, is the leading chieftain in the Baluch Confederacy. Mir Kamal Khan, the Jam of Las Bela, is the Arab ruler of a State now under the protection of the British Government. He succeeded his father, the late Jam, Sir Mir Khan, in 1895, and was formally invested with powers in January 1902.

The Chiefs and tribal headmen who at the viceregal entry rode with Colonel Deane, Chief Commissioner of the newly-formed North-West Frontier Province, were encamped, with other notables of the Punjab border, alongside the Baluchistan tents. Prominent among them were Shuja-ul-Mulk, the Mehtar of Chitral, who, since he was installed in September 1895, has attained his majority; Nawab Muhammad Sharif Khan of Dir; Nawab Safdar Khan of Nawagai; and Colonel Nawab Muhammad Aslam Khan, now retired from his arduous post of Political Officer in the Khyber, full of honours as an Aide-de-camp to His Majesty.

Owing to the recent death of the Deb Raja, and no successors having been appointed, the State of Bhutan was not represented.

Special mention must be made of the camp on the Alipur Road about two miles from the Viceroy's camp, which accommodated one of the most distinguished of the guests, the representative of the Maharaja of the important frontier State of Nepal, which provides the Indian Army with its brave Gurkha soldiers. The Maharaja, who occupies a quasi-religious position, being prevented by the traditions of the State from leaving his own territory, had sent his Prime Minister, Maharaja Chandra Shamsher Jang, as his representative. The latter is one of the nephews of the late Maharaja Sir Jang Bahadur, who visited England in 1850, and entertained the King-Emperor when Prince of Wales in Nepal in 1876. The British Government first entered into relations with Nepal as early as 1767, and these relations have never been more cordial and satisfactory than they are at the present time, a result which is due in no small measure to the diplomacy and ability of the enlightened minister who came to Delhi.

H. H. The Maharao Raja of Bundi.
G.C.I.E. K.C.S.I.

CHAPTER V

THE EXHIBITION OF INDIAN ARTS

IN framing the programme for the Delhi celebrations earlier in the year, the Viceroy was anxious that so useful an opportunity should not be lost—when the leaders of society and of public opinion throughout India would all be gathered in one place, and when so much wealth would be in circulation—of doing something for those art industries and fabrics for which India was once so famous, and the decline of which is sometimes brought as a charge against the British administration, though it is in reality no more than the local illustration of a law which may be observed in operation in every part of the world, wherever indigenous handicrafts are being ousted by machine-made articles, or where old-fashioned tastes and styles are succumbing to the fascination of what is at once foreign, novel, and relatively cheap. The Viceroy decided that the best method of effecting this object would be to hold at Delhi a great exhibition of all that was best in Indian art, as still produced or capable of production by the best native artificers, carefully selected in all parts of the country and presented with the opportunity and the means of showing their skill.

Such an exhibition would serve more than one useful purpose. It would attract many visitors, and possibly purchasers also, both from inside India and from the outside. It would provide for a more general and accurate survey of the condition of artistic industries in India than had for long been attempted by Government; and for estimating the extent to which they had been favourably or unfavourably affected by foreign competition and foreign demand. It would popularise fabrics or manufactures hardly known because of the remoteness and lack of resources of the artisans who produced them. To the latter it might also supply fresh ideas or patterns. In fact there were few classes of the community who might not benefit in some form or another. From the first the intention was that nothing should be exhibited save the best examples of each artistic handicraft; specimens being carefully chosen which would illustrate the perfection reached in the various branches of industrial art. The aims of the Indian Government were explained in a letter addressed to the Local Governments and Administrations in March 1902. "The main test," it was then said, "to be applied in each case will be that of artistic merit, the handicrafts selected being those that have already attained a certain pitch of proficiency and are capable of further development." In addition to such exhibits as would be offered for sale, arrangements were made to get together a collection of exhibits on loan, obtained from museums, or lent by private persons; and a special and successful appeal was made to native Chiefs and noblemen with this object. The loan collection was likewise to be restricted to the best examples of still existing handicrafts, which might serve as a standard of approved merit and a guide to Indian craftsmen in their future endeavours. Dr., now Sir George, Watt, Reporter on Economic Products to the Government of India, was appointed Director of the Exhibition, and was entrusted with the task of selecting the exhibits, as well as with the general organisation and control of the arrangements.

A convenient site for the Exhibition building was found in the Kudsia Bagh, an old Muhammadan garden, between the Kashmir Gate of the city and No. 1 Visitors' camp. Here, where the Kudsia Begum, the dancing girl who became a queen, wife of one Moghul emperor and the mother of another, had made for herself a palace and pleasaunce, there was now erected what the natives called the *Ajaib ghar*, "the house of marvels," where was to be displayed the unique collection of Indian art manufactures brought together by the Director and his assistants—costly enamels, embroideries and brocades, carpets made to the order of Moghul emperors, gold and silver plate, carvings in wood, marble, ivory, and jade, fabrics of silk, cotton, and wool, dyed and embroidered, jewellery of every description, from a Raja's richly gemmed necklet or sword hilt, to the peasant woman's bangle.

The Exhibition building itself, in common with every structure erected at Delhi by the Viceroy's orders for the ceremonials of the fortnight, was designed in careful accordance with the canons of Indo-Saracenic architecture; and, as will be seen from the illustration facing page 91, was in admirable keeping with the associations of the place. Within was a spacious hall, measuring 220 feet by 80 feet: four rooms assigned for special exhibitions to the Schools of Art in Madras, Bombay, the Punjab and Burma; two large galleries for the loan and jewellery collections; and other accommodation. In an outer verandah, representative craftsmen from all parts of India practised their various arts; brocade-weaving, carpet-making, silk-dyeing, calico-printing, wood-carving, etc. The ornamental tiles used in the building were obtained from Lahore, Multan, Halla, and Jaipur; and the fresco painting was executed by pupils of the Mayo School of Art at Lahore.

His Excellency the Viceroy formally opened the Exhibition on Tuesday, December 30th, the ceremony being attended by Their Royal Highnesses the Duke and Duchess of Connaught, the Grand Duke of Hesse, several of the ruling Chiefs and a large number of visitors from the various camps. Among those present were the Nizam of Hyderabad, the Maharaja of Kashmir, the Khan of Kalat, the Maharao of Bundi, the Maharajas of Bikaner, Kishangarh, and Alwar, the Maharao of Kota, the Maharaja of Gwalior, the Raja of Cochin, the Maharajas of Kolhapur and Idar, the Rao of Cutch, the Mir of Khairpur, the Maharaja of Patiala, the Rajas of Jind and Kapurthala, and the Maharaja of Kuch Behar. Standing at the entrance to the Exhibition and addressing the large audience which was seated outside the building, His Excellency spoke as follows:—

"YOUR ROYAL HIGHNESSES, YOUR HIGHNESSES, LADIES AND GENTLEMEN,—It is now my pleasant duty to proceed to the first of the functions of the present fortnight, and to declare open the Delhi Arts Exhibition. A good many of our visitors would scarcely believe that almost everything that we see before us, except the trees, is the creation of the last eight months. When I came here in April last to select the site, there was not a trace of this great building, of these terraces, and of all the amenities that we now see around. They have all sprung into existence for the sake of this Exhibition, and though the effects of the Exhibition will, I hope, not be so quickly wiped out, the *mise-en-scène* is, I am sorry to say, destined to disappear.

"Perhaps you will expect me to say a few words about the circumstances in which this Exhibition started into being. Ever since I have been in India I have made a careful study of the art industries and handicrafts of this country, once so famous and beautiful, and I have lamented, as many others have done, their progressive deterioration and decline. When it was settled that we were to hold this great gathering at Delhi, at which there would be assembled representatives of every Province and State in India, Indian Princes and Chiefs and nobles, high officials, native gentlemen, and visitors from all parts of the globe, it struck me that here at last was the long-sought opportunity of doing something to resuscitate these threatened handicrafts, to show to the world of what India is still capable, and, if possible, to arrest the process of decay. I accordingly sent for Dr. Watt, and I appointed him my right hand for the purpose. Far and wide throughout India have he and his assistant, Mr. Percy Brown, proceeded, travelling thousands of miles, everywhere interviewing the artisans, selecting specimens, giving orders, where necessary supplying models, and advancing money to those who needed it. Three conditions I laid down, to be observed like the laws of the Medes and Persians.

"First, I stipulated that this must be an Arts Exhibition, and nothing else. We could easily have given you a wonderful show illustrating the industrial and economic development of India. Dr. Watt has such an exhibition, and a very good one too, at Calcutta. We could have shown you timbers, and minerals, and raw stuffs, and hides, and manufactured articles, to any extent that you pleased. It would all have been very satisfying, but also very ugly. But I did not want that. I did not mean this to be an industrial or economic Exhibition. I meant it to be an Arts Exhibition, and that only.

"My second condition was that I would not have anything European or quasi-European in it. I declined to admit any of those horrible objects, such as lamps on gorgeous pedestals, coloured glass lustres, or fantastic statuettes, that find such a surprising vogue among certain classes in this country, but that are bad anywhere in the world, and worst of all in India, which has an art of its own. I laid down that I wanted only the work that represented the ideas, the traditions, the instincts, and the beliefs of the people. It is possible that a few articles that do not answer to my definition may have crept in, because the process of Europeanisation is going on apace in this country, and the number of teapots, cream jugs, napkin rings, salt cellars, and cigarette

Bourne & Shepherd

OPENING OF THE ARTS EXHIBITION

cases that the Indian artisan is called upon to turn out is appalling. But, generally speaking, my condition has been observed.

"Then my third condition was that I would only have the best. I did not want cheap cottons and wax-cloths, vulgar lacquer, trinkets and tinsel, brass gods and bowls made to order in Birmingham, or perhaps made in Birmingham itself. What I desired was an exhibition of all that is rare, characteristic, or beautiful in Indian art, our gold and silver ware, our metal work and enamels, and jewellery, our carving in wood and ivory and stone, our best pottery and tiles, our carpets of old Oriental patterns, our muslins and silks and embroideries, and the incomparable Indian brocades. All of these you will see inside this building. But please remember it is not a bazaar, but an Exhibition. Our object has been to encourage and revive good work, not to satisfy the requirements of the thinly lined purse.

"Such is the general character of the Exhibition. But we have added to it something much more important. Conscious that taste is declining, and that many of our modern models are debased and bad, we have endeavoured to set up, alongside the products of the present, the standards and samples of the past. This is the meaning of the Loan Collection, which has a hall to itself, in which you will see many beautiful specimens of old Indian artware, lent to us by the generosity of Indian Chiefs and connoisseurs, some of it coming from our own Indian Museums, and some from the unrivalled collection in the South Kensington Museum in London. Many of these objects are beautiful in themselves; but we hope that the Indian workmen who are here, and also the patrons who employ them, will study them not merely as objects of antiquarian or even artistic interest, but as supplying them with fresh, or, rather, resuscitated, ideas which may be useful to them in inspiring their own work in the future. For this may be laid down as a truism, that Indian art will never be revived by borrowing foreign ideals, but only by fidelity to its own.

"And now I may be asked, What is the object of this Exhibition, and what good do I expect to result from it? I will answer in a very few words. In so far as the decline of the Indian arts represents the ascendency of commercialism, the superiority of steam power to hand power, the triumph of the test of utility over that of taste, then I have not much hope. We are witnessing in India only one aspect of a process that is going on throughout the world, that has long ago extinguished the old manual industries of England, and that is rapidly extinguishing those of China and Japan. Nothing can stop it. The power-loom will drive out the hand-loom, and the factory will get the better of the workshop, just as surely as the steam-car is superseding the horsed carriage, and as the hand-pulled punkah is being replaced by the electric fan. All that is inevitable, and in an age which wants things cheap, and does not mind their being ugly, which cares a good deal for comfort, and not much for beauty, and which is never happy unless it is deserting its own models and traditions, and running about in quest of something foreign and strange, we may be certain that a great many of the old arts and handicrafts are doomed.

"There is another symptom that to my mind is even more ominous. I am one of those, as I have said, who believe that no national art is capable of continued existence unless it satisfies the ideals, and expresses the wants, of the nation that has produced it. No art can be kept alive by globe-trotters or curio-hunters alone. If it has got to that point, it becomes a mere mechanical reproduction of certain fashionable patterns: and when the fashion changes, and they cease to be popular, it dies. If Indian art, therefore, is to continue to flourish or is to be revived, it can only be if the Indian Chiefs and aristocracy, and people of culture and high degree, undertake to patronise it. So long as they prefer to fill their palaces with flaming Brussels carpets, with Tottenham Court Road furniture, with cheap Italian mosaics, with French oleographs, with Austrian lustres, and with German tissues and cheap brocades, I fear there is not much hope. I speak in no terms of reproach, because I think that in England we are just as bad in our pursuit of anything that takes our fancy in foreign lands. But I do say that if Indian arts and handicrafts are to be kept alive, it can never be by outside patronage alone. It can only be because they find a market within the country and express the ideas and culture of its people. I should like to see a movement spring up among the Indian Chiefs and nobility for the expurgation, or, at any rate, the purification, of modern tastes, and for a reversion to the old-fashioned but exquisite styles and patterns of their own country. Some day I have not a doubt that it will come. But it may then be too late.

"If these are the omens, what then is the aim of this Exhibition, and what purpose do I think that it will serve? I can answer in a word. The Exhibition is intended as an object-lesson. It is meant to show what India can still imagine, and create, and do. It is meant to show that the artistic sense is not dead among its workmen, but that all they want is a little stimulus and encouragement. It is meant to show that for the beautification of an Indian house or the furniture of an Indian home, there is no need to rush to the European shops at Calcutta or Bombay, but that in almost every Indian State and Province, in most Indian towns, and in many Indian villages, there still survives the art, and there still exist the artificers who can satisfy the artistic, as well as the utilitarian, tastes of their countrymen, and who are competent to keep alive this precious inheritance that we have received from the past. It is with this object that Dr. Watt and I have laboured in creating this Exhibition; and in now declaring it open, it only remains for me to express the earnest hope that it may in some measure fulfil the strictly patriotic purpose for which it has been designed."

After the opening ceremony, the Royal and Viceregal party entered the building and walked through the hall and galleries, frequently stopping to inspect some of the choicer exhibits. Under the orders of the Indian Government, a complete and sumptuously illustrated catalogue * of the Exhibition was prepared by Sir George Watt, and to this the reader must be referred for an adequate account of the collection, since it would be impossible here to describe even the most notable objects, where so many claimed attention, either as masterpieces of a by-gone day, as specimens of artistic craftsmanship of a purely Oriental type, still practised and to be wisely encouraged, or as the outcome of a conscientious and intelligent endeavour to revive, foster, or improve expiring or extinct industries. Sir George Watt's work is, however, much more than its name implies. It is a comprehensive analysis and narrative of contemporaneous Indian art, arranged in due sequence, and compiled and illustrated with a wealth of knowledge to be found in no other volume. It constitutes in itself a sufficient justification of the undertaking to which it was only originally designed as an adjunct.

A liberal response was made by the Chiefs, nobles, and native gentry to the Viceroy's appeal for the loan of artistic treasures in their possession. By order of the Nizam's Government a collection of silver, copper, and brass ware, gold and silver embroideries, textiles, etc., was made for the Exhibition; and the Minister, Maharaja Peshkar Sir Kishen Pershad Bahadur, lent some fine specimens of *bidri* ware. The Gaekwar of Baroda exhibited the carpet of pearls, which his predecessor, Maharaja Khande Rao Gaekwar, intended to present to the tomb of Muhammad. Among the articles lent by the Maharaja of Mysore, were some fine examples of embossed and encrusted silver plate, and old

* "Indian Art at Delhi, 1903," by Sir George Watt, published by the Superintendent of Government Printing, Calcutta.

carved ivories; while modern art was represented by wooden inlay work and other ornamentations prepared for His Highness's new palace. The Kashmir State sent seventy shawls for the loan exhibits, one of which was said to be worth Rs. 22,000; as well as some beautiful enamelled ware, and three silver images, obtained from the Buddhist Monastery at Leh in Maharaja Gulab Singh's time. General Sir Amar Singh also lent a superb ewer and other articles from his private collection.

Noticeable among the exhibits lent by the Chiefs of Rajputana were the large number of richly ornamented weapons, including a remarkable collection of matchlocks, swords, daggers, etc., from the Jodhpur armoury. The Maharana of Udaipur sent, among other things, two beautiful hookah bowls of jade, one set with carved emeralds, the other with rubies, which were greatly admired. But, indeed, almost every Native State in India had been induced to send some treasured rarity; and the researches of the Director and his assistants had brought to light articles, of the greatest historical and artistic interest, in places where their existence had never been suspected. Thus, the Raja of Chamba, a State in the Punjab hills, was found in possession of an exquisite set of daggers, with gold enamelled handles, given to his ancestor by the Emperor Akbar. These were lent to the Exhibition. The three specimens of ivory carving representing a tortoise and the God Krishna, made only fifty years ago in the Orissa State of Nayagarh, were amongst the most beautiful and artistic exhibits.

Nor were Sir George Watt's discoveries confined to the Native States. At Ajmer he came across what may probably be classed among the oldest examples known of ancient Hindu wood carving, namely, two doors which Akbar took from Chitor in 1580. From Bijapur came a carpet which is said to have been presented to the mosque there by the Emperor Aurungzeb, and some other carpets which, it is believed, were made in Kashmir two and a half centuries ago. Another interesting feature of the Exhibition was a collection of costumes worn by the wives of Rajas and Nawabs at their weddings, at various times during the last three hundred years. There were also a number of pictures by native artists, one of them being a contemporary record of Lord Lake's entry

H. H. The Maharaja of Bikaner.
K.C.I.E.

into Delhi after the battle of Laswari, which the Marquis Wellesley described as a triumph then unsurpassed in the history of our arms in India. This curious picture, which cleverly commemorates an elephant procession in the early part of the last century, was lent by the Maharaja of Alwar.

Mention may also be made of the loan exhibit from the Victoria and Albert Museum, South Kensington. At the request of the Viceroy, Sir Caspar Purdon Clarke, the Director, himself a leading authority on all questions relating to Oriental art, selected a number of the finest examples of Indian workmanship in the national collection, and sent them to Delhi. The two beautiful carpets from Warangal in the Deccan were shown at the great Exhibition of 1851, and are the finest at South Kensington. The vases and other articles of carved and jewelled jade were of the richest quality. A glass hookah stand, ornamented with flowers in bold relief, the background being delicately chipped away, was made probably for some Moghul Emperor or noble, and is unique. The brass and copper ware from Tibet and Chinese Turkestan was exceptionally interesting to the connoisseur. All articles sent from South Kensington, with the exception of the mosaics from the Diwan-i Am, referred to in Chapter VIII., were afterwards returned.

While the wish of the Indian Government to collect materials for a general survey of the industrial arts of the country was abundantly fulfilled, convincing evidence was soon afforded that the secondary purpose of the Exhibition had not been missed. The palace of art in the Kudsia Bagh was visited daily by enormous crowds. Indeed, the treasures it contained were such an irresistible attraction to the natives resident in, and visiting Delhi that, more than once, people had to be turned away at the doors as the building was full. During the short time for which it was open, 48,000 persons paid for admission. Of the exhibits that were for sale, many might have been disposed of for far higher sums than the prices marked, and as it was, purchases were made to the value of over 3½ lakhs of rupees. Some were acquired by the Government for Museums and Schools of Art; the Indian Chiefs, nobles, and gentry bought freely; and visitors from all parts of the world gladly availed themselves of the opportunity of obtaining, at a reasonable price, carefully selected examples of what is really good in Indian art workmanship.

To estimate the effects produced by the Exhibition directly and indirectly on the arts and crafts of the Indian Empire, and on the public taste, which, to a greater or less extent, reacts on the quantity and quality of the supply, would be impossible. Time alone will reveal whether the honest and enlightened endeavour of the Government, to encourage the producer and to stimulate a healthy demand for the best products of his skill, has been attended with success. On the other hand, it is satisfactory to think that something has been done which, by serving as a strong incentive to good workmanship, can hardly fail to have exerted a wholesome influence. The award of prizes, medals, and certificates of excellence to exhibitors and craftsmen, for the most meritorious articles exhibited, in each of the ten classes into which the Exhibition was divided, will have taught both the workers and those who employ them that there is really an improved standard of artistic merit, and that there is advantage in following it. The task of selecting the prize-winners was assigned to a judging Committee, composed of the following gentlemen:

President.

COLONEL SIR SWINTON JACOB.

Members.

GENERAL STUART BEATSON.
C. L. BURNS, ESQ.
CHEVALIER O. GHILARDI.
COLONEL T. H. HENDLEY, I.M.S.
R. D. MACKENZIE, ESQ.
MUNSHI MADHO LAL.
BHAI RAM SINGH.
E. THURSTON, ESQ.

Secretary.

R. E. V. ARBUTHNOT, ESQ.

Nineteen gold medals were placed at the disposal of the Committee, the Government of India presenting five, the Maharaja of Kuch Behar four, the Rajas of Kapurthala and Poonch, and Raja Sir Amar Singh, two each, Munshi Madho Lal three, and Raja Bahadur Ranajit Sinha of Nashipur one. These were awarded as follows:

CLASS I.—METAL WARES.

1. Metal ware (Copper and Brass) from Jaipur School of Art.
2. Niello work, bowl and dish—Saya Po of Toungoo.
3. Silver work—Maung Yin Maung of Rangoon.

CLASS II.—STONE WARE.

4. A carved sandstone house from Bharatpur, Bharatpur State.

CLASS III.—GLASS AND EARTHENWARE.

None.

CLASS IV.—WOOD WORK.

5. Model of a carved wooden façade from Bhavnagar, Bhavnagar State.
6. Wood carving—Mayo School of Art, Lahore.
7. Carved figure in wood of a Burmese Princess—Maung Than Yegyan of Rangoon.
8. Bombay Art Furnished Room—Bombay School of Art.
9. Carved sandal-wood casket—Shapur Subbrayappa and Sagar Dodda Putappa of Mysore.

CLASS V.—IVORY, HORN, LEATHER, ETC.

10. A collection of carved ivory by Fakir Chand Raghu Nath Dass of Delhi.
11 Ivory casket—School of Art, Trevandrum.

CLASS VI.—LAC, LACQUER, ETC.

None.

CLASS VII.—TEXTILES.

12. Gold kincobs—Bhagwan Das Gopi Nath of Benares.

CLASS VIII.—EMBROIDERY.

13. A pair of shawls—Trailokya Nath Das of Dacca and Murshidabad.
14. A collection of chikan work by Kedar Nath Ram Nath and Co. of Lucknow.
15. Collection of Kashmir shawls (woven and embroidered) from His Highness the Maharaja of Kashmir.

CLASS IX.—CARPETS.

16. Kashmir Manufacturing Co., Srinagar.
17. The Agra Central Jail.

CLASS X.—FINE ARTS.

18. Mr. G. K. Mhatre of Bombay, for the figure of a girl.
19. Bhagwant Singh of the Lucknow Industrial School, for clay modelling.

In addition to these prizes, 83 silver and 115 bronze medals were awarded, and 110 exhibits were commended. A sum of Rs. 4900, subscribed by ruling Chiefs and European and Indian gentlemen, was also distributed among the craftsmen who made the articles for which medals were given. A full list of the awards was published in the *Gazette of India*, April 25th, 1903, and will also be found in the official catalogue.

The Exhibition building was the scene of a gathering, not less interesting, though less crowded, than that of the opening day, when on Friday, January 2nd, the Viceroy gave an afternoon reception there to the native guests of the Indian Government. This was attended by almost all the Indian nobles and gentlemen other than ruling Chiefs, who were present at Delhi in an official capacity; and many of these were introduced upon this occasion to His Excellency and to His Royal Highness the Duke of Connaught. The Duchess of Connaught, Lady Curzon, Lord and Lady Ampthill, Lord and Lady Northcote, and many high officials and English visitors from the various camps were also present. Much satisfaction was caused by the provision of this special opportunity for personal conversation between the Viceroy and his Royal guests on the one hand, and the many distinguished and representative Indians who had been drawn together from all parts of the country on the other. The evening party in the viceregal camp, to be described in a subsequent chapter, effected the same object with the ruling Chiefs. Constant occasions presented themselves for intercourse with the European officials and guests; and thus among all those who were invited to Delhi, there was no section that was not enabled to pay its respects personally to the representative and to the brother of the Sovereign. The Kudsia building achieved not the least of many useful purposes by facilitating this object.

E. Vandyk, London, photo. Walker & Cockerell Ph. Sc.

H.H. The Maharaja of Gwalior,
A.D.C., G.C.S.I., G.C.V.O.

CHAPTER VI

THE IMPERIAL DURBAR

At an early hour on New Year's Day, 1903, the environs of Delhi were alive with the final dispositions for the supreme pageant that had brought together so many thousands of persons from all parts of the civilised world. Princes and notables, governors and high officials, were preparing for their several parts in the Imperial ceremony. Regiments and batteries were starting for their appointed stations. The hard-worked staffs of civilians and military men, on whose energy and power of organisation depended the successful marshalling of the great assemblage, were still strenuously engaged in what seemed the interminable toil of evolving order from confusion, and of guarding against all possible chance of unrehearsed mishap. Visitors and sightseers were braving the sharp cold of a Delhi winter's morning, in order that they might arrive in good time at the scene of the long-expected celebrations.

Soon the well-watered highways, leading from Delhi to the Amphitheatre on the open plain, some four miles to the north of the Kashmir Gate, as well as the side roads from the various camps, were filled with broad streams of people, in carriages, on horseback, and afoot, all making for the same goal. Others availed themselves of the light railway, on which a succession of trains ran to the station near the Amphitheatre. Along the Alipur Road, Rajas, escorted by their cavalry, appeared in richly painted and gilded state carriages drawn by four-horse teams. Vehicles of every denomination, from the English-built landau or pony-cart to lumbering bullock-waggons and the humbler *ekka*, carried an endless procession of spectators, among whom might be seen English and native officials, strangers from scenes as far apart as the banks of the Hudson and the Yarra, or the capital cities of Pretoria and Tokio; Pathans from the North-West frontier, Chiefs from the region hitherto known as Yaghistan—the "Land of the Outlaw;" bearded and ringleted warriors from the highlands of Baluchistan; men of strange speech and stranger garb from the borderlands of China and Tibet; Sheikhs and Sultans from the shores of the Arabian Sea; and types of every race within the confines of the Indian Empire.

New Year's Day was the first of the Muhammadan month of Shawal, when the festival of the Id-ul-Fitr signals the termination of the month of fasting: for during Ramazan, "ere the better moon arose," followers of the Prophet may not, unless on a journey, eat or drink during the hours between sunrise and sunset. On the previous night, like the watchers of whom Omar Khayyam wrote, "one spied the little crescent all were seeking"; and, accordingly, on the day of the Durbar, there was a great gathering, in the forenoon, for prayers at the Id-gah; on which account, and for the convenience of the Muhammadans who desired to attend, the opening of the ceremony was postponed from mid-day to half-past twelve. Long before that hour, however, thanks to the warnings given in advance and to the general success of the police in directing the stream of vehicles and pedestrians, the majority of the spectators, official and unofficial, had assembled at the great Amphitheatre. The Chiefs drove up to the entrances on the outer circumference, where each was received by the guard of honour to which he was entitled, and was conducted by a political officer to the place assigned to him. When over a hundred Chiefs had to be received with a dignity and attention befitting their rank, no slight strain was imposed upon the officers who had been entrusted with this duty; but so carefully had all the arrangements been planned and rehearsed that no mistake occurred and not a single complaint was received. As each Chief arrived he was presented with a translation in Urdu of the speech which the Viceroy was about to deliver at the Durbar. This had been printed on cardboard in gold characters. Each noble and durbari received a similar translation printed in red, so that there were few persons present, at least among those of education or rank, who could not follow the proceedings throughout, even though they were not familiar with the English language.

The military preparations were not less carefully planned and thorough. All the troops in camp paraded, in review order, at an early hour for the Durbar ceremonial. The two divisions of Infantry, each including thirteen battalions, marched to the ground and were formed up in line of quarter-column, opposite to, and about four hundred yards from, the entrance to the Amphitheatre, the line extending about a thousand yards. The place of the 2nd battalion, Gordon Highlanders, which furnished the guard of honour inside the Amphitheatre and the guards at the various entrances, was taken by the 28th Punjabis. This solid mass of Infantry was flanked on its right by the Corps troops, including the 38th Brigade Division (24th, 34th, and 72nd Batteries), Royal Field Artillery; and No. 3 Company and the Pontoon and Balloon Sections of the Bengal Sappers and Miners. Beyond these were the 1st Brigade Division (13th, 67th, and 69th Batteries), Royal Field Artillery. On the left flank of the Infantry divisions were, to the immediate left of the 2nd Division, the Imperial Service Infantry (seven battalions), and the Maler Kotla and Sirmur Sappers and Miners; to the left of these, the 39th Brigade Division (46th, 51st, and 54th Batteries), Royal Field Artillery. The total number of troops on the ground, or guarding its approaches, was 39,607.

Durbar Road, along which the Viceroy and the Duke of Connaught were to drive to the Amphitheatre, was lined by troops, in the following order, beginning with the section furthest from the Amphitheatre: Imperial Service Cavalry (fourteen squadrons), and Bikaner Camel Corps; Mounted Infantry (two British and four Native companies); Divisional Cavalry (eight squadrons), including the Guides Cavalry and the 5th Punjab Cavalry (each two squadrons), and a composite Regiment of the Central India Horse; Corps Cavalry (eight squadrons), including the 18th Bengal Lancers and one squadron each from the 1st and 2nd Punjab Cavalry and 10th and 14th Bengal Lancers; Volunteer Cavalry; the 1st Cavalry Brigade (12 squadrons) on the west, and 2nd

Cavalry Brigade (12 squadrons) on the east of the road, facing each other; the troops thus far lining both sides of the road; thence, up to the point where the road turned off toward the Amphitheatre, D., I., and H. Batteries, Royal Horse Artillery, on the east of the road only. The infantry portion of the viceregal Escort (1st battalion, Northamptonshire Regiment and the 15th Sikh Infantry) was drawn up on either side of the road outside the entrance to the Amphitheatre, and between it and the long line of infantry. After the arrivals of Their Royal Highnesses and the Viceroy, their cavalry Escorts also formed up here, behind the infantry.

Although situated on almost identically the same spot where, in 1877, Lord Lytton had proclaimed to the Princes of India the assumption by Queen Victoria of the Imperial Title, the building erected for Lord Curzon's Durbar differed greatly in design and structure, as will appear from the plan, from that which was found sufficient, a quarter of a century earlier, for the less crowded assemblage of his predecessor. In 1877, the Indian Governors, Lieutenant-Governors, ruling Chiefs, and higher officials were seated in a crescent-shaped structure, forming rather more than the quadrant of a circle and facing the Viceroy, while Lord Lytton addressed them from an isolated hexagonal Daïs erected slightly in advance of what would have been the centre of the circle. The remaining officials and spectators witnessed the proceedings from smaller blocks placed to the rear of the viceregal Daïs. The total number of persons who were accommodated in these various stands did not exceed 5000. A reference to the plans and drawings of Lord Lytton's Ampitheatre will show that it was an exceedingly well-designed and picturesque structure. But it possessed certain unavoidable drawbacks. Nearly half of the audience were behind the Viceroy, and did not catch a word that he said. His remarks were scarcely more audible in the tiers of seats in front of him, the nearest point of which was at a distance of over seventy-five yards from the Daïs. Nor was there in the design or in the decorations, which consisted exclusively of bunting, shields, flags, and streamers, anything suggestive of the East.

On the present occasion it was clear that a larger building and a different design were essential, both in order to accommodate the vastly

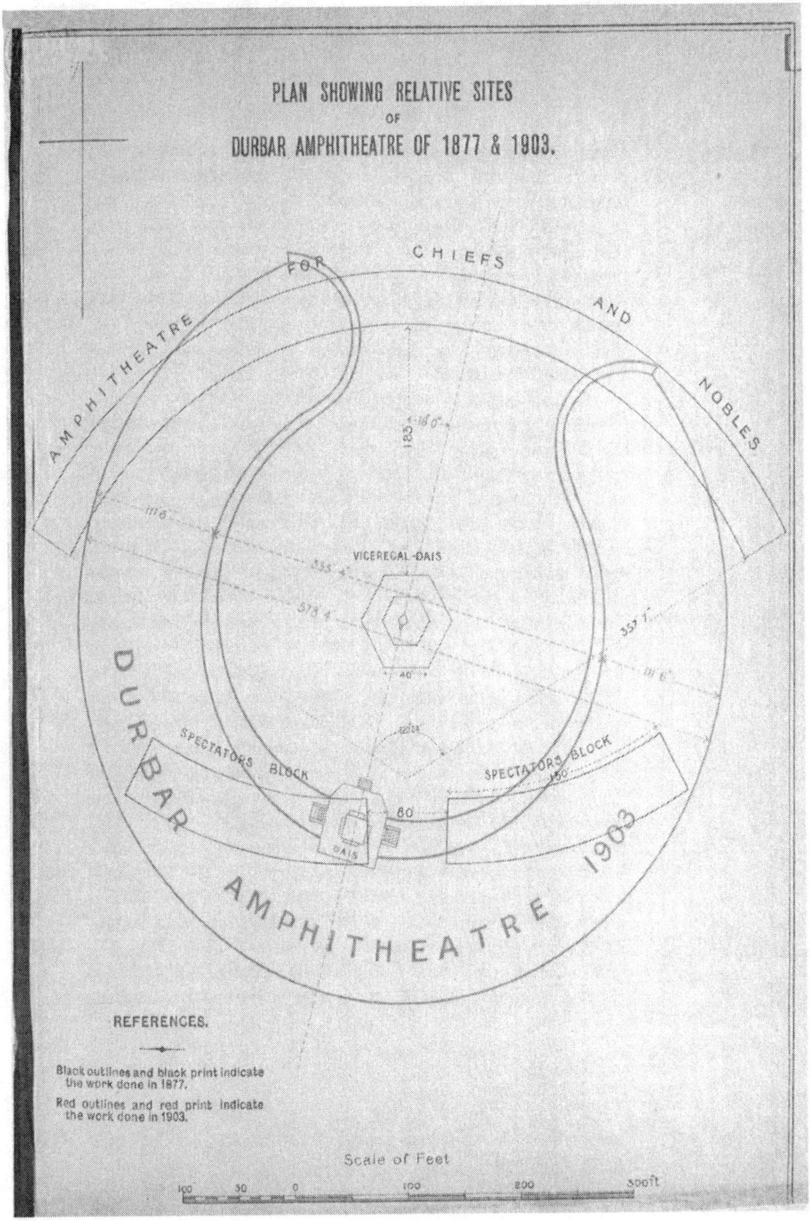
PLAN SHOWING RELATIVE SITES
OF
DURBAR AMPHITHEATRE OF 1877 & 1903.
AMPHITHEATRE FOR CHIEFS AND NOBLES
VICEREGAL DAIS
SPECTATORS BLOCK
SPECTATORS BLOCK
DAIS
DURBAR AMPHITHEATRE 1903
REFERENCES.
Black outlines and black print indicate the work done in 1877.
Red outlines and red print indicate the work done in 1903.
Scale of Feet
100 50 0 100 200 300ft

greater attendance that was expected, and to enable the Viceroy and the Duke of Connaught to associate with the assemblage some of the time-honoured features of an Indian Durbar. A year and a half before the Durbar was held, the matter had been considered by the Viceroy, who came to the conclusion that a building shaped like a horse-shoe would be the best adapted for the requisite purposes of hearing and action; and with the help of Colonel (now Sir Swinton) Jacob, so well known for his architectural works in northern India, a plan had been sketched and drawings prepared.

In April 1902, the Viceroy went to Delhi to inspect the site. The scene of Lord Lytton's Durbar had long ago relapsed into its pristine state and was scarcely distinguishable from the surrounding country. Indeed, many long residents in Delhi, whose business had never taken them outside of the city in that direction, were unaware of the exact locality. Upon arrival at the spot it was found that a small heap of bricks was all that remained of the Daïs of 1877, while the site of the crescent-shaped auditorium was only just traceable by a faint swelling in the ground above the level of the cultivated plain. It was decided to treat Lord Lytton's Daïs as the centre of the new arena, and to shift the axis of the latter to a point a little to the east of north. The mounds that marked the site of the former tiers of seats were to be absorbed in the necessarily larger erection that was to take their place.

As the engineers proceeded with the work, it was found desirable by the Viceroy to introduce a number of material alterations into the original plans. The drawings of Sir S. Jacob had provided for an Amphitheatre to be covered with a light canopy of blue and white canvas in stripes, with emblematic banners on the roof. It was decided to substitute for this a fabric of exclusively Saracenic design, every feature of which should be copied from one of the Moghul buildings at Delhi or Agra, and which, though constructed only of wood and iron, should simulate the appearance of white marble. As the works advanced, and as fresh models were prepared and submitted, further modifications were made in these plans; and the final design was not settled until the Viceroy's last visit of inspection to the site at the beginning of December 1902.

In order to protect the spectators from strong winds or rain, to both of which Delhi is liable at Christmas time, as well as from the mid-day sun, the entire space to be occupied by sitting or standing persons, amounting to 100,000 square feet, was now roofed over, the roofing being extended so as to cover the *terre-plein* at the back, thus providing accommodation for nearly 4000 additional spectators. The somewhat heavy and overcrowded pillars supporting the roof of the Amphitheatre seemed likely to obstruct the view of the Daïs. Accordingly, by the use of girders, the supports were greatly reduced in size and number, with the result that a full view of the proceedings was obtainable from every seat. An even more important alteration was made in the Saracenic pavilion that crowned the Daïs. The original design had provided for an octagonal structure in direct reproduction of the marble kiosques or *chatris* that are such conspicuous features in Moghul architecture. But the study of a model at once revealed that the too numerous pillars of such a building would have effectually screened the actors on the Daïs from a great many of the spectators; and Rai Bahadurs Bhai Ram Singh and Gunga Ram, who designed or carried out all these works with equal zeal and fidelity, were accordingly commissioned by the Viceroy to substitute a four-sided pavilion copied from one of Akbar's buildings at Agra. This answered its purpose admirably. On the occasion of the final inspection it was also decided to lighten the general effect of the Amphitheatre by reducing the number of cupolas raised upon the roof-ridge, and to admit no ornamentation, except a little gilding on the pillars and arches and the finials of the domes. With these exceptions the entire building was painted a creamy white. On the same occasion the arrangements of the Daïs, and of the broad platform sweeping up to it from the lowest tiers of seats, by which the Princes were to ascend for the ceremony of presentation at the close of the Durbar, were carefully reconsidered and rehearsed so as to leave nothing to chance or to accident on the final day. As regards the seating of the spectators, it may be mentioned that in the lowest row, where the Chiefs and leading officials were placed, the seats consisted of chairs specially manufactured for the occasion and upholstered in dark blue. Behind were four rows of cane-bottomed chairs, and in the higher tiers wooden benches cushioned with red upholstery. In front of the lowest tiers a crimson cloth covered the broad platform, two feet above the ground level, that ran completely round the arena and ascended the Daïs, which was two feet higher, on either hand by means of a broad sloping ramp.

The whole centre of the arena, except the space occupied by the carriage-drive, was covered with turf, and turf also had been planted on the slopes at the back of the Amphitheatre, between the broad flights of steps, strewn with red gravel, that gave access to the several blocks of seats. In the centre of the arena stood the Imperial flag-staff, 100 feet high. Erected round its base was a small stand or box from which Captain Sanford directed the bands. The Viceroy's flag-staff was placed behind the Daïs, and rose to a height of seventy feet above the platform, so that the flag, when unfurled, floated out above the summit of the central dome. The low white balustrade of pierced lattice work (known as *jali*) which ran along the edge both of the platforms and Daïs, and of the roof, had also been directly copied from the marble parapets of the the Saracenic mosques and tombs.

These details may perhaps prove of interest as explaining the history and evolution of a structure which excited the keenest interest among all those who saw it; which served its purpose of accommodating some 16,000 spectators, every one of whom could both see and hear, as well, in all probability, as any structure that has ever been raised; but which, having now disappeared, has nothing to recall it beyond the impression left on record by so many photographic cameras or artists' pencils.

Even to those who are thus acquainted with the external appearance of the Delhi structure, a truer idea of its size and proportions may be conveyed by comparing them with what is perhaps the most famous Amphitheatre in the world, namely, the Colosseum at Rome. The latter enclosed an arena, of elliptical shape, measuring along its major axis, 287 feet from end to end, and 180 feet across. The total area thus embraced was 40,495 square feet. The circular arena included within the horse-shoe theatre at Delhi, the open ends of which left an entrance 220 feet across, measured about 101,828 square feet. The interior space of the Colosseum might thus have been marked out inside the arena of the Delhi Amphitheatre, and there would still have been ample room to spare.

In its elevation, of course, the Durbar Amphitheatre offered no points of comparison with the Colosseum. It was built neither to stand the wear of centuries, nor to hold the far larger multitudes that flocked to see the pageants of imperial Rome. From the sixty or eighty rows of stone seats, tier upon tier, of the Colosseum, upwards of 80,000 people could applaud the contests of gladiators, the mimic sea-fights, the massacres of animals and human beings lavishly provided for their amusement. At Delhi it was not considered necessary to provide seats for more than about 13,430 spectators; with standing room for about 2570 others, a total of about 16,000. For the purpose of seeing and hearing, however, nearly every one of this total was equally well placed with his neighbour; for while those nearest to the Daïs could follow the proceedings more closely, those who were further away enjoyed a finer panoramic effect.

The illusion produced by the remarkable structure that has been described was so successful and so complete that, to an observer standing at the entrance between the two extremities of the horse-shoe, it seemed that over the wide, curved embankment, on which the rising tiers of seats were placed, there had been thrown a light roof of white marble, supported on two rows of marble pillars; while the platform and canopy in the hollow of the circle, equidistant from either end, appeared to be a solid structure of the same material. From a distance of miles the white circle of the Amphitheatre could be seen resting like a patch of snow on the drab surface of the plain. Nearer at hand its airy arches and light cupolas tipped with gold exercised a fascination that never seemed to diminish, and that added a touch of romantic beauty to the solemn scenes which were about to be enacted in this appropriate setting.

The location of the Daïs further marked a striking and significant difference between the ceremony of 1903 and the Imperial Assemblage of 1877. The Viceroy was now to sit, not, as then, apart from the ruling Princes and English governors of India, facing and addressing them from a distance, but in their very midst. As in the state procession, three days before, the position occupied by the ruling Chiefs was to be the prouder one of colleagues and partners, as it were, of the Sovereign's representative. They had come to Delhi not to pay a reluctant homage to alien rulers; but to take their part, with the Viceroy, as the chief actors in the performance of an Imperial function. In the presence of the King-Emperor's brother, and in the eyes of India and the world, they were to appear as the trusted supporters of the Indian Government and as the foremost of the feudatories of the Crown. It was this conception of the part to be played by them that had been placed before the Chiefs in advance by the Viceroy, and that had brought them as eager participants in the ceremony from all parts of India. Anything that might seem to qualify this conception of partnership and co-operation had been scrupulously eliminated; and in the face of confident prediction that many would not attend, that burning and insoluble problems of precedence would arise, and that, whatever they did, the Princes and Chiefs would never consent to play an active part in the proceedings or to agree to any order of coming forward, or even to come forward at all, there was neither the smallest hitch in the arrangements nor any room for doubt that there were no prouder or more contented actors in this memorable scene than the more than a hundred ruling Chiefs who had responded to the invitation of the Viceroy, and had come to Delhi to join him in rendering honour to the Sovereign. In no empire of which annals are extant can there ever have been gathered together such a concourse of ruling Princes, boasting such high and ancient lineage or representing so wide an extent of territory, all assembled in homage to a single throne.

The first block of seats to the right hand of the viceregal and royal party on the Daïs was allotted to the members of the Governor-General's Council and to His Excellency the Viceroy's guests. Here were to be seen the Duke and Duchess of Marlborough, the Duke and Duchess of Portland, and other European visitors. Lord Kitchener, Commander-in-Chief, also sat in the front row of this block. Behind these seats a curtained box had been prepared, which was occupied by the wives and female relatives of certain of the Indian Princes present at the Durbar. The Maharani of Bharatpur with her son, the present

Maharaja Kishen Singh, an infant aged only three years, sat in this box. The Maharani Scindia, the Maharani of Baroda and the ex-Maharani-Regent and the Maharani of Mysore, were also occupants; and it was a source of equal pleasure to the Chiefs and their families that arrangements should have been made, conformably with the most scrupulous restrictions of Indian *purdah*, to enable so many ladies of high rank to be present for the first time at a ceremony of this description.

The seats immediately to the left of the viceregal Daïs were occupied by the foreign representatives and distinguished guests, amongst whom were Their Excellencies the Governor-General of Portuguese India, and the Governor of the French Establishments in India, Sir R. Solomon from South Africa, Sir R. Baker from Australia, General Baron Yasukata Oku of Japan; Colonel Muhammad Ismail Khan, the Amir of Afghanistan's Envoy; General Chow Phya Surawongse, chief Aide-de-Camp to the King of Siam; Seyyid Timur bin Faisal, eldest son and heir of the Sultan of Maskat; and Maharaja Chandra Shamsher Jang, Rana Bahadur, Prime Minister of Nepal.

In the front row of Block W, the second to the right of the Daïs, the first seats were occupied by His Highness the Nizam of Hyderabad and his son, the Shahzada Osman Ali Khan. Colonel Sir David Barr, Resident at Hyderabad, was on the Shahzada's right; while, in the row of seats behind the Nizam, were his Minister, Maharaja Peshkar Sir Kishen Pershad, Lieutenant-Colonel Nawab Afsar-ud-Doula Bahadur, and other nobles and officials of the State. On Sir David Barr's right, also in the front row, were seated His Highness the Gaekwar of Baroda on whose robe of white silk shone the insignia of a Knight Grand Cross of the Star of India; his son, Shrimant Yuvraj Fateh Singh Rao Gaekwar; the Maharaja of Mysore, in a coat of gold brocade, and wearing superb necklaces of diamonds and pearls; Colonel, now Sir Donald, Robertson, the Resident in Mysore; and Mr. J. P. Hewett, the Chief Commissioner of the Central Provinces. Behind the Maharaja of Mysore sat his brother, the Yuvraja Shri Kantviava Narasaraja Wudyar; and behind the Chief Commissioner of the Central Provinces, four of the Chiefs under his political control.

In the corresponding block of seats in the left wing of the Amphi-

H.H. The Maharao of Kota.
K.C.S.I.

theatre were a group of Chiefs, whose States might be described as *propugnacula imperii*, outworks of the Empire. Here were seen, in the front row, the Maharaja of Jammu and Kashmir, lord of the lovely vale which the British Government made over, after the Sikh wars, to his grandfather, Gulab Singh; the Jam of Las Bela and the Khan of Kalat, whose territories march with the dominions of the Shah of Persia; the Raja of Manipur from the extreme eastern boundary between Assam and Upper Burma; the British Resident in Kashmir; and the Chief Commissioners of British Baluchistan and the North West Frontier Province: in the second row, sitting behind the latter, were the Mehtar of Chitral, and border chieftains from the country between the Black Mountain and the upper waters of the Oxus. Raja Sir Amar Singh, Commander-in-Chief of the Kashmir army, sat behind his brother, the Maharaja, with Raja Baldeo Singh of Poonch, his cousin, the chief feudatory of the Kashmir State.

Two blocks in the right wing, and the two opposite blocks on the left, were set apart, respectively, for the Rajputana and Central Indian Chiefs. The Maharana of Udaipur, who at considerable risk to his health had managed to reach Delhi, was unfortunately absent from his place among the Rajput Princes owing to serious illness, but all those who had ridden in the procession of elephants, or with the Imperial Cadets, on the day of the viceregal entry, were present, as well as the Maharawal of Dungarpur and the Raja Dhiraj of Shahpura. Mr. Martindale, Agent to the Governor-General in Rajputana, sat between the Maharao Raja of Bundi and the Maharaja of Bikaner.

Looking to the other wing of the Amphitheatre, one saw the Maharaja Holkar of Indore (who has since abdicated in favour of his son), seated between Major F. E. Younghusband, Resident at Indore, and the Agent to the Governor-General in Central India, Mr. C. S. Bayley; the Maharaja Scindia of Gwalior, on the Agent's left; the Maharaja of Datia, with a diamond armlet; the Maharaja of Charkhari, resplendent in a coat of orange yellow, girt with red *cummerbund;* and, next to the Maharaja of Orchha, the Begum of Bhopal, who, though she had been offered a seat amongst the ladies in *purdah*, chose rather to take her place closely veiled in the front row among her peers. In addition to the Central India

Chiefs who rode in the elephant procession, there were also present at the Durbar the Nawab of Jaora and the Raja of Rutlam, who sat behind the Viceroy among the Imperial Cadets; and, sitting in the Central India Block D, the Rana of Barwani, the Thakur of Piploda, and the Rao of Alipura.

Next beyond the Rajputana blocks, in the right wing of the Amphitheatre, were the Hindu Maharaja of Travancore, and Rajas of Cochin and Pudukota, grouped around the Governor of Madras and Lady Ampthill. Then came the Punjab Chiefs, conspicuous amongst whom were the snowy-bearded Raja of Nabha and the young Maharaja of Patiala, Sir Charles and Lady Rivaz also occupying seats in this block; and beyond these, the Chiefs who are attached politically to the Government of the United Provinces, the Maharaja of Benares, though not a ruling Chief, sitting here also.

In the left wing, next to the Central India blocks, were the Bombay Chiefs; the Maharaja of Kolhapur being on the right of His Excellency the Governor, and the Rao of Cutch next to Lady Northcote. A conspicuous figure in the adjoining block allotted to Bengal was the son and heir of the Maharaja of Sikkim, dressed in Chinese embroidered silks. Here also were the Maharaja of Kuch Behar and the Raja of Hill Tippera. In the last of the blocks, in the left wing, allotted to ruling Chiefs, were the Shan Sawbwas, in their curious costumes covered with gold plates, and the more plainly clad Chief of the Red Karens. The Lieutenant-Governor of Burma was also in this block.

Round the Imperial flag-staff in the centre of the arena were the massed bands of the following regiments:—

9th Lancers; 1st battalion, North Staffordshire Regiment; 2nd battalion, Gordon Highlanders; 1st battalion, Royal Irish Rifles; 2nd battalion, Argyll and Sutherland Highlanders; 2nd battalion, King's Royal Rifle Corps; 3rd battalion, Rifle Brigade; 1st battalion, Munster Fusiliers; 1st battalion, 2nd Gurkha Rifles; 1st battalion, 3rd Gurkha Rifles; 32nd Punjab Pioneers; and the 27th Baluch Light Infantry.

These bands had been specially selected from those placed at the disposition of the Director of military music, for the reason that all the regiments to which they belonged had served in the Mutiny campaigns. As trumpeters were needed for the performance of the proclamation music, the bands of the 4th Dragoon Guards and 15th Hussars were also included. In the interval before the Durbar commenced, the massed bands played the following programme:—March, "Under the Double Eagle" (Wagner); Huldegungsmarsch (Wagner); March in *Athalie* (Mendelssohn); March in *Rienzi* (Wagner); March in *Scipio* (Handel); Coronation March (Sanford).

From 9 o'clock onwards, carriages had begun to deposit their occupants at the outer entrance to the Amphitheatre. Soon after 10 o'clock, the first arrivals among the Chiefs appeared upon the scene. At 10.30 the Amphitheatre was already crowded, and the arena, into which no carriages were admitted, was filled with a brilliantly dressed crowd, who, having secured their seats, strolled about to exchange greetings or to survey the scene. Some admired the elegant outlines of the gleaming white Amphitheatre; others gazed at the rich dresses and jewels of the Princes, at the bright uniforms of the European officers and guests, or at the State robes and full-bottomed wigs of the High Court judges; others again found their emotions prepared for the scenes that were to follow by the solemn strains of the music of Wagner and Mendelssohn echoing round the arena from the instruments of 2000 performers. At 11 o'clock a bugle was sounded, and the arena now rapidly cleared. Round its vast circumference every seat was seen to be filled, save for the unoccupied space of the Daïs, with its gold embroidered floorcloth and its silver chairs, and for another empty space on the left side of the Amphitheatre, the meaning of which was soon to be made clear. Through the wide gap of the entrance between the outer points of the horse-shoe could be seen the serried ranks of the massed battalions on the distant plain, and behind them a tall mound which had been specially erected to accommodate native spectators who were not fortunate enough to obtain admittance to the arena, and which was packed with thousands. As soon as all within the arena had taken their seats, a sense of expectation pervaded the entire assemblage, and few were the feelings that were not tensely strung.

And now occurred an episode, all but unanticipated even by those who had observed its inclusion in the programme, and which can never be forgotten by a single man or woman of those who saw it.

In order to give to the veteran soldiers of the Mutiny, who nearly half a century before had fought and bled for the Empire, almost within sight of the very spot where its unity and grandeur were now being so majestically set forth, an opportunity to revisit the scene of their former deeds of daring, and to take part in the great solemnity which but for their valour might never have been held, the Viceroy had conceived the idea of inviting to Delhi, as the guests of Government, a selected number of the survivors of those immortal days and of assigning to them a prominent place in the Durbar. The original idea had been to extend the invitations to any old soldiers, without distinction of race or rank, who had fought on the British side during the Mutiny in any part of India. But when examination revealed that there were more than 1400 who answered to this description—a number which it was obviously impracticable to transport to Delhi from all parts of the continent, and entertain there—it was decided to confine the invitation to the officers and non-commissioned officers, European, Eurasian, and Indian, who had fought in the historic operations at Delhi and Lucknow. Of these, 27 Europeans and Eurasians and 387 Indians responded to the appeal. They were entertained as the guests of Government throughout the period of the celebrations, and were under the command of Colonel A. R. D. Mackenzie, C.B., himself a Delhi veteran, and for many years a retired resident in Simla.

There were some who disputed the wisdom of introducing on such an occasion the memories of an earlier and sadder day, and who from a distance penned captious criticisms upon the Viceroy's decision. No such view was entertained by a single person, European or Indian, at Delhi itself. To all such the appearance of this little band of war-scarred heroes was a remembrance that can never be obliterated: the place assigned to them in the ceremonial seemed almost an inspiration: the honour that they received was the spontaneous act of European and Indian alike, and was their common glory.

A few weak and trembling figures, hardly noticed by the audience, had been conducted to their seats in the empty space on the left horn of

Bourne & Shepherd

THE DURBAR. MARCH OF THE VETERANS

the Amphitheatre, when suddenly the main body appeared at the entrance. Preceded by the band of the 1st battalion, Munster Fusiliers, which, as the old 101st Foot, had shared their sufferings and triumphs nearly half a century ago, the veterans marched in. There was no order in the procession, save that the little knot of Europeans headed by Colonel Mackenzie walked in front. Some were in uniform, others in civil dress, but the medals that told of their bravery shone on the breasts of all. Then followed a motley band of natives in every variety of costume and uniform, many white-haired or bowed with age and with difficulty supported by their comrades. In the rear of the procession walked a cluster of Sikh veterans, clad entirely in white. As the little body of heroes straggled round the broad road of the arena, to which none had hitherto been admitted but themselves, the entire audience rose to their feet and greeted them with cheers again and again renewed; and when the strains of "See the Conquering Hero comes," to which they had entered, were succeeded by the pathetic notes of "Auld Lang Syne," as the veterans reached their appointed seats, few eyes were dry, and there was a choking in many throats. It may be added that there was one officer, and one alone, still serving on the active list of the Indian Army and present at Delhi, who might have headed the procession had he not been otherwise engaged. This was Lieutenant-General Sir R. Low, commanding in Bombay. Two days after the Durbar, the veterans were again paraded in front of the viceregal head-quarters in the central camp, where, at their own instance, they presented an address of thanks to the Viceroy, and were addressed by him. On that occasion Lord Curzon and the Duke of Connaught went round the ranks, and conversed with the men.

A few moments later the sound of bagpipes was heard, and the guard of honour of a hundred men of the 2nd battalion of the Gordon Highlanders under Major Staunton and Lieutenant Dick-Cunyngham, with Lieutenant Makgill-Crichton-Maitland carrying the King's colour, marched into the arena, preceded by their pipers, and formed up in two straight lines opposite the Daïs. Next, His Royal Highness the Grand Duke of Hesse drove up in a carriage and four with his Escort to the main entrance at the back of the Amphitheatre, and was provided with special seats for himself and staff on the open space to the right rear of the Daïs, in front of the seats for the Imperial Cadet Corps.

And now a gun was heard, the first of the royal salute that heralded the approach of the Duke and Duchess of Connaught. Their Royal Highnesses, driving in a carriage and four, with postilions, had left camp at 11.45 A.M., escorted by a squadron of the 9th Lancers and a squadron of the 19th Bengal Lancers. As the royal carriage approached the main entrance to the Amphitheatre, the troops outside presented arms, and in a moment the cavalcade swept into the arena, and moved at a trot towards the Daïs. Their Royal Highnesses were greeted by loud and enthusiastic cheering. As they alighted at the Daïs, the guard of honour presented arms, and the massed bands played the national anthem. The entire assemblage, which had risen to its feet as they entered, remained standing until Their Royal Highnesses, who were received by the Foreign Secretary, had taken their seats.

His Royal Highness was in field-marshal's uniform, with the collars of the Garter and the Star of India, and the riband of the Order of the Indian Empire, and carried a field-marshal's bâton in his hand. The Duchess of Connaught wore the Orders of Victoria and Albert and the English Coronation medal.

The massed bands next played the "Coronation March," a brilliant and effective composition by Captain Sanford.

A few minutes later, another body of horse was seen approaching the entrance to the arena, headed by the 4th Dragoon Guards; and the sunlight flashed along the lines of bayonets, as the troops outside again presented arms and gave a royal salute. It was the Viceroy arriving.

His Excellency Lord Curzon had left the viceregal camp soon after noon, driving in a carriage and four, escorted by the 4th Dragoon Guards, the Imperial Cadet Corps, the Body-guard, and the 11th Bengal Lancers. The Viceroy, who was accompanied by Lady Curzon in a dress of sky blue, wore full-dress uniform, with the collar of the Star of India, the riband of the Order of the Indian Empire, and the Stars of both Orders. Major Grimston, commanding the Body-guard, rode on the right of the viceregal carriage; Major-General Sir Pratap Singh, Maharaja of Idar, honorary Commandant of the Imperial Cadet Corps, on the left. On the arrival of the *cortège* at the entrance to the arena, the Dragoons and 11th Bengal Lancers formed up on either side of the road, outside, behind the Infantry of the viceregal Escort, already posted here. The viceregal carriage, escorted by the Imperial Cadet Corps on their coal-black chargers, and the Body-guard entirely mounted on bays, entered the arena and, amid renewed cheering, drove up to the Daïs. As the guard of honour of the Gordon Highlanders presented arms, the massed bands played "God save the King"; and punctually at 12.30 the viceregal flag fluttered from the flag-staff behind the middle cupola, while the right battery, Royal Field Artillery, outside the arena fired a royal salute of thirty-one guns. Meanwhile Their Excellencies had alighted from the carriage, where they were received by the officers of their staff, and ascended the steps of the Daïs. The Viceroy saluted and bowed to the Duke of Connaught, who had risen at the sound of the national anthem, and who saluted in return, and to the Duchess of Connaught. For a few moments the four figures on the Daïs stood facing the audience; then all took their seats. The Viceroy's silver chair of state, with silver footstool, was in the centre, and slightly to the front. The Duke of Connaught's silver chair was a little to the left. The seats of the Duchess of Connaught and Lady Curzon were somewhat to the rear on the right.

All present in the Amphitheatre had risen when the viceregal procession entered the arena, and now resumed their seats; but the measured boom of guns firing the salute was still audible as the Imperial Cadets, who had ridden out of the arena and dismounted, came marching back up the left horn of the Amphitheatre, headed by Sir Pratap Singh, to the chairs allotted to them at the back of the Daïs. The Cadets wore their handsome uniform of white and sky blue, with an aigrette in the front of the *pagri*, and formed a splendid and princely guard of honour. It was the first occasion, except for the state entry, three days before, on which the Cadets had taken official part in any function; and their fine appearance and magnificent uniform, setting off the distinction of high lineage and noble bearing, made a great impression on the public.

The last gun of the royal salute had been fired when the Foreign Secretary, Sir H. Barnes, stepping in front of the Daïs and bowing to the Viceroy, asked leave of His Excellency to open the Durbar. Permission being given, a preconcerted signal conveyed an order to the conductor of the massed bands. The hush that followed the royal salute was now broken by a musical "Summons to the Herald." In response came a flourish of trumpets from outside the Amphitheatre, where Major Maxwell, the Herald, and his twelve trumpeters, six European and six Indian, were posted alongside the Escort. A few seconds passed, and there appeared at the entrance a party of horsemen; the Herald himself, with his drummer (Trumpeter Nuttall, 5th Dragoon Guards) and the trumpeters behind. After halting, while the silver trumpets sounded another flourish, the Herald, followed by half of the trumpeters, rode slowly up to the Daïs by the right-hand wing; the drummer and the remaining half taking the opposite road. The band was now playing the "Herald's March," composed by Captain Sanford, to which the well-trained black chargers kept time till the two parties met and formed up in front of the Daïs, where the trumpets sounded a third flourish. Major Maxwell, a commanding figure considerably over six feet in height, wore a rich tabard, encrusted with the Royal Arms. In his right hand he held a mace of ebony and silver. White breeches and jack-boots and a white helmet, with gold and white *pagri*, completed his uniform. The British and native trumpeters wore coats of dark crimson velvet with the Royal and Imperial monogram—E. R. I.—embroidered on the front and back. The Englishmen wore white helmets and the natives white and gold *pagris*. From the trumpets and round the drums were suspended banderoles, blazoned with the Royal Arms, like those of the State trumpeters in England.

The Foreign Secretary now asked that the Herald might be permitted to read to the assembled multitude a Royal Proclamation; and the Viceroy having accorded his assent, Major Maxwell, wheeling round his horse till he faced the entrance, read as follows in tones that could be heard to the furthest limits of the Amphitheatre:

Bourne & Shepherd

THE DURBAR. READING THE PROCLAMATION

A Royal Proclamation for appointing a day for the celebration in His Majesty's Indian Dominions of the Solemnity of the Coronation of His Majesty.

EDWARD, R.I.

Whereas upon the death of our late Sovereign of happy memory, Queen Victoria, upon the twenty-second day of January in the Year of our Lord one thousand nine hundred and one, We did ascend the Throne under the style and title of Edward VII., by the Grace of God, King of the United Kingdom of Great Britain and Ireland, Defender of the Faith, Emperor of India;

And whereas, by Our Royal Proclamations bearing date the twenty-sixth day of June and the tenth day of December in the Year of our Lord one thousand nine hundred and one in the First Year of Our Reign, We did publish and declare Our Royal intention, by the Favour and Blessing of Almighty God, to celebrate the Solemnity of Our Royal Coronation upon the twenty-sixth day of June, one thousand nine hundred and two;

And whereas, by the Favour and Blessing of Almighty God, We were enabled to celebrate the said Solemnity upon Saturday, the ninth of August last;

And whereas it is Our wish and desire that the fact of the celebration of the said Solemnity should be publicly announced to all Our loving Subjects within Our Indian Dominions, and that opportunity should be given to Our Governors, Lieutenant-Governors, and Heads of Administrations, to the Princes, Chiefs, and Nobles of the Native States under Our Protection, and to the Representatives of all the Provinces of Our Indian Empire, to take part in the said Ceremonial;

Now We do, by this Our Royal Proclamation, make announcement thereof, and We do hereby charge and command Our right trusty and well-beloved Councillor, George Nathaniel, Lord Curzon of Kedleston, Our Viceroy and Governor-General of India, to hold at Delhi on the first of January, one thousand nine hundred and three, an Imperial Durbar for the purpose of declaring the completion of the said Solemnity of Our Coronation; and We direct that at the said Durbar this Proclamation shall be read for the information of all whom it may concern.

Given at Our Court at St. James, the first day of October, one thousand nine hundred and two, in the Second Year of Our Reign.

GOD SAVE THE KING-EMPEROR.

The last words of the Royal Proclamation were followed by another flourish of trumpets; the Royal Standard was run up to the top of the flag-staff in the centre of the arena and spread its glorious folds to the breeze; the massed bands played the national anthem, the guard of honour presented arms, and all present rose again to their feet. The Herald and his trumpeters meanwhile rode back to the entrance. Then, as the audience resumed their seats, the first gun of the Imperial salute was heard from the batteries outside. A hundred and one of these guns followed each other, broken at two intervals by a *feu-de-joie*, commencing along the whole front rank of the Infantry divisions, and continuing along the rear ranks of the leading companies.

While the salute was being fired, the massed bands inside the arena performed Kretschmer's "Kronungsmarsch," Meyerbeer's "Coronation March," and the "Coronation March" of Captain Sanford. After the first and second *feux-de-joie*, the opening and concluding bars of the national anthem were heard in the distance, played by the regimental bands posted outside. As the sound of the last gun rolled away, the combined bands on the plain repeated the familiar strains. A prolonged flourish of trumpets followed, and the second part of the ceremonies was about to begin.

Rising from his chair, His Excellency the Viceroy stood and faced the assemblage, over which absolute silence prevailed. In slow and measured tones that could be heard by the furthest spectator on the outer rim of the great Amphitheatre, although this was nearly one hundred and thirty yards away, he spoke as follows:

"Your Royal Highnesses, Princes, and Peoples of India,—Five months ago, in London, His Majesty King Edward VII., King of England and Emperor of India, was invested with the crown and sceptre of the English Kings. Only a few representatives of the Indian Empire had the good fortune to be present at that ceremony. To-day His Majesty has by his royal favour afforded an opportunity to all his Indian people to take part in similar rejoicings; and here, and elsewhere throughout India, are gathered together in honour of the event the Princes and Chiefs and nobles, who are the pillars of his throne, the European and Indian officials who conduct his administration with an integrity and devotion to duty beyond compare, the Army, British and

Native, which with such pre-eminent bravery defends his frontiers and fights his wars, and the vast body of the loyal inhabitants of India, of all races, who, amid a thousand varieties of circumstance and feeling and custom, are united in their spontaneous allegiance to the Imperial Crown. It was with the special object of thus solemnising his Coronation in India that His Majesty commanded me, as his Viceroy, to convene this great Durbar, and it is to signify the supreme value that he attaches to the occasion that he has honoured us by deputing his own brother, His Royal Highness the Duke of Connaught, to join in this celebration.

"It is twenty-six years since, on the anniversary of this day, in this city of Imperial memories and traditions, and on this very spot, Queen Victoria was proclaimed the first Empress of India. That act was a vindication of her profound interest in her Indian subjects, and of the accomplished unity of her Indian dominions under the paramountcy of the British Crown. To-day, a quarter of a century later, that Empire is not less, but more united. The Sovereign to whom we are met to render homage is not less dear to his Indian people, for they have seen his features and heard his voice. He has succeeded to a throne, not only the most illustrious, but the most stable in the world; and ill-informed would be the critic who would deny that not the least of the bases of its security—nay, I think, a principal condition of its strength—is the possession of the Indian Empire, and the faithful attachment and service of His Majesty's Indian people. Rich in her ancient traditions, India is also rich in the loyalty which has been kindled anew in her by the West. Amid the crowd of noble suitors who, through all the centuries, have sought her hand, she has given it only to the one who has also gained her trust.

"Nowhere else in the world would such a spectacle be possible as that which we witness here to-day. I do not speak of this great and imposing assemblage, unparalleled as I believe it to be. I refer to that which this gathering symbolises, and those to whose feelings it gives expression. Over one hundred rulers of separate States, whose united population amounts to sixty millions of people, and whose territories extend over fifty-five degrees of longitude, have come here to testify their allegiance to their common Sovereign. We greatly esteem the sentiments of loyalty that have brought them to Delhi from such great distances, and often at considerable sacrifice; and I shall presently be honoured by receiving from their own lips their message of personal congratulation to the King. The officers and soldiers present are drawn from a force in India of nearly two hundred and thirty thousand men, whose pride it is that they are the King's Army. The leaders of Indian society, official and unofficial, who are here, are the mouthpieces of a community of over two hundred and thirty million souls. In spirit, therefore, and one may almost say, through their rulers and deputies, in person, there is represented in this arena nearly one-fifth of the entire human race. All are animated by a single feeling, and all bow before a single throne. And should it be asked how it is that any one sentiment can draw together these vast and scattered forces and make them one, the answer is that loyalty to the Sovereign is synonymous with confidence in the equity and benignity of his rule. It is not merely the expression of an emotion, but the record of an experience and the declaration of a belief. For to the majority of these millions the King's Government has given freedom from invasion and anarchy; to others it has guaranteed their rights and privileges; to others it opens ever-widening avenues of honourable employment; to the masses it dispenses mercy in the hour of suffering; and to all it endeavours to give equal justice, immunity from oppression, and the blessings of enlightenment and peace. To have won such a dominion is a great achievement. To hold it by fair and righteous dealing is a greater. To weld it by prudent statesmanship into a single and compact whole will be, and is, the greatest of all.

"Such are the ideas and aims that are embodied in the summoning of this Coronation Durbar. It is now my duty to read to you the gracious Message which His Majesty has desired me to convey to his Indian people:

"It gives me much pleasure to send a Message of greeting to my Indian people, on the solemn occasion when they are celebrating my Coronation. Only a small number of the Indian Princes and representatives were able to be present at the Ceremony which took place in London; and I accordingly instructed my Viceroy and Governor-General to hold a great Durbar at Delhi, in order to afford an opportunity to all the Indian Princes, Chiefs, and peoples and to the Officials of my Government, to commemorate this auspicious event. Ever since my visit to India in 1875, I have regarded that Country and its peoples with deep affection; and I am conscious of their earnest and loyal devotion to my House and Throne. During recent years many evidences of their attachment have reached me: and my Indian Troops have rendered conspicuous services in the Wars and Victories of my Empire.

"I confidently hope that my beloved Son, the Prince of Wales, and the Princess of Wales, may before long be able to make themselves personally acquainted with India and the Country which I have always desired that they should see, and which they are equally anxious to visit. Gladly would I have come to India upon this eventful occasion myself had this been found possible. I have, however, sent my dear Brother, the Duke of Connaught, who is already so well known in India, in order that my Family may be represented at the Ceremony held to celebrate my Coronation.

"My desire, since I succeeded to the Throne of my revered Mother, the late Queen Victoria, the First Empress of India, has been to maintain unimpaired the same principles of humane and equitable administration which secured for her in so wonderful a degree the veneration and affection of her Indian Subjects. To all my Feudatories and Subjects throughout India I renew the assurance of my regard for their liberties, of respect for their dignities and rights, of interest in their advancement, and of devotion to their welfare, which are the supreme aim and object of my rule, and which, under the blessing of Almighty God, will lead to the increasing prosperity of my Indian Empire and the greater happiness of its People."

"Princes and peoples of India, these are the words of the Sovereign whose Coronation we are assembled to celebrate. They provide a stimulus and an inspiration to the officers who serve him, and they breathe the lessons of magnanimity and goodwill to all. To those of us who, like my colleagues and myself, are the direct instruments of His Majesty's Government, they suggest the spirit that should guide our conduct and infuse our administration. Never was there a time when we were more desirous that that administration should be characterised by generosity and leniency. Those who have suffered much deserve much; and those who have wrought well deserve well.

The Princes of India have offered us their soldiers and their own swords in the recent campaigns of the Empire; and in other struggles, such as those against drought and famine, they have conducted themselves with equal gallantry and credit. It is difficult to give to them more than they already enjoy, and impossible to add to a security whose inviolability is beyond dispute. Nevertheless, it has been a pleasure to us to propose that Government shall cease to exact any interest for a period of three years upon all loans that have been made or guaranteed by the Government of India to Native States in connection with the last famine; and we hope that this benefaction may be acceptable to those to whom it is offered. Other and more numerous classes there are in this great country to whom we would gladly extend, and to whom we hope before long to be in a position to announce relief. In the midst of a financial year it is not always expedient to make announcements, or easy to frame calculations. If, however, the present conditions continue, and if, as we have good reason to believe, we have entered upon a period of prosperity in Indian finance, then I trust that these early years of His Majesty's reign may not pass by without the Government of India being able to demonstrate their feelings of sympathy and regard for the Indian population by measures of financial relief, which their patient and loyal conduct in years of depression and distress renders it especially gratifying to me to contemplate. I need not now refer to other acts of consideration or favour which we have associated with the present occasion, since they are recorded elsewhere. But it is my privilege to make the announcement to the officers of the Army that henceforward the name of the Indian Staff Corps will cease to exist, and that they will belong to the single and homogeneous Indian Army of the King.

"Princes and peoples, if we turn our gaze for a moment to the future, a great development appears with little doubt to lie before this country. There is no Indian problem, be it of population or education or labour or subsistence, which it is not in the power of statesmanship to solve. The solution of many is even now proceeding before our eyes. If the combined arms of Great Britain and India can secure continued peace upon our borders, if unity prevails within them, between Princes and people, between European and Indian, and between rulers and ruled, and if the seasons fail not in their bounty, then nothing can arrest the march of progress. The India of the future will, under Providence, not be an India of diminishing plenty, of empty prospect, or of justifiable discontent; but one of expanding industry, of awakened faculties, of increasing prosperity, and of more widely distributed comfort and wealth. I have faith in the conscience and the purpose of my own country; and I believe in the almost illimitable capacities of this. But under no other conditions can this future be realised than the unchallenged supremacy of the paramount power, and under no other controlling authority is this capable of being maintained, than that of the British Crown.

"And now I will bring these remarks to a close. It is my earnest hope that this great assemblage may long be remembered by the peoples of India as having brought them into contact at a moment of great solemnity with the personality and the sentiments of their Sovereign. I hope that its memories will be those of happiness and rejoicing, and that the reign of King Edward VII., so auspiciously begun, will live in the annals of India and in the hearts of its people. We pray that, under the blessing of the Almighty Ruler of the Universe, his sovereignty and power may last for long years, that the well-being of his subjects may grow from day to day, that the administration of his officers may be stamped with wisdom and virtue, and that the security and beneficence of his dominion may endure for ever.

"Long live the King, Emperor of India!"

With these words the Viceroy resumed his seat amid loud plaudits from the entire assembly. He had spoken for exactly half an hour. Before delivering the King's Message, he removed the cocked hat which he had hitherto worn, resuming it when he had completed that portion of his address. The Royal Message was received with enthusiastic cheering, and frequent acclamations greeted the main passages in the remainder of the speech.

Scarcely had the Viceroy resumed his seat, when the Herald and trumpeters again rode up to the Daïs and sounded a flourish. Then, at a signal from His Excellency, Major Maxwell, raising his helmet, called with stentorian voice for three cheers for His Majesty the King-Emperor. With one movement, the entire concourse of 16,000 people sprang to their feet, and the volume of cheers, thrice repeated, rang from side to side of the great theatre. As the sound died away, it was taken up again outside, and the distant roar of the soldiers' cheers was heard from the long lines of the troops stationed on the plain. It seemed both an echo of the louder acclaim inside the arena, and an answer to it. Once again the bands in the Amphitheatre and those outside it gave forth the national anthem, after which the Herald and his trumpeters, having discharged their final duties, retired.

And now followed the third and concluding portion of the ceremony. Hitherto, with the exception of the Viceroy and the figures that moved with stately pageantry through their allotted parts in the arena, the vast majority of the audience had been spectators alone. The most illustrious among them were now to be actors also. The ceremony of presentation of the ruling Chiefs, never before attempted on an occasion like the present, and linked at this unique Durbar with the honourable duty of offering their several messages of congratulation and homage to the Sovereign, was about to begin. Sir H. Barnes, the Foreign Secretary, having sought permission to present the ruling Chiefs, one after another of these, in the order previously arranged, left his seat, attended in a few cases, where special permission had been sought and obtained, by a son or brother, or by a minister, and advanced to the Daïs, where the Viceroy and the Duke of Connaught received them standing. The name and style of each Chief were announced by the Foreign Secretary, and the Viceroy first shook hands with him, before receiving his message, while the Duke of Connaught followed with a similar greeting.

The political officers did not accompany the Chiefs beyond the foot of the ramp. It was decided that the latter should advance and offer the expression of their fealty alone. Moreover, no *nazars* were presented on this occasion. In his desire to emphasise the peculiar nature of the celebration, as the Sovereign's Durbar rather than that of his representative, and to exclude any feature that might detract from the honour of the Chiefs, the Viceroy had waived this inseparable adjunct of a viceregal Durbar. The Chiefs had settled among themselves and in consultation with their political officers the order in which, in their several groups, they would advance to the Daïs, and all questions of precedence between the territorial groups had been solved by the ingenious plan according to which the groups advanced alternately from either side of the Amphitheatre, the lowest in rank of one group passing by before the highest in rank of the next appeared. By this felicitous arrangement was secured what had been deemed impracticable at the Imperial Assemblage of 1877. On that occasion the Chiefs were spectators alone. It is true that at the conclusion of Lord Lytton's speech the Maharajas of Gwalior, Udaipur, and Jaipur, and Sir Salar

Jang, the Minister of Hyderabad, sprang from their seats and addressed the Viceroy in a few unrehearsed phrases; but every one was already making ready to leave the Amphitheatre, and, in the general confusion, what they said was unnoticed and unheard. The closing scene of the Imperial Durbar of 1903 was at once more dignified and more impressive.

For the most part the ruling Chiefs, on being presented to the Viceroy, merely requested his Excellency, in brief words, to convey their heartfelt congratulations to the King-Emperor, adding an assurance of their devotion and loyalty. Some, indeed, who had purposed to give more elaborate utterance to their sentiments, and had even brought a written speech with them, never got beyond this formula. Others, after essaying to deliver an ornate address in English, broke into Hindustani; improvising, in place of a studied oration, a few sentences which were not the less welcome because they came manifestly from the heart. But whatever the length or form of the address, no one who was near enough to the Daïs to observe the countenance and demeanour of the speakers could doubt the sincerity and enthusiasm of the congratulations which they had come forward to offer. Contentment, also, and pride at being able to play such a part in the Sovereign's Durbar, found expression, more eloquently than in words, in the eagerness with which, one after another, the Princes pressed forward to salute the Viceroy and the Duke of Connaught, and in visible marks of satisfaction which the most rigid prescriptions of Oriental etiquette could not altogether conceal.

Though it is unnecessary to repeat, in each case, the simple message of loyal congratulation offered by the majority of the Chiefs, the nature of which has been indicated, the more studied addresses may be placed on record.

His Highness the Nizam of Hyderabad, who was accompanied to the Daïs by his son the Shahzada Osman Ali Khan, and his Minister, Maharaja Peshkar Sir Kishen Pershad, said:

"It has afforded me very great pleasure to be present here on this auspicious and memorable occasion. I am sure Your Excellency is aware that it has been my life-long endeavour to maintain and strengthen the tradition of my house as the faithful ally of the British throne. As such, I would ask you to be so kind as to convey my most sincere congratulations to the King-Emperor's Most Gracious Majesty, and to assure him on my behalf that His Majesty will always find in me and my house an ally ever faithful and true in every respect."

His Highness the Gaekwar of Baroda, who was accompanied by his son, Shrimant Yuvraj Fateh Singh Rao Gaekwar, asked the Viceroy to convey to His Majesty the King-Emperor his hearty and loyal congratulations on his Coronation, and his good wishes for the new year.

His Highness the Maharaja of Mysore, who was accompanied by his brother, the Yuvraja Narasaraja Wudyar, said:

"On behalf of my mother and myself, I offer my most humble and loyal congratulations to His Majesty the King-Emperor on this momentous occasion."

His Highness the Maharaja of Kashmir, who was accompanied by his brother, Raja Sir Amar Sing, said:

"I congratulate Your Excellency, with my innermost sense of loyalty and devotion, on this happy occasion; and I beg Your Excellency to communicate the same to His Imperial Majesty King Edward VII. My heartiest prayers are that God Almighty may preserve the British Crown and give protection and peace to all Indians, great and small."

The Khan of Kalat, speaking in Persian, said:

"On behalf of myself and of my whole State, I congratulate Your Excellency on this auspicious occasion."

The Jam of Las Bela, in like manner, begged the Viceroy to convey his hearty congratulations to His Majesty the King-Emperor, with assurances of his loyalty and devotion to the throne.

The Maharaja of Bikaner, after requesting His Excellency to convey his loyal and respectful congratulations to His Majesty the King-Emperor, begged Lord Curzon to assure His Majesty that he and his people were always ready to serve and fight for His Majesty on all occasions.

Raja Deen Dayal & Sons

THE DURBAR. PRESENTATION OF THE NIZAM

Her Highness the Begum of Bhopal, who came to the Daïs accompanied by her two elder sons, Nawab Nasrulla Khan and Sahibzada Ubaidulla Khan, had obtained special permission as a *purdah* lady to offer her congratulations in writing, and laid at the Viceroy's feet, for presentation to His Majesty, a casket richly jewelled, and adorned with miniatures on ivory of the late Nawab consort and Her Highness's three sons. The casket contained an address in Urdu, with an English translation, in which Her Highness, after referring to the circumstance, auspicious in Muhammadan eyes, that the Durbar coincided with the Id-ul-Fitr, assured the Government, "as the well-wisher and sincere admirer of the British paramount Power, on this historic occasion, not only of the fidelity, devotion and affection of myself, my sons, my people, and of the women of my State, but also of the loyalty of the whole Muhammadan population of India; for faithfulness and obedience to the ruler are both strictly ordained by the Muhammadan religion."

The young Nawab of Jaora, who was accompanied by his uncle and Minister, Khan Bahadur Yar Muhammad Khan, said:

"Will Your Excellency be pleased to convey to His Majesty the King-Emperor my respectful and sincere congratulations on this auspicious occasion? I beg to tender my homage to my august Sovereign, with the assurance that the resources of my State will always be at his disposal, and that I am ready to lay down my life in his service."

The Maharaja of Orchha, who was accompanied by his eldest son, Raja Bahadur Bhagwant Singh, said:

"I am highly delighted in attending this grand assemblage to have the opportunity of expressing my sincere feelings of fidelity to the British Crown, and request Your Excellency to be good enough to submit my hearty congratulations, fealty and devotion to His Most Gracious Majesty the King-Emperor of India on the auspicious occasion of the celebration of His Most Gracious Majesty's Coronation, and to assure His Most Gracious Majesty, on my behalf, that I and my house adhere, and will continue to adhere, most firmly to the British Crown, with the same zeal of attachment and fealty imbibed in my old house since the very advent of British rule in India, and so will ever remain deserving and thankful for the Imperial favours."

The Maharaja of Datia, who was accompanied by his son, the Maharaj Kumar, and by his Minister, Rao Bahadur Janki Prasad, said:

"I cannot sufficiently express my heartfelt joy and deep gratitude that I feel at this auspicious moment. I beg Your Excellency kindly to convey my best and sincere respects to His Imperial Majesty the King-Emperor, and to assure His Majesty that I, His Majesty's loyal and faithful subject, am ever ready to do any kind of service that may be desired of me for the welfare of the British Empire. I hope His Imperial Majesty would be graciously pleased to regard us with the same fostering care as was shown to us by our beloved Queen-Empress. I offer my respects to His Royal Highness the Duke of Connaught, who has been pleased to favour us with his royal presence. I beg your Excellency to accept my hearty congratulations for the prudent arrangements that have been made for our comfort during the Coronation Durbar period."

The Maharaja of Kolhapur, who was accompanied by his brother, Piraji Rao Ghatge Sarjirao Vazarat Maab Meherban, Chief of Kagal (senior), said:

"I request Your Excellency to convey, on this auspicious occasion, my most loyal and respectful congratulations to Their Majesties, and my most sincere wishes for long and happy life to them and everlasting peace and prosperity to our grand Empire."

His Highness the Rao of Cutch, who was accompanied by his son, Kumar Shri Vijarajji, said:

"Will Your Excellency be graciously pleased to convey my heartfelt congratulations to His Majesty the King-Emperor on His accession to the throne, and add, at the same time, that I hope His Majesty's reign will be as glorious as was that of his illustrious mother?"

His Highness the Sultan of Shehr and Mokalla, who was accompanied by his son, Sultan Omar-bin-Awadth, said:

"In the name of the most exalted God.

"I praise God with excessive praises, and thank Him with numerous thanks.

"I beg to approach Your Imperial Majesty with the most respectful and devoted compliments, from which have arisen the fragrant and pleasing smell, tightening the bonds of the gardens of union and friendship, and the breezes of which have opened the buds of alliance and companionship with His Imperial Majesty, the Malik-ul-Azam, the Protector, the possessor of such noble qualifications that everybody, whether rich or poor, bears witness; the bearer of such a rank and position which are so high that they lower the dignity of the Pleiades in Heaven and bless the clouds with profuseness: the possessor of characters so noble, charming and attractive that even the morning breeze cannot excel in its fascinating and alluring charm, but, on the contrary, becomes indisposed; possessor of such etiquettes and behaviours that they, in comparison with those of the other Sovereigns of different nations, are far superior and excellent; spreader of the flag of equity and justice on the heads of all the communities, including Arabs and Ajams (the non-Arabs); the King of England, Scotland, and Ireland, Edward VII. May God bestow upon him dignity, success and pleasure in every place and every time, and preserve him with peace, security and safety. May the days of his reign ever shine as bright and brilliant as the sun, and may the nights of his reign be ever brilliant on the sky of the subjects of the Empire like the shining moon; and may his troops be ever successful in their day and night march, and may the scope of his presents include all the subjects, whether superior or inferior.

"Therefore (it is with great pride) that I, on behalf of myself, my children, relatives, in reality on behalf of all my loyal and devoted subjects, venture with due respect to approach Your Imperial Majesty with the loyal and respectful congratulations on the felicitous occasion of the Coronation of Your Imperial Majesty on the day of June 26th 1902 in the presence of the great assembly of the grandees and nobles of the Empire.

"Gladly there came a messenger who brought such tidings of pleasure which have completely charmed the mental eyes,

"That among the people who have taken part in the congratulatory (address),

"And among them who have distributed and procured for themselves a part of this felicity and happiness,

"He proclaimed that I have secured for myself the greatest share.

"Now I earnestly solicit the Almighty God that may the bonds of the sincere and devoted attachment among us remain ever tightened with increasing friendship, and may they last till eternity.

"Finally, I pray the Almighty God that He may bless this Coronation and Your Imperial Majesty's reign with peace, progress and prosperity to the Empire in general, and save it from the terrors of accidents and miserable calamities of Heaven, and may Your Imperial Majesty and Your Gracious Consort Queen Alexandra, together with the other members of Your Imperial Family, pass your lives in everlasting joys, pleasures, eternal prosperity and happiness.

"In conclusion, I sincerely thank the Almighty Creator and the Giver of blessings with numerous thanks."

The Nawab of Junagadh said:

"Please convey my most sincere and heartfelt congratulations to Their Imperial Majesties for their auspicious Coronation. To-day is a day of great rejoicing on account of Ramazan Id, and this rejoicing is doubly enhanced on account of the Coronation Durbar being held to-day. Please accept my congratulations for Your Excellency also, and kindly take the trouble of communicating my salutations and profound sense of devoted loyalty to Their Majesties and to their throne."

The Thakur Sahib of Bhavnagar said:

"I beg respectfully to offer my most loyal and devoted homage to His Imperial Majesty the King-Emperor on the most auspicious occasion of his Coronation in the ancient capital of our beloved Hindustan, and wish him and his illustrious Consort a long life and prosperous career."

The Sultan of Lahej, speaking in Arabic, said:

"It is my desire to express through Your Excellency my loyalty to His Majesty the King-Emperor Edward VII., and my congratulations on the great event of the celebration of his Coronation in India."

The Amir of D'thali, also speaking in Arabic, said:

"Will Your Excellency kindly convey to His Majesty the King-Emperor this expression of my loyalty to the great Government, and of the gladness I feel in being able to see on this day the brother of His Majesty?"

His Highness the Maharaja of Patiala, who was accompanied by his uncle, Kunwar Sir Ranbir Singh, said:

"I beg to offer my congratulations to the King-Emperor on this great occasion through Your Excellency, and beg that you will also convey the assurance that my State and my sword are ever at the service of His Majesty."

His Highness the Raja of Nabha, who was accompanied by his son, Tika Ripu Daman Singh, said:

"I pray Your Excellency to convey my hearty and loyal congratulations to Their Majesties the King-Emperor and Queen-Empress on the most auspicious occasion of their Coronation, to celebrate which we have assembled in this Durbar. Our joy would have been full had His Most Gracious Majesty honoured this assembly with his presence, but it is no small matter of joy and pride to us that His Majesty has most graciously sent Their Royal Highnesses the Duke and Duchess of Connaught to represent the Royal family. I beg leave also to felicitate Your Excellency on the success of this grand ceremony, which is the result of your own wise forethought and unremitting labours. I pray to the Gracious God to spare our benevolent Sovereign, His Majesty the King-Emperor, that he may long and prosperously reign over us."

This was his formal and prepared oration, but the old Sikh Chief burst out, with his well-known piety and loyalty:

"Now I can die in peace, as I have discharged the three duties of a true Sikh. I have lived according to the precepts of the Gurus, I have aided the State with my sword, and now I have paid my personal homage to my Sovereign."

The Raja of Faridkot said:

"May the Akalpurkh (God Almighty) confer blessings on this auspicious Coronation of His Imperial Majesty and prolong his valuable life and increase his prosperity; let his sway over his dominions in this world be strong and India be benefited materially under his rule. We the feudatory Chiefs of India, one and all are always ready to sacrifice everything for the security of his administration."

The Maharaj Kumar Sidkyong Tulku, son and heir of the Maharaja of Sikkim, said:

"May His Majesty King Edward VII., from the time of occupation of his Golden Throne, exercise power over the three Worlds (of Heaven,

Earth and Hell). May he live for thousands of cycles, and ever sustain all living creatures in joy and happiness."

The Maharaja of Kuch Behar, who was accompanied by his son, Maharaj Kumar Rajendra Narain, said:

"Will Your Excellency convey to His Gracious Majesty the King-Emperor my humble duty and respectful congratulations and loyalty to the throne on this auspicious occasion? May Their Majesties be spared long to rule over India."

The Raja of Hill Tippera, who was accompanied by his son, Jubraj Birendro Kishore Deb Burman, said:

"Through Your Excellency I have the pleasure to offer my most sincere congratulations to His Majesty the King-Emperor Edward VII., on the occasion of this solemn proclamation of his Coronation, and to convey to His Majesty my assurance that, following the example of my ancestors, I shall always be ready to place my humble resources at the service of the Empire. May His Majesty enjoy long life, peace and prosperity with all the members of the Royal Family."

The Nawab of Rampur, who was accompanied by his Minister, Shaikh Abdul Ghafur, said:

"Your Excellency,—I feel grateful for the privilege of having this opportunity, on the day of the Coronation Durbar, of expressing my dutiful and heartfelt loyalty to His Most Gracious Majesty King Edward VII., Emperor of India. May God, who preserved His Majesty's life in time of dire sickness and raised him up to be crowned our King and Emperor, continue to watch over his life and Empire and grant to His Majesty the King-Emperor and Her Majesty the Queen in ever-increasing measure health, happiness, and glory."

The Sawbwa of Keng Tung, speaking in the Hkun Shan language, said:

"The Keng Tung Sawbwa, whose territory is bounded by China, Siam and the French territories, begs to express the gratification which he feels in taking part in the ceremony connected with the Coronation of His Most Gracious Majesty King Edward VII. He offers his congratulations on the King-Emperor's recovery from his serious illness and on his being crowned as King-Emperor. He earnestly prays that

Bourne & Shepherd, photo. Walker & Boutall Ph. Sc.

Shan Chiefs at the Durbar

the King and the Queen and the Royal Family may be free from all illnesses and have length of days, and that the reign of His Majesty may last for very many years."

The Sawbwa of Möng Nai, speaking in Shan, said:

"The Möng Nai and Keng Tung Sawbwa, who was driven from his States by the despotism of the Burmese King, Thibaw, and was restored by the troops of the Great Queen, is deeply gratified by the opportunity now afforded him of expressing, through your Excellency, to her son His Majesty, the Great King, his loyal and profound gratification that the Great King is now completely restored to health and is able formally to assume authority over all the Eastern countries. May he and Her Majesty and all the Royal Family long be spared and live well and happy, and when His Majesty ascends to the village of the Nats may there be a glorious and happy reunion with his mother, who was the greatest of all Queens."

The Sawbwa of Yawng Hwe, speaking in Burmese, said:

"The Yawng Hwe Sawbwa deems it a very great privilege to have been permitted to join with the other Chiefs of the Empire, which is co-extensive with the globe, in offering his most loyal and heartfelt congratulations, through your Excellency, to His Most Great and Glorious Majesty, King of Kings, King Edward VII., who alone is worthy to have succeeded her sainted Majesty, the Great Queen, on the recovery which he has made from his grievous illness, and on his Coronation as King-Emperor of his vast dominions. He prays devoutly that the King, the Queen, the Prince of Wales and all the Royal Family may now and always have immunity from the ninety-six diseases, and great length of days, and that the reign of the King-Emperor may last for very many years."

The Sawbwa of South Hsenwi, speaking in Shan, said:

"It has given me very great gratification to appear as the solitary representative of the Northern Shan States at this great function. For myself, and for the other Chiefs who have not been permitted to come to his Coronation ceremony, I beg to express to Your Excellency our great gratification that His Majesty King Edward VII. should have so satisfactorily recovered from his severe illness, and our loyal congratulations on the occasion of this his Eastern Coronation ceremony, and we beg that you will transmit them to His Majesty. May he, the

Queen, and all the Royal Family have happiness, long life and immunity from all ills of whatsoever kind."

The Sawbwa of Möng Pawn, speaking in Shan, said:

"The Möng Pawn Sawbwa will remember to the last hour of his life the great ceremony at which it has been his privilege to be present. He begs that Your Excellency will transmit to His Great and Most Glorious Majesty, King Edward VII., the possessor of several precious rings, his congratulations on His Majesty's recovery from his serious illness and his present assumption of authority over all the lands of the East. May the King-Emperor live for ever and may his glory be as the glory of the Great Queen, in whose time we first came under the shelter of the British Flag. May the King-Emperor's sons, his grandsons, his younger brother, now present, whom we regard as the reflection of His Majesty, have length of days, freedom from the ninety-six diseases and eventual glorious rest."

Sawlawi, the Myoza of Gantarawadi, now raised to be Sawbwa of the Eastern Karenni, speaking in Karenni, said:

"May it please Your Excellency graciously to convey to His Most Great and Glorious Majesty, King of Kings, Ruler over countless Princes, the only Great King, son of the Supreme Queen, the heartfelt congratulations of myself, his most loyal servant, and of all the other Karenni Chiefs for whom I speak, his most humble servants, on His Majesty's recovery from his grievous illness and on his Coronation as Emperor of all the lands that surround Mount Meru. The badge of the Red Karen is the rising sun. His Majesty's glory is as the glory of the sun at noontide and it endureth for ever. His loyal servant prays most earnestly that His Majesty, Her Majesty the Queen, the Prince of Wales, the King-Emperor's Most Exalted Brother, now present, and all the rest of the Royal Family, may for ever be free from the ninety-six diseases and have length of happy days, and, above all, we pray daily that His Majesty the King-Emperor may reign over us for very many long years to come."

With the presentation of the last of the addresses, the Imperial Durbar came to an end. It had lasted one hour and three-quarters. The state equipages drove again into the arena. The Imperial Cadets reappeared on their black chargers, and the Viceroy's Body-guard, in their uniforms of scarlet and gold, took their former place. His

Excellency and Lady Curzon entered the carriage and departed with the same ceremonies as had been observed on their arrival, the first gun of the royal salute being fired as the Viceroy took his seat. The procession passed slowly out of the arena amid the plaudits of the crowd. For a few brief seconds the Duke and Duchess of Connaught stood alone on the Daïs. Then turning to right and to left, both bowed with unaffected grace and dignity to the assemblage, who responded with acclamations, again and again renewed, that bespoke their recognition of the princely act, and the popularity of the royal guests. Their Royal Highnesses then left the Amphitheatre, followed by His Royal Highness the Duke of Hesse, the foreign representatives, Lord Kitchener and the members of the Council, the heads of local governments and administrations; the ruling Chiefs; the Lieutenant-Generals commanding army corps. These drove in their carriages from the interior of the arena, while the remainder of the guests left by the exits to the rear of the Amphitheatre. The police arrangements were again excellent, and the immense crowd dispersed without difficulty or confusion. Soon after 3 P.M. the last of the spectators had disappeared, and the great arena was once more empty.

So ended the Coronation Durbar. From first to last it had passed off without flaw or mishap. Even at the time it left upon the senses an overwhelming impression of ordered solemnity, of pomp and splendour rarely equalled, of soul-stirring loyaltyand devotion. As time has passed, these emotions have deepened in the hearts of all those who were privileged to be present. It seems to them that such a display can hardly, if ever, have been witnessed before in the history of empires or nations; and that it is improbable that its like will ever be seen again. Whatever destiny may attend the British Empire in India, whether an even more glorious future awaits it, or whether the fate that has overtaken the whole of its predecessors be somewhere lurking in the womb of time, the great pageant of January 1st, 1903, must always stand forth as an abiding landmark in its annals, and as consecrating a supreme moment in the story of its greatness.

CHAPTER VII

TWO STATE CEREMONIES

THE Imperial celebration described in the preceding chapter was followed, the same evening, by a state dinner at the Viceroy's camp, when Lord Curzon entertained Their Royal Highnesses the Duke of Connaught and the Grand Duke of Hesse, and the officers of their staffs; Their Excellencies the Governors of Bombay and Madras, and the Commander-in-Chief; Their Honours the Lieutenant-Governors of the Punjab, Burma, United Provinces and Bengal, and other high officials; all the foreign representatives who had attended the Durbar; and a number of other distinguished persons, the following being the full list of His Excellency's guests:—

H.R.H. the Duke of Connaught and Strathearn.
H.R.H. the Grand Duke of Hesse.
H.E. the Right Hon. Lord Northcote, Governor of Bombay.
H.E. the Right Hon. Lord Ampthill, Governor of Madras.
H.E. Colonel Sir E. A. R. Galhardo, Governor-General of the Portuguese Settlements in India.
H.E. M. Victor Lanrezac, Governor of the French Settlements in India.
H.H. Sir C. Rivaz, Lieutenant-Governor of the Punjab.
H.E. General Lord Kitchener of Khartoum, Commander-in-Chief in India.
H.H. Sir F. Fryer, Lieutenant-Governor of Burma.
H.H. Sir J. La Touche, Lieutenant-Governor of the United Provinces of Agra and Oudh.
H.H. Mr. J. A. Bourdillon, officiating Lieutenant-Governor of Bengal.
H.H. Sir A. Fraser, Lieutenant-Governor designate of Bengal, President of the Police Commission.
Sir H. Barnes, Lieutenant-Governor designate of Burma.
The Hon. Sir F. Maclean, Chief Justice of Bengal.

H. H. the Maharaja of Orchha, G.C.I.E.

The Most Rev. Dr. R. S. Copleston, Bishop of Calcutta and Metropolitan of India and Ceylon.

The Hon. Mr. T. Raleigh, Member of Council.

The Hon. Sir Edward FitzGerald Law, Member of Council.

The Hon. Major-General Sir E. Elles, Member of Council.

The Hon. Mr. A. T. Arundel, Member of Council.

The Hon. Sir Denzil Ibbetson, Member of Council.

The Hon. Sir R. Solomon, Representative from South Africa.

The Hon. Sir R. Baker, Representative from Australia.

Lieut.-General Baron Yasukata Oku, Representative of His Majesty the Emperor of Japan.

General Chow Phya Surawongse, Representative of His Majesty the King of Siam.

The Duke of Marlborough.
The Duke of Portland.
The Earl of Pembroke.
The Earl of Jersey.
The Earl of Lonsdale.
The Earl of Durham.
The Earl of Dartrey.
The Earl of Crewe.
Lord Wolverton.
Lord Killanin.
Lord Davey.
Lord Elcho.

H.E. Rear-Admiral Sir Charles Drury, Commander-in-Chief of His Majesty's Naval Forces in the East Indies.

The Hon. Sir Lawrence Jenkins, Chief Justice of Bombay.

The Hon. Sir Arnold White, Chief Justice of Madras.

The Hon. Sir J. Stanley, Chief Justice of the United Provinces of Agra and Oudh.

The Right Rev. Dr. H. Whitehead, Bishop of Madras.

The Hon. Sir H. Winterbotham, Member of the Madras Council.

The Hon. Sir J. Monteath, Member of the Bombay Council.

The Hon. Mr. J. Thomson, Member of the Madras Council.

The Hon. Mr. E. M. H. Fulton, Member of the Bombay Council.

General Sir R. Low, Commanding the Forces, Bombay.

Lieut.-General Sir George Wolseley, Commanding the Forces, Madras.

Lieut.-General Sir Bindon Blood, Commanding the Forces, Punjab.

Lieut.-General D. McLeod, Commanding the Forces, Bengal.

The Hon. Lieut.-Colonel Sir David Barr, Resident at Hyderabad.

The Hon. Lieut.-Colonel Sir Donald Robertson, Resident in Mysore and Chief Commissioner of Coorg.

The Hon. Mr. A. H. T. Martindale, Agent to the Governor-General in Rajputana.

The Hon. Colonel C. E. Yate, Agent to the Governor-General and Chief Commissioner in Baluchistan.

The Hon. Mr. C. S. Bayley, Agent to the Governor-General in Central India.

The Hon. Lieut.-Colonel H. A. Deane, Agent to the Governor-General and Chief Commissioner in the North-West Frontier Province.

The Hon. Mr. J. B. Fuller, Chief Commissioner of Assam.

The Hon. Mr. J. P. Hewett, officiating Chief Commissioner of the Central Provinces.

The Right Rev. Dr. G. Lefroy, Bishop of Lahore.

The Right Hon. Sir Michael Hicks-Beach, Bart., M.P.

The Right Hon. Sir George Taubman-Goldie.

Sir John Dickson Poynder, Bart., M.P.

Sir Robert Mowbray, Bart., M.P.

Sir Edgar Vincent, M.P.

Sir Howard Vincent, M.P.

Sir Alfred Haslam, M.P.

Sir Christopher Furness, M.P.

Sir Charles Cayzer, M.P.

Sir Charles McLaren, M.P.

Mr. Stuart Samuel, M.P.

The Hon. W. Peel, M.P.

The Ven. W. E. Scott, Archdeacon of Bombay.

Sir Mancherjee Bhownaggree, M.P.

Brigadier-General J. S. Collins, General Officer Commanding the Viceroy's Escort.

Mr. S. E. Voigt, Consul-General for Sweden and Norway.

General R. E. Patterson, Consul-General for the United States of America.

Mr. C. C. Kilburn, Consul-General for Denmark.

Herr E. R Maurig von Sarnfeld, Consul-General for the Austro-Hungarian Empire.

Count A. Raybaudi Massiglia, Consul-General for Italy.

Mr. F. C. Pallachi, Consul-General for Greece.

Viscount de Wrem, Consul-General for Portugal.

Emin Bey Effendi, Consul-General for Turkey.

M. M. Gerard, Consul-General for Belgium.

Mofakhames Sultan Mahmud Khan, Consul-General for Persia.

Dr. Voretzsch, officiating Consul-General for Germany.

Colonel Sir Colin Scott-Moncrieff, President of the Irrigation Commission.

Sir Thomas Higham, Member of the Irrigation Commission.

Sir Evelyn Ruggles-Brise.

M. A. de Koster, Consul for the Netherlands.

Don Rafael Acquaroni y de Solis, Consul for Spain.

Mr. A. A. Apcar, Consul for Siam.

Mr. S. Hayashi, Consul for Japan.

Major R. E. Grimston, Commandant, Viceroy's Body-guard.

Major W. Weallens, Commanding the Viceroy's Guards.

Major T. E. Scott, Staff of Lieut.-General Baron Oku, Representative from Japan.

The Staff of H.R.H. the Duke of Connaught.

The Staff of H.R.H. the Grand Duke of Hesse.

The Aide-de-Camp in Waiting to the Governor of Bombay.

The Aide-de-Camp in Waiting to the Governor of Madras.

The Aide-de-Camp in Waiting to the Governor-General of the Portuguese Settlements in India.

The Aide-de-Camp in Waiting to the Governor of the French Settlements in India.

The Aide-de-Camp in Waiting to the Lieutenant-Governor of the Punjab.

The Aide-de-Camp in Waiting to the Commander-in-Chief in India.

The Aide-de-Camp in Waiting to Lieut.-General Baron Oku, Representative from Japan.

The Aide-de-Camp in Waiting to General Chow Phya Surawongse.

The Aide-de-Camp in Waiting to the Lieutenant-Governor of Burma.

The Aide-de-Camp in Waiting to the Lieutenant-Governor of Bengal.

The Aide-de-Camp in Waiting to the Lieutenant-Governor of the United Provinces of Agra and Oudh.

The Chaplain to the Bishop of Calcutta.

The Flag Lieutenant to the Naval Commander-in-Chief, East Indies.

Sir Walter Lawrence, Private Secretary to the Viceroy.

Lieut.-Colonel the Hon. E. Baring, Military Secretary to the Viceroy.

Aides-de-Camp.

At the conclusion of the dinner His Excellency the Viceroy, in proposing the toast of the King-Emperor, spoke as follows:

"YOUR ROYAL HIGHNESSES, YOUR EXCELLENCIES, MY LORDS, AND GENTLEMEN,—I rise to propose the health of His Majesty the King, Emperor of India. This afternoon we carried through, I hope with success, the great ceremony that had been devised for the celebration of His Majesty's Coronation in this country, and the spectacle was one that must have stirred the heart of every beholder. It brought home to every European or Indian inhabitant of this land the vivid reality of the constitution under which we live, and by which a far away and invisible mainspring guides with resistless energy and power every movement of this vast political machine; and I hope that it may also have impressed our various illustrious visitors and guests with the conviction that this Indian possession of His Majesty is no mere dead-weight tied on to the heels of the British Empire, but a Dominion, a Continent, an Empire by itself, rich in its own personality and memories, self-confident in its strength, and aglow with abundant potentialities for the future. To be King of the United Kingdom and of the British possessions beyond the Seas is a great and noble title. But to be Emperor of India is in no respect less, and is in some respects greater. For powerful Empires existed and flourished here, while Englishmen were still wandering painted in the woods, and when the British Colonies were wilderness and jungle; and

India has left a deeper mark upon the history, the philosophy, and the religion of mankind than any other territorial unit in the universe. That a British Sovereign should in the fulness of time have been able to do what no predecessor of his ever accomplished, what Alexander never dreamed of, what Akbar never performed, namely, to pacify, unify, and consolidate this great mass into a single homogeneous whole, is, in my judgment, the most impressive phenomenon in history, and the greatest wonder of the modern world.

"YOUR ROYAL HIGHNESSES, YOUR EXCELLENCIES, AND GENTLEMEN,—I venture to say that but one regret has filled all our minds here to-day. It is that His Majesty the King-Emperor has not been able to be present here in person to receive the homage of his loyal Feudatories, and the acclamations of his Indian people. There is, indeed, no necessity for an Emperor of India to come out here to be crowned. His Majesty was our acknowledged and Sovereign Lord as soon as the throne was vacant nearly two years ago. But India would dearly have loved to see the face of her Emperor and to listen to his voice; and some day we may hope that, as time and distance continue to dwindle under the magic finger of science, it may be found possible for the Viceroy on a future occasion like the present to be eliminated as a superfluous phantom, and for the real figure to appear upon the scene.

"However that may be, we are met here in honour of a Sovereign who, though he may be absent in person, is with us in spirit, and whose royal message, which I had the privilege of reading this afternoon, shows how proud he is of the allegiance and how devoted to the interests of his Indian people. At the Durbar it was my duty to address more particularly the various classes of His Majesty's Feudatories and subjects who had assembled to render him their homage and to listen to his words. But the presence at this table here to-night of so many illustrious representatives of foreign Powers and of eminent persons from all quarters of the globe, enables me to point to the fact that the possession of India draws with it other and outside responsibilities, and brings us into relation, I am glad to say peaceful and amicable relation, with all the Powers and Principalities of the East. We are honoured here by the company of a distinguished representative of the great and allied Empire of Japan, and by an Envoy from that enlightened monarch the King of Siam; and at our Durbar there were present to-day the Envoys or representatives of our friend and ally the Amir of Afghanistan, of the friendly Kingdom of Nepal, and of the Sultan of Maskat. Among our guests are the Governors-General of the Indian possessions of two powerful and allied nations, France and Portugal, with whom our relations are those of unbroken peacefulness and concord. Further, there have appeared for the first time at a gathering such as this, representatives of those great British Colonies beyond the seas, Australia and South Africa, whose star is destined to rise ever higher and higher, and whose Governments, as time passes on, must be brought into still closer connection with our own. Finally, we have here prominent members of the Imperial Legislature, of the British Lords and Commons, who have journeyed across the ocean to join hands with us in this great ceremonial. I think I am entitled, therefore, to claim that it is no mere local celebration, but a great and Imperial solemnity of far-reaching interest and application, that we have been enacting to-day, and it is before an audience that is typical of all that is best in the British Empire, of our established dominion in Asia, of the friendly sentiments of our neighbours, and of the sympathetic regard of our own kith and kin across the seas, that I now propose my toast.

"I give you all, Gentlemen, with feelings of profound respect, of devotion, and of enthusiasm, the health of His Majesty the King, Emperor of India."

The toast was drunk with all honours.

The Viceroy then rose to propose the health of His Royal Highness the Duke of Connaught. His Excellency said:

"YOUR ROYAL HIGHNESSES, YOUR EXCELLENCIES, MY LORDS, AND GENTLEMEN,—There is only one other toast that I shall present to you this evening. I said just now how greatly His Majesty the King-Emperor had regretted that he could not be present here in person at the celebration of his own Coronation. But as this was impossible, His Majesty took the one step that, had there been a plebiscite on the subject in India, we should all have voted for unanimously—namely, he deputed a member of the Royal Family, a near relative of his own, to represent his family on this occasion; and—the Prince and Princess of Wales finding it impossible to visit India in the present winter, though we hope that that is an honour only for a little while delayed—His Majesty's choice fell upon his Royal brother, the Duke of Connaught, whose presence at the ceremony to-day, and here again to-night, is regarded by all of us with quite exceptional pleasure and delight. These are our feelings, both because we regard His Royal Highness's visit as testifying in the most unmistakable way to the attitude and interest of the Sovereign, and also because there is no Prince, I might go further and say no officer—for, after all, His Royal Highness has been one of ourselves, and has served the Crown in India—who has more endeared himself to the people of all classes in this country, to soldiers and civilians, to Europeans and Natives, than His Royal Highness the Duke of Connaught. He comes back to us, therefore, not merely as the delegate of our illustrious Sovereign, but as the old friend whom all India reveres and loves; and if I may be permitted to diverge for one moment from the strict track of my toast, I would add that these sentiments on our part are enhanced by the knowledge that His Royal Highness has brought with him the gracious Princess whose popularity in India is not second even to his own. May I also say, though it is not perhaps absolutely germane to my toast, with what pleasure we see here another member of the Royal Family, His Royal Highness the Grand Duke of Hesse, himself a reigning sovereign, and a grandson of our late Queen, who has honoured us by joining our company, and whose presence is a compliment and a delight to us all.

"And now, to revert to the subject of my toast, I hope that His Royal Highness the Duke of Connaught will carry away to His Majesty the King a favourable impression of the prosperity and loyalty of his great Indian dominion. I can assure him that we regard it as the highest honour that he should have come out to be with us on this momentous occasion. When our Delhi functions are over, we hope to arrange for him a pleasant tour through the scenes and among the people to whom he is so much attached; and when he sails away from our shores, I hope that India will always keep the firm and agreeable resting-place in his memory that the Duchess and he already occupy, and will by their present visit confirm, in the affections of Europeans and Indians alike in this country.

"Gentlemen, I ask you to join with me in drinking the good health, pleasant journey, and safe return of our illustrious guest, His Royal Highness the Duke of Connaught."

The toast was drunk with enthusiasm.

His Royal Highness, who, on rising to respond to the toast, was very warmly received, said:

"YOUR EXCELLENCIES, YOUR ROYAL HIGHNESS, MY LORDS, AND GENTLEMEN,—I am indeed very sensible of the very kind manner in which you have proposed my health on this great and auspicious day. I can assure you that it was a great pleasure and satisfaction to myself when His Majesty the King informed me that it was his wish to send me out to India for the Coronation Durbar to represent his own family. I never expected that I should have such good fortune. My soldiering

H. H. The Maharaja of Datia, K.C.S.I.

days now are cast in a very different climate. Ireland is a very different place from India, and Dublin is a very different place from Delhi, and I was never more astonished than I was on being told that I should come out to India again. It is a great pleasure to me to come—a pleasure to come again to a country to which anybody at all interested, and having served the Crown in it, must feel deeply attached.

"There is also the feeling—I must say a somewhat sorrowful one—that when I was here before I had the good fortune to serve under three Viceroys and two Commanders-in-Chief, and that now I am no longer connected with India, except in my heart. But I think it requires very little assurance from me that I do, and always shall, take the very deepest interest in everything that affects the happiness and prosperity and the greatness of His Majesty's Indian Empire.

"I have many friends here, both British and Native, and to see them again—to see them well and getting on in the world—is a great satisfaction to me; and what especially gives me pleasure is to meet the Native Army once again. As you know, Sir, I was first connected with the Bengal Army, as it was then, in this Command—the Meerut Division—and with that of the Rawal Pindi Division; after that, for nearly four years, I had the Command of the Bombay Army, and, therefore, I may say that my interests are Indian, and not confined to one Presidency or another. But, during the twelve years since I was in India, the Indian troops have taken their share in the defence of our frontiers and of our interests both in India and beyond the seas, and I am happy to think that whether it was in Africa, whether it was in China, or whether it was on the frontiers of India, every branch of the Indian Army has known how to maintain its reputation, and I can say with confidence that the Indian Army is respected by the armies of all other nations. It is a bad day for any Army when it does not get the chance of active service, and it would be especially so for the Indian Army if they were to be locked up year after year in their own country. However, this is a slight digression from the toast. May I be allowed to say for the Duchess of Connaught that she, equally with myself, rejoices to be again in India, and that she was very proud to be present at the ceremony of to-day; and may I also, with reference to Your Excellency's remarks about my nephew, the Grand Duke of Hesse, say how highly he appreciates the pleasure of visiting India and of being your guest, and further may I, on this New Year's Day, tell you, Lord Curzon, how grateful we all are for your great hospitality and for the very kind and cordial welcome you have given us.

"I thank you all, Gentlemen, for the kind manner in which you have drunk my health."

More than one Sunday was spent in Delhi by the majority of the visitors in the various camps. But it had been arranged that one at least of these, that immediately following upon the Durbar, should not pass by without the holding of a solemn religious service of the Church of England, at which should be present all the British officers, civil and military, and the British troops who were at Delhi, as well as the great influx of European guests. The occasion was one that demanded no ordinary celebration, but that called for the association of the services of the Church, amid due and befitting surroundings, with the important event which this large concourse of Englishmen and Englishwomen had been gathered together to solemnize. Accordingly, on Sunday morning, January 4th, Divine Service was celebrated by the Most Reverend Dr. R. S. Copleston, Lord Bishop of Calcutta and Metropolitan in India, assisted by the Right Reverend Dr. G. Lefroy, Bishop of Lahore. No church at Delhi was large enough to contain more than a fraction of the congregation that was expected to attend. It had been decided, therefore, to utilise one of the two open expanses of level sward which had been prepared as polo-grounds; an artificial bank had been raised at its extremity to accommodate the massed bands; and the stand, erected in the centre between the two grounds, provided adequate sitting space for the great crowd of official and other guests, as well as a platform for the Metropolitan and his clergy. At 11 A.M. the Viceroy and Lady Curzon arrived with the Duke and Duchess of Connaught and the Grand Duke of Hesse. There were also present the Governors of Bombay and Madras, the Lieutenant-Governors and Chief Commissioners of Provinces, the Members of Council, and all the high officials of Government at Delhi, together with almost all the official and non-official Europeans invited to the Durbar or residing in Delhi. The Army was represented by Lord Kitchener, Commander-in-Chief; the Generals commanding in Bombay, Madras, the Punjab, and Bengal; and the European troops of the Church of England in camp. Officers entitled to wear uniform were ordered to appear in full dress, the troops being in review order. The total number of persons present was over 15,000. The troops were drawn up on the north and south sides of the ground facing the stand, so that the entire congregation was before and below the Metropolitan, as he conducted the service from a platform built out at the top of the steps. On this were gathered around him not only the Bishop of the Diocese, but the Bishops of Madras and Lucknow, the Archdeacons of Bombay and Lahore, and a large number of chaplains.

A special Order of Service had been appointed, impressive in its simplicity and rendered yet more solemn by the carefully chosen music of the bands and the singing of the military choir.

Meyerbeer's "Coronation March" and Viviani's "Silver Trumpets" were played as opening voluntaries; and the service began with the words, "The Lord is in His Holy temple: let all the earth keep silence before Him," followed by the singing of Psalm xciii.—*Dominus regnavit*. The choir of 520 male voices on the artificial mound was situated at a distance of over 300 yards from the main body of worshippers; and Captain Sanford, who conducted the music, and had arranged the chants for the musical bands, had ventured on the daring but entirely successful, experiment of making the men sing through megaphones, thereby attaining the intensity of 5000 voices. Two hymns were sung during the service, "O God, our help in ages past," and "Fight the good fight with all thy might." The lesson, taken from 1 Peter, ii. 13–7, was read by the Bishop of Lahore. Prayers were offered for the King-Emperor, for the Royal Family, for the Viceroy and Government of India, for the Clergy and Laity, for the Indian Princes and for all the peoples of India. After the second hymn, the Bishop of Calcutta delivered the following address:

"Amid the heart-stirring splendours and the intense human interests of this historic occasion, and as a definite element in its proceedings, we, brethren in Christ Jesus, are gathered together to worship the King of kings. We are here to thank God,—and we do thank Him with all our hearts—for what He has given us; for our King-Emperor, his health, and happy Coronation; and for all the blessings with which this season of national rejoicing has been enriched. Rising beyond even this thankfulness for the gifts that we enjoy, let us lift up our hearts to the Giver; as He reigns Himself in infinite Majesty and Love; and let us worship Him. Let us praise Him with the praise which is most acceptable to Him, and which best becomes us to offer;—the acknowledgment of His unspeakable Gift in the redemption of the world by Jesus Christ, His Son.

"If we left this undone, we should have failed to make our Indian celebration an adequate commemoration of what was done at Westminster. For that ceremony was an act of worship, a rite of the Christian religion; and it was such, not in form only, but with a reality which made itself felt and touched the religious sense of the Empire. To this aspect of the Coronation we are bound to bear our thankful witness.

"For among the vast multitudes of men of many creeds who make up the Indian Empire of King Edward, we, who are here, represent his Christian subjects. He is acclaimed as Emperor of India by all her creeds, not least for this reason, that he is the true successor of that august Mother of Kings and of peoples, who, in assuring her Indian subjects of the absolute religious freedom, which they hold from her as an inalienable inheritance, and which rests upon a principle of Government essentially Christian,—who in making, I say, that ever-memorable promise, did also in words as winning as they were noble, claim for herself the title and the blessings of a Christian. If we, brethren in Christ, remember that to-day, we shall certainly not lose thereby the respect, rather we shall secure the sympathy, of our fellow subjects who are not Christians.

"Of us then, Christian subjects of the King-Emperor, and servants and soldiers of Christ Jesus, what is it that this day demands? At this moment, throughout the Empire of King Edward, the general conscience of men is, in a true sense, awake. Our troubles, our efforts, our blessings, have all conspired to uplift the national heart to a high seriousness. And we, in this wonderful Durbar, have felt, many of us, such a touch of seriousness; such a call to conscience. Through all the pomp and the entertainments, we have felt, not far below the surface, the presence of an immense responsibility. We experience something of what the prophet expressed by the words: 'Thy heart shall fear and be enlarged.' Our hearts swell at the greatness of things; at the march of armies and the pageant of nations; at the accumulated results of history, the far-rolling waves of influence; at the vast promises of hope and the vast demands of duty. This greatness of things fills us with awe; we have a share in that thrill which has moved the conscience of the Empire: our hearts are lifted up not alone by pride.

"Let our answer be: 'We lift them up unto the Lord!' We acknowledge the call made upon us by these great emotions and these great realities. We will be more devoted than ever to duty, and to the service of other men; more pure, more Christlike, more worthy of the Lord. We Christians will try, in the plain familiar words,—but words how far reaching!—to 'let our light shine before men, that they may see our good works and glorify our Father which is in heaven.'"

The *Te Deum* was then chanted, the Metropolitan pronounced the benediction, and the service ended with the singing of the national anthem. Among the solemnities of the week none was more impressive than this simple ceremonial, conducted, with the forms familiar to all the participators from childhood, under the canopy of heaven.

CHAPTER VIII

IN THE PALACE OF THE GREAT MOGHUL

It occurred to Shah Jehan's omniscient mind, the author of the "Shah Jehan-nama" relates, that on the banks of the Jumna, in the environs of old Delhi, he would build himself a splendid Fort, with edifices like to those of Paradise. Labourers and skilled workmen, stone masons and sculptors, were collected from all quarters of the empire; and, in the thirteenth year of his auspicious reign (1638), the foundation-stone of a noble structure was laid. It took nine years and three months to finish, and cost sixty lakhs of rupees. The architectural beauties of the buildings within the Fort, and especially of the two Courts of Audience, have never failed to win the admiration of travellers, even of those whose eyes have feasted on the yet fairer proportions of the Taj Mahal at Agra, or whose imaginations have been impressed by the stupendous ruins—the monuments of a more heroic age—of Tughlukabad, and by what remains of the magnificence of the Turki Sultans who built the Kutab Minar, the tomb of Altamsh, and the Alai Darwaza.

Shah Jehan's palace fortress, beneath the walls of which the state procession had passed on the day of the viceregal entry, was to be the scene, later on, of two notable gatherings. Considered merely as brilliant spectacles, in which the inexhaustible glamour of the Orient was mingled with the steadier, if colder rays, of a civilisation that had its origin in the remote West, the Grand Chapter of the two Indian Orders and the State Ball must be reckoned among the most memorable incidents of the Delhi celebrations. The political significance of the investiture need not be expounded. To confer rank and title on those

H. H. The Maharaja of Kolhapur,
G.C.S.I., G.C.V.O.

who uphold the State by their prudence and goodwill, or protect it by their energy and courage, is a duty that no wise ruler will overlook. It enhances the value of these honours if they can be formally bestowed amid such a display of magnificence as was possible, when an Imperial assemblage had been convoked in such a city as Delhi, and when the palace of the Moghuls was available for the ceremony.

It was in the Diwan-i Am, or hall of public audience, in the palace of Shah Jehan, that the French traveller, François Bernier, in the middle of the seventeenth century, saw Aurungzeb enthroned, with Muhammadan Omrahs, Hindu Rajas, and ambassadors from foreign countries standing round in postures of profound reverence. Seated on the famous Peacock Throne, which was placed, when used in this court, on a canopied platform of marble inlaid with coloured stones, the Moghul emperors were wont to give audience to high and low. The space in front of the imperial platform was divided by a silver railing from the rest of the hall, and was reserved for the grandees of the State. The hall, which is built of red sand-stone, is 168 feet wide, from north to south, and 56 feet in depth; the throne platform projecting from a recess in the centre of the east wall, facing the entrance. On the north, west and south sides the hall is not closed in. Three rows of pillars, carrying scalloped arches, which turn longitudinally as well as transversely, support a roof made of crimson sand-stone slabs, laid flat on a deep-coved cornice. In the days of the Moghul emperors the space in front of the Diwan-i Am was shut in by a rail of similar sand-stone ornamented by gilt spikes. This enclosure, known as the Gulal Bari, was covered, on state occasions, with a canopy.

To provide the requisite space for the most imposing Chapter of the Indian Orders that has ever been held in India, and also for the subsequent ball, Shah Jehan's hall of public audience had been enlarged to three times its original size. The Viceroy had himself designed and superintended the execution of this task, ordering two replicas of the hall to be made in continuation of it. The only differences that struck the eye (so cleverly had the imitation been carried out) were that the central extension, constructed for the spectators at the Chapter, and for the dancers at the ball, was unencumbered by any pillars or arches, but was an open space from end to end, while in the third or outermost extension the pillars and arches were fashioned in less heavy style, so as to admit of this part of the building being used as a robing and assembly room on the occasion of the Investiture, and a refreshment buffet on the night of the ball. It had been represented to the Viceroy that the reproduction of the original hall in the manner proposed was almost an impossibility, that the colours could not be imitated or the requisite space obtained, and that the general effect of the crimson sand-stone would be so sombre, even when lighted by electricity, as to plunge the festivities which it was intended to hold there in gloom. Every one was ready with independent suggestions for painting, or stencilling, or decoration, or upholstery in every conceivable variety of style. The Viceroy, however, adhered resolutely to the decision that the entire building should be Moghul and nothing else: each pillar or moulding or section of roof was copied from some part of the existing structure; and the great crimson curtain, with the outline of a *mihrab*, or niche, *appliqué* in white upon it, that closed the entrance, was the *facsimile* of a design that has remained unchanged since the Moghul times.

So skilfully and successfully had these instructions been carried out that, when the invited guests entered the building on the night of the Investiture, they found, instead of the pillared pavilion, open on three sides, of the Moghul court of audience, an immense hall, walled in on every face, and covering a total area of about 168 square yards.

Right opposite there stood, as always, the marble platform under its glittering baldacchino; but it appeared to have receded, for one now counted six, and not three, rows of pillars in front of it, and so cleverly had the work been done that it was a puzzle to say which were the new pillars, and which the old. The Diwan-i Am, it was evident, had been enlarged; but in what way, or by what device, only those in the secret could tell. Next, one noted that a wooden floor had been laid in the central hall, and carpeted; and that a daïs had been constructed in front of the throne platform. Conspicuous on the daïs were two silver chairs of state, standing on a carpet of gold brocade. The more ornate chair, destined for the Grand Master of the Orders of the Star of India and the Indian Empire, stood exactly beneath the throne platform of the Great Moghul. It had been discussed whether the seat of the representative of the Sovereign could be placed upon the actual platform on which in old days stood the Peacock Throne; and it had even been suggested by some hyper-sensitive spirits that an unfortunate effect might be produced upon the Oriental mind if he were to occupy a lower level than that which was once graced by the presence of the Great Moghul. These sentimental considerations, however, had to yield to the facts that the throne platform is so lofty (it is only approached by a door in the wall at the back, and is inaccessible from the front) that a steep flight of steps would have been required for any one to ascend to it from the body of the hall, that its occupant or occupants would have been inconveniently elevated above the remaining actors or spectators, and that it would have been almost impossible from such an altitude to have conducted the intricate ceremonies of an Investiture. The chairs of state had accordingly been placed upon a low inlaid marble platform that ordinarily stands immediately below the throne, and upon which the tradition runs that the Wazir of the Emperor stood in former times to hand up petitions to his royal master seated above. The inlay in this platform (in the *pietra dura* style of the period), which had suffered very much in modern times, had been renovated by order of the Viceroy by artists from Agra, just previous to the Durbar, and is now in a perfect condition.

There was a further work of restoration which he had contemplated carrying out simultaneously in the Diwan-i Am, but which for want of time had to be postponed. One of the chief features in olden days of the recess in the wall from which the canopied throne projects into the Diwan-i Am was a series of mosaics inlaid, in Florentine designs of birds and flowers, in a background of black marble. These works of art have commonly been attributed to Augustin or Austin de Bordeaux, the French artificer, who is said to have been employed by the Emperor Shah Jehan both in the Delhi palace and in the Taj at Agra. The central panel represented the figure of Orpheus seated under a tree, surrounded by listening animals, and engaged in playing a violin. Whatever may have been the origin of these mosaics (the somewhat debased style of which has led some critics to attribute them to inferior artists and to a later period), there is no doubt about the historical fact that they figured in the wall behind the throne of the Moghul up till the date of the Mutiny. In that period of general chaos and destruction they were torn from their setting, and came into the possession of a British officer, who carried them off to England and sold them to the British Government for £500. Lord Curzon, aware that they had reposed for years, unnoticed and all but unknown, in the South Kensington, now the Victoria and Albert, Museum in London, sought their restoration from the British Government, with a view to replacing them in their original site before the Delhi ceremonials. The panels were generously surrendered by the Board of Education, in whose custody they were; but they did not reach Delhi in time to be reinserted before the Diwan-i Am was required for the purposes that are now being described. They have since been replaced.

To return to the history of the Chapter. In that portion of the hall which was formed by the original Diwan-i Am rows of chairs were ranged on either side of, and parallel to, the wide approach to the daïs, which was covered with a scarlet carpet embroidered in gold with the royal arms. Other rows of chairs, for spectators, were placed in the new part of the building, also on either side of the central gangway, but at right angles to it. The electric light arranged in the cornice of the coffered panels of the ceiling, and in clusters depending from the centre, threw a soft radiance on arch and pillar. The great white marble throne with its curving baldacchino stood out from the dark background with an almost dazzling brilliance; while a rich glow, reflected from the crimson columns and roof, suffused the remainder of the gigantic hall.

In the enlargement and adaptation of the latter, which have been described, not the most fastidious or critical eye could detect anything which, by a stretch of the imagination, could be construed as even an approach to vandalism, or as showing a lack of thoughtful care for the master builders of a bygone age. The whole of these works were additions to, and not alterations of, the Diwan-i Am; the original structure remained unaffected and almost untouched. Hardly had the

Dagg & Co

THE DIWAN-I AM, DELHI

last visitor left Delhi when these temporary creations were removed, and the Diwan-i Am of to-day presents not a trace of its recent and startling metamorphosis. To Colonel J. W. Thurburn, R.E., Secretary to the Punjab Government in the Public Works Department, and Rai Bahadur Gunga Ram, Superintendent of Works, was mainly due the credit for so cleverly carrying out the Viceroy's plans, without the slightest detriment to the Moghul fabric.

Nearly two thousand spectators were invited to attend the Grand Chapter of the Orders, which was to be opened at 9 P.M., on Saturday, January 3rd. Almost all the ruling Chiefs in Delhi were present, some as spectators, others as participants in the picturesque ceremonial that was about to ensue.

A guard of honour, furnished by the 2nd battalion, Gordon Highlanders, was drawn up at the entrance to the hall.

Shortly after 9 o'clock, the Grand Duke of Hesse arrived with his staff, and took a seat on the daïs. A little later Her Royal Highness the Duchess of Connaught and Lady Curzon drove up to the hall, and were conducted to seats on the daïs, a little to the right and rear of the two state chairs. Meanwhile the combined string bands of the 2nd battalion, King's Own Scottish Borderers and 2nd battalion, East Lancashire Regiment played the following pieces:

Grand March . . .	Tannhäuser . . .	*Wagner.*
Overture . . .	Poet and Peasant . . .	*Suppé.*
Three Dances . . .	Henry VIII. . . .	*German.*
Selection . . .	Faust . . .	*Gounod.*
Grand March . . .	Krönungsmarsch . . .	*Kretschmer.*

Both now, and during the ceremonies which were to follow, the music, which was under the able direction of Captain Sanford, admirably emphasised the solemnity of the scene. Shah Jehan, like his grandfather Akbar, "the patron," Abul Fazl says, "of all who practise this enchanting art," had encouraged the Court musicians; but the puritan Aurungzeb abolished them. They came to the palace, with lamentations, bearing a bier; and when Aurungzeb asked whom they had on it, they answered "Music is dead, and we go to the graveyard."

"Make the grave deep," said the Emperor, "that neither voice nor echo issues therefrom." On the night of the Grand Chapter, if never before, the wrong done to music was gloriously revenged.

The Viceroy, who is the Grand Master of both the Indian Orders, and the Duke of Connaught, together with the Knights Grand Commanders of the two Orders, had already met in the robing-room, and the other members were marshalled in the assembly room. In the robing-room, His Royal Highness, in accordance with the King-Emperor's command, invested Mr. Hugh Barnes with the insignia of a Knight Commander of the Royal Victorian Order, a distinction the more gratifying to the recipient as it was unexpected. The entire assemblage of spectators having now entered the hall, and taken their seats—all being in full uniform—a procession was formed of the members of the two Orders then present in Delhi; the trumpeters at the entrance sounded the "Star of India Flourish," the curtain was raised, and the procession passed slowly, two and two up the hall, the band playing the Grand March from Handel's "Scipio," and the long line being closed by the single figures, firstly of the Duke of Connaught, and lastly of the Grand Master. The Companions, Knights, and Grand Commanders, as the procession reached the upper part of the hall, filed off to their seats. As the Grand Master approached the daïs, the band played "God save the King," and all the spectators in the hall stood up till the Grand Master and the Duke of Connaught had taken their seats. The order of the procession was as follows:

J. B. Wood, Esq., Under-Secretary, Foreign Department.

L. W. Dane, Esq., Officiating Secretary, Foreign Department.

Sir Hugh Barnes, Secretary of the Orders.

COMPANIONS OF THE ORDER OF THE INDIAN EMPIRE.

Rai Bahadur Nanak Chand.
A. J. Dunlop, Esq.
K. Krishnaswami Rao.
A. Pedler, Esq.
The Hon. Mr. T. Conlan.
Lieutenant-Colonel W. J. R. Rainsford.
Major T. E. Scott, D.S.O.
F. W. Latimer, Esq.
J. S. Donald, Esq.
Major A. F. Pinhey.
Lieutenant-Colonel G. H. D. Gimlette.
A. L. P. Tucker, Esq.
S. Preston, Esq.
Commander G. E. Holland, D.S.O.
Sardar Mir Ausaf Ali Khan.
Lieutenant-Colonel G. K. Scott-Moncrieff.

Major J. R. Dunlop Smith.
Colonel S. C. F. Peile.
Rai Bahadur Kailash Chandar Bose.
Lieutenant-Colonel A. M. Crofts.
Diwan Bahadur P. Rajaratna Mudaliyar Avargal.

Maung On Gaing, A.T.M.
Khan Bahadur Kazi Jalal-ud-din.
V. P. Mudhava Rao.
Rai Bahadur Dhanpat Rai.

Captain A. B. Minchin.
E. F. Jacob, Esq.
Virchand Dipchand.
Major J. Ramsay.
B. Robertson, Esq.
Sahibzada M. Bakhtiyar Shah.
C. G. W. Hastings, Esq.
P. N. Krishna Murti.
Brigadier-General B. Duff, C.B.
Khan Bahadur Naoroji Pestanji Vakil.

The Hon. Mr. A. Anderson.
Raja Bhup Indra Bikram Singh, of Piyagpur.
Surgeon-General B. Franklin.
Sir Patrick Playfair, Kt.
Major W. R. Yielding, D.S.O.
The Hon. Mr. S. W. Edgerley.
Gangadhar Rao Madhav Chitnavis.
A. C. Hankin, Esq.
The Hon. Mr. F. J. E. Spring.
The Hon. Lieutenant-Colonel Sir G. M. J. Moore, Kt.
The Hon. Mr. Phiroz Shah Marwanji Mehta.
B. S. Carey, Esq.

Rao Sahib Thakur Bahadur Singh, of Masuda.
Diwan Ganpat Rai.

J. G. Scott, Esq.
The Hon. Mr. H. T. White.
H. H. Risley, Esq.
Colonel T. H. Hendley.

Fardunji Kuvarji Tarapurvala.
The Hon. Mr. H. A. Sim.
Captain W. S. Goodridge, R.N.
H. Marsh, Esq.
The Hon. Mr. W. C. Hughes.

Khan Bahadur Muhammad Yakub.
Lieutenant-Colonel M. J. Meade.
Khan Bahadur Kharsedji Rustamji Thanawala.
Khan Bahadur Dhanjibhai Fakirji Commodore.

Lieutenant-Colonel H. K. McKay.
Major Kunwar Bir Bikram Singh.
A. Pennycuick, Esq.
The Hon. Lieut.-Colonel D. P. Masson, V.D.
R. W. Carlyle, Esq.
Raja Balwant Singh, of Awa.
Rai Bahadur Daulat Ram.
Rustamji Dhanjibhai Mehta.
Major Nawab Muhammad Ali Beg.
The Hon. Rai Bahadur P. Ananda Charlu Avargal.

J. Eliot, Esq.
The Hon. Rai Bahadur Chunilal Venilal.
T. Higham, Esq.
R. M. Dane, Esq.
Munshi Hafiz Abdul Karim, C.V.O.
T. R. A. Thambu Chetti.
The Hon. Mr. C. E. Buckland.
Khan Bahadur Haq Nawaz Khan.
Fazalbhai Visram.
Lieutenant-Colonel E. H. Fenn.

P. G. Melitus, Esq.
The Hon. Diwan Bahadur S. Srinivasa Raghava Aiyangar.
Sheikh Baha-ud-din Nawab-i-Am.
Maharaja Harballabh Narayan Singh Bahadur, of Sonbursa, Bhagalpur.
Khan Bahadur Kadirdad Khan.
Major H. Daly.
The Hon. Mr. J. B. Fuller.
Major F. E. Younghusband.

Khan Bahadur Sheikh Hafiz Abdul Karim.
H. P. Todd-Naylor, Esq.
Ramkrishna Gopal Bhandarkar.
Colonel B. Scott.
Nawab Bahadur Saiyid Amir Husain.
Kumar Sri Kaluba.
G. Watt, Esq.
G. P. Rose, Esq.
Sardar Sultan Jan, Saddozai.
The Rev. E. Lafont.
The Hon. Mr. J. Buckingham.
Colonel S. S. Jacob.
Colonel J. C. F. Gordon.
Lieutenant-Colonel J. L. Walker.
Lieutenant-Colonel F. H. R. Drummond.
Colonel C. W. Muir, C.B.
Lieut.-Colonel Nawab Muhammad Aslam Khan, Wazirzada, A.D.C., Sardar Bahadur.
Hafiz Muhammad Hasan Khan.
Rai Bahadur Hittu Ram.
Mirza Ghulam Ahmad.

COMPANIONS OF THE ORDER OF THE STAR OF INDIA.

The Hon. Mr. J. Wilson.
S. Ismay, Esq.
J. O. Miller, Esq.
E. N. Baker, Esq.
The Hon. Mr. H. M. Winterbotham.
The Hon. Mr. J. P. Hewett, C.I.E.
The Hon. Lieutenant-Colonel D. Robertson.
Khan Bahadur Yar Muhammad Khan, of Jaora.
The Hon. Mr. A. W. Cruickshank.
The Hon. Raja Tasadduk Rasul Khan, of Barabanki.
Sardar Bahadur Kashi Rao Sarve.
H. A. Anderson, Esq.
H. F. D. Moule, Esq.
The Hon. Mr. J. Monteath.
The Hon. Mr. A. H. L. Fraser.
The Hon. Lieutenant-Colonel H. A. Deane.
The Hon. Lieutenant-Colonel D. W. K. Barr.
Rao Chhatra Pati Bahadur, Jagirda of Alipura.
Colonel L. J. H. Grey.
Raja Jai Krishan Das Bahadur.
The Hon. Mr. D. T. Roberts.
Brig.-Gen. G. L. R. Richardson, C.B., C.I.E.
The Hon. Mr. F. S. P. Lely.
The Hon. Mr. A. H. T. Martindale.
Surgeon-General D. Sinclair.
His Highness Raja Kirti Sah, of Tehri.
The Hon. Mr. A. T. Arundel.
L. W. King, Esq.
The Hon. Mr. J. A. Bourdillon.
M. M. Finucane, Esq.
Major A. H. McMahon, C.I.E.
Colonel J. A. Miley.
The Hon. Mr. C. W. Bolton.
J. M. Macpherson, Esq.
The Hon. Mr. C. L. Tupper.
The Hon. Mr. D. C. J. Ibbetson.
Sardar Jiwan Singh, Shahid, of Shahzadpur.
The Hon. Colonel C. E. Yate, C.M.G.
Colonel Sir C. C. Scott-Moncrieff, K.C.M.G.
Major-General Beresford Lovett, C.B.

KNIGHTS COMMANDERS OF THE ORDER OF THE INDIAN EMPIRE.

His Excellency Colonel Sir E. A. R. Galhardo, Governor-General of Portuguese India.
The Hon. Sir F. W. Maclean, Chief Justice of Bengal.
Major His Highness Maharaja Sir Ganga Singh Bahadur, of Bikaner.
The Hon. Kunwar Sir Harnam Singh Ahluwalia, of Kapurthala.

Nawab Sir Amir-ud-din, Khan Bahadur, of Loharu.

Baba Sir Khem Singh, Bedi, of Kullar.

Maharaja Sir Partab Narain Singh, of Ajudhya.

Sir M. M. Bhownagree, M.P.

Nawab Sidi Sir Ahmad Khan, of Janjira.

The Hon. Maharaja Sir Ravaneshwar Prasad Singh Bahadur, of Gidhaur.

The Hon. Nawab Sir Imam Bakhsh Khan, Mazari.

Thakur Sahib Sir Jaswant Singhji, of Limri.

Sardar Sir Naoroz Khan, of Kharan.

KNIGHTS COMMANDERS OF THE ORDER OF THE STAR OF INDIA.

The Hon. Sir J. D. La Touche.

Sultan Sir Ahmad-bin-Fadthl, of Lahej.

His Highness Maharao Sir Umed Singh Bahadur, of Kota.

The Hon. Sir C. M. Rivaz.

Sir J. F. Price.

His Highness Nawab Sir Rasul Khanji, of Junagadh.

His Highness Raja Sir Jagatjit SinghBahadur, of Kapurthala.

His Highness Maharaja Sir Bhawani Singh Bahadur, of Datia.

Sir E. C. Buck.

His Highness Raja Sir Rama Varma, of Cochin.

His Highness Maharao Sir Kesri Singh Bahadur, of Sirohi.

Thakur Sahib Sir Mansinghji, of Palitana.

Raja Sir Amar Singh, of Kashmir.

The Hon. Sir F. W. R. Fryer.

KNIGHTS GRAND COMMANDERS OF THE ORDER OF THE INDIAN EMPIRE.

His Highness Sir Sultan Muhammad Shah, Agha Khan.
Two Attendants.

Major-General Sir A. Gaselee, K.C.B.
Two Attendants.

His Excellency the Right Hon. Lord Ampthill.
Two Attendants.

His Highness Maharaja Sir Pratap Singh Bahadur, of Orchha.
Two Attendants.

His Excellency the Right Hon. Lord Northcote, C.B.
Two Attendants.

His Highness Maharaja Sir Prabhu Narayan Singh Bahadur, of Benares.
Two Attendants.

His Highness Thakur Sahib Sir Waghji Ravagi, of Morvi.
Two Attendants.

His Highness Thakur Sahib Sir Bhagwantsinghji, of Gondal.
Two Attendants.

His Highness Mir Sir Faiz Muhammad Khan, of Khairpur.
Two Attendants.

His Highness Maharaja Sir Bhanwar Pal Deo Bahadur, of Karauli.
Two Attendants.

His Highness Mir Sir Mahmud Khan, of Kalat.
Two Attendants.

His Highness Nawab Sir Muhammad Ibrahim Ali Khan Bahadur, of Tonk.
Two Attendants.

Lieutenant-Colonel His Highness Maharaja Sir Nripendra Narayan Bhup Bahadur, of Kuch Behar.
Two Attendants.

His Highness Maharao Sir Khengarji Bahadur, of Cutch.
Two Attendants.

KNIGHTS GRAND COMMANDERS OF THE ORDER OF THE STAR OF INDIA.

Major-Gen. His Highness Maharaja Sir Pratap Singh Bahadur, of Idar, K.C.B., A.D.C.
Two Attendants.

His Highness Maharaja Sir Vyankatesh Raman Singh Bahadur, of Rewa.
Two Attendants.

Colonel His Highness Maharaja Sir Madho Rao Scindia Bahadur, of Gwalior.
Two Attendants.

His Highness Maharaja Sir Shahu Chhatrapati, of Kolhapur.
Two Attendants.

Major-General His Highness Maharaja Sir Pratab Singh Bahadur, of Jammu and Kashmir.
Two Attendants.

His Highness Sir Bala Rama Varma Bahadur, of Travancore.
Two Attendants.

His Highness Maharaja Sir Madho Singh Bahadur, of Jaipur, G.C.I.E.
Two Attendants.

His Highness Maharaja Sir Shivaji Rao Holkar Bahadur, of Indore.
Two Attendants.

His Highness Maharaja Sir Sayaji Rao Gaekwar, of Baroda.
Two Attendants.

His Highness Nawab Mir Sir Mahbub Ali Khan Bahadur, Nizam of Hyderabad.
Two Attendants.

His Highness Raja Sir Hira Singh Bahadur, of Nabha.
Two Attendants.

AN OFFICER OF THE ROYAL STAFF.

His Royal Highness the Duke of Connaught.

Pages.

STAFF OF HIS ROYAL HIGHNESS

Sir Maurice FitzGerald.
Lieutenant-Colonel Jarvis.
Lieutenant Colonel Leslie.
Lieutenant-Colonel the Hon. C. Bingham.
Major Beevor, R.A.M.C.

STAFF OF THE GRAND MASTER.

Captain R. G. T. Baker-Carr, Aide-de-Camp to the Viceroy.
Colonel the Hon. E. Baring, Military Secretary to the Viceroy.
Captain C. Wigram, Aide-de-Camp to the Viceroy.
Sir Walter Lawrence, Private Secretary to the Viceroy.

His Excellency the Grand Master.

Pages.

Colonel the Hon. C. Harbord, Aide-de-Camp to the Viceroy.
Captain the Hon. R. Lindsay, Aide-de-Camp to the Viceroy.
Resaldar-Major Hukam Singh, Sardar Bahadur, Native Aide-de-Camp to the Viceroy.
Captain F. Adam, Aide-de-Camp to the Viceroy.
Captain the Hon. J. R. L. Yarde-Buller, Aide-de-Camp to the Viceroy.
Resaldar-Major Debi-Dayal Singh, Sardar Bahadur, Native Aide-de-Camp to the Viceroy.

His Highness Maharao Raja Sir Raghubir Singh Bahadur, of Bundi, G.C.I.E., K.C.S.I., who would have followed Major-General Sir Alfred Gaselee, K.C.B., among the Knights Grand Commanders of the Indian Empire, was absent owing to indisposition. Sir Hugh Barnes wore the white silk mantle and badge of the Secretary of the Order of the Star of India, with the insignia of a Knight of the Victorian Order. His Royal Highness the Duke of Connaught, who was in field marshal's uniform, wore the silk robe and insignia of a Grand Commander of the Order of the Star of India. His Excellency the Viceroy wore the sky-blue velvet robe and insignia of the Grand Master of this Most Exalted Order. The two pages who had been selected for the honour of attending His Royal Highness were the Raj Rana Man Singh, a young Rajput nobleman, aged ten, the son of the Thakur of Dilwara, and a boy of the same age, the Sipah Salar Saramadai Khandan Sri Raja Udai Bhan Singh Shamsher Jang Bahadur, brother to the Maharaj Rana of Dholpur. The pages of His Excellency the Grand Master were Mian Hari Singh, aged seven, the son of Raja Sir Amar Singh of Kashmir, who had himself acted as page to Lord Lytton at the Imperial Assemblage of 1877, and the Sahibzada Hamidulla Khan, aged eight, the youngest son of Her Highness the Begum of Bhopal. The keenest desire had been expressed by the princely and aristocratic families of India to provide pages from their youthful scions for this most historic occasion. Each page, by special desire of the Viceroy, was attired in the characteristic costume of his own court; and the gravity of their deportment no less than the magnificence of their costumes excited universal admiration. They took their seats on cushions of blue silk, placed behind the state chairs, with their backs to the marble throne.

His Excellency the Grand Master having taken his seat, the Secretary of the Order of the Star of India, Sir Hugh Barnes, approaching the daïs, reported that the business before the Chapter was the investiture of one Knight Grand Commander and twelve Knights Commanders of the Order of the Star of India and the decoration of fourteen Companions, of the same Most Exalted Order, each with the insignia of the class to which he was appointed. Having made this report, Sir H. Barnes delivered to the Grand Master the Sovereign's grant conferring on His Highness Raja Sir Rama Varma, K.C.S.I., of Cochin, the dignity of a Knight Grand Commander; after which, with the Under-Secretary in the Foreign Department and the Junior Knights Commanders, who were Sir James La Touche and Sir Charles Rivaz, he conducted His Highness to the front of the daïs, where the Raja made his reverence. The Sovereign's grant was now read by Sir H. Barnes, to whom the Grand Master had delivered it. The Secretary's next duty was to conduct the Raja to a table; where the junior of the two Knights Commanders decorated His Highness with the riband and badge; and the Senior Knight attached the Star of the Order to his breast. The two Knights Commanders next robed His Highness with the mantle of the Order; and, this done, His Highness was conducted by Sir H. Barnes to the daïs, to make further reverence. The Grand Master, remaining seated, then invested His Highness with the collar of a Knight Grand Commander, and in loud tones, which could be heard to the end of the hall, addressed him in the following terms:

"In the name of the King, Emperor of India, and by His Majesty's Command, I hereby invest you with the Honourable Insignia of the Order of the Star of India, of which Most Exalted Order His Majesty has been graciously pleased to appoint you to be a Knight Grand Commander."

When the admonition had been given, the newly-invested Knight Grand Commander made his reverence to the Grand Master, and was conducted by Sir Hugh Barnes to the seat appointed for him.

The new Knights Commanders of the Star of India were now to be invested with the insignia of the Second Class of this Most Exalted Order, namely, the following:

His Highness Raja Surindar Bikram Prakash Bahadur, of Sirmur.
The Hon. Lieutenant-Colonel David Willam Keith Barr, C.S.I., Indian Army.
The Hon. Mr. Denzil Charles Jelf Ibbetson, C.S.I., Indian Civil Service.
His Excellency Rear-Admiral Charles Carter Drury.
The Hon. Mr. Henry Martin Winterbotham, C.S.I., Indian Civil Service.
The Hon. Mr. James Monteath, C.S.I., Indian Civil Service.
The Hon. Lieutenant-Colonel Donald Robertson, C.S.I., Indian Army.
The Hon. Mr. Andrew Henderson Leith Fraser, C.S.I., Indian Civil Service.
Hugh Shakespear Barnes, Esq., C.S.I., Indian Civil Service.
Colonel Sir Colin Campbell Scott-Moncrieff, K.C.M.G., C.S.I., Royal Engineers (retired).
His Highness Raja Kirti Sah, C.S.I., of Tehri.
Kunwar Ranbir Singh, of Patiala.

These Rajas, noblemen, officers, and gentlemen, in groups of four were conducted by Mr. Louis Dane, officiating Secretary in the Foreign Department, and the two Junior Knights Commanders of the Order to the daïs, and were there presented by the Secretary of the Orders, one after another, to the Grand Master. The members of the group, in which Mr. Hugh Barnes was included, were presented by the officiating Foreign Secretary. Each, as he was presented, made his reverence to the Grand Master. Those who, in accordance with practice, either not being Europeans, or having been knighted already, were not to receive knighthood (namely, the Raja of Sirmur, Sir C. Scott-Moncrieff, the Raja of Tehri, and Kunwar Ranbir Singh) were straightway conducted by Mr. Wood, Under-Secretary in the Foreign Department, to the table; but upon Lieutenant-Colonel Barr, Mr. Ibbetson, Rear-Admiral Drury, Mr. Winterbotham, Mr. Monteath, Lieutenant-Colonel Robertson, Mr. Fraser, and Mr. Hugh Barnes, the Grand Master conferred, by accolade, the title, degree and honour of a Knight Bachelor of the United Kingdom of Great Britain and Ireland, each, when he had been knighted, being conducted by Mr. Dane to the table. Here the two Junior Knights Commanders fastened the Stars of the Order on the breast of each recipient and, when they had all been thus decorated, they were conducted by Mr. Dane to the daïs, where they made their reverence, and were addressed, collectively, by the Grand Master as follows:

"In the name of the King, Emperor of India, and by His Majesty's Command, I hereby invest you with the Honourable Insignia of the Order of the Star of India, of which Most Exalted Order His Majesty has been graciously pleased to appoint you to be Knights Commanders."

The Grand Master then invested them one by one, in the order of their precedence, with the riband and badge of the Order. When all the Knights in one group had been invested, they made their reverence to the Grand Master and were led to the seats provided for them by Mr.

Dane, who then, with the two Junior Knights Commanders, conducted another group to the daïs.

The investiture of the Knights Commanders of the Order of the Star of India having been finished, the Secretary presented to the Grand Master the badges of the Third Class of the Order for the Companions who were to be decorated.

These were the following:

The Hon. Mr. Charles Gerwien Bayne, Indian Civil Service.
The Hon. Mr. Thomas Raleigh.
The Hon. Mr. James Thomson, Indian Civil Service.
The Hon. Mr. Joseph Bampfylde Fuller, C.I.E., Indian Civil Service.
The Hon. Sir Edward FitzGerald Law, K.C.M.G.
The Hon. Mr. Charles Stuart Bayley, Indian Civil Service.
The Hon. Mr. Edward Townshend Candy, Indian Civil Service.
Major-General Trevor Bruce Tyler, Royal Artillery.
The Hon. Mr. William Henry Lockington Impey, Indian Civil Service.
The Hon. Mr. William Charles Macpherson, Indian Civil Service.
Major Hugh Daly, C.I.E., Indian Army.
Raja Ban Bihari Kapur, of Burdwan.
Nawab Mumtaz-ud-Daula Muhammad Faiyaz Ali Khan, of Pahasu, United Provinces.
Sardar Badan Singh, of Malaudh, Punjab.

The officiating Foreign Secretary conducted these gentlemen, in groups of five, to the front of the daïs, where the Secretary presented them one after the other to the Grand Master, announcing their names as he did so. Each gentleman made his reverence to the Grand Master; and forthwith the Grand Master handed a badge to the Secretary, who attached it in the proper place, whereupon the newly-decorated Companion made his reverence and withdrew.

After all the Companions had been decorated, the Secretary made representation that there was no further business before the Assembly of the Most Exalted Order of the Star of India. His Excellency the Grand Master and His Royal Highness the Duke of Connaught, with their staffs, and Their Highnesses the Raja of Nabha, the Maharaja of Jaipur, and the Maharaja of Travancore, with their attendants, thereupon left the Chapter hall for the robing-room in the following order, all others present in the hall rising from their seats and standing up while the procession passed out:

The Under-Secretary in the Foreign Department.

The Officiating Foreign Secretary.

The Secretary of the Order.

Aide-de-Camp to the Viceroy. Aide-de-Camp to the Viceroy.
Military Secretary to the Viceroy. Private Secretary to the Viceroy.

HIS EXCELLENCY THE GRAND MASTER.

Pages.

Aide-de-Camp to the Viceroy. Surgeon to the Viceroy.
Aide-de-Camp to the Viceroy. Aide-de-Camp to the Viceroy.
Native Aide-de-Camp to the Viceroy. Native Aide-de-Camp to the Viceroy.

An Officer of the Royal Staff.

HIS ROYAL HIGHNESS THE DUKE OF CONNAUGHT.

Pages.

Staff of His Royal Highness.

His Highness the Raja of Nabha.
Two Attendants.

His Highness the Maharaja of Jaipur.
Two Attendants.

His Highness the Maharaja of Travancore.
Two Attendants.

As His Excellency the Grand Master and His Royal Highness the Duke of Connaught passed down the Chapter hall, the bands played the Grand March "Krönungsmarsch" (Kretschmer's); and as the procession disappeared under the archway, the trumpeters sounded the "Star of India Flourish."

Having exchanged the sky-blue robes and the insignia of the Order of the Star of India for the deep blue, almost purple, mantles, and the insignia of the Order of the Indian Empire, His Excellency the Grand Master and His Royal Highness the Duke of Connaught, attended by their staffs, and preceded by the Maharajas of Jaipur and Travancore, and the Raja of Nabha with their attendants, re-entered the Chapter hall, in the following order:

The Under-Secretary in the Foreign Department.

The Officiating Foreign Secretary.

The Secretary of the Order.

His Highness the Maharaja of Travancore.
Two Attendants.

His Highness the Maharaja of Jaipur.
Two Attendants.

His Highness the Raja of Nabha.
Two Attendants.

An Officer of the Royal Staff.

HIS ROYAL HIGHNESS THE DUKE OF CONNAUGHT.

Pages.

Staff of His Royal Highness.

Aide-de-Camp to the Viceroy.	Aide-de-Camp to the Viceroy.
Military Secretary to the Viceroy.	Private Secretary to the Viceroy.

HIS EXCELLENCY THE GRAND MASTER.

Pages.

Aide-de-Camp to the Viceroy.	Aide-de-Camp to the Viceroy.
Aide-de-Camp to the Viceroy.	Aide-de-Camp to the Viceroy.
Native Aide-de-Camp to the Viceroy.	Native Aide-de-Camp to the Viceroy.

As the head of the procession appeared at the entrance, the State trumpeters sounded the "Star of India Flourish," and, as it advanced up the hall, the bands played a section of Kretschmer's "Krönungsmarsch," leaving off when His Excellency the Grand Master and His Royal Highness the Duke of Connaught had taken their seats, as before, on the daïs.

The Secretary of the Order of the Indian Empire now came forward and reported that the business before the Chapter was the investiture, under the Sovereign's grants, of three Knights Grand Commanders and eighteen Knights Commanders, and the decoration of twenty-six

Companions of the Most Eminent Order of the Indian Empire, with the insignia of their respective classes.

The Maharajas and Rajas who were to be invested with the insignia of the First Class, as Grand Commanders of the Indian Empire, were the following:

His Highness Maharao Sir Kesri Singh Bahadur, K.C.S.I., of Sirohi.
His Highness Maharaja Sir Bala Rama Varma, G.C.S.I., of Travancore.
His Highness Raja Sir Hira Singh Bahadur, G.C.S.I., of Nabha.

The Secretary of the Order next delivered to His Excellency the Grand Master the Sovereign's grant conferring on His Highness Maharao Sir Kesri Singh Bahadur, K.C.S.I, of Sirohi, the dignity of a Knight Grand Commander. The Secretary of the Order, with the Under-Secretary in the Foreign Department, and the two Junior Knights Commanders, Maharaja Sir Ganga Singh Bahadur, of Bikaner, and Kunwar Sir Harnam Singh, then conducted the Maharao to the daïs, where he made his reverence. The Secretary having read the Sovereign's grant in favour of the Maharao of Sirohi, conducted His Highness to the table; the junior of the two Knights Commanders decorated His Highness with the riband and badge; and the Senior Knight attached the Star of the Order to his breast. The two Knights Commanders next robed His Highness with the mantle of the Order, whereupon he was conducted by the Secretary to the daïs, there again to make his reverence. The collar of the Grand Knight Commander was delivered by the Under-Secretary to the Grand Master, who, remaining seated, invested His Highness with it, and addressed him as follows:

"In the name of the King, Emperor of India, and by His Majesty's Command, I hereby invest you with the Honourable Insignia of the Order of the Indian Empire, of which Most Eminent Order His Majesty has been graciously pleased to appoint you to be a Knight Grand Commander."

This admonition having been given, the newly-invested Knight Grand Commander made his reverence, and was then conducted by the Secretary to the seat appointed for him.

The like ceremonies were duly observed in the investiture of His

H. H. The Rao of Cutch, G.C.I.E.

Highness Maharaja Sir Bala Rama Varma, G.C.S.I., of Travancore, and His Highness Raja Sir Hira Singh Bahadur, G.C.S.I., of Nabha, as Knights Grand Commanders of the same Most Eminent Order.

The Maharajas, Rajas, nobles, officers, and gentlemen, who were now to be invested with the insignia of the Second Class of the Most Eminent Order of the Indian Empire as Knights of the Order, were the following:

Nawab Shahbaz Khan, Bugti.
James George Scott, Esq., C.I.E.
His Highness Maharaja Malkhan Singh Bahadur, of Charkhari.
The Hon. Maharaja Rameshwara Singh Bahadur, of Darbhanga.
Thomas Higham, Esq., C.I.E., M.I.C.E.
Colonel Samuel Swinton Jacob, C.I.E., Indian Army.
The Hon. Sir Lawrence Hugh Jenkins, Kt.
The Hon. Mr. Herbert Thirkell White, C.I.E., Indian Civil Service.
The Hon. Mr. Charles Lewis Tupper, C.S.I., Indian Civil Service.
Surgeon-General Benjamin Franklin, C.I.E., Indian Medical Service.
Walter Roper Lawrence, Esq., C.I.E., Indian Civil Service (retired).
John Eliot, Esq., C.I.E.
Raja Dhiraj Nahar Singhji, of Shahpura.
Gangadhar Rao Ganesh *alias* Bala Sahib Patwardhan, Chief of Miraj (Senior Branch).
Sardar Ghaus Bakhsh, Raisani.
Maharaja Harballabh Narayan Singh Bahadur, C.I.E., of Sonbursa.
Maharaja Peshkar Kishen Pershad.
Purna Narasingharao Krishna Murti, C.I.E.

In groups of four these were conducted by Mr. Dane and the two Junior Knights, His Highness Maharaja Sir Ganga Singh, of Bikaner, and Kunwar Sir Harnam Singh, of Kapurthala, to the daïs, where they were presented by the Secretary one after the other to the Grand Master. Each, as he was presented, made reverence to the Grand Master. Those who were not to be knighted, namely, Nawab Shahbaz Khan, the Maharajas of Charkhari and Darbhanga, Sir Lawrence Jenkins, the Raja of Shahpura, the Chief of Miraj, Sardar Ghaus Bakhsh, Raisani, Maharaja Harballabh Narayan Singh Bahadur, Maharaja Peskhar Kishen Pershad, and Mr. P. N. Krishna Murti, were straightway conducted by Mr. Wood and the two Junior Knights Commanders to the table.

But upon the others, namely, Mr. Scott, Mr. Higham, Colonel Jacob, the Hon. Mr. White, the Hon. Mr. Tupper, Surgeon-General Franklin, Mr. Walter Lawrence, and Mr. Eliot, the Grand Master, when they were brought before him for the purpose, conferred the title, degree, and honour of a Knight Bachelor of the United Kingdom of Great Britain and Ireland; and each, when he was knighted, was conducted to the table by the officiating Foreign Secretary.

At the table, the two Junior Knights fastened the Star of the Order to the breast of each Maharaja, Raja, noble, officer, and gentleman; and, after all had been thus decorated, they were conducted by the officiating Foreign Secretary to the daïs, where they made their reverence to the Grand Master, by whom they were addressed, collectively, as follows:

"In the name of the King, Emperor of India, and by His Majesty's Gracious Command, I hereby invest you with the Honourable Insignia of the Order of the Indian Empire, of which Most Eminent Order His Majesty has been graciously pleased to appoint you to be Knights Commanders."

The Grand Master then invested the new Knights successively with the riband and badge, in order of precedence. When all in one group had been invested, they made their reverence, and were led by the officiating Foreign Secretary to the seats appointed for them; the next group being then conducted to the daïs by him with the two Junior Knights Commanders.

The Chiefs, nobles, officers, and gentlemen, who were to be decorated with the badge of the Third Class of the Order of the Indian Empire as Companions of that Most Eminent Order, were the following:

Rao Bahadur C. Jambulingham Mudaliyar.
Lieutenant-Colonel Thomas Elwood Lindsay Bate, Indian Medical Service.
John Benton, Esq.
Rao Bahadur Pandit Sukhdeo Pershad.
Major Herbert Lionel Showers, Indian Army.
Major Percy Zachariah Cox, Indian Army.
Babu Nalin Bihari Sircar.
Frederick Gurr Maclean, Esq.
Algernon Elliott, Esq.
Lieutenant-Colonel William Loch, Bengal Infantry.
Lieutenant-Colonel John Hodding, V.D.

Bourne & Shepherd, photo — Walker & Boutall Ph. Sc.

Raja Sikandar Khan, C.I.E., of Nagar, and the Mir of Hunza, C.I.E.

Henry King Beauchamp, Esq.
Harjibhai Manekji Rustamji, Esq.
Nawab Muhammad Sharif Khan, of Dir.
Mehtar Shuja-ul-Mulk, of Chitral.
Mir Muhammad Nazim Khan, Mir of Hunza.
Raja Sikandar Khan, of Nagar.
William Dickson Cruickshank, Esq.
John O'Brien Saunders, Esq.
Henry Wenden, Esq.
Rao Bahadur Shyam Sundar Lal.
Diwan Bahadur Munshi Balmukund Das.
Robert Herriot Henderson, Esq.
Hkun Kyi, K.S.M., Sawbwa of Möng Nai.
Nawab Fateh Ali Khan, Kazilbash.
Faridoonji Jamshedji, Esq.

The Secretary presented to the Grand Master the badges of the Third Class of the Order for the Companions to be decorated, who were then conducted by Mr. Dane, in groups of six, in due order of precedence, to the daïs, where the Secretary presented them one after the other to the Grand Master, announcing their names. As each made his reverence the Grand Master handed a badge to the Secretary, who attached it in the proper place, and the newly-decorated Companion, again making reverence to the Grand Master, withdrew to one side. When all in one group had been decorated, they were led by Mr. Dane to the seats appointed for them, and he then conducted another group to the daïs.

After all the Companions had been decorated, the Secretary represented that there was no further business before the Assembly of the Most Eminent Order of the Indian Empire, and His Excellency the Grand Master, rising from his seat, commanded him to declare the Chapter dissolved. This being done, a procession of the Grand Master and the members of the two Orders was formed and left the Chapter hall, returning to the assembling room in the reverse order to that in which it entered; His Royal Highness the Duke of Connaught and the members of the two Orders, two and two in order of seniority, following His Excellency.

The bands played the Grand March from Handel's "Scipio" as His Excellency the Grand Master and His Royal Highness the Duke of

Connaught passed; the trumpeters, as the procession disappeared under the archway, sounded the "Star of India Flourish"; and, as the Grand Master entered the assembling room, the bands played the National Anthem.

After the Grand Master and the Knights Grand Commanders had unrobed in the robing-room, His Excellency and His Royal Highness the Duke of Connaught left the palace, successively, in the same manner and with the same ceremonies as they had come. The Knights Grand Commanders, and the Knights Commanders and Companions who were ruling Chiefs, were escorted to their carriages by officers deputed for the purpose, the guard of honour outside the building presenting arms to those entitled to this compliment. So ended the grandest ceremony ever enacted in the Palace of Delhi since the Empire of the great Moghuls became the heritage of the Sovereigns of Great Britain. It had lasted a little less than two hours.

THE STATE BALL.

The magnificent hall in which the gorgeous solemnities of the Grand Chapter had been performed was to witness, three nights later, on Tuesday, January 6th, a yet more brilliant sight. Throughout the Investiture two thousand spectators had sat in silence. Save for the processions passing to and from the robing-room, the subdued stir, as the newly-appointed Grand Commanders, Knights, and Companions, singly or in groups, were conducted before the Grand Master, and the clear tones of the latter ringing through the Hall, as he delivered the admonition or conferred the accolade, the myriad lights shone softly over an assemblage that was almost free from sound or movement. To the State Ball, above four thousand guests were invited. Indian Chiefs and nobles, glittering with priceless gems, officers in brilliant uniforms, with Orders and medals, and such an array of British rank and beauty as Delhi had never before seen, again filled the hall of audience and the edifice annexed to it; but this time it was a gaily animated throng, joining in the dance, promenading the columned arcades, or occupying every point from which a view of the unequalled spectacle could be obtained. In spite of the extraordinary number of people, there never seemed to be any crush on the dancing floor, and there was no lack either of opportunity or of candidates for the principal enjoyment of the evening.

The main hall of the Diwan-i Am, now divested of its investiture trappings, had assumed the form of a lounge—where, amid palm-trees and flowers, those who were not dancing either moved about, or chatted or sat at ease. The daïs had been left in front of the marble throne and was a rendezvous throughout the evening for the royal and princely guests. At either end of the great dancing hall, bands occupied two galleries which had been specially built for the purpose. The assembly and robing rooms of a few nights earlier had disappeared and been replaced by a spacious annexe furnished with refreshment tables, sofas, and chairs, where a thousand guests could without difficulty find accommodation. The Ball was attended by the Viceroy and Lady Curzon, the Duke and Duchess of Connaught, the Governors of Bombay and Madras, the Lieutenant-Governors, and other high officials and their wives and families, the Governors of the French and Portuguese Settlements and their Staffs, the Foreign and Consular representatives, and by the following among many other English guests:

Duke and Duchess of Marlborough, Duke and Duchess of Portland, the Dowager Marchioness of Headfort and Lady Beatrix Taylour, Earl and Countess of Pembroke and Lady Beatrix Herbert, Earl of Scarborough, Earl and Countess of Jersey and Lady Beatrice Villiers, Earl and Countess of Powis, Earl and Countess of Lonsdale, Earl of Durham and Lady Anne Lambton, Earl and Countess of Dartrey and Lady Edith Dawson, Earl and Countess of Crewe, Dowager Countess of Kingston and Lady Edith King-Tenison, Hon. G. Peel, Lord Stanley, M.P., and Lady Alice Stanley, Lord Elcho, Lord Errington, Lady Mary Cooke, Lady Mary Lygon, Lady Ulrica Duncombe, Lord and Lady Wolverton, Lord Lamington, Lord and Lady Llangattock, Lord and Lady Playfair, Lord and Lady Davey, Lord Killanin, Lord William Seymour, Hon. W. Peel, M.P., Emily Lady Ampthill, Hon. D. Marjoribanks, Sir Michael Hicks Beach, M.P., and Lady Lucy Hicks Beach, Sir G. Taubman Goldie, Lady Miller, Hon. F. Curzon, Hon.

Spencer Lyttelton, Sir John Dickson Poynder, M.P., and Lady Poynder, Sir Robert Mowbray, M.P., Sir E. Ruggles Brise, Sir Edgar Vincent, M.P., Sir R. and Miss Baker (from Australia), Sir Howard Vincent, M.P., Sir R. and Lady Solomon (from South Africa), and Sir C. Cayzer, M.P.

The ruling Chiefs who attended included the Nizam, the Gaekwar, the Maharajas of Mysore, Kashmir, and Jaipur, the Maharao Raja of Bundi, the Maharao of Kota, the Maharajas of Bikaner, Karauli, Kishangarh, and Alwar, the Maharawal of Jaisalmer, the Maharaj Rana of Dholpur, the Maharawal of Dungarpur, the Raj Rana of Jhalawar, the Maharajas of Gwalior, Orchha, and Charkhari, the Raja of Dewas (senior), the Nawab of Jaora, the Raja of Pudukota, the Maharajas of Kolhapur and Idar, the Rao of Cutch, the Thakur Sahib of Gondal, the Nawabs of Bahawalpur and Loharu, the Raja of Sirmur, the Maharaj Kumar of Sikkim, and the Maharajas of Kuch Behar and Benares.

A combined string band, composed of bandsmen from the 15th Hussars, first battalion Northamptonshire Regiment, first battalion Royal Irish Rifles, second battalion Royal Irish Rifles, and third battalion Rifle Brigade, played alternately with the Viceroy's band.

The programme of dance music was as follows:

Lancers	Mikado	*Sullivan.*
Valse	Beauty's Eyes	*Leslie.*
Valse	Jeunesse Dorée	*Waldteufel.*
Polka	Black and Tan	*Lowthian.*
Valse	Morgenblatter	*Strauss.*
Lancers	Belle of New York	*Kerker.*
Valse	Blue Danube	*Strauss.*
Valse	Le Sang Roumain	*Ivanovici.*
Valse	Sourire d'Avril	*Depret.*
Valse	Sobre las Olas	*Rosas.*
Valse	L'Amour et la Vie à Vienne	*Komzak.*
Lancers	Army and Navy	
Valse	Delhi	*Cowie.*
Valse	Moonlight on the Rhine	*Voelstedt.*
Polka	Bismarck	*Ziehrer.*
Valse	Ensueno Seductor	*Rosas.*
Lancers	Toreador	*Williams.*
Valse	Bleue	*Margis.*
Valse	Abschied von Munchen	*Gungl.*

H. A. Mirza & Sons

THE DIWAN-I KHAS, DELHI

Polka	Chic		*Coote.*
Valse	Schatz		*Strauss.*
Valse	La Svengali		*Roeder.*
Gallop	Post Horn and John Peel		*Koenig.*

The guests were invited for 9.30 P.M., and soon after 10 P.M. the Ball opened with the State Lancers, the dancers being Lord Curzon and the Duchess of Connaught, the Duke of Connaught and Lady Curzon, Lord Northcote and Lady Ampthill, the Grand Duke of Hesse and Lady Northcote, Lord Kitchener and Mrs. Bourdillon, Sir Charles Rivaz and Lady La Touche, Lord Ampthill and the Duchess of Portland, Sir Frederic Fryer and the Duchess of Marlborough.

An even more fairy sight was witnessed when it was announced that supper was ready, and when the principal guests began to wend their way from an opening at the north end of the Diwan-i Am, down a long covered passage, towards the celebrated white marble hall of private audience, or Diwan-i Khas. On either side of the passage stood troopers of the 4th Dragoon Guards, and at intervals were recesses fitted with lounges and seats. At the end of this long vista there suddenly burst upon the view the astonishing loveliness, the exquisite and incomparable grace, of the Diwan-i Khas. This, as is well known, is one of the most beautiful buildings in the world, and the most ornate of all the structures of Shah Jehan. In it in later Moghul times was placed the Peacock Throne. It has suffered cruelly and often since the days of its founder. The more costly stones which once formed the tracery on the marble columns were picked out, long ago, by the daggers of Persian, Mahratta, and Afghan plunderers, and have been replaced by baser material; but the consummate grace of the design was such as not even the rudest vandals could destroy. On the panels, above the arches, one may still read, inscribed in letters of gold, the Persian couplet composed by the Wazir Saad-ulla Khan:

> "If there be a paradise on the face of the earth
> It is this, it is this, it is this."

Some of the historical associations that cling to the Diwan-i Khas were recalled, many years ago, by Colonel Sleeman, in a passage written while a descendant of Shah Jehan still reigned at Delhi. "Here, thought I, as I entered this apartment, sat Aurungzeb when he ordered the assassination of his brothers Dara and Murad, and the imprisonment and destruction by slow poison of his son Muhammad, who had so often fought bravely by his side in battle. Here, also, but a few months before, sat the great Shah Jehan, to receive the insolent commands of this same grandson Muhammad, when flushed with victory, and to offer him the throne, merely to disappoint the hopes of the youth's father, Aurungzeb. Here stood in chains the graceful Suleiman, to receive his sentence of death by slow poison with his poor young brother, Sipihr Shikoh. Here sat Muhammad Shah, bandying compliments with his ferocious conqueror, Nadir Shah, who had destroyed his armies, plundered his treasury, stripped his throne, and ordered the murder of a hundred thousand of the helpless inhabitants of his capital." The court of private audience has passed through many vicissitudes of splendour and sadness; but never since the golden prime of the Great Moghuls can this enchanted pavilion have been fairer to behold than on this evening, when uniformed and bejewelled figures moved to and fro between its gleaming arches and across its polished floor.

Here also, as in the Diwan-i Am, the utmost care had been taken to combine the requisite structural additions or modifications with the most scrupulous regard for the original fabric. The central hall, or Diwan-i Khas, itself was left entirely untouched. It contained no object save the solitary white marble platform or throne. Less reverent had been the treatment accorded to it a quarter of a century earlier, when a ball was held there on January 12th, 1876, in honour of the then Prince of Wales, now King Edward VII. On that occasion the Diwan-i Khas itself was used as the ball-room; and it was in preparation for this event that the carved wooden ceiling which had been introduced in place of the famous silver ceiling of the Moghuls (torn down long ago by the predatory hands of Mahrattas) was repainted in black, red and gold, instead of white and gold, and that many of the coloured and gilded arabesques on the pillars and walls were painted over by modern and inferior artists.

For the Ball of January 6th, 1903, no such treatment had been permitted. The original building, as has been said, remained intact. The open marble terraces on either side of it, however, had been roofed over, and the archways in their temporary walls had been filled with glazed wood work, minutely copying, and scarcely distinguishable from the marble lattices in the central hall. Even the screen of perforated marble, above which are the celebrated carved Mizan-i-Adal or Scales of Justice, had been successfully reproduced, and the Persian inscriptions could, with difficulty, be detected from their prototypes. The marble channel down the centre of the floor, through which water originally flowed to the Hummum or royal baths at the northern end, had been boarded over: and the comfort of the guests had been so far considered, in anticipation of a possibly cold night, that hot water pipes had been laid below the boarding. The Viceregal and Royal party supped in the beautiful chamber, formerly one of the royal apartments, immediately behind the marble lattice surmounted by the sculptured scales. Like the Diwan-i Am, the entire building was lit by the electric light, which illuminated, with a brilliance that they had never previously known, every pillar and cornice, every pattern and inscription, of these exquisite chambers; and as the Viceroy with his principal guests, on leaving the supper table, paused for a while in the central hall, which filled rapidly with a gay throng, the effect of the glittering crowd in these unique and almost ætherial surroundings was such as those who witnessed it can never before have seen.

Dancing was kept up with great spirit into the early hours of the morning. Their Royal Highnesses the Duke and Duchess of Connaught left soon after midnight; but the Viceroy and Lady Curzon stayed longer, and a new day dawned before the last of the guests had departed.

Many of the visitors at Delhi who attended every one of the ceremonials throughout the crowded fortnight left with the impression that the State Ball in the Diwan-i Am and Diwan-i Khas was the most beautiful of all. It was not of course so solemn or inspiring as the Durbar. It was less picturesque and quaint than the review of native retainers. The elephant procession in the State Entry was more grandiose and almost barbaric. But there was something unique and incomparable in the collection of this brilliant crowd of splendidly dressed men and women—the chivalry of the East and West commingled together —in the rich and sumptuous glory of the surroundings in one hall, and the radiant loveliness of the other, in the sound of the music, and the movement of the dance, and, above all, in the spirit of gaiety and exhilaration that pervaded the entire proceedings. Persons who had witnessed the Imperial balls in the palaces of St. Petersburg and Moscow—admittedly the stateliest pageants in Europe—conceded that they had never seen anything to compare with this; and when the success of the entertainment, and the universal pleasure which it gave, are contrasted with the dire prognostications that had freely prevailed in advance as to impossible movement, inadequate provision, and insufferable crowds, it will probably be held that upon none of the Delhi festivities had their organisers more reason to congratulate themselves than upon the State Ball in the old palace of the Moghuls.

Kitchener

CHAPTER IX

THE ARMY AT DELHI

THE magnificence of the celebrations at Delhi, as the reader must already be aware, was in no small measure due to the presence of a large and exceptionally efficient military force. The British and Native troops encamped outside Delhi numbered upwards of 39,500 men. At the time of the Imperial Assemblage, in 1877, only 13,900 men were assembled for the purpose; but as, on the present occasion, army manœuvres on a large scale had taken place in the country between Umballa and Delhi in the weeks preceding the Durbar, it was found possible to collect at the latter centre a force which was far stronger, in point of numbers, and at the same time more fully representative of the various components of His Majesty's Army. An account of the manœuvres carried out by the Northern and Southern Armies between November 24th and December 22nd, 1902, does not fall within the scope of the present narrative; but there are one or two points of special interest, which may be noted. It was the first time that an opportunity had been afforded for a large army in India to apply the principles and employ the methods learnt during the war in South Africa; and this was done under the eyes of Lord Kitchener, who acted as Director-General of the manœuvres and Umpire-in-Chief, and of a large number of officers who had taken part in that memorable conflict. The heavy Artillery included, for the first time at manœuvres, 30-pounders, 6-inch howitzers and 5-inch guns, and the new 10-pounder gun for Mountain Batteries. Mounted Infantry, trained in the new schools, and mounted Gurkhas were employed; as well as a camel corps. And never before since the short service system was introduced, owing to the large number of men who had extended their service, could British corps in India have shown such a proportion of seasoned material in the ranks.

From the troops mobilised for manœuvres (comprising two Cavalry and three Infantry Divisions, with Artillery, Corps Troops, &c.), one Cavalry and two Infantry Divisions, the Imperial Service and Corps Troops were retained at Delhi for the Durbar celebrations, and a Volunteer contingent was added to the force; the detailed strength of which was as follows:

	Officers.		Ranks.	
	British.	Native.	British.	Native.
Army Staff	28	—	6	12
Viceroy's Escort	67	28	1,347	1,155
Cavalry Division	95	83	1,215	2,260
First Infantry Division	201	121	3,991	6,104
Second Infantry Division	199	120	5,193	5,902
Corps Troops	63	31	1,119	1,621
Imperial Service Troops	23	230	—	6,057
Mounted Volunteers	13	—	163	—
Dismounted Volunteers	34	—	710	—
Sappers and Miners	14	15	21	898
Third Bengal Cavalry, Camp Details	6	12	—	450
	743	640	13,765	24,459

The exact composition of the Durbar troops, which were under the command of Major-General D. J. S. McLeod, C.B., D.S.O., will be given in the account of the grand parade; the positions of the various military camps are shown on the map. During the manœuvres the troops had been without tents, but while halted at Delhi for the Durbar they were allowed these on the field-service scale.

On Thursday, January 8th, all the troops in the Durbar camps were reviewed by His Excellency the Viceroy. The parade ground lay three-quarters of a mile to the north of the village of Azadpur, and about midway between the Durbar Amphitheatre and Shalimar Gardens, "the abode of joy" laid out by Shah Jehan in imitation of his father's more famous pleasance in Kashmir. Close at hand is the battle-field of Badli-ki-Sarai, where on June 8th, 1857, Sir Henry Barnard defeated the mutineers, before advancing to occupy the position they held on the Ridge. As many as fifty thousand spectators witnessed the review. Two grand stands had been erected for 4000 people; benches were provided for as many more, and a large enclosure was reserved for carriages. Most of the ruling Chiefs in Delhi attended, several of them being on parade at the head of their Imperial Service contingents.

The whole of the troops assembled in camp, including the Viceroy's Escort, which His Excellency had placed at the Commander-in-Chief's disposal for the occasion, were ordered to take part in the grand parade, in review order. By a quarter past ten they were formed up, facing south-west, in the order given below, from right to left:

The Cavalry Division, with three batteries of Royal Horse Artillery and the Imperial Service Cavalry, in line of brigade column of mass, on the extreme right; Major-General A. Boyce Combe, C.B., in command.

The Royal Artillery, including three Brigade Divisions, Royal Field Artillery, a Brigade Division, Royal Garrison Artillery (30-pounder guns), one British and one Native Brigade Division, mountain guns, and two Brigade Divisions, Royal Garrison Artillery, heavy (5 and 6-inch) guns; in line of brigade divisions in column of batteries at half interval; Brigadier-General J. Leach, Commanding.

Sappers and Miners, in quarter column, with Balloon and Pontoon sections in rear.

Two divisions of Infantry and the Imperial Service Infantry, in line of brigades in mass, on the extreme left; Brigadier-General Sir J. Wolfe Murray, K.C.B., and Major-General Sir Alfred Gaselee, G.C.I.E., K.C.B., Commanding.

The strength of the troops on parade is given below:

Details.	British Officers.	British W. O.s, N. C. O.s and men.	Native Officers, N. C. O.s and men.	Total, Officers and men.	Horses.	Mules.	Bullocks.	Guns.
Staff	101	1	—	102	102	—	—	—
Royal Horse Artillery	18	216	—	234	282	—	—	18
British Cavalry	44	1,049	—	1,093	1,093	—	—	—
Native Cavalry	82	—	3,190	3,272	3,272	—	—	—
Imperial Service Cavalry	—	—	1,450	1,450	1,450	—	—	—
Royal Field Artillery	53	905	—	958	862	—	—	54
R. G. A. 30-pounders	6	104	64	174	140	—	—	8
Mountain Artillery	26	154	423	603	54	204	—	28
R. G. A. 5-inch guns	9	113	116	238	—	—	224	8
R. G. A. 6-inch guns	7	128	80	215	—	—	160	8
S. & M. Pontoons; Balloons	11	14	952	977	65	72	90	—
Mounted Volunteers	13	163	—	176	176	—	—	—
Mounted Infantry	16	154	310	480	480	—	—	—
British Infantry	206	6,289	—	6,495	36	—	—	—
Native Infantry	148	—	9,347	9,495	60	—	—	—
Imperial Service Infantry	—	—	2,970	2,970	21	—	—	—
Volunteers	34	650	—	684	3	—	—	—
Total	774	9,940	18,902	29,616	8,096	276	474	124

His Excellency Lord Kitchener, Commander-in-Chief, with the Army Head-Quarters staff and his personal staff, rode on to the parade ground, and took command of the troops, shortly after 10 A.M. A few minutes afterwards Her Royal Highness the Duchess of Connaught drove up with Lady Curzon, and witnessed the parade and march past from a carriage, which was placed a little to the left of the flag-staff. At half-past ten His Excellency the Viceroy, accompanied by Field-Marshal H.R.H. the Duke of Connaught, H.R.H. the Grand Duke of Hesse, and Their Excellencies the Governors of Bombay and Madras, and escorted by the Imperial Cadet Corps and the Viceregal Body-guard, rode on to the parade ground. His Excellency wore morning dress with the Star of Grand Master of the Order of the Star of India. The Duke of Connaught was in field-marshal's uniform. Major-General Sir Edmond Elles, military member of Council, Brigadier-General

Collins, commanding the Viceregal Escort, and Colonel the Hon. E. Baring, Military Secretary to the Viceroy, also accompanied the Viceregal party. On the Viceroy's arrival on the parade ground, a royal salute was fired by a battery in position clear of the left of the line of troops. The first gun was fired as the Viceroy reached the ground; the last as His Excellency arrived at the saluting-point, when the bands played the national anthem.

The troops then marched past, in the order given below, headed by Lord Kitchener, Commander-in-Chief, and the Head-Quarters staff; the Cavalry in line of regiments, the Artillery in line of brigade divisions, and the Infantry in column of double companies:

HEAD-QUARTERS STAFF.

Deputy Assistant Quartermaster-General.
Major M. Cowper.

Native Aide-de-Camp.	*Native Aide-de-Camp.*
Risaldar Ajab Khan Bahadur.	Risaldar-Major Sher Singh.

Aide-de-Camp (Madras).	*Aide-de-Camp (Bengal).*	*Aide-de-Camp (Punjab).*	*Aide-de-Camp (Bombay).*
Captain E. de H. Smith.	Captain E. B. Cook.	Major C. P. Campbell.	Major C. E. Baynes.
Aide-de-Camp.	*Aide-de-Camp.*	*Aide-de-Camp.*	*D.A.Q.M.G. for Mobilization.*
Major R. J. Marker, D.S.O.	Major F. A. Maxwell, V.C., D.S.O.	Captain V. R. Brooke, D.S.O.	Major G. de S. Barrow.
D.A.A.G. Royal Engineers.	*Assistant Military Secretary.*	*Assistant Adjutant-General.*	*Principal Veterinary Officer.*
Major J. A. Tanner, D.S.O.	Lieut.-Col. W. R. Birdwood.	Lieut.-Col. C. de C. Hamilton.	Lieut.-Col. B. L. Glover, C.B.
Military Secretary.	*Director of Military Education.*	*A.Q.M.G. Intelligence.*	*Deputy Adjutant-General.*
Col. H. I. W. Hamilton, D.S.O., A.D.C.	Col. W. B. Capper.	Colonel J. E. Nixon, C.B.	Brigadier-General B. Duff, C.B., C.I.E.
Inspector-General of Volunteers.	*Director-General of Supply and Transport.*	*Inspector-General of Cavalry.*	*Director-General of Ordnance.*
Major-General W. Hill, C.B.	Major-General L. W. Christopher, C.B.	Major-General Sir E. L. Elliot, K.C.B., D.S.O.	Major-General C. H. Scott, C.B.

Director-General, Military Works.	*Principal Medical Officer.*	*Inspector-General of Artillery.*
Major-General W. T. Shone, C.B., D.S.O.	Surgeon-General Sir T. J. Gallwey, M.D., K.C.M.G., C.B.	Major-General T. B. Tyler, C.S.I.

Quartermaster-General.
Major-General G. Henry, C.B.

Major-General Commanding, Bengal.
Major-General D. J. S. McLeod, C.B., D.S.O.

Adjutant-General.
Major-General H. L. Smith-Dorrien, D.S.O.

Lieutenant-General Commanding, Madras.
Lieutenant-General Sir G. B. Wolseley, K.C.B.

Lieutenant-General Commanding, Punjab.
Lieutenant-General Sir B. Blood, K.C.B.

Lieutenant-General Commanding, Bombay.
Lieutenant-General Sir R. C. Low, G.C.B.

HIS EXCELLENCY THE COMMANDER-IN-CHIEF.

CAVALRY DIVISION.

MASSED BANDS, CAVALRY DIVISION.

(Conducted by Bandmaster C. W. C. Lee, *4th Dragoon Guards.*)

Aide-de-Camp.
Lieutenant S. Boyce Combe.

Staff Captain Royal Horse Artillery.
Captain R. Greathed.

D.A.Q.M.G. Intelligence.
Major A. W. Warden.

D.A.Q.M.G.
Captain C. O. Swanston.

Deputy Assistant Adjutant-General.
Major J. B. Edwards, D.S.O.

Assistant Quartermaster-General.
Lieutenant-Colonel S. D. Gordon.

Assistant Adjutant-General.
Lieutenant-Colonel G. F. N. Tinley.

Colonel-on-Staff Royal Horse Artillery.
Colonel A. H. Hewat.

General Officer Commanding.
Major-General A. Boyce Combe, C.B.

"D" BATTERY, ROYAL HORSE ARTILLERY.
Major A. H. Short.

"H" BATTERY, ROYAL HORSE ARTILLERY.
Major R. St. C. Lecky.

"I" BATTERY, ROYAL HORSE ARTILLERY.
Captain B. Vincent.

1ST CAVALRY BRIGADE.

Orderly Officer.
Lieutenant A. S. Trower.

Deputy Assistant Quartermaster-General.
Captain L. M. Dunbar.

Deputy Assistant Adjutant-General.
Major A. G. Medley.

Officer Commanding.
Colonel M. O. Little.

4TH DRAGOON GUARDS.
Major F. B. L. Woodwright.

Lawrie & Co.

THE PARADE OF TROOPS. ARRIVAL OF THE VICEROY

15TH HUSSARS.
Lieutenant-Colonel T. Ch. de Crespigny.

4TH BOMBAY CAVALRY.
Major F. Wadeson.

9TH BENGAL LANCERS.
Lieutenant-Colonel F. W. P. Angelo.

2ND CAVALRY BRIGADE.

Orderly Officer.
Lieutenant H. F. Gordon, C.I.E.

Deputy Assistant Quartermaster-General.
Major C. M. Cartwright.

Deputy Assistant Adjutant-General.
Major H. Kennard.

Officer Commanding.
Colonel J. C. F. Gordon.

9TH LANCERS.
Major-General H. A. Bushman, C.B., Honorary Colonel.
Lieutenant-Colonel S. W. Follett.

8TH BENGAL LANCERS.
Lieutenant-Colonel E. H. Rivett-Carnac.

11TH, P.W.O., BENGAL LANCERS.
Lieutenant-Colonel F. G. Delamain.

19TH BENGAL LANCERS.
Lieutenant-Colonel H. S. Massey.

3RD CAVALRY BRIGADE.

Orderly Officer.
Captain A. H. Buist.

Deputy Assistant Quartermaster-General.
Major H. A. Merewether.

Deputy Assistant Adjutant-General.
Major J. A. Douglas.

General Officer Commanding.
Brigadier-General G. L. R. Richardson, C.B., C.S.I., C.I.E.

COMPOSITE REGIMENT, GUIDES CAVALRY, 5TH PUNJAB CAVALRY.
Lieutenant-Colonel G. J. Younghusband, C.B.

CENTRAL INDIA HORSE.
Lieutenant-Colonel F. H. R. Drummond, C.I.E.

18TH BENGAL LANCERS.
Lieutenant-Colonel G. A. Money.

Composite Regiment, 1st Punjab Cavalry, 2nd Punjab Cavalry, 10th Bengal Lancers, 14th Bengal Lancers.
Major G. H. Weller.

4th CAVALRY BRIGADE.

Orderly Officer.
Lieutenant W. Graham.

Deputy Assistant Quartermaster-General.
Captain C. E. E. F. K. Macquoid, D.S.O.

Deputy Assistant Adjutant-General.
Major C. F. Campbell.

General Officer Commanding.
Brigadier-General S. B. Beatson, C.B.

IMPERIAL SERVICE CAVALRY.

Alwar Lancers.
Bhoor Singh (Commandant).

Bhopal Lancers.
Major Mirza Karim Beg, Bahadur (Commandant).

Gwalior Lancers.
Keshao Rao Bhonslay (Commandant).

Hyderabad Lancers.
Abdulla Beg Mahir Jang, Bahadur (Commandant).

Jodhpur Lancers.
Thakur Jas Singh, Sardar Bahadur (Commandant).

Mysore Lancers.
Saiyid Hafiz, Bahadur (Commandant).

Patiala Lancers.
Nand Singh, Bahadur (Commandant).

Rampur Lancers.
Muhammad Wazir Khan (Commandant).

ROYAL ARTILLERY.

Aide-de-Camp.
Captain R. G. Keyworth.

Staff Captain.
Captain C. E. Parry.

Brigade Major.
Captain H. R. Palmer.

Colonel-on-Staff.
Colonel J. A. Coxhead, C.B.

General Officer Commanding.
Brigadier-General J. Leach.

1st Brigade Division, Royal Field Artillery.
13th, 67th, and 69th Batteries.
Lieutenant-Colonel S. D. Rainsford.

38th Brigade Division, Royal Field Artillery.
24th, 34th, and 72nd Batteries.
Lieutenant-Colonel D. C. Carter.

39th Brigade Division, Royal Field Artillery.
46th, 51st, and 54th Batteries.
Lieutenant-Colonel H. S. Dawkins.

30-Pounders, Brigade Division, Royal Garrison Artillery.
71st and 72nd, Royal Garrison Artillery.
Major F. R. Thackeray.

MOUNTAIN ARTILLERY.

Staff Captain.
Captain T. E. Marshall.

Colonel-on-Staff.
Lieutenant-Colonel E. Gunner.

British Brigade Division.
6th and 7th Mountain Batteries, Royal Garrison Artillery.
Major M. F. Fegen.

Native Brigade Division.
Peshawar, Quetta, and Kashmir Mountain Batteries.
Lieutenant-Colonel W. Keene, D.S.O.

Brigade Division, Royal Garrison Artillery, 5" Guns.

Adjutant.
Captain R. A. Tancred.

Colonel-on-Staff.
Lieutenant-Colonel R. A. G. Harrison.

91st and 104th, Royal Garrison Artillery.
Major F. J. Græme.

Brigade Division, Royal Garrison Artillery, 8" Guns.
42nd and 51st, Royal Garrison Artillery.
Major A. J. Mullins.

Sappers and Miners, Pontoons and Balloons.
Lieutenant-Colonel Barton, D.S.O.

2nd Company, Queen's Own Madras Sappers and Miners.
1st Company, Bengal Sappers and Miners.
3rd Company, Bengal Sappers and Miners.
Sirmoor Sappers and Miners.
Maler Kotla Sappers and Miners.
Pontoon Section.
Balloon Section.

MOUNTED VOLUNTEERS.
Lieutenant-Colonel A. Grey.

BEHAR LIGHT HORSE.
CAWNPUR LIGHT HORSE.
SURMA VALLEY LIGHT HORSE.
CALCUTTA LIGHT HORSE.
BOMBAY LIGHT HORSE.
PUNJAB LIGHT HORSE.
ASSAM VALLEY LIGHT HORSE.
NORTHERN BENGAL MOUNTED RIFLES.
DEHRA DUN MOUNTED RIFLES.
CHOTA NAGPUR MOUNTED RIFLES.
OUDH LIGHT HORSE.

MOUNTED INFANTRY.
Major H. Stannell.

FIRST INFANTRY DIVISION.

Aide-de-Camp.
Captain W. F. O'Connor.

Deputy Assistant Adjutant and Quartermaster-General, Divisional Troops.
Captain A. W. Dunlop.

Chief Supply and Transport Officer.
Captain F. W. Hawks.

Deputy Assistant Quartermaster-General.
Major W. G. Home.

Deputy Assistant Adjutant-General.
Major B. A. Johnstone.

Assistant Adjutant-General.
Colonel A. W. L. Bayly, C.B., D.S.O., A.-D.-C.

General Officer Commanding.
Brigadier-General Sir J. Wolfe Murray, K.C.B.

1ST INFANTRY BRIGADE.

MASSED BANDS.
(Conducted by Bandmaster A. Shackleford, *2nd Welsh Regiment.*)

Orderly Officer.
Lieutenant R. J. H. Baddeley.

Deputy Assistant Quartermaster-General.
Major H. C. Bernard.

Deputy Assistant Adjutant-General.
Captain W. Glasgow.

General Officer Commanding.
Brigadier-General F. H. Plowden.

1ST BATTALION, SOUTH WALES BORDERERS.
Lieutenant-Colonel C. V. Trevor.

2ND BATTALION, WELSH REGIMENT.
Lieutenant-Colonel W. V. Dickinson.

4TH RAJPUTS.
Lieutenant-Colonel H. Read.

32ND PIONEERS.
Major H. Brander.

Raja Deen Dayal & Sons

THE PARADE OF TROOPS. NABHA INFANTRY

2ND INFANTRY BRIGADE.

MASSED BANDS.

(Conducted by Bandmaster H. W. Davis, *2nd Argyll and Sutherland Highlanders.*)

Orderly Officer.	*Deputy Assistant Quartermaster-General.*	*Deputy Assistant Adjutant-General.*
Captain R. L. Haymes.	Captain R. M. Ovens.	Major H. R. Mead.

Officer Commanding.
Brigadier-General C. H. Des Vœux.

2ND BATTALION GORDON HIGHLANDERS.
Lieutenant-Colonel W. A. Scott, C.B.

2ND BATTALION, ARGYLL AND SUTHERLAND HIGHLANDERS.
Lieutenant-Colonel J. H. Campbell.

27TH BALUCHIS.
Lieutenant-Colonel G. E. Even.

23RD PIONEERS.
Lieutenant-Colonel A. F. Hogge.

3RD INFANTRY BRIGADE.

MASSED BANDS.

(Conducted by Bandmaster A. Williams, *1st Royal Irish Rifles.*)

Orderly Officer.	*Deputy Assistant Quartermaster-General.*	*Deputy Assistant Adjutant-General.*
Captain B. P. Elwood.	Captain J. Wilson.	Major J. M. Stewart.

General Officer Commanding.
Brigadier-General Sir J. Willcocks, K.C.M.G.

1ST BATTALION, ROYAL IRISH RIFLES.
Lieutenant-Colonel H. F. Swaine.

1ST BATTALION, 3RD GURKHAS.
Lieutenant-Colonel H. Ross.

6TH JAT LIGHT INFANTRY.
Lieutenant-Colonel C. H. Westmoreland.

13TH RAJPUTS.
Lieutenant-Colonel W. T. Fairbrother.

7TH INFANTRY BRIGADE.

MASSED BANDS.

(Conducted by Bandmaster A. Weyer, *1st Northampton Regiment.*)

Orderly Officer.	*Deputy Assistant Quartermaster-General.*	*Deputy Assistant Adjutant-General.*
Lieutenant H. St. G. M. McRae.	Major T. McKay.	Major Slade Thomson.

Officer Commanding.
Colonel H. N. McRae, C.B., A.-D.-C.

1st Battalion, Northampton Regiment.
Lieutenant-Colonel W. F. Fawcett.

15th Sikhs.
Lieutenant-Colonel G. F. Rowcroft.

34th Pioneers.
Lieutenant-Colonel H. B. Borradaile.

SECOND INFANTRY DIVISION.

Native Aide-de-Camp.	*Aide-de-Camp.*	*Chief Supply and Transport Officer.*
Risaldar Sher Khan.	Captain B. T. Pell, D.S.O.	Major Rideout.

Deputy Assistant Quartermaster-General.	*Deputy Assistant Adjutant-General.*	*Assistant Quarter-master-General.*	*Asssistant Adjutant-General.*
Major W. G. L. Benyon, D.S.O.	Major H. A. Iggulden.	Lieutenant-Colonel F. C. Beatson, C.B.	Lieutenant-Colonel J. W. Hawkins.

General Officer Commanding.
Major-General Sir A. Gaselee, G.C.I.E., K.C.B.

4th INFANTRY BRIGADE.

Massed Bands.

(Conducted by Bandmaster G. B. Bartlett, *1st Norfolk Regiment.*)

Orderly Officer.	*Deputy Assistant Quartermaster-General.*	*Deputy Assistant Adjutant-General.*
Captain C. J. C. Barrett.	Captain R. E. Dyer.	Major W. G. Ley.

General Officer Commanding.
Brigadier-General H. A. Abbott, C.B.

1st Battalion, Norfolk Regiment.
Lieutenant-Colonel A. C. Becher.

1st Battalion, Bedford Regiment.
Lieutenant-Colonel H. Lyons, V.C.

20th Punjab Infantry.
Colonel J. B. Wood.

38th Dogras.
Major K. P. Burne.

5TH INFANTRY BRIGADE.

MASSED BANDS.

(Conducted by Bandmaster J. H. Sage, *2nd King's Royal Rifle Corps.*)

Orderly Officer.	*Deputy Assistant Quartermaster-General.*	*Deputy Assistant Adjutant-General.*
Lieutenant H. S. Becher.	Captain F. W. Evatt.	Major R. Strachey.

General Officer Commanding.
Brigadier-General H. P. Leach, C.B., D.S.O.

2ND BATTALION, KING'S ROYAL RIFLE CORPS.
Lieutenant-Colonel H. Gore-Brown.

3RD BATTALION, RIFLE BRIGADE.
Lieutenant-Colonel G. Cockburn, D.S.O.

1ST BATTALION, 2ND GURKHAS.
Lieutenant-Colonel D. C. F. Macintyre.

1ST BATTALION, 39TH GARHWAL RIFLES.
Lieutenant-Colonel A. C. O'Donnell.

6TH INFANTRY BRIGADE.

MASSED BANDS.

(Conducted by Bandmaster F. Andrews, *2nd Yorkshire Regiment.*)

Orderly Officer.	*Deputy Assistant Quartermaster-General.*	*Deputy Assistant Adjutant-General.*
Captain K. L. W. Mackenzie.	Captain A. B. Whatman, D.S.O.	Captain F. A. Smith.

Officer Commanding.
Colonel A. A. Pearson.

2ND BATTALION YORKSHIRE REGIMENT.
Lieutenant-Colonel J. A. Fearon.

1ST BATTALION NORTH STAFFORD REGIMENT.
Lieutenant-Colonel H. S. B. Hodgkinson.

28TH MADRAS INFANTRY.
Lieutenant-Colonel W. H. Lowry.

4TH INFANTRY, HYDERABAD CONTINGENT.
Lieutenant-Colonel M. T. Shewen.

FRONTIER BATTALION.
Colonel A. A. Barrett.

8TH BRIGADE.

MASSED BANDS.

(Conducted by Bandmaster F. Andrews, *2nd Yorkshire Regiment.*)

Orderly Officer.	*Deputy Assistant Quartermaster-General.*	*Deputy Assistant Adjutant-General.*
Lieutenant J. Fairlie.	Major W. L. Conran.	Major T. P. England.

General Officer Commanding.
Brigadier-General G. H. More-Molyneux, C.B., D.S.O.

VOLUNTEER CONTINGENT.
Lieutenant-Colonel F. Goodwin.

28TH PUNJAB INFANTRY.
Lieutenant-Colonel W. E. Phillips.

IMPERIAL SERVICE INFANTRY.

ALWAR INFANTRY.
Natha Singh, Bahadur (Commandant).

BHARATPUR INFANTRY.
Girdhar Singh (Commandant).

JIND INFANTRY.
Gurnam Singh, Sardar Bahadur (Commandant).

KAPURTHALA INFANTRY.
Narayan Singh (Commandant).

KASHMIR INFANTRY.
Sardar Sumandar Khan (Commandant).

NABHA INFANTRY.
Hardas Singh (Commandant).

PATIALA INFANTRY.
Sunda Singh, Bahadur (Commandant).

The march past of the army of 29,616 men, headed by its illustrious Commander and his brilliant staff, was the grandest military spectacle, one may well believe, ever witnessed on a plain which has been not unfitly described as a veritable Ἄρεως ὀρχήστρα, the dancing floor of Mars, and it produced a marked effect on the assembled spectators, more especially on the large number of Indians of the more warlike races, who had made their way to the parade ground. Cavalry, artillery, and infantry swept by in imposing and irresistible strength. His Excellency

H. H. The Maharaja of Patiala.

the Commander-in-Chief, after saluting the Viceroy, wheeled to the right, followed by an Aide-de-Camp, and joined the Viceregal party, reining in his charger next to the Duke of Connaught. Later on, the cavalry were to be seen to still better advantage; but as they paced slowly by, sabres flashing in the sunlight, the pennons of the lances fluttering in the air, English Dragoons, Hussars and Lancers, followed by the *élite* of the Indian Light Horse, and preceded by three splendid Batteries of Royal Horse Artillery, the mounted troops presented as fine a spectacle as could be seen anywhere in the world.

The Imperial Service Cavalry, too, made a goodly show; and as with the Imperial Service Infantry, it was evident that marked progress has been made, during the last few years, in the efficiency of this force, which has already given such signal proof of its usefulness, not only on the Indian frontier but also in China and in Somaliland.

At the head of the Bhopal Lancers rode the Nawab Nasrulla Khan and the Sahibzada Ubaidulla Khan, the two sons of Her Highness the Begum.

The Jodhpur Lancers were to have been led by the Maharaja, but His Highness was unfortunately on the sick list. Honorary Colonel His Highness the Maharaja Scindia rode at the head of his smart corps of Gwalior Lancers. The young Maharaja of Patiala, mounted on a white Arab, and arrayed in a robe of pale yellow silk, with a sea green turban, led the Patiala Cavalry. The Maharajas of Mysore and Alwar also rode at the head of their corps. The Rampur Lancers were to have been led past by the Nawab of that State, but he was unfortunately prevented from attending the parade by the illness of a member of his family.

After the Imperial Service Cavalry came the Field, Garrison, and Mountain Artillery. In our old battles in India, as an historical writer points out, describing the battle of Mehidpur, where Holkar's forces were routed by Sir John Malcolm, it was almost invariably the case that the enemy outmatched the English in the number and weight of their guns; and victories were won by advancing in the face of a deadly fire, and carrying their batteries at the point of the bayonet. The Artillery that now marched past the Viceroy, for the most part British Batteries, served by British gunners, might be pointed to as showing how vastly the conditions have changed. It could have been matched nowhere in Asia. The horse teams dragging the long 30-pounders of the 71st and 72nd Batteries, Royal Garrison Artillery, were driven by natives. The Kashmir Mountain Batteries were led past by Raja Sir Amar Singh, Commander-in-Chief of the Kashmir Army, and brother to the Maharaja. The heavy guns of the 91st, 104th, 42nd and 51st Batteries were drawn by bullocks; twelve to each 5-inch gun, and eighteen to each 6-inch gun; the native drivers sitting on the yokes. The Sirmoor Sappers and Miners were led past by Captain Rajkumar Bir Bikram Singh, the Maler Kotla Sappers and Miners by the Nawab's only son, Sahibzada Muhammad Ibrahim Khan Bahadur. The Maharaja of Bikaner rode past at the head of a detachment of his camel corps, for only a remnant of this now famous force was at Delhi, the main body being then on its way to Somaliland.

Next came two divisions of Infantry, British and Indian, the spectators noting with approval the distinctive appearance and style of each regiment, many of them bearing names that are famous in the annals, not merely of India, but of the Empire; and the Imperial Service Infantry closed the long procession. The ruling Chiefs of Alwar, Bharatpur, Jind, Nabha, and Patiala each led past his own contingent, while Raja Sir Amar Singh rode at the head of his brother's Kashmir Infantry. Some of those who saw the Raja of Jind leading his troops may have remembered that his grandfather, Raja Sarup Singh, marching in the vanguard of the Army, was actually the first man who appeared in arms before Delhi, on the English side, after the outbreak of the Mutiny. The appearance of the young Maharaja of Patiala, as he rode up to the flag-staff for the second time, was the signal for loud applause. His Highness then joined the Viceregal party. Still louder cheers followed when the venerable Chief of Nabha, on a fine charger, rode up; a picture of Sikh chivalry of the olden time. He, too, joined the Viceroy at the saluting flag, dismounting with the courtesy for which he is conspicuous. After marching past, the Infantry left the parade ground to line the road to the Viceregal camp.

The mounted troops now trotted past, the Cavalry by wings, the

Artillery as before. The whole of the Cavalry then formed in four lines of brigades, one behind the other; and each, in turn, advanced at the gallop until about 100 yards from the saluting-base, halted, gave a royal salute, and, wheeling troops outwards, cleared the way for the next brigade. The same manœuvre was executed by the Royal Horse Artillery. After this, the whole of the Cavalry, in line of masses, with the Brigade Division of the Royal Horse Artillery on the right, advanced at the gallop, led by the Commander-in-Chief with the Head-Quarters staff, and halted at a similar distance in front of the Viceroy, and gave a royal salute. It was the most impressive moment of the whole parade.

The Viceroy now rode forward and congratulated Lord Kitchener on the efficiency and smartness of the troops under his command, and on the excellence of their conduct while at Delhi.

A final salute of thirty-one guns was fired, the national anthem was played, and His Excellency the Viceroy, accompanied by Their Royal Highnesses the Duke of Connaught and the Grand Duke of Hesse, rode back to camp between lines of Infantry.

The review, which had lasted for about two and a half hours, had been a complete success from every standpoint: and the spectacle of the long line of seasoned warriors, British and Indian, stretching away into the haze on either hand and set in that background of indefinable mystery and colour which only an Indian sun shining down on sandy plains can give, is one that must have impressed itself deeply on the memories of those who were present. It was anticipated that the dust cloud which the movement of such a mighty host would produce would have completely concealed the troops from view; but the dust had been opportunely laid by the slight shower which fell two days before, and the ground was kept watered by a large army of *bhistis*, so that every movement was as clear as though it had taken place on Laffan's Plain.

The following General Order by the Commander-in-Chief was published the same evening:

"His Excellency the Commander-in-Chief has much pleasure in announcing to the Army that His Excellency the Viceroy has expressed his great admiration of the appearance and conduct of the troops on parade to-day, and that Field-Marshal His Royal Highness the Duke of Connaught has requested him to inform the troops how highly he appreciated their smart and soldier-like bearing, reflecting credit upon themselves, and upon the entire Army in India.

"It is a pleasure to His Excellency the Commander-in-Chief to convey these complimentary remarks to the troops, who, by their efforts, made the parade, in his opinion, a complete success."

H. H. The Maharaja of Patiala

CHAPTER X

SPECTACLES, INTERLUDES, ASSEMBLIES

ALL the more important ceremonies performed at Delhi, in connection with the Coronation Durbar, have been described in the preceding pages, with the exception of an evening party that was given in honour of the Indian Chiefs by the Viceroy in camp on January 9th, and the state departure on the following day, which must be recorded in a concluding chapter. But apart from the official celebrations and events of the fortnight, there was a succession of spectacles, popular entertainments and festivities, polo, cricket, and football matches, and other interludes, as well as certain gatherings of a religious or semi-political character, which have now to be chronicled.

On the night of Friday, January 2nd, the city of Delhi was illuminated, and there was a grand display of fireworks on the Champ de Mars between the Jama Musjid and Elgin Road. The battlements and gateways of the Fort, the galleries of Shah Jehan's cathedral mosque, Government offices and public buildings, the shops in Chandni Chauk, and offices and houses in other quarters of the city, were outlined with myriads of *chirags* or tiny oil lamps, a form of illumination in which the native of India has always excelled. But it was the fireworks, of course, that most enthralled the great mass of spectators. The pyrotechnic art has long been practised in India; and few festivities or popular rejoicings can be celebrated without recourse to the skill of the local manufacturer, who is to be found in every Indian town of any size. On this occasion, however, it was felt desirable to give to the natives—whose festival this was intended particularly to be—something that they had never seen before in their own country, and on a scale beyond the resources of indigenous artists. Accordingly the famous firm of Messrs. C. T. Brock and Co., of the Crystal Palace, London, had been commissioned to arrange a display, which should surpass anything ever before seen in the land.

The Viceroy and Lady Curzon, with their guests and a number of other residents in camp, viewed the fireworks from the arcades of the Jama Musjid. The roof of the Civil Hospital was also crowded with English spectators, while some of the stands in Khas Road, which had been put up for the state entry, were now reserved for the ruling Chiefs. An enormous crowd of natives on foot watched the display, manifesting its approval of each item of the programme with a mighty roar of admiration. The fireworks included "Special Colossal Fire Portraits" of the King-Emperor and Queen Alexandra, Lord and Lady Curzon, the Duke and Duchess of Connaught, and Lord Kitchener; showers of rockets and shells, cascades of coloured fire, the Star of India, and a variety of other devices, which can have left no doubt in the mind of a citizen of Delhi as to the indisputable supremacy of the master-folk in the fire game (*atash bazi*).

No one who was present can fail to remember the spectacle as some great flight of rockets burst high in the heavens, and for a few seconds turned the darkness almost into day. The red battlements and bastions of Shah Jehan's Fort framed one entire side of the picture. On the other side the white marble domes of the great mosque shone out with a sudden and startling radiance against the sombre background of the night. In the middle, between them, was a vast sea of turbaned heads and upturned faces—numbering hundreds of thousands—and a roar that rose and fell like the voice of a storm.

On Wednesday, January 7th, the Amphitheatre was the scene of a spectacle which, for its historical interest, as well as for unexpected scenic effects of a purely Asiatic type, might be accounted the most curious and even remarkable of all the celebrations at Delhi. This was the review of native Chiefs' retainers which was held on the morning of that day. Here the picturesque splendour of Indian courts, and whatever they retain of mediæval pomp and profusion, were presented with no contrasts of Western order and organisation. The Viceroy, in inviting the Chiefs to Delhi, had suggested that they should bring with them as many of their old-world retinues and trappings as were still in use, and had promised to reserve a special occasion, which should be dedicated not to the India of the present or of Great Britain, but to the India of the Chiefs and of the past. Some forty States responded to the invitation by sending their contingents, and two thousand horsemen and one thousand five hundred foot marched past, with 160 elephants and about the same number of camels. There were warriors in chain mail; war elephants plated with armour or bristling with spears and knives; men with sword and buckler, with spear and lance, with bows and arrows, or with clubs and staves; half naked Nagas or militant ascetics, armed with long blades from Rajputana; Akalis, soldier devotees from the Sikh States; drummers, trumpeters and pipers on foot or mounted on horses, elephants, or camels; wild-looking Arabs, who went by executing a war dance; musqueteers with blunderbuss and matchlock; acrobatic troopers, who stood on their saddles; cavaliers *à la haute école*, whose steeds pranced by on their hind legs; retainers carrying palanquins and litters, resplendent with gold and silver, or with velvet, embroidery and silk; musicians, evoking weird sounds from horns and trumpets; dancers executing dances, and bards reciting songs; fan-bearers and bannermen; led horses in great numbers, and even dogs and hounds—so they went by, one contingent after another sweeping round the arena, in such marvellous garb and bizarre equipment that it seemed as though a page of Froissart's Chronicle, specially dedicated to India, were being unrolled before one's eyes. Now and again the moving panorama of Oriental pageantry was interrupted by the steady tramp of Imperial Service troops; but for the most part it was a chapter lifted straight from the past.

The seats in the great Amphitheatre were crowded with spectators; the Viceroy and Lady Curzon, Their Royal Highnesses the Duke and Duchess of Connaught, nearly all the ruling Chiefs, Lord Kitchener, Governors, Lieutenant-Governors, and other high officials being present. The various contingents entered the arena, not in accordance with the rank of their respective Chiefs, but in an order corresponding to the distance that they had marched from their camps, those from the more remote camps coming first. Thus the first to go past were the retainers of the Maharaja of Kolhapur, whose banner was borne on a curiously painted elephant. Standard-bearers, mounted on camels, carried the banners of the Rao of Cutch, one of which had been given to an ancestor by the Moghul Emperor Shah Alam, the other to the then Rao by Lord Lytton at the Imperial Assemblage of 1877. Cutch also furnished four men walking on enormously elongated stilts, the relic of a day when warriors thus equipped fought with men on the backs of elephants. The entire Cutch procession was, indeed, faithfully reproduced from a painting in the possession of the Rao, which depicts the ceremonies practised by his ancestors. The Sultan of Shehr and Mokalla's Arab horsemen were followed by the retainers of Mysore, carrying spears and state umbrellas. The Gaekwar of Baroda sent his gold and silver cannon. Fifteen elephants, with heads and trunks painted a brilliant green, marched with the Gwalior contingent, which also included horsemen in a uniform that dates from the time of Shivaji. Behind Holkar's elephants came his gold and silver chairs of state, and his yellow-coated body-guard. A great green standard, bearing verses from the Koran, was held aloft on one of the Bhopal elephants by men in chain armour, wearing spiked helmets. Among the Central India Chiefs the Maharaja of Rewa made the bravest show, and next to him came the States of Datia and Orchha. The Rewa retainers escorted a dozen silver state litters, one of which was fashioned in the image of a tiger, as well as an immense carriage, with golden roof, drawn by a pair of elephants. From Rewa also came an individual in armour, from which protruded immense spikes, mounted on an elephant. A notable feature in the Orchha contingent was an elephant bearing on its back the figure of a gilt dragon. One of the Datia elephants was clad in chain armour, and bore an iron howdah. Another reared up on his hind legs to salute the Viceregal party as he passed the Daïs. The Rajput Chiefs contributed many picturesque and interesting features. Sixty lancers in chain armour rode with the Jaipur contingent. Among the retainers of the Chief of Bundi was a horseman carrying a flagon of water from the sacred Ganges. Bikaner sent mail-clad sowars mounted on camels

Lawrie & Co.

THE RETAINERS' REVIEW. KISHANGARH HORSEMEN

caparisoned with yellow saddle-cloths, and carrying small swivel guns. Fifteen Nagas from Kota, their bare skins smeared with ochre, and striped like tigers, engaged in mimic combat with sword and shield as they leaped around the arena. The Maharaja of Kishangarh's horsemen are shown in one of the illustrations; he also sent men on foot wearing long heavily quilted coats and head-gear—a sure protection against sword-cuts—and carrying shields of rhinoceros hide. Alwar furnished one of the most diversified contingents. It included a huge two-storied elephant carriage with glass windows, and several performing horses, one of which passed the Daïs with a series of jumps on its hind legs. These animals were not taught these tricks for any circus purpose; they were schooled in olden times for direct use in warfare.

Following the Rajput contingents, came Shans from the land of pagodas, wearing large plaited straw hats, and beating mellow-toned gongs. Next to appear were the retainers of the Maharaja of Benares and the Raja of Tehri. The former sent a quite exceptional contribution, both in the number of his elephants and in the richness of their howdahs. Some of his footmen were armed with clubs and carried hand grenades. Among the Punjab States, Faridkot sent a camel carriage, escorted by a mounted body-guard; Nabha, seven elephants, one of which bore chandeliers on its tusks, and falconers with hawks and greyhounds; Jind, horsemen with banner and drums, trumpeters blowing fantastic horns, and wild-looking Akalis each with a small arsenal of weapons about him; and Patiala, a contingent headed by three elephants, the third bearing the sacred writings.

Last came the *cortège* of Kashmir retainers, amongst whom were mounted men from Gilgit and Yasin, Buddhist Devil Dancers, wearing hideous masks, from Ladakh; and two veritable giants, one 7 ft. 8 in., the other 8 ft. high. These might opportunely have been placed in juxtaposition to the little Nabha dwarf.

There was no conscious absurdity or burlesque about this review. Each separate section that marched past represented, as faithfully as possible, the order and composition of such ceremonial processions as may still be seen, in the various States, on the occasion of a great festival. The extraordinary and unprecedented novelty of the display at Delhi consisted in the combination of these picturesque survivals—replete with interest for the antiquary and the historian—of an Oriental magnificence which is gradually but surely passing away. This review of the native Chiefs' retainers, which in all probability can never be reproduced—owing partly to the change that is everywhere passing over India, and is rendering these relics of a bygone age obsolete and unfashionable, partly to the incongruity that was sometimes manifest even at Delhi, as, for instance, when some of the elephants and retainers went by to the sound of the latest European tunes—seemed to sum up in a single pageant the most wonderful sights recorded by a long line of Indian travellers from the days of Tom Coryat and Pietro della Valle. Political officers from each of the principal groups of States that were represented constituted a committee to organise this remarkable spectacle: but the chief control was vested in Major Dunlop Smith, Political Agent for the Phulkian States: and to him and his fellow workers the admirable arrangements were due.

An assault at arms was held at the Amphitheatre on Saturday and Monday, January 3rd and 5th. Cups were presented by His Excellency the Viceroy for a riding and jumping competition by sections, open to non-commissioned officers and men of all British Cavalry, including Volunteer mounted corps, in India; and for tent-pegging by sections, open to all Native Cavalry regiments in India and Imperial Service Cavalry. The preliminary ties for these competitions had been played off at various Cavalry stations in the country, leaving four teams to compete in the final test at Delhi for the riding and jumping prize, and five for the tent-pegging. In addition to these contests, the programme of the assault at arms included Musical Drives by the I. and J. Batteries, Royal Horse Artillery; Musical Rides by the 4th Dragoon Guards and the 15th Hussars: Cavalry displays by the 8th Bengal Lancers (Bengal Command); 9th Bengal Lancers (Punjab Command), the Poona Horse (Bombay Command), and the Central India Horse; club swinging and running drill by the 15th Sikhs; and a gymnastic display by the Army gymnastic staff and special classes selected from the various Commands.

Thirty teams had entered for the Indian Cavalry tent-pegging competition, the result of the final contest in the Amphitheatre on January 3rd being as follows:

(1) 15th Bengal Lancers, 1st Prize.
(2) 3rd Bengal Cavalry, 2nd Prize.
(3) 2nd Punjab Cavalry.
(4) Hyderabad Imperial Service Lancers.
(5) 13th Bengal Lancers.

For the British Cavalry riding and jumping competitions, sixteen teams had entered. The result of the final contest, which took place in the Amphitheatre on the second day of the assault at arms, was as follows:

(1) 5th Dragoon Guards, 1st Prize.
(2) "J" Battery, Royal Horse Artillery, 2nd Prize.
(3) 15th Hussars.
(4) "I" Battery, Royal Horse Artillery.

Cups were also presented by the Viceroy for association football, open to all British corps serving in India, and for hockey, open to all Native troops. For these competitions, tournaments had been held in each command, leaving four winning teams for each event to play the final matches at Delhi.

In the football matches, the Punjab Command was represented by the 2nd battalion Gordon Highlanders; Bengal by the Royal Irish Rifles; Madras by the 2nd battalion, Essex Regiment; and Bombay by the 1st battalion, Cheshire Regiment. On December 23rd, the Royal Irish Rifles defeated the Cheshire Regiment by one goal to *nil;* and on the following day the Gordon Highlanders scored three goals against none by the Essex Regiment. A match between the Highlanders and the Royal Irish Rifles, on January 6th, ended in a drawn game, each side scoring one goal; but in the final match on the following day the team of the 2nd battalion Gordon Highlanders won the cup by three goals to one.

In the hockey tournament, after a series of matches in the various Commands, the 38th Dogras (Punjab), 33rd Punjab Infantry (Bengal), 11th Madras Infantry, and 22nd Bombay Infantry were left to compete in the match at Delhi. In the final match, played between the 33rd Punjab Infantry and the 22nd Bombay Infantry, played on January 5th, the Punjabis won the Viceroy's cup by four goals to one.

But it was the polo tournament at Delhi which attracted the greatest crowds; and, indeed, it was in every way proper and fitting that the royal Indian game should have a prominent place among the festivities connected with the Coronation Durbar. In the days of Akbar, Abul Fazl relates, there were superficial observers who looked on polo as a mere amusement; but men, he says, of loftier mind saw in it a means of learning promptitude and decision, a test of worth, and a stronger link in the bond of friendship. Polo added to the splendour of the court; and it served to reveal hidden talents. For these reasons, Akbar himself took delight in the game. According to Abul Fazl, the Emperor was an unrivalled player, and would often astonish the courtiers by hitting the ball as it flew through the air. Sometimes he would play polo at night, with balls of *palas* wood set on fire. History also records the name and deeds of a Sultan of Delhi, Kutb-ud-Din Aibak, who, long before Akbar's time, lost his life when playing polo, his horse falling with him, and the pommel of the saddle crushing his ribs. This was at a match played at Lahore in 1046 A.D.; but it seems safe to assume that eight or nine centuries, at least, have gone by since the first polo match was played at Delhi. We may doubt, however, if the game was ever played under such perfect conditions as were possible during the Coronation Durbar week. The Delhi polo tournament brought together the finest teams in India; and among the competitors for the Viceroy's international cup, open to the world, was a famous team from England. The two match grounds specially laid out for the occasion, as well as the practice grounds, were as true as a billiard table; and the Polo Club House, with its spacious stands, became, from the beginning, the general meeting place, every afternoon, for both residents and visitors.

All the arrangements connected with polo were in charge of the following Committee:

President.

Colonel C. W. Muir.

Members.

H.H. the Maharaja of Idar.

Lieutenant-Colonel the Hon. E. Baring, Military Secretary.

Captain D. G. M. Campbell, 9th Lancers.

Lieut.-Colonel T. O. W. C. de Crespigny, 15th Hussars.

Lawrie & Co.

THE RETAINERS' REVIEW. KISHANGARH HORSEMEN

J. D. West, Esq.
D. N. Graham, Esq.
Brigadier-General Stuart Beatson.
Lieut.-Colonel G. A. Money, 18th Bengal Lancers.
Major S. H. Climo, 24th Punjab Infantry.
Lieut.-Colonel J. H. E. Reid, King's Own Scottish Borderers.
Major A. B. Mayne, Central India Horse.
Captain A. d'A. G. Bannerman.

Honorary Secretaries.

Major R. St. C. Lecky, Royal Horse Artillery.
Captain J. C. D. Pinney, Central India Horse.

The grounds had been most carefully prepared; an army of coolies, under anxious supervision, beginning to work on them before the end of the rainy season, so that by Christmas the turf might have excited the envy of Hurlingham. The Club House, a well-designed building erected on an eminence between the two match grounds, contained a large reception room, refreshment rooms, and spacious verandahs to the east and west. On either side, broad terraces sloped down to the level of the field, with rows of seats for spectators, for whom there were also two other stands, each holding 2000 chairs. Four of the rooms had flat terraced roofs, from which the Viceroy and his Royal guests witnessed more than one hard fought game. The cost of the building, of laying out the grounds, turfing, maintenance, etc., amounted in all to Rs.60,000, but this was more than covered by subscriptions and entrance fees. The Club was open from December 15th to January 15th, to all civil and military officers, ruling Chiefs, a limited number of their Sardars, and all gentlemen on the Government House list, on payment of Rs.20, ladies being charged Rs.10. Spectators who did not join the Club were admitted to one of the enclosures on payment of Rs.10 for the whole time or two and a half rupees each day. To other parts of the polo grounds, set aside for spectators, soldiers in uniform were admitted free, other persons being charged eight annas a day.

Besides the international polo cup, His Excellency the Viceroy also presented a cup for a competition open to all Regiments of the Native Army in India.

The following teams competed for the international cup:

Hyderabad, Bhavnagar Imperial Service Lancers, Royal Horse Guards (Blues), Bikaner, Bhopal Imperial Service Lancers, Jodhpur, Shahpur Tiwanas, Patiala, Imperial Cadet Corps, Kuch Behar, Alwar, 3rd Battalion, Rifle Brigade, 4th Dragoon Guards, 15th Hussars.

The results of the first ties were as follows:

Hyderabad vs. *Bhavnagar Imperial Service Lancers.*

Hyderabad won by 18 goals and 9 subsidiaries, to 1 goal and 1 subsidiary.

Bhopal Imperial Service Lancers vs. *Jodhpur.*

Jodhpur won by 12 goals and 6 subsidiaries, to 1 goal and 1 subsidiary.

Shahpur Tiwanas vs. *Patiala.*

Patiala won by 14 goals and 3 subsidiaries, to 1 goal and 1 subsidiary.

Royal Horse Guards (Blues) vs. *Bikaner.*

Bikaner won by 4 goals and 2 subsidiaries, to 2 goals and 2 subsidiaries.

Imperial Cadet Corps vs. *Kuch Behar.*

The Imperial Cadet Corps won by 12 goals to 4.

The Rifle Brigade, which was to have played the Alwar team, scratched. The 4th Dragoon Guards and 15th Hussars were byes.

The second ties had the following results:

Jodhpur vs. *Patiala.*

Jodhpur won by 6 goals and 2 subsidiaries, to 3 goals and 2 subsidiaries.

Hyderabad vs. *Bikaner.*

Bikaner won by 5 goals and 6 subsidiaries, to 5 goals and 2 subsidiaries.

Imperial Cadet Corps vs. *Alwar.*

Alwar won by 7 goals and 3 subsidiaries, to 1 subsidiary.

4th Dragoon Guards vs. *15th Hussars.*

The Dragoons won by 4 goals and 4 subsidiaries, to 2 goals and 3 subsidiaries.

In the semi-finals the scores were as follows:

Alwar vs. *4th Dragoon Guards.*

Alwar won by 6 goals to 2.

Jodhpur vs. *Bikaner.*

Jodhpur won by 6 goals and 5 subsidiaries, to 1 goal and 1 subsidiary.

The final match for the Viceroy's international cup was played on January 9th, when the Alwar team beat Jodhpur by seven goals and six subsidiaries, to two goals.

The following were the players in these two teams, and it is probable that no finer team than the Alwar four has ever been seen:

Alwar Team.	*Jodhpur Team.*
(1) Moti Lal.	(1) Thakur Ogham Singh.
(2) H. H. the Maharaja of Alwar.	(2) Thakur Dhonkal Singh.
(3) Captain R. L. Ricketts.	(3) Thakur Ghuman Singh.
back Rao Raja Amar Singh.	*back* H. H. the Maharaja of Jodhpur.

The following Regiments were entered for the Indian Army cup presented by the Viceroy:

8th Bengal Lancers.
2nd Gurkhas, scratched.
1st Bengal Lancers.
3rd Bengal Cavalry.
2nd Punjab Cavalry, scratched.
18th Bengal Lancers.
3rd Bombay Cavalry.
4th Bengal Lancers.
2nd Central India Horse.
Poona Horse.
9th Bengal Lancers.
19th Bengal Lancers.
1st Lancers, Hyderabad Contingent, scratched.
11th Bengal Lancers.
1st Central India Horse.

The first ties resulted as follows:

8th Bengal Lancers vs. *4th Bengal Lancers.*

8th Bengal Lancers won by 9 goals and 7 subsidiaries, to 3 goals and 2 subsidiaries.

3rd Bengal Cavalry vs. *9th Bengal Lancers.*

3rd Bengal Cavalry won by 11 goals and 1 subsidiary, to 2 goals and 5 subsidiaries.

3rd Bombay Cavalry vs. *11th Bengal Lancers.*

3rd Bombay Cavalry won by 4 goals and 4 subsidiaries, to 2 goals and 1 subsidiary.

The second ties resulted as follows:

18th Bengal Lancers vs. *19th Bengal Lancers.*

18th Bengal Lancers won by 5 goals and 4 subsidiaries, to 3 goals and 1 subsidiary.

3rd Bombay Cavalry vs. *1st Central India Horse.*

Bombay won by 5 goals and 3 subsidiaries, to 2 goals and 1 subsidiary.

8th Bengal Lancers vs. *2nd Central India Horse.*

Central India Horse won by 6 goals and 3 subsidiaries, to 5 goals and 2 subsidiaries.

Poona Horse vs. *3rd Bengal Cavalry.*

Poona Horse won by 11 goals and 6 subsidiaries, to 3 goals and 3 subsidiaries.

In the semi-final the following matches were played:

Poona Horse vs. *2nd Central India Horse.*

Poona Horse won by 5 goals and 4 subsidiaries, to 3 goals and 2 subsidiaries.

18th Bengal Lancers vs. *3rd Bombay Cavalry.*

Bengal won by 5 goals and 5 subsidiaries, to 2 subsidiaries.

The final was as follows:

Poona Horse vs. *18th Bengal Lancers.*

Poona Horse won by 4 goals and 4 subsidiaries, to 3 goals and 1 subsidiary.

The Viceroy and Lady Curzon, with Their Royal Highnesses the Duke and Duchess of Connaught, and a distinguished party, watched the concluding match for the international cup from the roof of the pavilion, where members of the Club and other visitors were entertained by the Rajputana Chiefs and Political officers. The final match for the football cup was played on an adjoining ground, where most of the troops in camp had collected to see the deciding contest between the Gordon Highlanders and Royal Irish Rifles. On the same afternoon polo teams from Gilgit and Hunza and also from Manipur gave an exhibition of polo as played in those remote regions at the opposite extremities of the Indian Empire. In both it seems to have found a home for centuries, having probably made its way up to the petty Hindu Kush States from Kashmir, where it must have been introduced by the Moghul sovereigns. From both quarters it returned almost simultaneously to India soon after 1860, and was introduced to English sportsmen, at Srinagar on the one side and Calcutta on the other. The diminutive ponies that are used in the Indian Hill States, the unlimited number of players, the extraordinary narrowness of the grounds, the rough equipment both of ponies and riders, and the general absence of

F. Bremner

THE RETAINERS' REVIEW

rules, render the game a very different spectacle from that to which we are accustomed. But it gives openings for a skill and a daring that are not excelled by any experiences of the European game. At the conclusion of the cup match the Viceroy made a short speech, saying that it had given him great pleasure to offer cups for the competitions, and congratulating the winners on their success. The Duchess of Connaught then presented the prizes for the various contests:

International Polo cup.—Alwar State Team.
Army Polo cup.—Poona Horse.
Jumping Competition.—5th Dragoon Guards, first; "J" Battery, Royal Horse Artillery, second.
Tent-pegging.—15th Bengal Lancers, first; 3rd Punjab Cavalry, second.
Hockey.—33rd Punjab Infantry.
Best Man-at-Arms amongst Volunteers.—Sergeant Collinson, Cawnpore Light Horse.

On January 5th, 6th, and 7th, a cricket match was played on the polo ground, between a team representing the Gentlemen of India, and the Oxford University Authentics, who were touring in India during the cold weather season, and was won by the latter, the score being as follows:

GENTLEMEN OF INDIA.

1st Innings.		*2nd Innings.*	
H. C. Cheetham, c Hollins, b Williams	11	b Powys-Keck	3
S. R. Hignell, b Simpson-Hayward	18	c Headlam, b Powys-Keck	0
K. O. Goldie, b Powys-Keck	37	c Hornby, b Williams	6
B. N. Bosworth-Smith, b Simpson-Hayward	2	b Williams	30
W. Troup, retired hurt	5	absent hurt	0
W. J. Marsham, b Williams	7	l-b-w, b Powys-Keck	68
C. T. Studd, c Headlam, b Powys-Keck	11	b Powys-Keck	4
H. F. French, c Hornby, b Williams	11	b Williams	1
J. D. Guise, b Williams	0	b Powys-Keck	6
A. F. Ffoulkes, b Williams	0	c and b Simpson-Hayward	5
H. R. Hoare, not out	3	not out	0
Extras	13	Extras	20
TOTAL	118	TOTAL	143

OXFORD UNIVERSITY AUTHENTICS.

H. B. Chinnery, hit wicket	9	b Hoare	5
A. H. Hornby, b Guise	54	not out	73
F. H. Hollins, b Guise	22	b Hoare	7
R. A. Williams, b Studd	0		
R. H. Raphael, run out	10	b Guise	11
K. J. Key, st French, b Hoare	17	not out	2
G. H. Simpson-Hayward, b Hoare	7	b Hoare	31
J. E. Tomkinson, c Goldie, b Hoare	12		
J. N. Ridley, c and b Hoare	0		
C. Headlam, hit wicket	1		
H. J. Powys-Keck, not out	0		
Extras	3	Extras	0
TOTAL	135	TOTAL	129

Mention may also be made here of the unveiling, by Sir Charles Rivaz, Lieutenant-Governor of the Punjab, of a statue of the late Queen-Empress Victoria, presented to the city of Delhi by Mr. James Cousins Skinner, a grandson of the famous Colonel James Skinner, who, after serving under Scindia's French Generals, de Boigne and Perron, entered the Company's service, and greatly distinguished himself as a leader of irregular cavalry. Colonel Skinner, of Skinner's Horse, was the son of a Scotch ensign in the Indian Army, his mother being a Rajput lady; but in spite of his parentage and his swarthy complexion, his friend Sir John Malcolm told him, "You are as good an Englishman as I am." The statue of the Queen-Empress presented by Mr. James Skinner is the work of Mr. Albert Turner, and it now stands in the middle of the Chandni Chauk, in front of the Town Hall.

The proud and proven loyalty of the Sikhs found notable expression at Delhi in a religious ceremony, which, though witnessed by only a small party of Englishmen, and not included in any official programme, deserves more than a passing reference. The occasion was the anniversary of the birth of Govind Singh, the tenth and last apostle of the Sikhs; and the ceremony took place at the Sis Ganj, a small Sikh temple, on the spot where Teg Bahadur, Govind Singh's father and predecessor, was put to death, in 1675, by order of the Emperor

Aurungzeb. It is related, in Sikh chronicles, that when Teg Bahadur, whose name signifies "Brave to wield the sword," was held in confinement, a short time before his martyrdom, he went one morning to the upper storey of his prison and looked over the city. This was duly reported by his guards to the Emperor. Aurungzeb thereupon accused his prisoner of an offence against the laws of Oriental etiquette, for his eyes had been turned in the direction of the imperial zenana, and he might have seen, or perhaps desired to see, the ladies of the Great Moghul's household. To this, it is said, Teg Bahadur replied: "Aurungzeb, Emperor, I was on the upper storey of my prison. I gazed not at the zenana. I was looking toward the south, in the direction of the white faces, who, one day, are coming from over seas to tear down your *purdahs* and overthrow your empire." This prophecy was carefully borne in mind by Govind Singh, Teg Bahadur's son, and by those who came after him; and the words gave a battle cry to the Sikh soldiers who fought alongside of our own troops at the siege and capture of Delhi in 1857. The name of Teg Bahadur, it will be seen, was associated in a remarkable way with the objects of the meeting held here on January 3rd, 1903. With the exception of the Raja of Kapurthala all the Sikh ruling Chiefs, the Maharaja of Patiala, the Rajas of Jind, Nabha, and Faridkot, and the Sardar of the Kalsia State, drove in carriages to the Sis Ganj, with a long procession of mace-bearers, spear-men, drummers, trumpeters and Sikh bards; the Granth, the sacred book of the Sikhs, being carried on an elephant, as far as the Mori Gate, and taken thence in a carriage by itself to the temple, where it was received with military honours by a company of the 1st Jind Imperial Service Infantry, the regimental band playing "God save the King." The Granth was borne reverently into the temple, which was crowded with worshippers, both men and women. The Chiefs followed barefooted, and a short service was held. Passages were recited from the Sikh scriptures, the Guru of Anandpur in the Hoshiarpur district delivered a homily, and the venerable Raja of Nabha addressed the congregation. Speaking with deep emotion, he referred at length to the story of Teg Bahadur, his prophecy and martyrdom. The Sikhs, His Highness said, if they were worthy of the favour of God and of their forefathers, must renew their pledge of loyalty to the King of the "white faces," who had done so much for them. The Raja's speech made a marked impression at the time; and it has since become known that the outburst of enthusiastic loyalty at the gathering in the Sis Ganj has had a far-reaching effect on the whole body of the Sikh people.

H. H. The Nawab of Junagadh,
K. C. S. I.

CHAPTER XI

LOCAL CELEBRATIONS

WHILE the Viceroy and the high officials of the administration, the ruling Chiefs, and leading men from all parts of the Indian Empire assembled at the ancient capital of Delhi to celebrate the Coronation of the King-Emperor, the event was also made the occasion of public ceremonies and rejoicings by all classes of the people throughout the length and breadth of the land, both in British territory and in the Native States. These rejoicings are described in a despatch from the Government of India to the Secretary of State, which is printed as Appendix IV to this volume. In British territory the Royal Proclamation was publicly read, in English and in the vernacular, at the headquarters of all the Local Governments and administrations, and of each district; troops in garrison were paraded; royal salutes of 101 guns were fired wherever this was practicable; public buildings were illuminated; the poor were fed, and, by the particular desire of the Viceroy, entertainments were given to school children, in order that the auspicious event might be more deeply impressed on the minds of the rising generation. By an act of grace, 16,188 prisoners were released from the jails in British India; and similar clemency was shown in all the Native States. Wherever honours had been conferred on English or Indian residents in a locality, the fact was publicly announced; and in many cases certificates of merit were presented by the senior civil officer to those who had earned such distinctions. Everywhere public bodies and private persons gladly undertook to provide the whole or a large proportion of the cost of the local celebrations; and thanks to their liberality, it is certain that among all classes of the population there were few left untouched by that sense of the unity of the Empire, and of the privileges of common citizenship, which it was the main object of the Imperial Durbar at Delhi to demonstrate.

The celebrations at the three presidency towns of Calcutta, Madras and Bombay, and at the provincial capitals of Allahabad, Lahore, Rangoon, Nagpur, Shillong and Peshawar were marked by displays of enthusiastic loyalty. At Calcutta, however, only the more formal ceremonies, including a parade of troops, the reading of the Proclamation, the presentation of certificates of honour and the release of 462 prisoners from the presidency and Alipur jails were performed on New Year's Day; the general festivities being postponed till the return of the Viceroy and the Lieutenant-Governor, from the great ceremony at Delhi. Then, from January 26th to January 29th, the city of palaces on the Hugli was *en fête.* Upwards of half a lakh of rupees was subscribed by the general public, of which Rs.28,677 were spent in entertaining school children, while 25,000 poor Hindus and 20,000 Muhammadans were fed on the Maidan at the expense of Babu Bhajan Lal Lohia. On January 26th, the Viceroy gave a costume ball at Government House on the hundredth anniversary of the great ball given on January 26th, 1803, by Lord Wellesley, then Governor-General, to celebrate both the opening of Government House, which had just been completed, and the conclusion of the Peace of Amiens, news of which had reached India a short time before. This was the famous ball of which so minute an account is to be found in the "Travels of Lord Valentia," who was among those present. The costumes of a hundred years ago were faithfully reproduced by the Viceroy and all his guests. Lord Curzon appeared in an exact copy of the uniform worn by Lord Wellesley as depicted in the paintings at Government House; and his staff were also attired in a direct reproduction of the staff costume of that day. The celebrations, however, which appealed most closely to the populace were the fireworks and the illuminations. The former were given on the racecourse before an immense crowd of natives, by Messrs. C. T. Brock, who reproduced several of their Delhi pieces. On the night of the illuminations, all the public buildings of Calcutta and the principal European and native streets were a blaze of light, the natives pursuing their own effective method of illumination in their own quarters. The Viceroy and Lady Curzon and their party drove in procession through the streets at 10 P.M. on a prescribed route, which was over five miles long.

At Bombay, in addition to the formal ceremonies, there was a People's Fair on the Esplanade, lasting from December 26th to January 4th; a grand illumination on the night of January 1st, and a display of fireworks on January 6th; while each of the various communities and public bodies organised special festivities and gatherings. By the whole population, January 1st was kept as a gala day, one and all striving to outvie each other in demonstrating their loyalty to the King-Emperor. The Royal Proclamation was read at noon, at the Town Hall, by the sheriff, Mr. Leslie Crawford.

At Madras, a durbar was held on January 1st, in the banqueting-hall, when the Proclamation was read by the Hon. Mr. Gabriel Stokes, Chief Secretary to the Government of Madras. Throughout the day there were religious services, musical entertainments, dramatic performances, distributions of food and clothing to the poor, and treats for the school children. The main thoroughfares of the city, public buildings, and houses of business were decorated, and in the evening there were illuminations and a display of fireworks on the island of St. Thomas.

At Allahabad, Mr. Percy Gray, the Commissioner of the Division, held a durbar in the Mayo Hall, where he read the Royal Proclamation in the presence of a large gathering, which included leading native gentlemen from the city and neighbouring districts. In the afternoon there was an elephant procession; and in the evening, a meeting of the residents and a display of fireworks at the Khusru Bagh.

At Lahore, the capital of the Punjab, the Royal Proclamation was read on the parade ground of the 1st Punjab Volunteers, by Mr. C. H. Atkins, the Deputy Commissioner, the city and civil station were illuminated, and several leading members of the native community distributed food to the poor.

At Rangoon there was a parade of the troops in garrison, and the

Royal Proclamation was read by the senior puisne judge of the Chief Court. Certificates of honour were presented; a feast was given to poor Europeans and natives, each of whom received a small present in money; nearly 14,000 school children were entertained, and the day ended with illuminations and fireworks. On the following evening a display of pyrotechnics, as practised for a thousand years in the Celestial Empire, was, as in Calcutta, given by the Chinese community.

To add a full report of the festivities and rejoicings in other cities and towns of India, and in the rural districts, would be impossible. Everywhere the loyalty of the people, the liberality of the moneyed classes, and even of those who could not so well afford to be generous, and the enthusiasm with which officials and private persons strove to make the celebration a success, were conspicuously shown. The reports, too, which were received from various centres, as well as the columns of the local newspapers, afforded ample testimony that the great mass of the population, and especially the poor and the children, had good cause to remember the occasion with gratitude. Here, however, there is only space to record some of the festivities that took place in a few localities in each province, outside the capitals, and in the Native States. In the Bombay Presidency, four scholarships for the local school of Art and Industry were founded at Surat in honour of the King-Emperor and Queen Alexandra. In many places, as at Bassein, Ratnagiri and Kanara, portraits of Their Majesties were displayed, and decorated with garlands. At Shahpur, the Brahmins, who recited Sanskrit *mantras* for their long life, received gratuities from the local committee. At Ahmednagar, the Fort, where the Boer prisoners were kept, was illuminated. At Poona, the district magistrate held a durbar in the Council Hall; thousands of poor people were fed at the cost of Mr. Kaluram Bhau Mansaram, a wealthy citizen, and bonfires were lit on the neighbouring heights. In the Ratnagiri district, medals, portraits of Their Majesties, and short biographies of Queen Victoria in the Marathi language, were distributed among the school children; and in many of the villages larger portraits of the King-Emperor and Queen Alexandra were placed in sedan chairs and carried in procession through the place. Where there were no troops the police paraded and gave a *feu de joie;* or, as reported from one township, private persons, who had gun licences, fired a salute. At Karachi, nearly two thousand people met on the Queen's Lawn in the grounds of Frere Hall, to hear the Proclamation, which was read in English by the Collector, and in Sindhi by Mr. Tahilram Khemchand, president of the municipality; and, in addition to the festivities of the day, the event was commemorated by a handsome donation to the Lady Dufferin Hospital.

In the Madras Presidency, durbars were held by the Collector at the head-quarters of each district; portraits of Their Majesties were carried in procession on elephants, or were placed on decorated vehicles, and, as at Kurnool, dragged through the town by the people themselves; there were illuminations and fireworks; and, everywhere, the poor were fed and treats were provided for the school children. At Madura, the durbar was held in the palace of Tirumala Naick, under the central dome, where the hereditary priests from the great temple presented offerings of flowers after the custom that obtained at the coronations of the old Pandyan kings. At many places in the Presidency, the event will be commemorated by public buildings and monuments erected at the expense of loyal citizens and societies; such as an "Edward Reading Room" at Karikal, a public hall at Anantpur, "Coronation wells" at Saidapet, an "Edward library" at Nandyal, a "Coronation Hall" at Krishnagiri, and "Coronation lamps" in many places in the Tinnevelly district.

The celebrations throughout Bengal were marked by the heartiest demonstrations of loyalty. In the Presidency division, the festivities were continued at most places for several days. Well-to-do men in the districts illuminated their houses, entertained their friends, and gave alms to the poor. Hindus and Muhammadans everywhere offered up prayers for the long life and prosperity of Their Majesties. Processions of school children, bearing flags, and singing songs in the vernacular specially composed for the occasion, paraded the towns; and large sums were collected for charitable purposes. The durbar at Hooghly, presided over by the Commissioner of Burdwan, was attended by the Administrator of the French settlement of Chandernagore. At Narajole, in the Midnapur district, over 18,000 poor people were fed by

Raja Narendra Lal Khan. In Orissa, a central durbar was held for the whole division at Cuttack, at which fourteen of the tributary Chiefs were present. The Commissioner rode to the durbar in a procession of forty elephants. At Chittagong, Babu Revati Raman Rai, a Hindu zamindar and merchant, entertained the students, feasted the prisoners in jail, and the Christian orphans and poor under the Roman Catholic mission, and distributed clothes among indigent Christian widows and children; while a Muhammadan merchant, Munshi Yakub Ali, Dubash, fed all the poor of his faith for three days together.

In the United Provinces most successful arrangements were made by local committees at the head-quarters of each district for the popular festivities which, in addition to official gatherings, marked the occasion. The example of a ruling Chief, the Nawab of Rampur, who remitted Rs. 1,76,255 arrears of revenue, was generously emulated by a large number of landholders, who made considerable remissions of rent due by tenants. Many *raises* distributed blankets to the poor and to *pardanishin* women in distressed circumstances. Illuminations and fireworks were general throughout the provinces; the display of fireworks on an island in the river at Cawnpur being described as especially fine. Numbers of old soldiers attended the durbars held by the Commissioners and district officials. The report received from Fyzabad mentions that a retired native officer, eighty-five years of age, his breast covered with medals, wearing a uniform of days long gone by, was greeted with loud and prolonged cheers, as he was led before the Deputy Commissioner.

The Punjab, at the accession of Queen Victoria, was ruled by Ranjit Singh; and his successors, a few years later, defied the armed strength of England, and invaded British territory. Throughout this land of the five rivers, which now, under British administration, enjoys a prosperity it never knew before, the celebration of the King-Emperor's accession was the signal for a notable outburst of enthusiastic loyalty. Everywhere in the province, in Hindu temple, Sikh *gurdwara*, and Muhammadan mosque, no less than in Christian churches, heartfelt prayers were offered for His Majesty's preservation and long reign. At the head-quarters of every district the poor of all creeds were fed; there

Bourne & Shepherd, phot. Walker & Boutall Ph. Sc.

The Khan of Dir, C.I.E., The Mehtar of Chitral, C.I.E., and the Khan of Nawagai.

were treats for the school children; and all public buildings and many private houses were illuminated. Special mention is made in the reports of the elaborate illuminations of the Golden Temple of the Sikhs at Amritsar, and of an enormous bonfire on Mount Tilla in the Jhelum District, in which 400 *maunds* of wood blazed for two days and nights. The Jhelum district, indeed, was profuse in its display of liberal loyalty; for it is reported that in some parts, the school children, *mirabile dictu*, were quite unable to consume the quantity of sweets provided for their delectation. In Gujrat, one native gentleman offered to pay the fines of a number of wrong-doers, who had been imprisoned in default; and in Montgomery four others remitted debts due to them. At Sialkot, Sardar Bagel Singh, a retired police officer, endowed a bed in the civil hospital; at Amritsar, a wealthy citizen provided an institution for the relief of the poor; and there were many other instances of open-handed philanthropy. The manly races of the Punjab, it may be added, almost everywhere included athletic sports, wrestling matches, tent-pegging, horse races, cricket and football in their programme of festivities.

In the adjoining North-West Frontier Province the celebrations were much of the same kind; but mention may be made of the Khattak sword dance at Kohat, and the Waziri dance at Bannu. At Peshawar, the capital, troops were paraded, a durbar was held by the Deputy Commissioner, and congratulatory addresses were presented by the various communities of the city.

In Burma, among the forms of popular festivity peculiar to the province, may be mentioned the *pwes* or dramatic entertainments, lasting, in some places, many days in succession, boat races in many-oared native craft, and banquets for Buddhist monks, in accordance with time-honoured custom. At Mandalay, beside the parade of troops, the reading of the Proclamation by the Judicial Commissioner, and the firing of a royal salute of 101 guns, nearly 10,000 of the poor were fed, the whole town was illuminated, even the lowliest inhabitants burning a few candles or an oil lamp in front of their houses; on January 2nd, there was a treat for 6000 school children; and, on the following day, Burmese boat races on the moat. At Ma-ubin, in the Prome district, the ceremonies of an Imperial coronation according to the Burmese custom were performed; and a procession, arranged in imitation of the ceremonial of the old Burmese court, marched to the Durbar Hall, where the Proclamation was read. At Toungoo, the good-natured Burmese, with characteristic kind-heartedness, took the prisoners, who had just been released, to a pavilion erected for the purpose, and gave them a hearty meal.

A noteworthy feature of the celebrations in the Central Provinces was the presentation, to every one who attended the district durbars, of a photograph of the King-Emperor, a gift which seemed everywhere to be highly appreciated. In Jubbulpur, owing to the prevalence of plague, the feeding of the poor, by attracting large crowds, might have been attended with danger to the public health, and blankets were distributed instead; but in other places, great numbers of poor people were fed, and everywhere the population took part eagerly in the general rejoicing. In honour of the occasion, Raja Gokaldass of Jubbulpur, remitted debts to the value of over five lakhs of rupees. In Nagpur, Shrimati Gunga Bai gave Rs. 2000 toward the erection of a fountain in Needham Park, and an additional sum towards the lighting installation of the city.

In Assam, the efforts of the district officials to bring home the importance of the occasion to the minds of the people appear to have been attended with marked success; and the rejoicings will long be remembered by tribes like the Lushais, Nagas, Garos and Kasis, many of whom came in, from long distances, to pay their homage to the Emperor. At Shillong, the capital, there were the usual formalities and festivities; and in the districts, the celebrations included durbars, feeding of the poor, feasts for school children, national dances and sports, and in the evening, illuminations of the towns, and the lighting of bonfires on the hill peaks.

The Agent to the Governor-General in Baluchistan reported that durbars had been held on January 1st at Quetta, Sibi, Duki, Fort Sandeman, and other places. Numbers of people from across the Afghan border came into Sibi to take part in the festivities there. In several places there were horse and foot races and other games; food was distributed among the poor, there were entertainments for the children, fireworks and illuminations, and prayers for Their Majesties in the mosques and temples.

Even the convict settlement in the Andaman Islands had its share in the rejoicings. Indeed, a large number of convicts had particular reasons of their own for remembering the celebration of the King-Emperor's accession, for 261 life convicts and 121 term convicts were released absolutely. New Year's Day was a holiday for every one in the settlement, even for the prisoners in jail and the chain gangs. King's dinners were provided for all, troops, lascars, police, convicts, and the native Andamanese. The free people in the islands subscribed liberally for illuminations and festivities. The native officers of the police subscribed a sum to be divided among a number of the poorest and most helpless ex-convicts. The free native population subscribed Rs. 300 for the annual presentation of two silver medals at the Port Blair boys' and girls' schools. The Andamanese aboriginals, a race of savages who, as a rule, shun all intercourse with civilised people, were entertained at a banquet, arranged in accordance with aboriginal tastes. Colonel Sir R. C. Temple, Bart., the Chief Commissioner of the Andamans and Nicobars, was present, and made a speech in the Andamanese language; his endeavour to get at the hearts of his audience, which was composed of savages in the lowest scale of humanity, being, it was reported, eminently successful.

If in the States under the rule of Indian Princes the celebrations were organised on even less formal lines than in British territory, the universal demonstration of loyalty and the spontaneous outburst of rejoicing must be considered in the highest degree gratifying. It was a resonant antiphon, so to speak, to the acclamations of the Imperial Durbar at Delhi, and to the rejoicings throughout the provinces directly under English administration; and the ring and volume of this grand echo were indeed remarkable. Though space cannot be found here for a full account of what was done, some conception of the warmth and sincerity of the observances and displays in the Native States may be gathered from such extracts as can be given from reports sent in by Political Residents and Agents.

The celebrations at the Nizam's capital and throughout his

dominions were duly carried out in accordance with an edict issued early in December by the Nizam, which gave the following orders:

"All offices, whether in the city or in the districts, will be closed on account of the auspicious Durbar from the 5th to the 8th Shawal 1320 Hijri. (January 5th to January 8th).

"Arrangements will be made to illuminate, at Government expense, all Government offices and other places in the city. Food will be distributed to the poor and the indigent through the Ecclesiastical Department, and arrangements for the entertainment of school children will be made by the Educational Department. It is hoped that all jagirdars, nobles, merchants, and others will illuminate their houses and buildings on this auspicious occasion.

"The poor and the indigent will be fed and school children entertained at Government expense at the head-quarters of each suba. His Highness's Government is pleased to grant permission to celebrate this auspicious occasion to all raiyats, merchants, and others residing in places outside the head-quarter stations, who may intend to participate in these rejoicings.

"On the day mentioned above, which will be a day of great rejoicings and congratulations, convicts whose conduct has been good will be released, and all the other convicts throughout His Highness's dominions will receive this concession that on account of the auspicious day they will be provided with better food than they usually obtain.

"The Managers and Emams of mosques and people of all other religions should assemble at their places of worship on the auspicious day referred to in order to pray at the threshold of the true King of Kings (God) for the long life and prosperity of His Most Gracious Majesty, the King-Emperor. The people of Islam especially will have an opportunity to offer their prayers as directed above, because the Durbar will probably be held on the day of the *Id*, and consequently large numbers of Muhammadans will have assembled at every Mosque, whether in the city or in the districts, to offer *Id* prayers. Therefore it appears necessary that the Muhammadans should generally embrace this opportunity for offering prayers for the well-being of the Emperor of India, since, having regard to the blessings of this world with which all people are favoured during His Majesty's reign, it is incumbent upon every individual to join with his co-religionists and express his gratitude by means of prayers."

In the British military cantonment of Secunderabad, which is situated within the limits of the Nizam's dominions, the troops in garrison were paraded and His Majesty's Proclamation was read. A religious service was held at St. George's Church, Hyderabad, and in the afternoon there was a durbar at the British Residency, which was attended by some forty-four nobles and officials of the Hyderabad State, by the officers commanding units of the Nizam's regular troops, by the

British officers commanding corps and batteries quartered at Secunderabad and Bolarum, and the staff officers and heads of departments in the two garrisons, by the clergy and sixty non-officials. At this assembly Major W. Haig, First Assistant to the Resident, read the Royal Proclamation, and the names of persons to whom Coronation certificates had been granted. In Berar there were durbars and illuminations at Amraoti and at all the district and taluq head-quarters.

At Baroda, on January 1st, 1903, there was a durbar at the Residency; and the Royal Proclamation was read at durbars held at the head-quarters of the Kadi, Naosari and Amreli Divisions. One hundred and thirty-seven criminal prisoners were released on January 1st, 1903. His Highness the Gaekwar, on his return to his capital, held a grand durbar in the Palace at Baroda, where the Royal Proclamation was publicly read in the presence of the Resident and European officers of the station, and a large assembly of State officials and leading inhabitants of Baroda, the State artillery firing an Imperial salute.

In Mysore, durbars were held on January 1st, 1903, by the Deputy Commissioners at all district head-quarters, and by Amildars at the head-quarters of each taluq, at which the Royal Proclamation was read. In municipal towns, the poor were fed, sweets were distributed among the school children, athletic sports were held, and at night there were fireworks and illuminations. Sixty-six prisoners were released from the State jails; and the sentences on 432 prisoners were partially remitted. At all the Hindu temples and Muhammadan mosques, prayers were offered for the long life and prosperity of the King-Emperor and the Queen.

At Mercara, the picturesque capital of Coorg, there was, in addition to the ordinary festivities, a procession through the town, in which two great portraits of the King-Emperor and the Queen were the chief feature.

In Kashmir the actual date of His Majesty's Coronation, August 9th, had been celebrated at the summer station of Gulmarg by a state banquet, which was graced by the presence of Lady Curzon, followed by a display of fireworks and the illumination of the huge hill of Apharwat, 14,400 feet high, which rises behind Gulmarg. The

Maharaja and his brother, Raja Sir Amar Singh, attended the celebrations. The poor to the number of some 10,000 had been fed on June 26th at Srinagar. Again, on January 1st, at the beautiful capital of Kashmir, the Assistant Resident held a durbar on the polo ground, which was attended by all the leading people of the city, Europeans and natives, the State troops parading at the same time. In the afternoon athletic sports were held, and in the evening Srinagar was illuminated. At Jammu, a royal salute of 101 guns was fired from the Bahugarh Fort, five thousand of the poor were fed, and by order of the Maharaja a durbar was held in the Mandi Mubarak, where the Royal Proclamation was read in the presence of a large assembly. Similar ceremonies were observed in other parts of the State.

The reports from Rajputana show that nowhere in the Empire was the occasion more zealously celebrated. At Udaipur, the capital of Mewar, the Royal Proclamation was read in the Victoria Hall in the presence of the principal State officials and residents of the city, and a royal salute was fired. The day was observed as a general holiday, the poor were fed, and eleven prisoners were released. At Jaipur, the Proclamation was read by the Secretary of the Council at a durbar in the Sarbatta Palace, and a royal salute was fired from the Nahargarh Palace. At Jodhpur 101 prisoners were released on the firing of the salute. In Bundi, in addition to other observances, prayers for Their Majesties were offered up by Hindus in their temples, and Muhammadans in their mosques. There were general rejoicings throughout Bikaner, alms were given to the poor, the fort and city of Bikaner were illuminated, and a durbar was held, the authority of the Maharaja, who was at Delhi, being symbolised, according to the Rajputana custom, by his sword and shield, placed on the *gadi*. The Maharao of Kota, in honour of the occasion, remitted all arrears of land revenue outstanding up to the end of 1899–1900, the arrears of that year alone amounting to Rs. 15,92,000. Elaborate festivities were organised in Kishangarh, including a durbar in the Phul Mahal Palace, illuminations of the capital and suburbs, and a Coronation fair, at which there were nautches, dramatic performances, and war dances. The celebrations at Dungarpur were attended by about a thousand Bhils from the interior,

D'Cruz, photo. Walker & Boutall Ph. Sc.

H. H. The Maharaja of Travancore,
G.C.S.I., G.C.I.E.

who sang and danced after their own primitive fashion; 600 poor were fed, thirty-six prisoners were released, it being carefully explained to them that this clemency was owing to His Majesty's Coronation, and a durbar was held, at which the Proclamation was read, and poems in Sanskrit and Gujarati recited in praise of His Majesty and the British Raj. Similar rejoicings took place throughout the districts of Ajmer-Merwara, and in the States of Alwar, Banswara, Bharatpur, Dholpur, Jaisalmer, Jhalawar, Karauli, Partabgarh, Shahpura, Sirohi and Tonk.

At the Indore Residency, the head-quarters of the Central India Agency, a durbar was held in the absence of the Agent to the Governor-General by one of his Assistants. Congratulatory addresses were received, and 215 prisoners were released from the Agency jail.

The reports from Gwalior mention the firing of royal salutes, the closing of public offices from January 1st to January 4th, and the release of fifty prisoners from the State jails. In the State of Indore, arrears of land revenue amounting to upwards of 55 lakhs of rupees, and over 17 lakhs of outstanding debts due by traders were remitted; eighty-one prisoners were released, the Palace at the capital and other buildings were illuminated, and the foundation stone of a Town Hall in Indore city was laid. In Bhopal, a royal salute was fired from the fort, the Royal Proclamation was read at a public durbar, offices were closed for four days, and the poor were fed. Similar celebrations are reported from other States of Central India.

The Coronation was celebrated throughout Travancore on January 1st; and in several towns permanent memorials of the event were started. It is estimated that a million people were fed in the State in honour of the occasion. At a durbar at Trivandrum, the capital, the Royal Proclamation was read in English and in Malayalam. Entertainments were provided for 3500 school boys and for 2000 school girls; who sang songs and recited *slokas*, praying for the long life and prosperity of Their Majesties, and His Highness the Maharaja.

In Cochin, the Coronation was celebrated at all important towns. At Ernakulam, the capital, the Royal Proclamation was read in durbar: nearly 40,000 of the poor were fed; there were boat races and illuminations, and prayers for Their Majesties were offered in the temples and mosques, and in the Roman Catholic and Syrian churches. In this State, Christians of different denominations form about one-fourth of the population. At Chittur, there was a procession through the town, headed by five elephants carrying portraits of Their Majesties, with the sepoys of the Nair Brigade as escort, and the foundation stone was laid of a Hall which is being erected in honour of the event.

At Kolhapur, a durbar was held at the Residency, which was attended by all those Sardars and State officials who had not gone with the Maharaja to Delhi, the State battery fired a royal salute, money was distributed among the poor, and public buildings were illuminated.

At the capital of Cutch, the Royal Proclamation was read at a public meeting in the Alfred High School, and at a parade of the British Indian troops cantoned at Bhuj. Khan Bahadur Pestonji Sorabji Bhujwalla, in honour of the Coronation, had undertaken to build a school-house in the Bhuj Sadr Bazar, and the foundation stone was laid on January 1st. In the Khairpur State, school children and the poor were fed at the capital and elsewhere. A durbar was held at the capital of Junagadh, a treat was provided for 2500 school children, the poor were fed, and the Palace and other public buildings were illuminated. By order of the Thakur Sahib of Bhavnagar, a durbar was held in the Moti Bagh Palace at his capital, the poor were fed, and 15,000 school children were feasted. At the capital of Cambay, the occasion will be commemorated by the laying out of an "Edward VII. Coronation garden." A durbar was held at the Fort of Janjira, at which the increase of the Nawab's dynastic salute was announced; and, in addition to the distribution of food to the poor, illuminations, etc., portraits of Their Majesties were given to the school children.

In the State of Patiala, durbars were held on January 1st, at the capital and at the chief towns of the five districts, at which the Royal Proclamation was read, and addresses were delivered, the speakers dwelling on the blessings of English rule, and on the loyalty of the Maharaja and people of Patiala. Imperial salutes of 101 guns were fired from the forts of Patiala, Bhatinda, and Kanaud. A large number of poor men and *pardanishin* women were fed at the State expense;

and many prisoners were released, money being given to take them to their homes. The capital was illuminated, and bonfires were lit on the hills. Special mention must also be made of the liberal measures of relief and assistance granted by the Patiala State, in honour of the Coronation, to the distressed cultivators in the Narnaul ilaqua, who have suffered greatly from long continued scarcity. Arrears of revenue to the amount of 3¾ lakhs were remitted; and an expenditure of two lakhs was sanctioned for the construction of a good road from Narnaul to Charkhi Dadri.

In Bahawalpur, the Royal Proclamation was read at a durbar held on January 1st, 1903, in the Municipal Hall of the capital, in the presence of a large assembly. All public offices were closed from January 1st to January 8th; food was distributed among the poor, and in the jails; twenty-five prisoners were released, and as many more were granted partial remissions of sentences; sweetmeats were distributed among school boys; and in all temples and mosques throughout Bahawalpur prayers were offered for the long life and welfare of the King-Emperor and the Royal Family.

At Sangrur, the capital of the Jind State, a durbar was held in the State Diwan-Khana on January 1st, 1903, at which the Royal Proclamation was read; prayers for the Royal Family were offered in the temples; Sangrur and the chief towns in the State were illuminated; twenty-one prisoners were released; and fines amounting to Rs. 1,097 and debts to the State amounting to 2¼ lakhs were remitted.

At the capital of Nabha the Royal Proclamation was read at a durbar, twenty-seven prisoners were released, and the city was illuminated, as were other towns in the State. The poor were fed for three days at the capital, and for one day in each of the districts. Khilats were conferred on the officials who went with the Raja to Delhi, and they were all granted six weeks' pay.

At Faridkot, in addition to prayers for the King-Emperor and the Royal Family, supplication was thoughtfully made for the success of the Viceroy, as well as for the Punjab Government. Fifty-one prisoners were released from the Faridkot jail.

The Nawab of Loharu in honour of the Coronation opened an

English charitable dispensary, the first institution of the kind ever established in his State.

In Rampur, the Nawab celebrated the Coronation by remitting nearly two lakhs of his revenue demand, and by releasing a number of prisoners from jail.

By order of the Maharaja of Kuch Behar, a durbar was held in his palace, on January 1st, 1903, to which all the officers of the State, then at the capital, were invited, as well as the Rajguns, Pundits, leading Jotedars and merchants. A proclamation issued by the Maharaja was read, after which the band in front of the Durbar Hall played the national anthem, and a royal salute of 101 guns was fired.

At Khatmandu, the capital of Nepal, a royal salute was fired. The far off Shan States in Burma all celebrated the occasion in their own way; and in the Chin Hills the bonfires that were lit on every prominent peak for over a hundred miles are said to have created a great impression.

The Political Agent in the Persian Gulf reported that January 1st was observed as a public holiday at the Residency and by British subjects at Bushire. The leading Persian officials and merchants, and British Indian subjects at Bunder Abbas offered their congratulations to the British Vice-Consul, and the Deputy-Governor dined at the Vice-Consulate. At Maskat, the flag-staffs at the various consulates were dressed; a salute of 101 guns was fired by order of the Sultan, who afterwards paid a complimentary visit to the British Agency, and the shops of British subjects were illuminated. His Highness the Sultan sent the following telegram to His Excellency the Viceroy at Delhi: "I beg Your Excellency will accept for yourself and convey to His Majesty the King my heartfelt congratulations on this august occasion." A telegram conveying the loyal congratulations of the Hindu community at Maskat was despatched to the Political Agent, who was at that time at Delhi. At Meshed, the head-quarters of His Majesty's Consul-General and Agent of the Governor-General for Khorasan and Seistan, the Coronation had been officially commemorated in August 1902; but on January 1st, 1903, a dinner was given at the Consulate to the European community, and 120 British Indians, Afghans and

Persians were entertained at the native Attaché's house, where the Consul-General made a speech, in which he referred to the Delhi Durbar, and—Abdulla Khan, the Amir of Afghanistan's Agent, being present—to the strong friendship existing between that ruler and His Majesty's Government.

In Turkish Arabia, at Baghdad and Kerbela, the residences of His Majesty's Consular representatives and of the leading British subjects were all illuminated, and the day was observed as a general holiday. At both places also the Consuls of foreign powers were entertained by their British colleagues.

The result of all these celebrations, so unanimous and so widespread, was that there was scarcely a hamlet in the remotest parts of the Indian Empire to which the news of the Delhi ceremonial and the consciousness of the event that it commemorated did not penetrate. As the fortunate visitors at Delhi returned to their homes, they were overwhelmed with questions as to the wonderful scenes that they had witnessed: and in some places, notably at Dacca, the ancient capital of Bengal, so greatly was the popular imagination stirred that the inhabitants were not satisfied until they had organised a local reproduction of the Delhi Durbar, with elephant procession, high officials, and native Chiefs all included. In many parts of India the subject retained its interest for months, and an officer returning a year later to his charge in the United Provinces reported that it was still the main topic of conversation in his district. It would be safe to assert that no incident has ever occurred in the history of India which was brought more vividly home to the minds of so large a proportion of its 300,000,000 inhabitants.

CHAPTER XII

CONCLUSION

The closing scenes of the Delhi celebrations have still to be recorded. On Friday, January 9th, 1903, the eve of the Viceroy's departure, an evening party was given in the viceregal tents to which all the ruling Chiefs were invited, as well as a large number of high officials and distinguished visitors to Delhi. It has already been explained that one of the objects of this gathering was to provide an opportunity for the personal meetings between the Viceroy and the Chiefs, which, under ordinary conditions, would have been afforded by their visits to His Excellency, and his return visits to all entitled to this privilege. Such visits, it was found, would have encroached so much on the limited time at the Viceroy's disposal as to be practically impossible within the short space of ten days. Indeed it was calculated that had the exchange of visits taken place in the case of all the Chiefs entitled to it, another ten days would have been required for the purpose—so great were the distances that would have had to be traversed between the different camps, and so large the number of ruling Chiefs to visit and be visited. There would have had to be no fewer than 160 of these formal exchanges of civility. In excusing himself from his share in these ceremonial courtesies, which were the less necessary in the case of a Viceroy who had already during the four years for which he had been in India exchanged them with almost every one of the ruling Princes, Lord Curzon was careful to absolve them also from the corresponding obligation of paying a state call upon him. In these circumstances the farewell party at the viceregal camp provided a happy means of filling

H.H. The Raja of Cochin.
G.C.S.I.

the gap; while the English and foreign guests of the Indian Government who, for the most part, had only seen the ruling Chiefs at state celebrations, were also enabled by this arrangement to meet them at a less formal gathering.

This assembly, which was held in the magnificent reception tents of the viceregal camp, was in many respects quite unique. Never before had almost all the great potentates in India, Rajputs, Pathans, Mahrattas, Arabs, and Shans, been collected together in one apartment. The spectacle was most brilliant as the Chiefs, in the full dress costumes of their respective nationalities, for the most part bedecked with a profusion of jewels, moved about with their attendant nobles amid the crowd of European ladies in full toilette and officers in uniform.

Not the least interesting feature of the evening was the brief but impressive ceremony at which His Royal Highness the Duke of Connaught, as Great Master of the Most Honourable Order of the Bath, invested the Nizam of Hyderabad with the Grand Cross of that Order; also Major-General Edward Locke Elliot, Inspector-General of Cavalry, and Major-General Charles Comyn Egerton, then commanding the Punjab Frontier Force and Frontier District, with the insignia of Knights of the Order. His Royal Highness next invested His Highness the Maharaja of Kolhapur as a Knight Grand Commander of the Royal Victorian Order, and presented gold medals to certain of the Chiefs who had attended the Coronation in London in 1902; these were Their Highnesses the Maharajas of Kolhapur, Idar, and Kuch Behar. His Highness the Aga Khan also received his medal on this occasion. At the close of this ceremony His Excellency the Viceroy proceeded by the King-Emperor's command to confer the honour of Knighthood on the Hon. Mr. William Ovens Clark, Chief Judge of the Punjab Chief Court; the Hon. Mr. Montagu Cornish Turner, President of the Bengal Chamber of Commerce; Lieutenant-Colonel James Lewis Walker, late Commandant of the 2nd Punjab Rifle Volunteers; and Mr. George Watt, Director of the Exhibition of Indian Arts.

On the following morning, Saturday, January 10th, His Excellency the Viceroy and Their Royal Highnesses the Duke and Duchess of Connaught left Delhi, Lord Curzon proceeding upon tour, and Their

Royal Highnesses travelling to Peshawar. The departure was public, and the proceedings at the railway station were precisely similar to those of the day of arrival. The route from the viceregal camp to the railway station was lined with troops; Lansdowne Road to its junction with Alipur Road, by the Infantry of the Viceroy's Escort, and the rest of the way, along the Alipur and Kudsia Roads, through the Mori Gate, over the Dufferin Bridge and along Queen's Road, by the Infantry of the 2nd Division, the bands of the same Division being posted at different points on the route. A guard of honour of the 2nd battalion, Munster Fusiliers, with the regimental band, was drawn up in front of the viceregal reception tents. At 10-45 A.M. the Viceroy and the Duchess of Connaught in one carriage, followed by the Duke of Connaught and Lady Curzon in another, started for the railway station, accompanied by their staffs and escorted by the Imperial Cadet Corps, the Viceroy's Body-guard and the Cavalry of the viceregal escort, a royal salute of 31 guns being fired by a field battery posted on the Ridge. Outside the station, a guard of honour of the Northamptonshire Regiment, posted there with the band, presented arms as His Excellency and Their Royal Highnesses entered the station; and as they reached the platform the band of the Norfolk Regiment played the national anthem.

All the high officials, including the Governors of Madras and Bombay, the Commander-in-Chief, the Lieutenant-Governors and other heads of administrations, as well as, with one or two exceptions caused by illness, all the ruling Chiefs who had attended the Durbar, and the Representatives of foreign States, had assembled at the station. Military officers and civil officials entitled to wear uniform were in full dress, and the Indian Princes again and for the last time at Delhi wore their robes of state.

First to leave, by special train for Peshawar, were Their Royal Highnesses the Duke and Duchess of Connaught. His Royal Highness, before departing, shook hands with the ruling Chiefs and high officials present, and then, having bidden farewell to the Viceroy and Lady Curzon, entered his carriage, the band playing the national anthem, and a battery on the Fort ramparts firing a royal salute as the train steamed away.

His Excellency the Viceroy, who was to start a quarter of an hour later in the opposite direction, now bade farewell to each of the ruling Chiefs, and to the high officials, as well as to the officers and members of the Imperial Cadet Corps. As His Excellency's train left the platform, the band again played the national anthem, a second royal salute was fired and three hearty cheers for His Excellency were given by all those present.

The eventful fortnight, during which the Coronation of His Majesty the King-Emperor had been celebrated with such imposing magnificence and amid such striking demonstrations of loyalty—echoed, as we have seen, throughout the length and breadth of India—had come to an end, and all that now remained was for the vast army of visitors both European and Indian, to disperse as quickly as possible, and for hard-worked officials to clear away the camps and restore Delhi to its normal condition.

On the eve of the Viceroy's departure the following official order was issued and circulated:

"His Excellency the Viceroy in leaving desires to take the opportunity of thanking all officers, both military and civil, who have been engaged in organising or in carrying out the series of events connected with the Coronation Durbar and rejoicings, for the conspicuous zeal, energy, and devotion with which they have performed their duties, and to congratulate them upon the complete success that has attended their labours. His Royal Highness the Duke of Connaught has graciously requested that his name may be associated with this message of felicitation."

A further appreciation of the services rendered by the staff of civil and military officers, to whose energy and foresight must be ascribed the successful management of this great assemblage, was recorded in a despatch, dated May 7th, 1903, to the Secretary of State, in which the Government of India dealt fully with the political aspects and effects of the Delhi commemoration. The despatch is printed among the papers in the Appendix, and may be left to speak for itself on these all important features of the Durbar. Special mention is there made of the work of the Central and Executive Committees, and in particular of Sir Hugh Barnes and Major-General Henry of the former, and of Major H. Hudson and Captain A. D. Bannerman of the latter. Sir Hugh Barnes, now Lieutenant-Governor of Burma, was also in charge of all matters of ceremonial; and the thoroughness of his preparations, the laborious attention paid even to the minutest detail, and the vigilance which provided against every possible *contretemps*, were apparent to all observers when each successive spectacle equalled its predecessor as a triumph of organisation. Sir Hugh Barnes was ably assisted in his most arduous task by a large staff of political officers from all parts of India, whose names are given in Appendix VI. These officers acted as intermediaries between Sir Hugh Barnes and the authorities of the Durbar organisation, on the one hand, and the Chiefs and local administrations with whom they were connected, on the other. Each of them had to pay a daily visit to the camp of the Chief or Chiefs for whom he was responsible, and this might be as much as seven miles away; he had to rehearse and attend all official ceremonies, to receive the Chiefs with due ceremony on arrival and departure, and whenever they went forth in state; and generally to look after everything that conduced to their comfort and dignity. The construction and management of the camps of the ruling Chiefs were not the least of the duties committed to their charge, and in many cases their difficulties were not a little increased by the mutual jealousies so often included among the cherished traditions of Indian courts, and apt to be inflamed by propinquity, or the recriminations of followers over rights of way, access to wells, and other small but troublesome matters.

Very onerous, too, was the burden of work and anxiety imposed on the local and provincial authorities who were responsible for the maintenance of public order, the proper working of police and sanitary regulations, the control of communications both within the camp and with other parts of India; and on the special officers appointed to supervise the commissariat, posts and telegraphs, public health, lighting, water supply, etc. Among those who subsequently received the thanks of Government for their services during an exceptionally trying time were Mr. Gordon Walker, the Commissioner, and Major M. W. Douglas,

H. H. The Thakar Sahib of Morvi.
G.C.I.E.

the Deputy Commissioner of Delhi, who were also active members of the Central and Executive Committees; Colonel H. F. Lyons Montgomery, Director of Supply and Transport; Lieutenant-Colonel C. J. Bamber, Sanitary Commissioner; Lieutenant-Colonel Thornhill, Executive Sanitary Officer; Rai Bahadur Ganga Ram, in charge of Public Works; Rai Bahadur Daulat Ram, Superintendent of the Post Offices; Mr. O. Lees, of the Telegraph Department; and Mr. C. Brown, Inspector-General of Police in the Punjab.

The Police force employed on all duties connected with the Durbar included 36 British officers, 165 Inspectors and Deputy Inspectors, European and Native, and 3661 Sergeants and constables. In the management of the traffic on roads, which were at all times crowded with vehicles and horsemen, and always liable to be blocked by a string of camels, an elephant, or a lumbering train of bullock carts; in the arrangements for parking carriages at the Amphitheatre, in the Fort, outside the Polo Club, and on the night of the firework display; in the supremely exacting task of directing the dispersal of immense crowds at the termination of each ceremony and gathering, as well as in the prevention of crime, the Police, most ably handled by Mr. C. Brown and the officers under him, did excellent work. The success of the police arrangements was all the more remarkable when it is remembered that the majority of the constables who were drafted into Delhi had spent their lives in country districts and had no previous experience of the work that they were now expected to perform. The almost total absence of crime during the fortnight was largely due to the vigilance of the special detective agency under Mr. H. L. Kemball, of the Thagi and Dakaiti Department, which had under careful observation every notorious thief and doubtful character in Delhi, and stopped on the railway line a large number of others who were converging from all parts of India.

For the better management of the vast encampment, and to provide a means of checking certain inconveniences and dangers to public order and comfort, which are not offences under the ordinary law of India, legislative sanction was sought and obtained for a special measure, entered in the Punjab statutes as the Delhi Durbar Police Act, 1902.

Colonel H. B. Thornhill was appointed special magistrate in the Camp, and the more serious cases which came under the cognisance of the police were taken before him. In order that minor offences might be promptly dealt with, the Punjab Government invested a number of officers with the powers of a magistrate of the first class, and, under section 260 of the Criminal Procedure Code, with power to try cases summarily. How light was the work imposed upon them may be seen from the despatch, already quoted, that is printed in Appendix III to this volume.

The Postal arrangements for the Durbar camps were carried out on a very elaborate scale by Rai Bahadur Daulat Ram. In all, twenty-seven post offices were opened in connection with the Durbar, with a staff which comprised a chief superintendent, 7 superintendents, 5 inspectors, 25 postmasters, 181 deputy postmasters, assistant postmasters and clerks, 145 postmen, 45 packers, 30 cycle and orderly peons, 12 overseers, and 73 menials. The enquiry bureau at the Durbar head office had a most onerous charge. It collected the names and addresses of the thousands of visitors to Delhi, received and circulated instructions for the proper delivery of letters, etc., and performed all the functions of the enquiry branch in a dead letter office. Among the clerks employed in it were men who could read almost every known vernacular used in the Indian Empire, from Kashmiri to Burmese, to say nothing of Persian and various foreign languages, and the problems that it was called upon to solve were often curiously intricate. It is estimated that the entire volume of extra unregistered correspondence delivered at Delhi, which may be differentiated as being due to the holding of the Durbar, amounted to 2½ million articles. The extra number of parcels, value-payable packets, and registered articles received was upwards of 76,000, while the extra number of money orders issued was about 28,000, the value being Rs. 6,68,500. The total postal revenue attributed to the Durbar shows a considerable excess over the additional expenditure incurred.

Timely provision had been made by the Indian Telegraph Department to meet the pressure of abnormal traffic. Supplemental wires were erected between Delhi and Bombay, Karachi, Sukkur,

Lahore, Allahabad, Cawnpore, and Calcutta. Delhi was already provided with five permanent telegraph offices; but, for the convenience of visitors and officials at the Durbar, local offices were also opened at the central camp, the Viceroy's camp, the Consular and Press camp, Maiden's Hotel (No. 1, Visitors' camp), Badli supply depôt, central supply depôt, Azadpur, Bombay Chiefs' camp, Central India Chiefs' camp, Mysore camp, and Rajputana Chiefs' camp, these eleven offices all working into and being controlled by a large office in the central camp. A network of telephone wires was also spread over the camps, and proved invaluable in facilitating and expediting the work of the Durbar officials. Altogether over 5000 miles of wire were erected throughout India in connection with the telegraphic requirements of the Durbar. Military telegraphists were largely employed as signallers, and military cyclists as orderlies for the delivery of telegrams. In the central camp telegraph office, one wing was entirely devoted to working by automatic instruments, which, more than anything else, enabled the department to cope with the enormous volume of traffic set in motion by the enterprise of the newspaper press. Fifty special correspondents were constantly handing in voluminous messages; and their requirements were met in every case with a promptitude that gave general satisfaction. Officials and the public at large had equal reason to be satisfied with the telegraphic service; and the Viceroy, writing to Mr. F. Maclean, the Director-General, congratulated him on "the splendid work done by the department under circumstances of wholly unprecedented strain."

Special mention must also be made of the Durbar light railway, a 2′ 6″ gauge steam tramway that was laid between the principal points of the great encampment. The railway consisted of a main line laid from near the Kashmir gate to the polo ground, a distance of four miles, with two branches, one to the Amphitheatre and the other to the review ground. The total length of single track laid was 11.23 miles, and during the Durbar period trains were run at intervals of 15 minutes throughout the day from 8 A.M. till 10 P.M., the total number of passengers carried being over 100,000. The line was constructed by Captain Hepper, of the Royal Engineers, and was worked by a small staff of officers belonging to the same corps.

The principal honours conferred, in addition to the promotions in the Order of the Bath which are mentioned in the present chapter, have been recorded in the account of the Investiture held by the Grand Master of the Orders of the Star of India and Indian Empire in the Diwan-i Am. Other distinctions, favours, and concessions which were announced on the day of the Durbar will be found in the Appendix of official papers, together with those specially conferred at a later date in recognition of services rendered in connection with the organisation and management of the Coronation celebrations.

By order of His Majesty the King-Emperor a silver medal was struck in honour of the Coronation Durbar, and was distributed by the Viceroy to the officers on special duty in connection with the Durbar, to the official guests of Government who were present, and to representative officers and men of the Army present at Delhi who were selected by the Commander-in-Chief. The Viceroy, the Duke of Connaught, the ruling Chiefs, and certain high officials received reproductions of the medal in gold. The total number distributed was about 2500, and the medal is, by His Majesty's direction, to take precedence of all war medals and to be worn immediately on the left of the English Coronation Medal. The crowned head of the King-Emperor on the obverse of the medal was copied from that designed for the coinage of India and the British Colonies, while the reverse bore the following legend in Persian:

بفضل مالكِ مُلك ادوردِ سابع قيصرِ هند

Transliterated into English characters this reads "Ba faṣl-i málik-i mulk Edward-i sábi' Kaisar-i Hind;" that is to say—"By the grace of the King of the Country, Edward VII., Emperor of India." This, it should be explained, is an *Abjad Toghra*, or chronogram, in which the numerical values conventionally assigned to each letter give, when added together, a date, in this case A.D. 1901, the year of His Majesty's succession. Chronograms of this description abound in Arabic, Persian, and Indian literature; and, as a method of recording dates, they have often been made use of by Oriental historians.

The chronogram adopted on this occasion was devised by Colonel

The Delhi Durbar Medal

Ranking, I.M.S., Secretary to the Board of Examiners. It is written in the Royal Turkish or Rumi character, which was considered more suitable than the Ajami or Persian; and, as will be seen from the enlarged copy on the cover of this book, is a fine example of Oriental calligraphy. The whole design for the reverse of the medal was prepared in Srinagar by Rahat Ju, a Kashmiri seal engraver, under the personal supervision of Mr. Dane, then Resident in Kashmir, who was responsible for the original suggestion of a chronogram. The floral wreath shows the rose, thistle, shamrock, and lotus intertwined.

The breaking up of the camps, after the Viceroy's departure from Delhi, was an affair of a few days. Tents were struck, the troops returned to their winter quarters, the Princes and their retinues scattered to every part of the Indian Empire, and every train that left Delhi bore away more than its full complement of passengers. In less than a month the Amphitheatre had been stripped, and solitary chimneys left standing where they had been built, to be dissolved by the summer rains, were almost the only surviving traces of the great encampment that had covered so many square miles of ground; the elegant gardens that had taken months to prepare quickly reverted to wilderness, and the network of roads and railways that had been specially constructed for the use of a fortnight vanished from the scene. Over the greater part of the area has since been resumed the sway of the humble cultivator and his plough. It is likely, however, that the historic arena of the two Imperial Durbars of 1877 and 1903 will receive a permanent commemoration. For it is the intention of the Viceroy, if possible, to convert it into a garden, and to erect a lofty pillar, with befitting inscriptions, on the site of these two great events.

Upon the vast crowd of spectators who dispersed to all quarters of the world the impression created by the grandeur and solemnity of the scenes in which they had taken part and by a sense, to which the slowest imagination must have thrilled, of the deep-seated and far-reaching forces that were symbolised thereby, was at once profound and indescribable. The whole fabric of the British Empire in India, from its foundation to its topmost pinnacle, seemed to be revealed through the pageantry of the Delhi ceremonies, as in a vision. Justice and toleration were its bases; loyalty and contentment the superstructure that had slowly but surely risen upon them.

Great Empires have been raised in Asia, have flourished and decayed. Medes and Parthians, Turks and Moghuls, have ruled over immense dominions which in turn have been shattered and broken in pieces. Ancient Delhi itself is an epitome of more than one such chapter in the history of the past. To-day the Indian Empire stands forth as the heir of these vanished traditions, strong and unchallenged, no more immune from danger than were its predecessors, but possessing sources of vitality that were denied to them. Not the least of these, indeed by far the greatest of all, is loyalty to a common Sovereign, alien, it may be, in race (as nearly all the great monarchs of India have been) to the majority of the peoples over whom he is called upon to rule, but consecrated in the allegiance and affections of all by the memory of two hundred years of British dominion and by the personal devotion inspired by the Royal House. That India is not behind the rest of the Empire in this loyalty and devotion was the great lesson of the Imperial Durbar. It showed to the world that unity has at last been achieved among the millions of India, and that the mysterious influence that has accomplished this result is no other than the British Crown. It left upon British and Indians alike the impression, amounting to a conviction, that this is no accidental or fleeting phenomenon, but that it is preordained and will endure.

General View of the Imperial Coronation Durbar, Jan. 1st 1903.

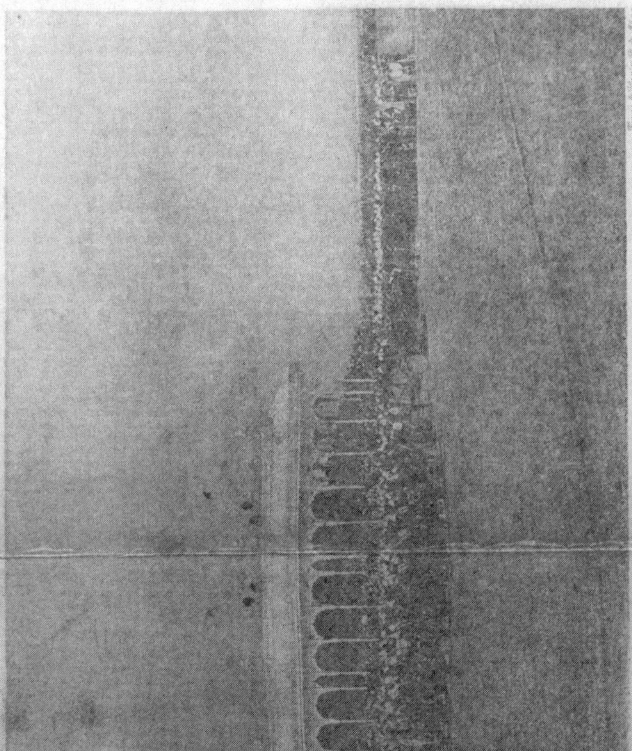

APPENDICES

APPENDIX I

PROCEEDINGS OF THE COUNCIL OF THE GOVERNOR-GENERAL OF INDIA, ASSEMBLED FOR THE PURPOSE OF MAKING LAWS AND REGULATIONS.

SPEECHES BY HIS EXCELLENCY THE VICEROY.

ON the meeting of the Council at the Viceregal Lodge, Simla, on Friday, September 5th, 1902, before the business of the Council was proceeded with, His Excellency THE PRESIDENT addressed the Honourable Members as follows:

"I desire to take advantage of the present occasion to say a few words about the great function, or combination of functions, at Delhi, which will fill so large a part of our attention during the next few months, and which will bring together so immense, and probably unprecedented, a concourse of the Indian peoples at the old Moghul capital in January next. His Majesty the King has already been happily crowned in England; and he is as much already our King and Emperor as he was the day after the death of the late Queen-Empress. No ceremony can increase his titles or add to the legality of his position. Why, then, it may be asked, should we have in India a celebration of his Coronation at all? Public opinion has, I think, already answered this question to its own satisfaction. But perhaps I may also be permitted to contribute a few words to the reply. To the East there is nothing strange, but something familiar and even sacred, in the practice that brings Sovereigns into communion with their people in a ceremony of public solemnity and rejoicing, after they have succeeded to their high estate. Every Sovereign of India, or of parts of India, did it in the old days. Every Chief in India—the illustration may even be carried as far as the titled noblemen and zamindars—does it now; and the installation durbar is an accepted and acceptable feature of ceremonial life from one end of the country to the other. If this is so in all the grades of our social hierarchy, how much more important and desirable it is that it should obtain in the highest. I find, for my part, in such a ceremony much more than a mere official recognition of the fact that one monarch has died and another succeeded. To millions of the people in their remote and contracted lives this can make but little difference. But the community of interest between a Sovereign and his people—to which such a function testifies, and which it serves to keep alive—is most vital and most important. Society in all ages has sought a head to whom it has been prepared to pay reverence, and kingship is the popular form that has

2 H

been assumed by this almost universal instinct. But it is in proportion as the superiority thus willingly acknowledged by the subject ceases to be merely official and titular, and as the King becomes the representative as well as the figure-head of his people, that the relationship is of value to both of them. The life and vigour of a nation are summed up before the world in the person of its Sovereign. He it is who symbolises its unity, and speaks for it in the gate. Here in India, it is for the first time under the British Crown that this unity has been attained, and that the entire Continent has acknowledged a single ruler. The political force and the moral grandeur of the nation are indisputably increased by this form of cohesion, and both are raised in the estimation of the world by a demonstration of its reality. There is another point of view from which I regard such a display as having far more than a superficial value. In all our various divisions in this country—divisions of race and class and custom and creed—the one thing that holds us together, and subordinates the things that make for separation to the compelling force of union, is loyalty to a common head, membership of the same body politic, fellow-citizenship of the same Empire. The more we realise this, the happier will be our individual lives, and the more assured our national destinies. It is, therefore, as an act of supreme public solemnity, demonstrating to ourselves our union and to the world our strength, that I regard the Delhi ceremonial, and certainly as no mere pageant, intended to dazzle the senses for a few hours or days, and then to be forgotten. To my mind Lord Lytton, who was the first in British times to inaugurate such an Imperial Durbar as we propose to hold, though in different circumstances and on a smaller scale, set an example characterised both by statesmanship and imagination. I have not a doubt that much good flowed from the Imperial Assemblage of January 1st, 1877; and, under the blessing of Providence, I firmly believe that similar and even larger results will follow from the ceremony of January 1st, 1903.

"Of course the occasion would be made both more solemn and more historic if the King-Emperor were able to be present in person and could place the Crown of all the Indias upon his own brow. Long ago, when we were first formulating our plans, I ventured to present this aspect of the case to His Majesty. The idea was most agreeable to him, and he would have greatly rejoiced to be able to carry it out. His love for this country has always been great, and I venture to affirm that he is as proud to be the first Emperor of all India, as the late Queen Victoria was to be its first Empress. But the duties of State are too absorbing to permit His Majesty to be absent from England for so many weeks as would have been required, and he was compelled to desist from gratifying a wish that would otherwise have had for him the greatest attractions. In these circumstances, the news will be received with delight that His Majesty has deputed his brother, the Duke of Connaught, to represent the Royal Family at the approaching Durbar. The presence of the Duke and Duchess, who have already spent so many happy years in this country, and who are so universally loved by all classes of the people, will lend to our proceedings a distinction that they would otherwise have lacked, and will bring home more directly to all India the vivid personal interest of the Sovereign. We shall feel that the King is in a certain sense with us in the person of his brother, and that, as it was not in his power either to attend himself, or to depute the Heir-Apparent, whom we all hope to welcome at a later date, His Majesty has taken the best means of testifying to India his profound sympathy and regard.

"There is another point of view from which I think that such a gathering as that which will take place at Delhi will be of value. The weak spot of India is what I may call its watertight compartment system. Each Province, each Native State, is more or less shut off by solid bulkheads, even from its neighbour. The spread of railways and the relaxation of social restrictions are tending to break these down. But they are still very strong. Princes who live in the South have rarely, if ever, in their lives, seen or visited the States of the North. Perhaps among the latter there are Chiefs who have rarely left their homes. It cannot but be a good thing that they should meet and get to know each other and exchange ideas: and yet no opportunity of meeting on a large scale is possible, unless it be afforded by a State occasion such as this. If we look at the Continent of Europe, we shall see what immense strides have been made in the development of common interests and in the cause of peace, since the European rulers have taken to meeting each other on important occasions. Where they used in the old days to set their armies in motion upon the slightest breath of suspicion, they now have a talk and exchange toasts at official banquets. Greece did the same thing in ancient times, and in a way peculiar to herself: for it cannot be doubted that the national spirit, which held all those little States together and enabled them to stand up against the greatest military empires of the old world, was largely bred and nurtured at the Pan-Hellenic gatherings known as the Olympic Games.

"Again, in this country I think that it is an equal benefit to the British administrators from different Provinces to meet. There is many a man in Madras who has never seen the Punjab, or even in Bombay who is wholly ignorant of Bengal. The Viceroy is almost the only man in India who has the chance of knowing the whole country and of applying the comparative test. People are apt to complain of uniformity in government. I can assure them that the differentiations of system and plan in India are amazing. I am not the person to wish to blot them out; but I do say confidently that an occasion like the Delhi Durbar, when soldiers and civilians from all parts of India will meet, not for a few hours or a day, but for a fortnight, and can compare notes and exchange ideas with each other, will be fraught with incalculable advantage both to the participants and to the administration which they serve.

"These appear to me, apart from the act of homage to the Sovereign, to be the principal benefits that will accrue to India as a whole from the Durbar. I have, as is known, endeavoured still further to utilise the opportunity in a practical spirit by arranging for a great Exhibition of Indian Art Manufactures to be held at Delhi at the same time. I confidently assure the public that they will be greatly astonished at the range, the variety and the beauty of this Exhibition. Whether it is true that the old Indian arts are being killed by European competition—a charge that is frequently brought by those who do not make the smallest effort to keep them alive themselves—or whether they are perishing from this apathy, or whether India merely provides, as I suspect, an illustration of a world-wide law—the fact remains that the process of extinction has not been carried nearly so far as many suppose, and that the artificers still exist in India, even in these days of commercial ideals and debauched taste, who are capable of satisfying the demand for the artistic and beautiful and rare, if such a demand there be. I cannot pretend by a single Exhibition to create it; but if it already be in existence—as I cannot but think—though perhaps dormant and abashed, then we may do a good deal by an opportunity such as this to revive and stimulate it; for we shall, I hope, both advertise to the world what we are capable of turning out, and also—which is much more important—encourage the aptitudes and educate the taste of our own people.

"And now I wish to say a few words about an even more practical aspect of the case, viz., the charge that will thereby be imposed upon the revenues of India. I have seen statements made about this subject that have startled even my hardened mind. It seems to be quite a popular thing to allege in certain quarters that the Durbar is going to cost India at least a crore, while in one responsible organ I read that Lord Curzon was going to throw away upon senseless pomp and show a sum of two millions sterling. Of course, too, our old friend Nero, who is alleged to have fiddled while Rome burned, has often been brought out for my special delectation. Personally, I deprecate the tendency to apply to every act of State, great or small, the sordid test of its actual equivalent in pice, annas, and rupees. There are some things for which no expenditure can be too great, just as there are others for which none can be too small. But I quite recognise that these abstract considerations will not appeal to everybody, and that there is both seriousness and sincerity in the contention that, desirable and even necessary as the function may be, the public money should not be needlessly squandered upon it. This plea seems to me to be so reasonable that I propose to give to it the answer that it deserves.

"It emanates, I think, from two classes of persons—from those who think that no money ought to be spent at Delhi at all while parts of India are suffering from drought or scarcity, and from those who are anxious that, while some money is spent, it should not be too much. I will deal with the first class first.

"A few weeks ago it is true that we were in the greatest anxiety and trepidation as to what might be in store for us in Guzerat, in parts of the Dekkhan, in Ajmer, and in portions of the Central Provinces and the Punjab. But I can truthfully say that the past three weeks have been, on the whole, the happiest that I have spent since I came to India; for by the merciful and continuous fall of rain in those tracts where it was most needed we have, I believe, escaped all chance of real or widespread famine in the forthcoming winter; and though here and there we may be confronted with distress, yet nothing in the shape of a national calamity is to be feared. But even supposing that this rain had not fallen, or that I am all wrong in my prognostications now, does any one suppose for a moment that because we are going to expend a certain number of lakhs of rupees at Delhi, one penny less would have been devoted to the relief and sustenance of the destitute in other parts of India? At the beginning of the Famine of 1899, I gave the assurance on behalf of Government that not one rupee would be stinted or spared that could be devoted to the alleviation of distress and the saving of human life. That promise we faithfully fulfilled; and even if famine burst upon us now, or while the Durbar was proceeding, we should not take from the public purse a single anna that would otherwise be consecrated to the service of the poor. They have the first claim upon our consideration; and that claim we should regard it as an obligation of honour to discharge.

"Then there is the second class of critics, who recognise that the Durbar must cost something, but are apprehensive lest it should be run on too exorbitant a scale. I am old enough to remember that the same criticism was rife at the time of Lord Lytton's Assemblage in the autumn of 1876. Famine was at that time abroad in the land, and loud were the denunciations, both in the Indian Press and even in Parliament at home, of his alleged extravagance and folly. And yet I have seen calculations made by Lord Lytton which show that, when all recoveries had been made, the net cost to India of the Delhi Assemblage was only £50,000, and of the entire rejoicings throughout India, Delhi included, £100,000.

"In one respect we are in a somewhat different position now. The Assemblage of 1877 was an almost exclusively Official Assemblage. I have tried to gather at the impending Durbar representatives of all the leading classes of the community from every part of India. I want to make it a celebration not of officials alone but of the public. This means that we shall have at Delhi in the forthcoming winter larger camps, more guests, and, as a consequence, greater outlay than in 1877. Quite apart from our own arrangements, the improvement in communications and the social progress that have taken place in the last twenty-five years will bring together a much larger concourse of persons. Nearly every one would like to be present; and the number who will actually be present will be very large. All these features will tend to increase the scale of the proceedings.

"Notwithstanding these considerations, I desire to assure the public, who have a right to know, that the proposed arrangements are being run on strictly businesslike and economical lines. I remember hearing Lord Salisbury, in a speech at the Mansion House before I left England, eulogise our future Commander-in-Chief, Lord Kitchener, for his ability to run a campaign on commercial principles. I think that in respect of the Durbar we may lay a similar flattering unction to our souls. The whole of the buildings and structures at Delhi that are being erected for the special purposes of the gathering are being made of materials that will retain their value after their preliminary use, and will be offered for public sale. In many cases recoveries of from sixty to eighty per cent. of the initial outlay are thus expected. The tents, carriages and horses, which have had to be made or collected in such enormous numbers for the convenience of visitors, will be similarly disposed of; and here in many cases I expect that we shall retrieve a hundred per cent. of the value. The entire electric plant for lighting the camps and the Fort is part of the machinery that has been ordered by the Military Department for instituting the great experiment of ventilating and lighting the barracks in India by electricity. Down to the smallest detail, we are so arranging that the money will not be thrown away, but in some form or other will come back. Then I take another form of recovery. As we all know, railways are, for the most part, Government property in this country; and whether we work them ourselves or through others, the whole or a considerable proportion of the profits come into our hands. I think that the critics may be invited to pause and wait to see the traffic receipts of December, January and February next before they continue their lamentations. I shall be very much surprised if these returns do not put back into the pocket of Government the major portion of what it has spent. There are also the Postal and Telegraphic services, the profits of which pass into the Government chest, and from which we shall receive largely increased returns. Finally, I would invite those who are so fearful of an unremunerative outlay to open their eyes to what is going on, and has been going on, for months past, in all parts of India. I assert that hundreds of thousands of Indian workmen and artisans are receiving full employment and good wages in preparing for this Durbar. Go to the cotton-mills of Cawnpore, Jubbulpore and Lahore, where the tents are made; to the factories, where the harness and saddlery are turned out; to the carriage-builders, where the landaus and victorias are being built by the hundred; to the carpet factories, where the durries and rugs are being woven; to the furniture-makers, where the camp equipage is manufactured. Go to every Native State, where the durzis and embroiderers will be found working double time. Go to any town or even village in India where a native art-industry exists, and has perhaps hitherto languished, but where you will find the coppersmiths and silversmiths, the carvers in wood and ivory and stone, the enamellers and painters and lacquerers, hard at work. Go to all these places, and then form an opinion as to the effect upon Indian labour of the Delhi Durbar. Supposing we were to follow the advice of some of our friends and to issue a proclamation suspending the entire proceedings to-morrow, I predict that a cry of protest and of appeal would be heard from one end of the country to the other, and that, without benefiting a single individual, we should deprive the Indian artisan of one of the greatest opportunities that he has enjoyed for generations, and inflict upon him a cruel and senseless injury.

"I have thus argued that a large portion of the expenditure to be incurred at Delhi will be nominal only, and that we shall take back or give back to India with one hand what we expend with the other. Let me deal with the actual figures. In the Budget of last March we provided for an outlay of 26½ lakhs upon the Durbar. This is the sum that in the fertile imagination of some writers has been magnified to one crore, and even to two millions sterling. I do not include in this outlay the sum of 4 lakhs which have been devoted to the Arts Exhibition, because I do not suppose that any one will be found to argue that that is an expenditure of public money upon the Coronation. The greater part of it will be recovered; and in any year, Coronation or otherwise, it would have been a prudent and remunerative expenditure of the public money. Neither do I take the 8½ lakhs provided for the troops. For we should not, of course, have expended that sum in bringing so large a number of troops to Delhi for the Durbar alone. It is being expended in the main upon the great military manœuvres that are an inseparable feature of modern military training, and that will take place during the month preceding the Durbar, in the same way as the manœuvres held by Lord Dufferin in the same neighbourhood, independently either of Durbar or of Coronation, in the year 1886. There remain, then, the 26½ lakhs, supplemented by such local expenditure as may be imposed upon Local Governments by their preparations: and of the total sum, as I have pointed out, the greater part will most certainly be reimbursed. The actual net cost of the proceedings at Delhi it is, of course, impossible at this date to calculate or forecast, but I hope I have said enough to show that it will be almost immeasurably less than the dimensions which a too tropical imagination has allowed it to assume; and that a great State ceremonial will never have been conducted in India upon more economical lines.

"I cannot help thinking that the sensitiveness about expenditure here, which I hope that

I may have succeeded in allaying, has been to some extent fomented by the impression that prevailed till a little while ago that India might also be called upon to pay for a portion of the entertainment of the Indian visitors and Military Contingent, who recently proceeded to England to take part in the Coronation festivities there. This was a subject upon which the Government of India placed themselves some time ago in communication with the Home Government; and, as a sequel to this exchange of opinion, it was with pleasure that we heard that the Secretary of State had persuaded the Imperial Exchequer to assume the entire cost of all charges that had been incurred in England in connection with the Indian visitors. These include the entertainment of the Indian Chiefs and representatives, and of the Contingent representing the Army and Volunteers, as well as the entire cost of the India Office ceremony. The principle that each country should pay for its own guests is, in my opinion, incontestably right; and it will, I hope, be accepted and acted upon in the future.

"I have now said enough, I hope, to show that neither is Rome burning—on the contrary, I believe that she stands on the threshold of an era of great prosperity—nor, most certainly, is Nero fiddling. I do not indulge much in prophecy in India; and I cannot say what unforeseen vicissitudes, internal or external, may lie in store for us. But, humanly speaking, we need not anticipate anything that is likely, during the few months that intervene between now and January next, to prevent us from joining in the Delhi gathering with clear consciences and joyous hearts. It only now remains for us to endeavour to make our celebration in India not less successful than that which has just been carried through in England. A good many eyes in a good many parts of the globe will be directed upon Delhi in January next; and we shall have an opportunity, not merely of testifying the enthusiastic loyalty of India to the King-Emperor, in the presence of his brother, but also of demonstrating to the world that India is not sunk in torpor or stagnation, but is alive with an ever-expanding force and energy. That all India should approach these ceremonies with one heart, and mind, and voice is my most earnest prayer; and that those who cannot take part in them at Delhi should hold similar rejoicings and be similarly entertained in the neighbourhood of their own homes, it is our hope and desire to arrange.

"There is one small matter personal to myself, which I may perhaps be allowed to mention before I conclude, because it also has a wider bearing. I have seen it assumed in many quarters that as soon as the Durbar is over, and this anxiety has been removed, I am likely to resign my office and to flit away to England, in the pursuit of personal or political ambitions there. Indeed, I scarcely know how many times during the past two years similar stories have been flying about. Both the authors of these rumours and those who give credit to them do me an unconscious injustice in assuming that I could think of taking my hand off the plough before the end of the furrow is in sight. Not once since I have been in India has any such idea entered my mind. Barring contingencies which cannot be foreseen, I have no intention whatever of so acting. Much of the work to which my colleagues and myself have set our hands is still incomplete. So long as I receive from them an assistance which has never swerved or abated, and so long as health and strength are given to me to pursue the task, I should regard it as an abnegation of duty to lay it down. Whether the work be worth doing for the sake of the country, it is not for me to say. But

I may be permitted to add that, to me, at any rate, it appeals as the highest and most sacred of trusts."

At the meeting of the Council at Government House, Calcutta, on Wednesday, March 25th, 1903, during the discussion of the Financial Statement for 1903-1904, His Excellency THE PRESIDENT, in the course of his speech, said:

"There is another point of view from which I would for a moment invite the Council and the outside public to regard the relief which has been announced in this Budget; since I think that here again we may find a useful corrective to some of the dangers of premature criticism. How often have we not been told in certain quarters in the past three months that the Delhi Durbar was a foolish and even wicked extravagance, because we spend the money of the people—how much or how little I shall presently show—without announcing to them a substantial benefit in return. I am not sure that my honourable friend Mr. Charlu is not a little unsound on this point himself, for he generously offered to let bygones be bygones, as though there was something that we would rather like to forget. That is not at all our view. I may remark that I should have been glad enough to make the announcement at the Durbar, but that it is the usual practice of modern Governments to connect relief of taxation with Budget Statements, and with the beginning or end of the financial year. I should have thought that this was tolerably clear from my Durbar speech. However, our eager and incredulous friends would not wait even for three months. In their view the golden opportunity had been thrown away, and the Government that had sacrificed it had proved its indifference to the public interest. I feel tempted to wonder whether the Durbar, which I firmly believe that $\frac{9}{10}$ths, I think I might say $\frac{99}{100}$ths, of those who either saw it or know anything about it, regard as having been a unique success, will be relieved from the charge of failure at the hands of the minority who have hitherto so represented it, now that the solitary cause which was alleged to have been responsible for that failure has disappeared, by the announcement in March of the bounty which they would have preferred to secure in January. When the Durbar is cited in the history of the future, even from the narrow point of view of material result alone, will it be quoted by the class of opinion of which I am speaking as a success because it heralded the present relief, or as a failure because it fell short by three months of anticipating it? I do not fancy that there can be much doubt as to the response.

"These remarks lead me by a natural transition to say something about the Durbar itself. And first I must devote a few words to the cost. As I said in my speech in September last, though this is not the test which I would dream of applying myself as the final or crucial touchstone to a ceremony which I at any rate regard as having had a profound political significance, and an almost immeasurable political effect, yet I have no right to object to its being applied by others, and I realise that even symbolism presents itself to many minds in terms of rupees and pies. If, however, we apply this standard, then I do not hesitate to claim an absolute vindication for all that I said last autumn. I remarked then that of the 26½ lakhs estimated for Imperial expenditure, we should recover the greater part, and I added that a great State ceremonial would never have been conducted in India upon more economical lines. These prophecies were not universally accepted at the time, but they have turned out to be scrupulously correct. And indeed they over-estimated, rather than understated, the actual outlay. The net charge against Imperial Revenues for the entire Durbar works out at little more than 12½ lakhs, or £84,000. If to this we add the expenses incurred by Local Governments for their Provincial Camps, over which, from the circumstances of the case, the Government of India could exercise little control, and which amounted to a net total of a little over 14¾ lakhs, or £99,000, we get a net final charge, Imperial and Provincial, of about £180,000 for the Durbar. Is there any one who will tell me that this is an excessive charge upon a population of over 230 millions in British India, exclusive of the Native States, for celebrating the Coronation of their Sovereign? In Great Britain, with a population of 41 millions of people, they voted, I believe, £100,000 for a similar purpose, or a charge of less than ½d. per head of the people. They also spent £70,000 in entertaining the representatives who came from India to attend the ceremony. In India, we have spent £180,000 with a population of nearly 300 millions in all, or about ⅙th of a penny per head of the entire community. Is this too heavy a price for the people to pay for the Coronation of their Emperor? Has a similar sum never been spent upon an Indian marriage or upon an Indian accession? Why, the sum is only about one-seventh part of the relief which we are going to give, not once, but in each succeeding year, to the Indian people by our relief of taxation. Each one of them paid in January a great deal less than a farthing for the Coronation of his Emperor. But he goes away in March with nearly eight times that sum in his pocket per annum. Spread over such enormous masses, the bounty may, in individual cases, seem small, but the recipient, I am sure, would be the first to recognise the degree to which he has gained; and I expect, if we could consult him, that he would at once respond by a request to have a Durbar every year, if only it was likely to be attended with similar results. There are, I know, some who say that this is all very well, but that we must look at what the Durbar cost the Princes and their people. Well, I do not know what it cost them, nor does anybody else, though I have seen a good many extravagant and random calculations. But I do know that these sums were voluntarily spent, that they were all spent in the country, that they diffused employment and radiated contentment far and wide, and that it would be impossible to get up a protest or a petition against them in a single Native State or in any part of the Indian Continent.

"But I would ask whether we may not leave this somewhat sordid field of controversy and pause for a moment to inquire what was the effect of the Durbar itself. I have deprecated the financial criterion. Here let me deprecate the ceremonial criterion also. I have read a great deal since January about pomp and pageantry, and the idea of some persons seems to be that the Durbar was intended only to show the magnificence of the Empire and the trappings of the East. How strangely we often misread each other in the world! I suppose that reams of paper and gallons of ink have been expended upon the delineation of the splendours of the Durbar. May I make a confession? I have never read these accounts without a positive pang. For all the while I have been thinking about something else. I hope I am not a rhapsodist or a dreamer. But to me, and I hope to the majority of us, the Durbar meant not a panorama or a procession. It was a landmark in the history of the people, and a chapter in the ritual of the State. What was it intended for? It was meant to remind all the Princes and peoples of the Asiatic Empire of the British Crown that they had passed under the dominion of a new and single Sovereign, to enable them to solemnise that great and momentous event, and to receive the Royal assurance and greeting. And what was its effect? They learned that under that benign influence they were one, that they were not scattered atoms in a heterogeneous and cumbersome mass, but co-ordinate units in a harmonious and majestic whole. The scales of isolation and prejudice and distrust fell from their eyes, and from the Arab Sheikhs of Aden on the west to the Shan Chiefs of the Mekong on the borders of China, they felt the thrill of a common loyalty, and the inspiration of a single aim. Was there nothing in this? Is it nothing that the Sovereign at his Coronation should exchange pledges with his assembled lieges, of protection and respect on the one side, of spontaneous allegiance on the other? Is it nothing that the citizens of the Empire should learn what that Empire means? Even if we take the rest of India, which could not be present at Delhi, but held its own rejoicings in its own place, is it nothing to lift an entire people for a little space out of the rut of their narrow and parochial lives, and to let them catch a glimpse of a higher ideal, an appreciation of the hidden laws that regulate the march of nations and the destinies of men? I believe that the Durbar, more than any event in modern history, showed to the Indian people the path which, under the guidance of Providence, they are treading; taught the Indian Empire its unity; and impressed the world with its moral as well as material force. It will not be forgotten. The sound of the trumpets has already died away. The Captains and the Kings have departed. But the effect produced by this overwhelming display of unity and patriotism is still alive and will not perish. Everywhere it is known that upon the throne of the East is seated a power that has made of the sentiments, the aspirations, and the interests of 300 millions of Asiatics a living thing, and the units in that great aggregation have learned that in their incorporation lies their strength. As a disinterested spectator of the Durbar remarked, 'Not until to-day did I realise that the destinies of the East still lie, as they always have done, in the hollow of India's hand.' I think, too, that the Durbar taught the lesson, not only of power but of duty. There was not an officer of Government there present, there was not a Ruling Prince, nor a thoughtful spectator, who must not at one moment or other have felt that participation in so great a conception carried with it responsibility as well as pride, and that he owed something in return for whatever of dignity, or security, or opportunity the Empire had given to him.

"Passing from the Durbar, Hon'ble Members may like to hear something of the results of the Art Exhibition which we held at Delhi at the same time, and which was designed exclusively in the interests of the indigenous arts and industries of this country. What effect the Exhibition will have upon the future of Indian Art, it is, of course, impossible as yet to determine. But that it had a wonderful success in calling the attention of the outside public, foreign as well as Native, to the still vital capacities of Indian Art, is, I think, certain. Though the Exhibition was open but a short time, no fewer than 48,000 persons paid for admission, the cash sales amounted to over 3 lakhs of rupees, and the total receipts to more than 4 lakhs. The building cost something more than 1½ lakhs, and, apart from that, the net cost of the Exhibition was only ½ lakh. I think, therefore, that we may fairly claim, for a very moderate outlay, to have given an impetus to Indian Art, which ought not to fade away; while the presence, in so many museums and private collections, of the beautiful objects that were purchased from the Exhibition ought to act as a timely advertisement to the still unexhausted skill of our craftsmen and artisans.

"Among the most contented of the participators at Delhi were the Ruling Chiefs of India, and not the least contented of them, I venture to say, was the Chief of premier rank, His Highness the Nizam of Hyderabad. I have had no previous opportunity of alluding to the agreement that I was fortunate enough to be able to conclude with him a little while before the Durbar. I may, perhaps, indulge in a brief reference to it now.

"It was an agreement regulating the future of the districts hitherto designated the Assigned Districts of Hyderabad, and more popularly known as Berar. The papers concerning that agreement have been made public; and it is open to any one to form his opinion of the arrangement arrived at, and of the steps by which it was attained. I believe that it has generally been accepted as an agreement honourable to both parties, and bringing to a satisfactory termination a state of affairs that had for half a century been neither satisfactory nor profitable to either. I will only add here, as the correspondence has shown, that the agreement, following upon a friendly exchange of views between His Highness the Nizam and myself, represented the free and unfettered disposition of both parties, and that no trace of any opposite influence entered at any moment into its negotiation. His Highness is not less gratified with the agreement than we are, and if both parties are equally content, then I think that there is nothing unreasonable in asking the public to join in our felicitations. There are few questions of delicacy or difficulty connected with Native States in which it has not been my experience that the Chief is ready to discuss them in the most frank and courteous spirit with the head of the Government of India."

APPENDIX II

The Gazette of India

EXTRAORDINARY—PUBLISHED BY AUTHORITY

DELHI: THURSDAY, JANUARY 1, 1903

.FOREIGN DEPARTMENT

NOTIFICATIONS.

Camp Delhi; the 1st January, 1903.

THE following addition to the Table of Salutes to Native Princes and Chiefs have been approved by His Majesty's Government, and are published for general information :

Permanent Salutes.

The Nawab of JANJIRA	11 guns.
The Sawbwa of KENG TUNG	9 "
The Sawbwa of MÖNG NAI	9 "
The Sawbwa of HSI PAW	9 "

Personal Salutes.

SHANKAR RAO CHIMNAJI, Pant Sachiv of BHOR . .	9 "
Maharana JASWANT SINGHJI HARISINGHJI of DANTA .	9 "
Nawab Sir AMIR-UD-DIN AHMAD KHAN Bahadur, K.C.I.E., of LOHARU	9 "

ORDER OF THE BATH

The KING-EMPEROR has been graciously pleased to give orders for the following appointment to and promotions in the Most Honourable Order of the Bath :

To be an Honorary Member of the Civil Division of the first class, or Knight Grand Cross of the said Most Honourable Order:

His Highness Asaf Jah Muzaffar-ul-Mamalik Nizam-ul-Mulk Nizam-ud-Daula Nawab Mir Sir MAHBUB ALI KHAN Bahadur Fateh Jang, G.C.S.I., of HYDERABAD.

To be Ordinary Members of the Military Division of the second class, or Knights Commanders of the said Most Honourable Order:

Major-General CHARLES COMYN EGERTON, C.B., D.S.O., A.D.C., Indian Staff Corps, Commanding Punjab Frontier Force and Frontier District.

Colonel ARTHUR GEORGE HAMMOND, V.C., C.B., D.S.O., Unemployed Supernumerary List, Indian Staff Corps.

L. W. DANE,

Officiating Secretary to the Government of India.

STAR OF INDIA

NOTIFICATIONS.

Camp Delhi; the 1st January, 1903.

The KING-EMPEROR has been graciously pleased to make the following promotions in and appointments to the Most Exalted Order of the Star of India, on the occasion of the Durbar to be held this day at Delhi in His Majesty's Indian Empire, in commemoration of His Majesty's Coronation:

To be Knights Grand Commanders.

The Right Honourable GEORGE FRANCIS HAMILTON, commonly called Lord GEORGE FRANCIS HAMILTON, M.P., His Majesty's Secretary of State for India.

His Highness Raja Sir RAMA VARMA, K.C.S.I., of COCHIN.

To be Knights Commanders.

The Honourable Mr. DENZIL CHARLES JELF IBBETSON, C.S.I., Indian Civil Service, an Ordinary Member of the Council of the Governor-General.

Rear-Admiral CHARLES CARTER DRURY, Royal Navy, Commander-in-Chief of His Majesty's Naval Forces in the East Indies.

The Honourable Mr. HENRY MARTIN WINTERBOTHAM, C.S.I., Indian Civil Service, Member of the Council of the Governor of Fort St. George.

The Honourable Mr. JAMES MONTEATH, C.S.I., India Civil Service, Member of the Council of the Governor of Bombay.

The Honourable Lieutenant-Colonel DONALD ROBERTSON, C.S.I., Indian Staff Corps, Resident in Mysore and Chief Commissioner of Coorg.

The Honourable Mr. ANDREW HENDERSON LEITH FRASER, C.S.I., Indian Civil Service, Chief Commissioner of the Central Provinces; President of the Police Commission.

HUGH SHAKESPEAR BARNES, Esquire, C.S.I., Indian Civil Service, Secretary to the Government of India in the Foreign Department.

Surgeon-General WILLIAM ROE HOOPER, C.S.I., Indian Medical Service (retired), President of the Medical Board at the India Office.

Colonel Sir COLIN CAMPBELL SCOTT-MONCRIEFF, K.C.M.G., C.S.I., Royal Engineers (retired), President of the Indian Irrigation Commission.

His Highness Raja KIRTI SAH, C.S.I., of TEHRI, Garhwal.

Kunwar RANBIR SINGH, of Patiala.

To be Companions.

The Honourable Sir EDWARD FITZGERALD LAW, K.C.M.G., an Ordinary Member of the Council of the Governor-General.

The Honourable Mr. CHARLES STUART BAYLEY, Indian Civil Service, Agent to the Governor-General in Central India.

The Honourable Mr. EDWARD TOWNSHEND CANDY, Indian Civil Service, Puisne Judge of the High Court of Judicature at Bombay—a Member of the Police Commission.

The Honourable Mr. GABRIEL STOKES, Indian Civil Service, Chief Secretary to the Government of Madras, and an Additional Member of the Council of the Governor of Fort St. George for making Laws and Regulations.

Major-General TREVOR BRUCE TYLER, Royal Artillery, Inspector-General of Artillery in India.

HARVEY ADAMSON, Esquire, Indian Civil Service, Judicial Commissioner of Upper Burma.

The Honourable Mr. WILLIAM HENRY LOCKINGTON IMPEY, Indian Civil Service, Officiating Chief Secretary to the Government of the United Provinces, and a Member of the Council of the Lieutenant-Governor of the United Provinces for making Laws and Regulations.

The Honourable Mr. WILLIAM CHARLES MACPHERSON, Indian Civil Service, Officiating Secretary to the Government of Bengal, General and Revenue Departments, and a Member of the Council of the Lieutenant-Governor of Bengal for making Laws and Regulations.

Colonel ST. GEORGE CORBET GORE, Royal Engineers, Surveyor-General of India.

Lieutenant-Colonel JAMES ALEXANDER LAWRENCE MONTGOMERY, Indian Staff Corps, Commissioner of the Rawalpindi Division of the Punjab—a Member of the Police Commission.

REGINALD HENRY CRADDOCK, Esquire, Indian Civil Service, Commissioner of the Jubbulpore Division of the Central Provinces.

Colonel HENRY DOVETON HUTCHINSON, Indian Staff Corps, Assistant Military Secretary (for Indian Affairs) at the War Office.

Major HUGH DALY, C.I.E., Indian Staff Corps, Deputy Secretary to the Government of India in the Foreign Department.

Raja BAN BIHARI KAPUR, of Burdwan.

Nawab Mumtaz-ud-Daula MUHAMMAD FAIYAZ ALI KHAN, of Pahasu in the Bulandshahr District, lately a Member of the Council of the Lieutenant-Governor of the United Provinces for making Laws and Regulations.

Sardar BADAN SINGH, of Malaudh in the Ludhiana District of the Punjab.

It had been the KING-EMPEROR'S intention to appoint His Highness Raja BIJE SEN Bahadur, of MANDI, to be a Knight Commander of the Most Exalted Order of the Star of India. Raja Bije Sen died on the 10th December.

By Order of the Grand Master,
H. S. BARNES,
Secretary to the Most Exalted Order of the Star of India.

INDIAN EMPIRE

NOTIFICATIONS.

Camp Delhi; the 1st January, 1903.

The KING-EMPEROR has been graciously pleased to make the following promotions in and appointments to the Most Eminent Order of the Indian Empire, on the occasion of the Durbar to be held this day at Delhi in His Majesty's Indian Empire, in commemoration of His Majesty's Coronation:

To be Knights Grand Commanders.

His Highness Sri Padmanabha Dasa Vanji Sir BALA RAMA VARMA Kulashekhara Kiritapati Mani Sultan Maharaja Raja Rama Raja Bahadur Shamsher Jang, G.C.S.I., of TRAVANCORE.

His Highness Farzand-i-Arjumand Akidat Paiwand Daulat-i-Inglishia Barar Bans Sarmur Raja-i-Rajagan Raja Sir HIRA SINGH Malwandar Bahadur, G.C.S.I., of NABHA.

To be Knights Commanders.

The Honourable Sir LAWRENCE HUGH JENKINS, *Kt.*, Chief Justice of the High Court of Judicature at Bombay.

The Honourable Mr. HERBERT THIRKELL WHITE, C.I.E., Indian Civil Service, Chief Judge of the Chief Court of Lower Burma.

The Honourable Mr. CHARLES LEWIS TUPPER, C.S.I., Indian Civil Service, Financial Commissioner of the Punjab, and a Member of the Council of the Lieutenant-Governor of the Punjab for making Laws and Regulations.

Surgeon-General BENJAMIN FRANKLIN, C.I.E., Indian Medical Service, Honorary Physician to the King, Director-General, Indian Medical Service, and Sanitary Commissioner with the Government of India.

The Honourable Mr. FREDERICK AUGUSTUS NICHOLSON, C.I.E., Indian Civil Service, First Member of the Board of Revenue, Madras, and an Additional Member of the Council of the Governor of Fort St. George for making Laws and Regulations.

ARTHUR UPTON FANSHAWE, Esquire, C.S.I., Indian Civil Service, Director-General of the Post Office of India.

WALTER ROPER LAWRENCE, Esquire, C.I.E., Indian Civil Service (retired), Private Secretary to His Excellency the Viceroy.

JOHN ELIOT, Esquire, C.I.E., F.R.S., Meteorological Reporter to the Government of India, and Director-General of the Indian Observatories.

Raja-Dhiraj NAHAR SINGHJI of SHAHPURA in Rajputana.

GANGADHAR RAO GANESH, *alias* BALA SAHIB PATWARDHAN, Chief of MIRAJ (Senior Branch) in the Southern Mahratta Country.

Sardar GHAUS BAKHSH, Raisani, the Premier Chief of the Sarawans, Baluchistan.

Maharaja HARBALLABH NARAYAN SINGH Bahadur, C.I.E., of Sonbursa, Bengal.

Maharaja Peshkar KISHAN PARSHAD, Minister to His Highness the Nizam of Hyderabad.

PURNA NARASINGHARAO KRISHNA MURTI, C.I.E., Diwan of Mysore.

Maharaja GODE NARAYANA GAJAPATI RAO, C.I.E., of Vizagapatam.

To be Companions.

Colonel ERNEST DEBRATH, Indian Staff Corps, Joint Secretary to the Government of India in the Military Department.

The Honourable Mr. PRATUL CHANDAR CHATTARJI, Rai Bahadur, Judge of the Chief Court of the Punjab.

FREDERICK GURR MACLEAN, Esquire, M.I.E.E., Director-General of Telegraphs in India.

WALTER BERNARD DE WINTON, Esquire, Chief Engineer and Secretary to the Government of Madras in the Public Works Department.

Colonel TREVREDYN RASHLEIGH WYNNE, Agent and Chief Engineer of the Bengal-Nagpur Railway, Honorary Aide-de-Camp to the Viceroy, and Commandant of the Bengal-Nagpur Railway Volunteer Rifle Corps.

ALGERNON ELLIOTT, Esquire, Officiating Commissioner of the Hyderabad Assigned Districts.

Major (temporary Lieutenant-Colonel) CHARLES ARNOLD KEMBALL, Indian Staff Corps, Officiating Political Resident in the Persian Gulf.

HERBERT WILLIAM CAMERON CARNDUFF, Esquire, Indian Civil Service, Deputy Secretary to the Government of India in the Legislative Department, and lately acting as Private Secretary to the Viceroy.

Lieutenant-Colonel WILLIAM LOCH, General List, Infantry, Principal of the Mayo College at Ajmer.

Lieutenant-Colonel GERALD BOMFORD, M.D., Indian Medical Service, Principal of the Medical College, Calcutta.

Lieutenant-Colonel JOHN HODDING, V.D., Honorary Aide-de-Camp to the Lieutenant-Governor of Bengal, Commandant of the Behar Light Horse.

EDWARD GILES, Esquire, M.A., Director of Public Instruction, Bombay.

HENRY KING BEAUCHAMP, Esquire, Editor of the *Madras Mail*, and Sheriff of Madras.

HARJIBHAI MANEKJI RUSTAMJI, Esquire, Sheriff of Calcutta.

HAVILLAND LEMESURIER, Esquire, Indian Civil Service, lately Magistrate and Collector of Patna, and Chairman of the Patna Municipality.

ROBERT NATHAN, Esquire, Indian Civil Service, lately Under-Secretary to the Government of India in the Home Department, and Secretary to the Indian Universities Commission.

Major ALFRED WILLIAM ALCOCK, M.B., F.R.S., Indian Medical Service, Superintendent of the Indian Museum.

ARTHUR HILL, Esquire, F.C.H., M.I.C.E., Executive Engineer, 1st grade, Bombay Presidency.

DOUGLAS DONALD, Esquire, Commandant of the Border Military Police and Samana Rifles, Kohat.

JAGADISH CHANDRA BOSE, Esquire, M.A., D.Sc., Professor of the Presidency College at Calcutta.

Nawab MUHAMMAD SHARIF KHAN, Khan of DIR.

Mehtar SHUJA-UL-MULK of CHITRAL.

Mir MUHAMMAD NAZIM KHAN, Mir of HUNZA.

Raja SIKANDAR KHAN of NAGAR.

WILLIAM DICKSON CRUICKSHANK, Esquire, Secretary and Treasurer of the Bank of Bengal.

THOMAS JEWELL BENNETT, Esquire, Editor of the *Times of India*, Bombay.

JOHN O'BRIEN SAUNDERS, Esquire, Proprietor and Editor of the *Englishman*, Calcutta.

HENRY WENDEN, Esquire, Agent of the Great Indian Peninsula Railway.

CHARLES HENRY WILSON, Esquire, Manager of the Hong Kong and Shanghai Banking Corporation, and Vice-President of the Rangoon Municipal Committee.

Khan Bahadur Maulvi KHUDA BAKHSH, of Patna.

Rao Bahadur SHYAM SUNDAR LAL, Diwan of Kishangarh in Rajputana.

Rao Bahadur Munshi BALMUKUND DAS, Diwan Bahadur, Member of the Alwar State Council.

ROBERT HERRIOT HENDERSON, Esquire, Superintendent of the Tarrapur Tea Company's Gardens in the Cachar District, Assam.

Nawab Hafiz MUHAMMAD ABDULLA KHAN, Alizai, of Dera Ismail Khan, Honorary Commandant of the 15th Bengal Cavalry.

HKUN KYI, K.S.M., Sawbwa of MONG NAI in the Southern Shan States.

Mir MEHRULLA KHAN, Raisani, Nazim of Mekran, Baluchistan.

Nawab FATEH ALI KHAN, Kazilbash, of Lahore.

Mahamahopadhyaya Pandit GANGA DHAR SHASTRI, Professor of the Sanskrit College at Benares.

FARIDOONJI JAMSHEDJI, Esquire, Private Secretary to His Highness the Nizam's Minister at Hyderabad.

CHARLES HENRY WEST, Esquire, Personal Assistant to the Adjutant-General in India.

It had been the KING-EMPEROR's intention to appoint Sir JOHN WOODBURN, K.C.S.I., to be a Knight Grand Commander of the Most Eminent Order of the Indian Empire, in recognition of his long and distinguished services in India. Sir John Woodburn died at Calcutta on the 21st November. He held, at the time, the high office of Lieutenant-Governor of Bengal.

It had been the KING-EMPEROR's intention to confer a Companionship of the Most Eminent Order of the Indian Empire on Mr. HARRY CHARLES HILL, in recognition of the able manner in which he had conducted his duties, during his long service in the Forest Department in India. Mr. Hill died on the 7th November, whilst on leave in England. He held, at the time, the important post of Inspector-General of Forests.

By Order of the Grand Master,

H. S. BARNES,

Secretary to the Most Eminent Order of the Indian Empire.

FOREIGN DEPARTMENT

NOTIFICATION.

Camp Delhi; the 1st January, 1903.

The KING-EMPEROR has been pleased to confer the honour of Knighthood on—

The Honourable Mr. JAMES ACWORTH DAVIES, Indian Civil Service, Puisne Judge of the High Court of Judicature at Fort St. George.

The Honourable Mr. WILLIAM OVENS CLARK, Indian Civil Service, Chief Judge of the Chief Court of the Punjab.

The Honourable Mr. MONTAGU CORNISH TURNER, President of the Bengal Chamber of Commerce, and an Additional Member of the Council of the Governor-General for making Laws and Regulations.

Lieutenant-Colonel WILLIAM EARNSHAW COOPER, C.I.E., Commandant, Cawnpore Volunteer Rifles.

Lieutenant-Colonel JAMES LEWIS WALKER, C.I.E., late of the 2nd Punjab Volunteer Rifles.

GEORGE WATT, Esq., M.B., C.I.E., Reporter on Economic Products to the Government of India.

HARKISANDAS NAROTTAMDAS, Esquire, lately Sheriff of Bombay.

WILLIAM GODSELL, Esquire, Auditor of Accounts, India Office.

L. W. DANE,

Officiating Secretary to the Government of India.

KAISAR-I-HIND MEDAL

NOTIFICATIONS.

Camp Delhi; the 1st January, 1903.

His Excellency the Viceroy and Governor-General of India is pleased to announce that the King-Emperor has been graciously pleased to award the Kaisar-i-Hind Medal for Public Service in India of the First Class to—

Her Excellency the Lady Curzon of Kedleston, C.I.

The Reverend Samuel Scott Allnutt, M.A., Cambridge Mission, Delhi.

Albert Frederick Ashton, Esquire, Deputy Commissioner, Northern India Salt Revenue Department.

Lieutenant-Colonel Charles Hutton Dawson, Indian Staff Corps, Political Superintendent, Hilly Tracts, Mewar.

Captain Alain C. Joly de Lotbiniere, R.E., Deputy Chief Engineer in Mysore.

James Douglas, Esquire, of Bombay.

The Reverend J. A. Graham, M.A., Kalimpong, Bengal.

Pandit Jwála Prasád, Magistrate and Collector of Jalaun, United Provinces.

Clarence Kirkpatrick, Esquire, Barrister-at-Law, Member of the Municipal Committee of Delhi.

Lieutenant-Colonel Robert William Steele Lyons, M.D., Indian Medical Service, Civil Surgeon and Superintendent, Lunatic Asylum, Dharwar, Bombay Presidency.

Merwanjee Cowasjee, Esquire, Municipal Commissioner and Honorary Magistrate, Rangoon.

John Nisbet, Esquire, lately a Conservator of Forests in Burma.

Major David Semple, M.D., R.A.M.C., Director of the Pasteur Institute, Kasauli.

The Reverend J. D. W. Sewell, S.J., Manager of St. Joseph's College, Trichinopoly, Madras Presidency.

The Reverend David Whitton, Principal of the Hislop College, Nagpur, Central Provinces.

His Excellency the Viceroy and Governor-General is pleased to award the Kaisar-i-Hind Medal for Public Service in India of the Second Class to—

Mrs. Adams-Wylie, widow of the late Lieutenant Adams-Wylie, of the Indian Medical Service, Bombay.

The Reverend Adam Andrew, Missionary, United Free Church of Scotland, Chingleput, Madras Presidency.

Mir Aziz Hasan, Honorary Magistrate and Member of the Municipal and District Boards, Etawah, United Provinces.

Babu Baijnath Goenka, Banker and Zamindar, of Monghyr, Bengal.

Edward Robert Kaye Blenkinsop, Esquire, Indian Civil Service, Settlement Officer, Raipur, Central Provinces.

Rao Bahadur Chandasing Kansing, Honorary Magistrate, Hyderabad, Sind.

Thakur Durjan Singh, Member of the Alwar State Council, Alwar, Rajputana.

George Eaglesome, Esquire, Head Master of the Lawrence School, Abu, Rajputana.

The Reverend Father Etienne Freynet, Superintendent, Roman Catholic Leper Asylum, Rangoon, Burma.

The Reverend Robert Jones, B.A., of the Welsh Mission in the Khásia Hills, Shillong, Assam.

Miss F. Joss, Church of Scotland Mission, Gujrat, Punjab.

Miss Ellen Elizabeth Mitchell, M.D., American Baptist Mission, Moulmein, Burma.

Miss Mitcheson, Zenana Medical Mission, Peshawar, North-West Frontier Province.

Miss Margaret O'Hara, M.D., Canadian Presbyterian Mission, Dhar, Central India.

Dr. T. L. Pennell, Medical Missionary, Church Missionary Society, Bannu, North-West Frontier Province.

Bhai Ram Singh, Vice-Principal, Mayo School of Art, Lahore, Punjab.

Santokh Singh, Kurmi, Malguzar, Raipur District, Central Provinces.

Bibi Soghra, of Bihar, Patna, Bengal.

Muhammad Zahur-ul-Husain, Member of the Municipal Board, Allahabad, United Provinces.

H. H. RISLEY,

Officiating Secretary to the Government of India,
Home Department.

MILITARY DEPARTMENT

Camp Delhi; the 1st January, 1903.

SPECIAL AND MISCELLANEOUS.

The Viceroy and Governor-General in Council has much gratification in announcing the following favours and concessions to different branches of the Army in India in connection with the Coronation of the KING-EMPEROR:

1. His Majesty has graciously approved of the designation of the Indian Staff Corps being abolished. Officers belonging to that Corps will in future be designated "Officers of the Indian Army."

2. His Majesty has been graciously pleased to direct that a limited number of Native officers of the Indian Army shall be annually appointed for duty as orderly officers in attendance upon Himself, the arrangement commencing with the year 1903. The rules governing the appointment of these Native officers will be as follows:

(1) The number appointed annually will be six. Each will be allowed a batman. They will remain for one season in London, *viz.*, from April to August, and

be annually replaced by other selections. Half of the Native officers will be drawn from the Cavalry, and half from the Infantry, Artillery, and Sappers and Miners.

(2) They will be provided with a residence in the neighbourhood of Buckingham Palace.

(3) They will be under the general control and supervision of the Assistant Military Secretary for Indian Affairs, and under the personal orders of the Equerry in Waiting upon the King.

(4) They will wear regimental uniform and a special aiguilette during the period of the special service.

3. The honorary rank of Captain will in future be granted on retirement to all Risaldar-Majors and Subadar-Majors in possession of the 1st class of the Order of British India, and that of Lieutenant on all other Native officers in possession of the same decoration.

4. In token of the appreciation in which the services of the Native Army are held by His Majesty, the Order of British India will be temporarily increased by fifty appointments, *viz.*, ten in the first class, and forty in the second class of the Order. These appointments will be absorbed on the death or promotion of the recipients.

5. In token of the appreciation in which the services of the Imperial Service Troops are held by His Majesty, an establishment of ten first class, and twenty second class appointments in the Order of British India has been sanctioned for them. This establishment will include holders on the retired list as well as those on the active list.

Appointments to the Order will be honorary, and will not carry any allowances from the British Government, but allowances hitherto enjoyed will continue to be drawn by members during their lifetime.

The Order will be the same as that bestowed on the officers of the Regular Army.

6. An extra meritorious service medal, with a gratuity of Rs. 25, for dafadars and havildars only, will be granted on the following scale:

To each regiment of Cavalry, corps of Sappers and Miners and battalion of Infantry (including local corps)*	1
To the three Body-Guards and Aden troop combined	1
To the four Punjab Frontier Force Batteries and Frontier Garrison Artillery	2
To the six other Native Mountain Batteries	3
To the four Hyderabad Contingent Batteries	1
To the native driver establishment of British Mountain Batteries	1

7. To the rank and file of the Native Army will be granted extra long service and good-conduct medals, with gratuities of Rs. 25, on the following scale:

To each regiment of Cavalry, corps of Sappers and Miners, and battalion of Infantry (including local corps)*	2
To the three Body-Guards and Aden troop combined	1

* The Malwar Bhil Corps and the Nepal Escort will be grouped together as one unit.

To the four Punjab Frontier Force Batteries and Frontier Garrison Artillery	2
To the six other Native Mountain Batteries	3
To the four Hyderabad Contingent Batteries	1
To the native driver establishment of British Mountain Batteries	1
To the whole of the native combatants of batteries and companies, Royal Horse Artillery, Royal Field Artillery, and ammunition column units in India	4
To the corps of Sub-Marine Mining Lascars, including serangs and tindals	1

8. The grants of medals in paragraphs 6 and 7 will be special ones for the year 1903 only, and the conditions of the grant will be the same as laid down in Army Regulations, India, Volume I., Part II., Articles 334 to 340, and Army Regulations, India, Volume II., Part A, paragraph 1107, *et seq.*

9. A money grant, as stated below, will be made to all British and Native corps. The money is to be spent in such manner as may be thought most suitable by Officers Commanding in each case:

	R
Royal Horse Artillery Battery	80
Royal Field Artillery Battery	80
Royal Garrison Artillery Company	70
Mountain Artillery Battery	60
Heavy Artillery Battery	60
British Cavalry Regiment	300
British Infantry Battalion	450
Sappers and Miners (European)	1 per head.
Native Mountain Battery	60
Frontier Garrison Artillery	35
Field Battery, Hyderabad Contingent	35
Drivers (Native) of British Mountain Batteries	35
Body-Guards	20
Native Cavalry Regiment	150
Corps of Guides	300
Native Infantry Battalion	200
Deoli and Erinpura Irregular Cavalry	40
Malwar Bhil Corps	150
Aden Troop	20
Nepal Escort	20
Local Corps, other than those specified above	200
Company of Sappers and Miners	40
Drivers (Native) of heavy batteries	35
Corps of Sub-Marine Mining Lascars	35
Coast Defence Lascars	80

	R
Drivers, Head-Quarter Units of ammunition columns . .	7 per unit.
„ Ordinary Units of ammunition columns . . .	5 „
British Non-Commissioned Officers of Indian Sub-Marine Mining Company	1 per head.

10. In consideration of the excellent services rendered by the Native Mountain Artillery, the six batteries named in the margin will be formed into a group, and be granted the following privileges now enjoyed by the mountain batteries of the Punjab Frontier Force:

Quetta Mountain Battery.
Jullundur „ „
Gujrat „ „
Lahore „ „
Muree „ „
Abbottabad „ „

(*i*) The rank and pay of Subadar-Major will be granted to the senior Subadar of the six batteries, and the senior, or other selected trumpeter, will be granted the rank and pay of Trumpet Major.

(*ii*) The British officers will in future be entitled to 90 instead of 60 days' privilege leave in the year when quartered at Dera Ismail Khan, Bannu, and in the Tochi Valley.

11. As a mark of Royal clemency on this auspicious occasion, particular classes of military offenders, of both the British and Native Armies, will be released at daybreak on the 1st January, 1903, or their punishments will be mitigated under orders published by His Excellency the Commander-in-Chief.

12. His Excellency the Commander-in-Chief will issue any subsidiary orders necessary for giving effect to the above measures.

The following special promotions in the Native Army and admissions to the Order of British India are notified:

I.—For supernumerary promotion to the rank of Subadar-Major:

Subadar Sher Singh, Sardar Bahadur, Lahore Mountain Battery.

II.—For supernumerary promotion to the rank of Risaldar-Major:

Risaldar Ramchander Rao Mahadik, Sardar Bahadur, the 1st (The Duke of Connaught's Own) Bombay Lancers.

III.—For supernumerary promotion to the rank of Risaldar:

Jemadar Ajab Khan, Bahadur, 9th Bengal Lancers (Hodson's Horse).
Jemadar Dhangri, 11th (Prince of Wales's Own) Bengal Lancers.

IV.—For supernumerary promotion to the rank of Subadar or Ressaidar:

Jemadar Gul Mawaz Khan, 18th Bengal Lancers.
Jemadar Mir Hidayat Ali, 1st Lancers, Hyderabad Contingent.
Jemadar Kehar Singh, Governor-General's Body-Guard.
Jemadar Bhao Sawanth, 3rd Bombay Light Infantry.
Jemadar Banna, Merwara Battalion.
Jemadar Gangadin Pande, 1st Brahman Infantry.

V.—For promotion in and admission to the Order of British India:

(a) For promotion to the 1st class, with the title of "Sardar Bahadur."

1. Risaldar-Major Muhammad Beg, Bahadur, 1st Madras Lancers.
2. Risaldar-Major Muizzuddin Khan, Bahadur, 15th (Cureton's Multani) Bengal Lancers.
3. Subadar Ghulam Muhammad, Bahadur, Derajat Mountain Battery.
4. Risaldar-Major Shaikh Farid, Bahadur, 1st Madras Lancers.
5. Risaldar-Major Baldeo Singh, Bahadur, 14th Bengal Lancers (Murray's Jat Horse).
6. Subadar Bhola Tiwari, Bahadur, 1st Brahman Infantry.
7. Subadar Tura-Baz Khan, Bahadur, 20th (Duke of Cambridge's Own) Punjab Infantry.
8. Subadar Jag Singh, Bahadur, Bengal Sappers and Miners.
9. Subadar-Major Devasahayam, Bahadur, "Queen's Own" Madras Sappers and Miners.
10. Subadar-Major Hira Singh, Bahadur, Bengal Sappers and Miners.

(b) For admission to the 2nd class, with the title of "Bahadur."

1. Subadar Ram Singh, 15th (Ludhiana) Sikh Infantry.
2. Risaldar-Major Faiz Talab Khan, the Queen's Own Corps of Guides (Cavalry).
3. Risaldar-Major Niyaz Muhammad Khan, 15th (Cureton's Multani) Bengal Lancers.
4. Risaldar-Major Wazir Ali Khan, 1st (Duke of York's Own) Bengal Lancers.
5. Risaldar Ishar Singh, The Queen's Own Corps of Guides (Cavalry).
6. Risaldar-Major Malik Ghulam Muhammad Khan, 2nd Central India Horse.
7. Subadar Hanbir Thapa, 2nd Battalion, 1st Gurkha Rifles.
8. Subadar Prem Singh, 32nd Punjab Pioneers.
9. Risaldar-Major Umdah Singh, 2nd Punjab Cavalry.
10. Subadar-Major Karnabir Thapa, 43rd Gurkha Rifles.
11. Subadar-Major Molar Ram, 6th Jat Light Infantry.
12. Subadar-Major Jan Muhammad, 29th (Duke of Connaught's Own) Baluch Infantry.
13. Subadar Baldeo Singh, 8th Rajput Infantry.
14. Subadar Mauladad Khan, 26th Baluch Infantry.
15. Subadar Nathu Sunar, 1st Battalion, 39th Garhwal Rifles.
16. Subadar Zargun Shah, 1st Punjab Infantry.
17. Ressaidar Sajjat Khan, 3rd (Queen's Own) Bombay Light Cavalry.
18. Subadar-Major Kalandar Khan, 28th Punjab Infantry.
19. Ressaidar Mir Baz Khan, 11th (Prince of Wales' Own) Bengal Lancers.
20. Ressaidar Mazhar Ali Khan, 1st (Duke of York's Own) Bengal Lancers.
21. Subadar Kandasami, 1st Madras Pioneers.
22. Ressaidar Mirza Umrao Beg, 1st (Duke of Connaught's Own) Bombay Lancers.
23. Subadar Shaikh Ebrahim, 16th Bombay Infantry.
24. Second-class Senior Hospital Assistant Debi-ditta Saithhi, Indian Subordinate Medical Department.
25. Subadar-Major Kaberaj Karki, 44th Gurkha Rifles.

26. Subadar-Major Shiubaran Singh, 2nd (Queen's Own) Rajput Light Infantry.
27. Risaldar-Major Har-ji Ram, 7th Bengal Lancers.
28. Subadar Bihari Singh, 2nd Infantry, Hyderabad Contingent.
29. Risaldar Gopal Singh, 10th (Duke of Cambridge's Own) Bengal Lancers (Hodson's Horse).
30. Subadar-Major Ram Kishan Bisht, 2nd Battalion, 39th Garhwal Rifles.
31. Subadar Balaji Mule, 1st Bombay Grenadiers.
32. Subadar Muhammad Sulaiman, 20th Madras Infantry.
33. First-class Senior Hospital Assistant Pati Ram, Rai Bahadur, Indian Subordinate Medical Department.
34. Subadar Dost Muhammad, 24th (Duchess of Connaught's Own) Baluchistan Infantry.
35. Subadar Balwant Singh, 23rd Punjab Pioneers.
36. Ressaidar Dewa Singh, 9th Bengal Lancers (Hodson's Horse).
37. Subadar Adhar Singh, 7th (Duke of Connaught's Own) Rajput Infantry.
38. Subadar Shaikh Ismail, 1st Infantry, Hyderabad Contingent.
39. Subadar Ashik Ali Khan, 17th (Mussulman) Rajput Infantry.
40. Subadar Ahmed Kutti, 2nd Moplah Rifles.

The following promotions in and admissions to the Order of British India among Native officers of the Imperial Service Troops are notified.

For promotion to the first class, with the title of "Sardar Bahadur."

Mirza Karim Beg, Commandant, Bhopal Lancers.
Sundar Singh, Commandant, Patiala Infantry.
Gurnam Singh, Commandant, Jind Infantry.
Jas Singh, Commandant, Jodhpur Lancers.
Natha Singh, Sardar Bahadur, Commandant, Alwar Infantry.
Nand Singh, Commandant, Patiala Lancers.

For admission to the second class, with the title of "Bahadur."

Narain Singh, Commandant, Kapurthala Infantry.
Mahomed Bakhsh Khan, Assistant Commandant, Maler Kotla Sappers.
Hardas Singh, Commandant, Nabha Infantry.
A. P. Edibam, Commandant, Gwalior Transport.
Farman Ali Khan, General, Kashmir Infantry, Adjutant-General, Kashmir Army.
Bhagwan Singh, Lieutenant-Colonel, Kashmir Infantry.
Saiyid Hafiz, Commandant, Mysore Lancers.

The King-Emperor has been graciously pleased to grant to His Highness Farzandi-i Arjumand Akidat Paiwand Daulat-i-Inglishia Barar Bans Sarmur Raja-i-Rajagan Raja Sir Hira Singh Malwandar Bahadur, G.C.S.I., of Nabha, the honorary rank of Colonel of the 14th (Ferozepore) Sikh Infantry.

The King-Emperor has been graciously pleased to grant to His Highness Maharao Sir Umed Singh Bahadur, K.C.S.I., of Kota, the honorary rank of Major in the Deoli Irregular Force.

E. G. BARROW, *Major-General,*
Secretary to the Government of India.

FOREIGN DEPARTMENT

NOTIFICATIONS.

Camp Delhi; the 1st January, 1903.

His Excellency the Viceroy and Governor-General is pleased to confer upon Sawlawi, Myoza of Gantarawadi, or Eastern Karenni, the hereditary title of SAWBWA, to be attached to the Chiefship.

His Excellency the Viceroy and Governor-General is pleased to confer upon the Zamindar of Burdwan, the hereditary title of MAHARAJA-DHIRAJ, to be attached to the Estate.

His Excellency the Viceroy and Governor-General is pleased to confer upon Raja Sriram Chandra Bhunj Deo, Chief of the Moharbhanj State, in the Orissa Tributary Mahals, the title of MAHARAJA, as a personal distinction.

His Excellency the Viceroy and Governor-General is pleased to confer upon Rani Dhankuar Ba Sahiba, of the Barwani State, in Central India, the title of MAHARANI, as a personal distinction.

His Excellency the Viceroy and Governor-General is pleased to confer upon Nawab Khwaja Salimullah, of Dacca, in the Bengal Presidency, the title of NAWAB BAHADUR, as a personal distinction.

His Excellency the Viceroy and Governor-General is pleased to confer the title of RAJA as a personal distinction upon—

Rao Bahadur Chhatarpati, C.S.I., Jagidar of Alipura, in Central India.

Rao Bahadur Thakur Mangal Singh, of Lawa, in Rajputana.

U Kine Singh, Seim of Nongkhlao, in the Khasi Hills, Assam.

Rao Jogendra Narain Roy, Zamindar of Lalgola, in the Murshidabad District.

Lal Raghuraj Singh, of Mankapur, in the Gonda District of the United Provinces.

His Excellency the Viceroy and Governor-General is pleased to confer the title of NAWAB as a personal distinction upon—

Khan Bahadur Sardar Khair Bakhsh, Chief of the Marri tribe in Baluchistan.

Sardar Kaisar Khan, Chief of the Magasi tribe in Baluchistan.

His Excellency the Viceroy and Governor-General is pleased to confer upon Bismillah Begam Sahiba, wife of Nawab Gulam Mahomed Ghouse, Khan Bahadur, brother of the Prince of Arcot, the title of NAWAB BEGAM, as a personal distinction.

His Excellency the Viceroy and Governor-General is pleased to confer the title of SHAMS-UL-ULAMA as a personal distinction upon—

Khan Sahib Maulvi Saadat Husain, of the Calcutta Madrassa.

Mufti Maulvi Abdulla, of the Oriental College, Lahore.

Maulvi Abdul Hakim, of the Oriental College, Lahore.

His Excellency the Viceroy and Governor-General is pleased to confer upon Pandit Shiva Chandra Sarvabhauma, of Bhatpara, 24-Parganas, in the Bengal Presidency, the title of MAHAMAHOPADHYAYA, as a personal distinction.

His Excellency the Viceroy and Governor-General is pleased to confer the title of DEWAN BAHADUR as a personal distinction upon—

N. Subramanyam, Administrator-General and Official Trustee, Madras, and Commissioner of the Madras Municipality.

M. R. Ry. Rao Bahadur Amembala Vencataramana Poi Avargal, Acting District and Sessions Judge of Kurnool, in the Madras Presidency.

Rai Bahadur Seth Kastur Chand Daga, of Bikaner.

His Excellency the Viceroy and Governor-General is pleased to confer the title of SARDAR BAHADUR as a personal distinction upon—

Rai Bahadur Gopal Singh, Naib Commandant, Bhamo Battalion, Burma Military Police.

Risaldar Partab Singh, Extra Assistant Commissioner in the Punjab.

His Excellency the Viceroy and Governor-General is pleased to confer upon Rai Bahadur Mehta Jagjiwan Jiwan, Dewan of Jaisalmer, the title of DEWAN, as a personal distinction.

His Excellency the Viceroy and Governor-General is pleased to confer the title of KHAN BAHADUR as a personal distinction upon—

Khan Sahib Din Muhammad, Extra Assistant Commissioner, Kasur, in the Lahore District of the Punjab.

Khan Sahib Haji Kalandar Khan, of Gundapur, in the North-West Frontier Province.

Haji Mahommed Abdul Hadi Badsha Sahib, a Commissioner of the Madras Municipality.

Maulvi Shams-ul-Zoha, Honorary Magistrate of the Sadar Bench, and Vice-Chairman of the District Board, Birbhum, in the Bengal Presidency.

Jan Mahomed Nawaz *walad* Ghulam Mahomed Dahar, Zamindar, Taluka Ubauro, Sukkur District, in the Bombay Presidency.

Ardeshir Dorabji Daviervala, landholder of Umbargaon, Thana District, in the Bombay Presidency.

Chaudhri Amir Husain Khan, of Sahespur, Bijnor District, in the United Provinces.

Maulvi Majid Bakht Mazumdar, Honorary Magistrate, in the Sylhet District, in Assam.

Hormusji Maneckji Bhiwindiwala, Abkari Contractor and Salt Merchant, Bombay.

Navroji Kavasji Kalyanvalla, Assistant Surgeon, Ahmedabad, in the Bombay Presidency.

Ardesir Dinshaji Chinoy, Extra Assistant Commissioner in Berar.

His Excellency the Viceroy and Governor-General is pleased to confer the title of RAO BAHADUR as a personal distinction upon—

Chaube Jagat Raj, Jagirdar of Paldeo, in Central India.

Rao Sahib Balwant Rao Bhuskate, Chairman of the Municipality of Burhanpur, in the Central Provinces.

Rao Sahib Nirbhe Singh Mandloi, of Sohagpur, in the Central Provinces.

Babu Sansar Chander Sen, Member of the Jaipur State Council.

Telagani Kothandarama Naidu, Dewan of the Sandur State.

Dayabhai Harjiwandas Nanavati, Accountant-General of the Baroda State.

Lal Janardhan Singh, Secretary to His Highness the Maharaja of Rewa, in Central India.

Panamalai Subachari Krishna Rao, District Judge, Civil and Military Station of Bangalore.

Pasupaleti Vencata Krishnayya Naidu Garu, Vice-President of the Guntur Taluk Board, and Chairman of the Guntur Municipal Council, Madras Presidency.

Khandubhai Gulabbhai Desai, retired Executive Engineer, Public Works Department, Bombay Presidency.

Wadhumal Chandiram, retired Deputy Collector, Talti, in the Tarkana District of the Bombay Presidency.

Bilaram Sachanand, retired Assistant Judge, Shikarpur, Sind.

G. C. Hanumantha Gowd, Member of the District Board, Bellary, in the Madras Presidency.

Annaji Aiyengar Krishnaswami Aiyengar, Assistant Commissioner, Salt and Abkari Department, Madras Presidency.

Duruseti Seshagiri Rao Pantulu Garu, High Court Vakil, Coconada, in the Madras Presidency.

M. R. R. M. Rangachariyar, Professor of Sanskrit at the Presidency College, Madras.

Moreshwar Raghoba Talpade, Postal Superintendent, Bombay Presidency.

Pandit Vishnu Sadaseo Baputt, Sub-Assistant Superintendent of Telegraphs.

Narayen Kesheo, Station Master, Great Indian Peninsula Railway.

His Excellency the Viceroy and Governor-General is pleased to confer the title of RAI BAHADUR as a personal distinction upon—

Rai Sahib Banamali Chakarbatti, Superintendent of the Toshakhana of the Government of India.

Rai Sahib Bhik Chand, Honorary Magistrate and Member of the Municipal Committee of Quetta.

Subadar-Major Har Singh Thapa, Northern Shan States Battalion, Burma Military Police.

Subadar-Major Kehr Singh Rana, Ruby Mines Battalion, Burma Military Police.

Inspector Hari Singh, of the Andaman and Nicobar Military Police.

Babu Jogesh Chunder Mitter, late District and Sessions Judge, Dacca, in the Bengal Presidency.

Lala Nand Kishor, Inspector of Schools, Jullundur Circle, Punjab.

Lala Moti Ram, Extra-Assistant Commissioner, Multan, in the Punjab.

Anant Lal, Extra-Assistant Commissioner in the Central Provinces.

Babu Sitanath Roy, of Calcutta.

Babu Rajendra Chandra Shastri, Librarian, Bengal Library.

Munshi Takht Singh, of Hatta, in the Central Provinces.

Babu Surjyakumar Chaudhuri, Senior Superintendent in the Department of Finance and Commerce.

Babu Kedar Nath Mookerjee, Household and Aide-de-Camp's Office, Government House.

His Excellency the Viceroy and Governor-General is pleased to confer the title of KHAN SAHIB as a personal distinction upon—

Maulvi Muhammad Mujib Ullah, Vice-Chairman of the Municipal Board of Gorakhpur, in the United Provinces.

Muhammad Naim Khan of Kailaspur, Saharanpur District, in the United Provinces.

Mir Rahim Khan, of the Kurd tribe in Baluchistan.

Haji Mulla Mastak, Jogizai, of Zhob, in Baluchistan.

Munshi Mahboob Alum, Supervisor, Allahabad-Fyzabad Chord Railway.

Mir Alim Kazi, retired Extra-Assistant Commissioner, of Haripur, Hazara District, in the North-West Frontier Province.

Sheikh Imam-ud-din, Superintendent of Police, Jammu.

Mir Akbar Shah, retired Tahsildar, Peshawar.

Pestonji Dorabji, Engine Driver, Great Indian Peninsula Railway.

His Excellency the Viceroy and Governor-General is pleased to confer the title of RAO SAHIB as a personal distinction upon—

Ganpatram Gavrishankar Shastri, retired Deputy Educational Inspector, Ahmedabad, in the Bombay Presidency.

Ganesh Hari Sugwekar, Member and Vice-President of the Taluka Local Board of Karjat, Neral, in the Bombay Presidency.

Anandrao Tukaram, Deshmukh of Jarur, in the Amraoti District of Berar.

Vijaragavaloo Chetty, Permanent Way Inspector, Madras Railway.

His Excellency the Viceroy and Governor-General is pleased to confer the title of RAI SAHIB as a personal distinction upon—

Babu Haran Chandra Rakshit, of Calcutta.

Darshan Singh, Zamindar, of the Pilibhit District, in the United Provinces.

Din Dayal, Honorary Magistrate and Vice-Chairman of the District Board, Lucknow.

Lala Ralla Ram, Honorary Assistant Examiner, Public Works Accounts, Punjab.

Lala Sheo Pershad, Assistant Superintendent, Northern India Salt Revenue Department.

Lala Radha Kishen, Member of the Municipal Committee, Peshawar.

Lala Kunj Behari, Thapar, Secretary of the Punjab Public Library, Lahore.

Babu Surendra, Nath Gupta, Honorary Assistant Engineer in the Public Works Department, Assam.

Babu Charu Chandar Mitter, Treasurer and Accountant, Foreign Department.

Babu Fanindra Mohan Basu, Head Clerk, Meteorological Office, Calcutta.

Lala Janki Pershad, Supervisor, Public Works Department, Simla.

Rikhiram Naik, Malguzar, Bilheri, in the Central Provinces.

Tarak Nath Ghose, Civil Assistant Surgeon, of the Prince of Wales' Hospital, Benares.

Babu Kailas Chandra Das, Senior Hospital Assistant, Sylhet, in Assam.

Kumud Behary Samanto, Civil Hospital Assistant, Bengal Presidency.

Babu Doorlub Chunder Mozumdar, retired Sub-Assistant Auditor, East Indian Railway.

Babu Hari Chand, Sub-Engineer, Kalka-Simla Railway.

Munshi Govind Jewan, Treasurer and Mir Munshi, 1st Bengal Lancers.

His Excellency the Viceroy and Governor-General is pleased to confer the title of KYET-THAYE-ZAUNG SHWE SALWE YA MIN as a personal distinction upon—

Maung Yaing, Extra Assistant Conservator of Forests, Burma.

Maung Pyat, retired Myoôk, and Honorary Magistrate, Bassein.

Maung Yo, Vice-President of the Paungdè Municipality.

His Excellency the Viceroy and Governor-General is pleased to confer the title of THUYE GAUNG NGWE DA YA MIN as a personal distinction upon—

Sao Möng Kak, Chief Minister of the State of Keng Tung.

Labang Ma Grong, Taungôk of the Southern Tracts, Bhamo-Kachin Hills.

His Excellency the Viceroy and Governor-General is pleased to confer the title of AHMUDAN GAUNG TAYEIK ZA MIN as a personal distinction upon—

Hkun Shwe Kya, Ngwegunhmu of Loi Ai in the Myelat, Southern Shan States.
Maung Nyo Hlaing, Ngwegunhmu of Maw in the Myelat, Southern Shan States.

The following concessions have been sanctioned by His Excellency the Viceroy and Governor-General in Council as rewards for distinguished services, and are published for general information :

To the Hon. Sir V. Bashyam Aiyangar, Kt., C.I.E., Judge of the High Court, Madras.	An assignment of land revenue of the value of Rs. 5,000 a year, for life.
To B. Srinivasa, retired Inspector of Police, Madras.	An assignment of land revenue of the value of Rs. 1,200 a year, for life.
To Bhivrao, Madhavrao Potnis, a 1st class Sardar of the Deccan.	The grant of a Saranjam, valued at Rs. 3,000 a year, for life.
To Mr. J. P. Warburton, late District Superintendent of Police, Punjab.	The remission of the *nazarana* payable on 20 squares of land on the Chenab canal.
To Rai Bahadur Daulat Ram, C.I.E., Superintendent of Post Offices, Simla Division.	The remission of the *nazarana* payable on 15 squares of land on the Jhelum canal.
To Khan Bahadur Ahmad Yar Khan, Wazir to the Jam of Las Bela.	The remission of the *nazarana* payable on 15 squares of land on the Jhelum canal.
To Khan Bahadur Kazi Jalal-ud-din Khan, C.I.E., Political Adviser to His Highness the Khan of Kalat.	A jagir of the approximate value of Rs. 1,250 a year, for life, in the Sarela village in Pishin.

L. W. DANE,
Officiating Secretary to the Government of India.

HOME DEPARTMENT

JAILS.

Camp Delhi; the 1st January, 1903.

RESOLUTION.

The Governor-General in Council has been pleased to issue orders, as follows, for the release, as an act of clemency and grace, of a certain number of prisoners, both criminal and civil, and the remission of a portion of the sentences of other prisoners in all the Jails throughout British India, and in the Penal Settlement of Port Blair, on the auspicious occasion of the Coronation of the King-Emperor.

2. Local Governments and Administrations have been desired to release on this day 10 per cent. of all the convicts under sentence, provided that their conduct during imprisonment has been good, and that their release is not likely to give rise to a revival of

blood feuds or professional crime. Under these orders 9123 offenders will be released. Special consideration has been given to the question of the release of Burmans convicted of dakaiti and similar offences, during the disturbances which followed the annexation of Upper Burma, and the release of 127 such convicts has been decided on. Apart from the foregoing concessions, His Excellency in Council has, as additional measures of clemency and grace, directed the release (1) of 1238 female convicts whose offences were not of a serious nature; (2) of 4909 persons under sentence of one month's imprisonment or less, who have on this day worked out half their sentence; and (3) of 276 persons under sentence of not more than six months' imprisonment, whose offences were more or less attributable to conditions of scarcity. The Governor-General in Council has also directed the absolute release of 352 male and female convicts in the Andamans, and the conditional release of 31 convicts under sentence for dakaiti. The total number of convicts of all classes at Port Blair, who will be released in connection with the celebration of the Coronation of the King-Emperor, will thus be nearly 400.

3. The Governor-General in Council has also been pleased to extend a measure of grace and clemency to convicts in Indian Jails who, in the interests of society, cannot now be released, by directing that they be granted remissions of their punishments, graduated according to the character of the sentence in each case, which may extend to a month's remission for each year of imprisonment passed in jail. His Excellency in Council has further sanctioned, in the case of all well-behaved convicts in the Penal Settlement of Port Blair, certain concessions which will mitigate the severity of their sentences, and will improve their prospects of earning further privileges by continued good behaviour.

4. The Governor-General in Council has been pleased to order the release of all persons confined in prison in execution of decrees of the Civil Courts whose debts do not exceed the sum of ₨100, provided that they are poor and not fraudulent; and the payment by Government of the debt or debts for which they are detained. One hundred and thirty-two civil prisoners will accordingly be discharged, and their debts, aggregating ₨8,590, will be paid by Government.

5. The total number of prisoners who will to-day be released from British Jails, including the Andamans, is 16,188.

H. H. RISLEY,

Officiating Secretary to the Government of India.

APPENDIX III

[No. 58 of 1903]

GOVERNMENT OF INDIA

FOREIGN DEPARTMENT

INTERNAL

To

The Right Hon. LORD GEORGE F. HAMILTON, G.C.S.I.,

His Majesty's Secretary of State for India.

Simla, *the 7th May, 1903.*

My Lord,

We have the honour to furnish Your Lordship, for the information of His Majesty's Government, with an account of the celebrations held at Delhi in December and January last in honour of the Coronation of His Majesty the King, Emperor of India. Copies of the official programmes are enclosed, and, as Your Lordship is aware, a commission to write an official history of the proceedings has been entrusted to Mr. Stephen Wheeler. As a narrative, therefore, this despatch is intentionally brief, and it relates more particularly to the political aspects of this great event.

2. It was in November 1901, that the intention to hold an Imperial Durbar with the above-named object was first publicly announced. The occasion was the notification of the issue of invitations by His Majesty the King-Emperor to a limited number of Indian Chiefs to attend his Coronation in England; and it was at the same time explained that in order to afford the remaining Chiefs, who could not be present in London, an opportunity of testifying their loyalty to his Throne and Person, His Majesty had instructed the Viceroy to hold a celebration in India at a date subsequent to the English ceremony. In February 1902, a Proclamation was published in the "Gazette of India," naming Delhi as the place, and the 1st January 1903, as the date, of the proposed gathering; and this was followed by invitations to attend, addressed by His Excellency the Viceroy to the heads of Local Governments and Administrations, and to the Ruling Chiefs of India. In September 1902, the news was made public that His Majesty had graciously deputed His Royal Highness the Duke of Connaught to represent the Royal Family upon this momentous occasion;

and the utmost satisfaction was everywhere expressed at this evidence of the warm personal interest taken by His Majesty in the approaching ceremony, and at the high compliment to India which the choice implied.

3. Throughout the summer, and still more after the successful celebration of His Majesty's Coronation in London on 9th August, 1902, our preparations for the forthcoming event in India continued apace; and before the end of the year they had reached so advanced a stage, that the most important functions had been several times rehearsed on the spot, and there remained only the arrival of the principal actors on the scene, and the occurrence of favourable weather, to ensure the triumphant realisation of our plans.

4. By the 27th December, the principal Ruling Chiefs of India, many representatives of foreign Powers, the leading officials of our Government, and a strong force from the Indian Army had assembled at Delhi, and on the 29th of the month, the ceremonies were inaugurated by the State Entry of His Excellency the Viceroy and Their Royal Highnesses the Duke and Duchess of Connaught. His Excellency arrived shortly in advance of Their Royal Highnesses. He was met at the station by the Ruling Chiefs, foreign representatives, and leading officials, and, attended by them, he received Their Royal Highnesses, who had journeyed direct from Bombay. The route of the Entry lay through the principal streets of the city. Preceded by their Escorts, the Imperial Cadet Corps, the Viceroy's Body Guard, and their respective staffs, His Excellency and Their Royal Highnesses headed the Procession on magnificently appointed State elephants. Then followed 51 Ruling Chiefs similarly mounted and riding two abreast, His Royal Highness the Grand Duke of Hesse, whose presence at Delhi, as the guest of the Viceroy, was heartily welcomed as an additional evidence of the interest of the Royal Family, the Governors, Lieutenant-Governors, and Chief Commissioners of every province of the Indian Empire, and the Commander-in-Chief, each with his Escort, the Members of the Viceroy's Council, the Lieutenant-General Commanding Bengal, the Chiefs from Baluchistan and the North-West Frontier, while the elephant retinues of the Chiefs brought up the rear. In this order the procession slowly passed, under a cloudless sky, through the avenues of the city. The Ruling Chiefs who did not join in the Procession were accommodated in a suitable stand in front of the Town Hall. The galleries of the Jumma Musjid had been placed by the courtesy of the Managing Committee, at the disposal of the Viceroy for the accommodation of English and European guests. The streets were lined throughout their entire length by troops, and behind the troops there was an immense concourse of spectators. It would be safe to say that no such crowd of persons has ever before been assembled at Delhi. Traffic had been suspended from an early hour, and for four miles the streets, the mosques, the temples, specially erected stands, and every roof and balcony commanding a view, were thronged. Portraits of Their Majesties and loyal mottoes were freely displayed in the native quarters. The brilliance of the spectacle was only equalled by the order and enthusiasm that prevailed. The welcome accorded to Their Royal Highnesses was particularly marked, the affection with which their former stay in this country is remembered, enhancing the cordiality of the greeting which all classes were eager to pay to such illustrious representatives of the Royal

House. After nearly two hours the Procession, which had passed out of the city, reached its destination in the various Camps, and dispersed.

5. Continuing with the chronological order of events, on the 30th December the Viceroy opened an Exhibition of Indian Art in the Kudsia Gardens. The exhibits were contained in a handsome building specially erected in the Moghul style, and the collection and arrangement had been carried out with great ability by Sir George Watt. The results exceeded our most sanguine anticipations. Unique specimens of ancient art, mostly chosen from the treasures of Native States, and now shown to the public for the first time, were exhibited side by side with a collection of the best art wares of the present day, the object being, as explained in the speech of His Excellency the Viceroy, a copy of which we enclose, on the one hand to demonstrate the capabilities of indigenous art and on the other hand to raise the existing standard by a comparison with the best models of the past. Our sincere thanks are due to the many Chiefs and Native gentlemen who contributed to the loan collections, and who stimulated competition by the offer of rewards to the competing artisans. Many of the latter, together with selected Native officials from all parts of the country, were assisted to visit the Exhibition; and to the public at large, we are glad to say, it afforded considerable attraction. Forty-eight thousand persons paid for admission, and purchases to the value of Rs. 3,62,332 were made. As permanent results, we are hopeful that a much needed impetus may have been given to many deserving branches of Indian art, and that craftsmen and patrons alike will be encouraged to revive the ancient traditions, and to adapt them to the requirements of modern life.

6. Omitting the Durbar, to which we shall refer later, the next important event was the Grand Chapter of the two Indian Orders of the Star of India and the Indian Empire held on the night of the 3rd January in the Diwan-i-Am, or Hall of Public Audience, in the Palace Fort of the Emperor Shah Jehan. This magnificent structure had, without the smallest injury to or alteration of its own features, been enlarged by temporary additions to three times its original size, and had been connected for the occasion by a covered passage with the white marble Diwan-i-Khas, or Hall of Private Audience. So skilfully were these additions made under the supervision of Colonel J. W. Thurburn, R.E., Secretary to the Punjab Government in the Public Works Department, and Rai Bahadur Ganga Ram, Superintendent of Works, that a stranger could hardly distinguish the new building from the old—even in the blaze of light in which the ceremony was held.

The Chapter was attended by 11 Knights Grand Commanders of the Star of India, 15 Knights Grand Commanders of the Indian Empire, 14 Knights Commanders of the Star of India, and 16 of the Indian Empire, 41 Companions of the former, and 110 of the latter Order. It was by far the largest Chapter that has ever been held in India. Nearly 2000 spectators were present. No less than 74 admissions or promotions in the Orders were made. Among those so honoured were the Chiefs of Charkhari, Cochin, Miraj (Senior Branch), Nabha, Shahpura, Sirmur, Sirohi, Tehri, and Travancore, the Khan of Dir, the Mirs of Hunza and Nagar, and the Mehtar of Chitral.

On the night of the 6th January, the Palace was again the scene of a State Ball, which, from the number of distinguished persons present and the unique surroundings, has had no equal in this country. Most of the Ruling Chiefs attended, and in all more than 4000 persons were present.

7. The 4th January being Sunday, Divine Service was celebrated at a specially arranged State ceremony, held in the open air, by the Metropolitan, assisted by the Bishop of Lahore. It was attended by His Excellency the Viceroy, Their Royal Highnesses, and all the officials and European troops present in Delhi.

8. On the 8th January, a Grand Review of the whole body of troops assembled was held on a level plain in the vicinity of the Camps. There were present about 34,000 troops of all ranks under His Excellency the Commander-in-Chief. Stands were erected for the accommodation of spectators, and many thousands also attended in carriages, on horseback, and on foot. His Excellency the Viceroy rode on to the ground at 11 A.M. with Their Royal Highnesses the Duke of Connaught and the Grand Duke of Hesse, and took the salute as the troops marched past. The Review was in all respects a most brilliant success, and produced a marked effect on the many warlike classes present. The Imperial Service Troops were well represented, the Contingents from Alwar, Bhopal, Bikaner, Gwalior, Jind, Nabha, Patiala, and Sirmur being led past the saluting-point by their Chiefs or other members of the ruling family. The enthusiasm created by the appearance of Chiefs of all ages, from the youthful prince who now occupies the Patiala *gadi* to the venerable figure of the veteran Sikh Chief of Nabha, will long be remembered by both Chiefs and people, and must tend to strengthen the military ties that unite the different constituents of the Indian Empire.

At Lord Lytton's Imperial Assemblage in 1877, an improvised Review of the Retainers of Native Chiefs preceded the Military Review. On the present occasion a separate morning was set apart for the Retainers' Review, and this ceremony, which took place on the 7th January, was one of the most picturesque and interesting of the celebrations of the fortnight. Some 40 States sent contingents, and great trouble had been taken to give a faithful representation of the old fashioned arms and equipment that are now passing out of use.

9. Owing to the enormous extent of ground covered by the various Camps, and to the press of daily and even hourly engagements, it was impossible for His Excellency the Viceroy to receive and return the visits of the unprecedented number of Chiefs and nobles who were present at Delhi. In order, however, to provide an opportunity of meeting all these distinguished personages, and to enable them to meet each other, two parties were given by His Excellency for the Indian guests—one at the Kudsia Gardens on the afternoon of the 2nd January for official guests other than Chiefs, and one for Ruling Chiefs on the evening of the 9th January at the Viceroy's Camp.

On the latter occasion an Investiture was held, at which His Royal Highness the Duke of Connaught, as Great Master of the Most Honourable Order of the Bath, invested the Nizam of Hyderabad with the Grand Cross of that Order, an honour which was intensely appreciated by His Highness, and the Maharaja of Kolhapur with the Grand Cross of the Royal Victorian Order. His Royal Highness also presented gold medals to various Chiefs who had attended His Majesty's Coronation in England, and, by His Majesty's command, His Excellency the Viceroy conferred the honour of Knighthood on several gentlemen.

10. Apart from official functions, the public rejoicings assumed various forms. Thus, on the 2nd January, there was an illumination of the city and a display of fireworks. A military assault-at-arms was held on the 3rd and the 5th January; and on most days there were numerously attended athletic contests, such as polo, football, and hockey, for which prizes were presented by the Viceroy. For the first time in Indian history might be seen on the same ground the game of polo, as still played in the remote mountain States of Hunza and Nagar on one side of India and Manipur on the other, and as borrowed from them and subsequently developed by the English both in India and in England. Concerts also were given by the military massed bands, numbering 2000 performers, under the direction of Captain G. B. Sanford.

11. From careful enquiries made at the time, we estimate that in addition to the normal population of the city, which was returned at the recent Census as 208,000, not less than 173,000 persons were attracted to Delhi by the Durbar. These figures afford a striking contrast to the 68,000 who were reckoned as having been drawn to Delhi by the Imperial Assemblage of 1877. Lists of the individuals invited by Government or attending officially will be found among the enclosures to this despatch; but the following additional details will be of interest. Of the principal Ruling Chiefs 103 were invited and 100 attended. Minor Chiefs were, as a rule, not invited; and any, to whom for financial reasons the visit to Delhi might have proved burdensome, were excused. In view of the recent heavy calls that had been made upon some of the Chiefs, mainly in consequence of famine, we were careful to explain that there was no occasion for ostentatious display and in a few cases we helped to relieve a temporary encumbrance by advancing the necessary funds.

Invitations to attend or to send representatives were also addressed to His Majesty the Shah of Persia and His Majesty the King of Siam, and to Their Highnesses the Amir of Afghanistan, the Sultan of Maskat, and the Maharaja Dhiraj of Nepal. These States were eventually represented by General Chow Phya Surawongse, the chief personal Aide-de-Camp of the King of Siam, Colonel Muhammad Ismail Khan, the Amir of Afghanistan's Envoy with the Viceroy, the son and heir of the Sultan of Maskat, and the Prime Minister of Nepal. An invitation to depute a representative was also addressed, through His Britannic Majesty's Minister at Tokio, to the allied Government of His Imperial Majesty the Emperor of Japan. The result was a Mission headed by General Baron Yasukata Oku, who, we have reason to believe, appreciated the military manœuvres which preceded the Durbar as highly as did the Indian Army his presence among them.

We also felt that the occasion was one in which it was eminently desirable that our fellow subjects in the colonies of Australia and South Africa with whom we have so many connections, and who are certain in the future to be brought into much closer contact with India, should be afforded an opportunity of participating. The invitations which the Viceroy addressed to their Governments were responded to by the deputation of Sir Richard Baker, President of the Federal Senate, from the former, and Sir Richard Solomon, Attorney-General of the Transvaal, from the latter.

Their Excellencies Colonel Sir Eduardo Galhardo, K.C.I.E., Governor-General of Portuguese India, and Mons. Victor Lanrezac, Governor of the French Settlements in

India, and the leading members of the Foreign Consular Body in India, also honoured us by assisting at the ceremonies as our guests.

Further, with a view to giving to the world at large a full, immediate, and unbiased account of the celebrations, we invited the leading journals of the United Kingdom and India to depute their representatives to attend the Durbar as our guests; and we extended similar hospitality and facilities to any other influential journals which applied to us. We have every reason to be grateful to those who profited by our invitation, for the admirable accounts of our proceedings which they circulated by telegraph and post to all parts of the world.

12. In inviting the attendance of the heads of Local Governments and Administrations, we intimated that they should be accompanied by a limited number of the members of their administration, leading officials, Native noblemen and gentlemen, and heads of representative bodies.

All the Europeans thus invited were treated as the personal guests of the head of the province or administration to which they belonged, and were accommodated in the head-quarters or Central Camp of the province. The Ruling Chiefs with the Political Officers attached to them were encamped in separate camps grouped territorially, and the Native noblemen, officials, and others were for the most part in separate Provincial camps, while some secured accommodation in the city and civil station of Delhi.

The Central Camps, including those of His Excellency the Viceroy, the various Local Governments and Administrations, the Commander-in-Chief and the Provincial Commands, and the Foreign and Press Camp, occupied a site historic in the annals of 1857, below the famous Ridge. The population of these camps alone, including followers, numbered over 13,000; and considerations of space and sanitation demanded the location elsewhere of the Provincial Camps with their 35,000 inhabitants, of the Military Camps with their strength of 56,000, and of the miscellaneous camps, which sheltered another 12,000. The most convenient sites were selected, but, even so, they extended over an area of 40 square miles, while the remaining 57,000 of additional population found quarters in the city and civil station. A map, showing the location of the different camps, with the railways and roads, is one of the enclosures with this despatch.

13. It will be readily understood that an encampment of this size entailed elaborate preparations. Many thousands of tents had to be collected. Camp sites had to be levelled and forty miles of new roads were constructed. A 2′ 6″ gauge light railway, seven miles in length, was built to connect the city with the Central Camp and the Durbar Amphitheatre, and carried 102,098 passengers from first to last, exclusive of 850 holders of season tickets; extensions were also made from existing main lines to facilitate the delivery of the heavy material for the camp. The existing water supply was supplemented by seventy-two reservoirs, forty-five wells, and thirty-eight miles of pipes; and 2475 persons were employed as a special sanitary staff. Special telegraph, telephone, and postal services were organised; and the Central Camp, the Fort, and the principal streets of the city were lighted by electricity, plant which had already been ordered by our Military Department, for the lighting and ventilation of barracks, being utilised for the purpose. The food supply was catered for partly by private enterprise, and partly by the Supply and Transport

Department. For the Durbar itself a temporary Amphitheatre in white and gold was erected, according to a plan prepared by the Viceroy, with the assistance of Sir Swinton Jacob. This structure, which turned out to be pre-eminently well adapted for its purpose and which was also utilised for the Retainers' Review and the military Assault-at-Arms, was designed exclusively in the Indo-Saracenic or Moghul style, every detail being copied from buildings at Delhi or Agra. It was erected on approximately the same site as Lord Lytton's Amphitheatre in 1877; but it was entirely different in size and shape, and it held three times the number of spectators, since it provided seating and standing accommodation for no fewer than 16,000 persons. A plan of the Amphitheatre, showing the seating arrangements, is enclosed.

The whole of the arrangements were under the supervision of a Central and an Executive Committee. The former was the initiatory and controlling authority, and its decisions were carried out by the Executive Committee or by the Government Department concerned. Thus the Home Department undertook the control of the Police arrangements, the Military Works Department that of the electric installation, and the Military Department that of the markets managed by the Supply and Transport Corps, while the control of ceremonies remained with the Foreign Department.

To make provision for the peace and the maintenance of good order at the Coronation Durbar, and to provide a simple and speedy procedure for dealing with the various petty offences that were likely to occur in the camps, a short Act, called the Delhi Durbar Police Act, 1902, was passed by the Punjab Legislative Council, and of this we enclose a copy.

In other ways we received valuable assistance from the Punjab Government, which deputed its Sanitary Commissioner to take charge of the Sanitation and Conservancy of the Camps, its Inspector-General of Police to control the Police arrangements, and its Chief Engineer to supervise the buildings, water supply, and roads. The further special agency included a Camp Officer in executive charge of each Camp; a Special Magistrate for the Central Camp and one for each group of Provincial Camps; an Executive Sanitary Officer, a Health Officer, and a Plague Officer; a Railway Officer for the construction and management of the light railway; and a staff of Attachés to attend to the details of the various ceremonies and to the reception of the Chiefs.

14. How successful were the exertions of all these different agents, and how fortune waited upon their enterprise, may be illustrated by the fact that, so far as we are aware, among the vast crowds temporarily assembled at Delhi, with few of the advantages offered by great European cities, not a single serious accident occurred. The proceedings were also favoured with the most agreeable weather, rain only falling upon a single night, and then only in sufficient quantity to lay the dust, and to add greatly to the comfort as well as to the spectacular effect of the great Military Review. Though the temperature was cold at night in the concluding weeks of December, it continued to get warmer every day, and throughout the fortnight of official celebrations may be said to have been perfect.

15. From this description of the preliminaries, we now pass to an account of the Durbar itself. Of the picturesque side of this memorable gathering we need say but little. The long lines of troops; the wide plain filled with a multitude of all races of the Empire; the great assembly in the Amphitheatre, where the Chiefs, Governors, Colonial and foreign

representatives, and leading officials occupied seats on either side of the Viceroy's Daïs; the emotion stirred by the entry of the small band of Mutiny heroes; these have all been described in the columns of the Press. Similarly full justice has there been rendered to the combined magnificence and variety of a display which brought together, in their national dresses or garbs of State, figures so widely separated by race and residence as the Arab Sheikhs of the Aden Protectorate, the Baluch and Pathan Chieftains of the Indian border, the heirs or representatives of the States of Nepal, Sikkim, and Maskat, and the picturesquely clad Shan Chieftains from the Salwin and the Mekong. To Muhammadans the day was the anniversary of the Id-ul-Fitr, and to allow of their devotions, the Durbar was fixed for noon. Punctually to the hour His Excellency the Viceroy drove into the arena escorted by his Body-Guard and the Imperial Cadet Corps, and ascended the Daïs, whither he had been preceded, in a separate procession, by Their Royal Highnesses the Duke and Duchess of Connaught. The Herald then advanced on horseback accompanied by his trumpeters, and by command of the Viceroy read aloud the Proclamation, announcing the Coronation of His Majesty the King, Emperor of India. On the conclusion of the Proclamation, the Royal Standard was unfurled to the sound of the National Anthem and an Imperial Salute of 101 guns. His Excellency then addressed the Assemblage, gathered, as he said, that day to symbolise and give expression to the united loyalty of the Empire to His Majesty's mighty and benevolent rule. The announcement of the gracious message which His Majesty had desired to be conveyed to his Indian people was received with enthusiastic cheering, and repeated applause greeted the Viceroy's references to the Princes and people of India, to the great future lying before the country, and to the favours which the Government desired to associate with the occasion. Translations of His Excellency's speech in Urdu had been distributed to the Ruling Chiefs and Native gentlemen on their arrival at the Amphitheatre, so that they might more readily follow the proceedings.

At the conclusion of the address, of which copies in English and Urdu are included in the enclosures to this despatch, three cheers for His Majesty were given by the audience and repeated with overpowering effect by the troops and spectators outside. The Ruling Chiefs were then presented to His Excellency the Viceroy and His Royal Highness the Duke of Connaught. This proceeding, which was in reality a reversion to the time-honoured practice of Indian Accession Durbars, had been introduced by the Viceroy and specially explained by him to the Chiefs, in order to enable them to play a personal part in the proceedings, and to testify individually their sentiments of loyalty and devotion to the Throne, by tendering to the Representative and to the Brother of His Majesty with their own lips the congratulations and heartfelt vows of attachment evoked by the moving character of the scene, in which they thus became chief actors instead of mere spectators. The suggestion was cordially welcomed by the Chiefs as soon as they realised its import. The whole of them came forward, without exception, attended in some cases by a son or a Minister, and in accents of unmistakable pleasure and sincerity offered their dutiful and loyal congratulations to His Majesty on his accession to the Throne, and expressed their satisfaction at being present at the great and notable solemnity held to proclaim the fact to the Princes and people of India. This ceremony, which was perhaps the most impressive feature of the Durbar, brought the latter to a close.

16. On the evening of the same day a State Dinner was given by His Excellency the Viceroy in his Camp to the principal official guests, and the health of His Majesty the King-Emperor and of His Royal Highness the Duke of Connaught were proposed by His Excellency, and enthusiastically received. We enclose copies of the speeches made by the Viceroy on this occasion and of the Duke of Connaught's reply.

17. His Excellency the Viceroy and Their Royal Highnesses the Duke and Duchess of Connaught left Delhi on Saturday, the 10th January, the same ceremonies being observed at their departure as on their arrival.

18. There thus came to an end the most imposing ceremony, or rather series of ceremonies, that has ever been held in India in British or perhaps in any times. The conception of the Durbar, the control of the arrangements and supervision of the thousand and one details which were essential to success, were the work of the Viceroy, who made himself responsible for the entire undertaking, and visited Delhi no fewer than four times in the nine months preceding the Durbar. As regards the policy which underlay the conception and inspired the execution of a scheme with which we regard it as a privilege to have been associated, we cannot better describe it than in His Excellency's own words during the recent Budget Debate on the 25th March, 1903:

"But to me, and I hope to the majority of us, the Durbar meant not a panorama or a procession. It was a landmark in the history of the people, and a chapter in the ritual of the State. What was it intended for? It was meant to remind all the Princes and peoples of the Asiatic Empire of the British Crown that they had passed under the dominion of a new and single Sovereign, to enable them to solemnise that great and momentous event, and to receive the Royal assurance and greeting. And what was its effect? They learned that under that benign influence they were one, that they were not scattered atoms in a heterogeneous and cumbersome mass, but co-ordinate units in a harmonious and majestic whole. The scales of isolation and prejudice and distrust fell from their eyes, and from the Arab Sheikhs of Aden on the west to the Shan Chiefs of the Mekong on the borders of China, they felt the thrill of a common loyalty and the inspiration of a single aim. Was there nothing in this? Is it nothing that the Sovereign at his Coronation should exchange pledges with his assembled lieges, of protection and respect on the one side, of spontaneous allegiance on the other? Is it nothing that the citizens of the Empire should learn what that Empire means? Even if we take the rest of India, which could not be present at Delhi, but held its own rejoicings in its own place, is it nothing to lift an entire people for a little space out of the rut of their narrow and parochial lives, and to let them catch a glimpse of a higher ideal, an appreciation of the hidden laws that regulate the march of nations and the destinies of men? I believe that the Durbar, more than any event in modern history, showed to the Indian people the path which, under the guidance of Providence, they are treading, taught the Indian Empire its unity, and impressed the world with its moral as well as material force. It will not be forgotten. The sound of the trumpets has already died away. The Captains and the Kings have departed. But the effect produced by this overwhelming display of unity and patriotism is still alive, and will not perish. Everywhere it is known that upon the throne of the East is seated a power that has made of the sentiments, the aspirations, and the interests of 300 millions of

Asiatics a living thing, and the units in that great aggregation have learned that in their incorporation lies their strength. As a disinterested spectator of the Durbar remarked, 'Not until to-day did I realise that the destinies of the East still lie, as they always have done, in the hollow of India's hand.' I think, too, that the Durbar taught the lesson not only of power but of duty. There was not an officer of Government there present, there was not a Ruling Prince, nor a thoughtful spectator, who must not at one moment or other have felt that participation in so great a conception carried with it responsibility as well as pride, and that he owed something in return for whatever of dignity or security or opportunity the Empire had given to him."

19. The feelings of loyalty and devotion to the Throne and of pride in the might of an Empire, of which they realised that they were integral parts, were clearly testified by the remarks made by the Chiefs as they tendered to the Viceroy and His Royal Highness the Duke of Connaught their felicitations and assurances of homage to the Crown. Sometimes a Chief had rehearsed a short speech, but the power of the moment was upon him, and his formal utterance melted into a simple but heartfelt and obviously sincere expression of the pride and pleasure that he felt in assisting as a partner in the toils and joys of Empire, and in tendering his congratulations to the Sovereign. Could any studied oration have been more eloquent than the few words of the aged Raja of Nabha? "Now," said he, "I can die in peace, as I have discharged the three duties of a true Sikh,—I have lived according to the precepts of the Gurus, I have aided the State with my sword, and now I have paid my personal homage to my Sovereign."

Her Highness the Begum of Bhopal, who took her place, veiled, among the other Chiefs, presented a written address in which, after referring to the auspicious circumstance in the eyes of Muhammadans that the Durbar should coincide with their Id, she, "as the well-wisher and sincere admirer of the British Paramount Power," assured Government, "on this historic occasion, not only of the fidelity, devotion and affection of myself, my sons, my people and of the women of my State, but also of the loyalty of the whole Muhammadan population of India, for faithfulness and obedience to the Ruler are both strictly ordained by the Muhammadan religion."

We could multiply such quotations from every speech made that day, but as these will be collected in the Official History, we will only now refer to an address subsequently delivered by His Highness the Nizam on his return from Delhi to Hyderabad, in which he said: "It was a source of great pleasure to me that I was enabled to take my part in the Coronation Durbar of His Majesty the Emperor of India (may his generosity last for ever) and after the custom of my ancestors to show, in a simple, straightforward, and soldierly manner, by word and deed, my historical friendship and loyalty. * * * I also count this journey particularly fortunate in that it enabled me to meet at Delhi my contemporary Chiefs and high officers."

20. We trust we have brought home to Your Lordship the extent to which the ceremony of the Durbar was regarded by the Ruling Chiefs and by those who took part in it as a solemn and almost religious observance, and also as a great ceremonial of Imperial and awe-inspiring significance. The occasion was wholly dissevered from the ideas or associations of an ordinary Durbar. It was felt that this was the Sovereign's

Durbar, held by his orders for the celebration of the most auspicious event in his reign. Accordingly it was the message of the Sovereign that excited the loudest applause at the Durbar. Every mention of his name evoked a similar demonstration, while the reception accorded to his Royal Brother was pregnant with the same lesson. No one who was present can have failed to carry away the conviction that the most potent force in the union of Great Britain with India is the veneration and affection that are entertained for the Throne.

If such was the immediate effect of the ceremony on those Princes and Chiefs of India whose lives had been passed under the immediate hegemony of the British Government, its influence upon those who have more recently come under our sway, or who are not so intimately connected with our rule, was even more marked. The Afghan Envoy at the Durbar inquired if the representatives of foreign Powers were present, for, said he, this assembly, resembling the final gathering at the Day of Judgment, could only bring home to them the futility of opposing a Power, which could thus assemble without force or compulsion, but simply by the ties of loyalty and affection, an entire universe of peoples and creeds. Much the same ideas were expressed by the Prime Minister of Nepal; while the representatives of the distant Gilgit tribes laughed when they thought of the day when they had attempted to pit their puny strength against even a feudatory of such a Power.

The effect of the display of military power at the Review was no less remarkable, and undoubtedly impressed the representatives of foreign Powers who were present. We attach special importance to the impression caused by the eagerness of the Chiefs to appear in public at the head of their troops as feudatories of the Empire. The interest taken by the Chiefs as a body in the contingents of the Imperial Service Troops was noticeable and cannot fail greatly to promote this most useful and patriotic movement. Their appearance on parade was highly creditable, so much so, indeed, that the Baluch Chiefs remarked that they only differed, if at all, from the regular army in the greater perfection of their equipment and drill.

We believe that these impressions were no mere transient phases of sensuous emotion, but that the striking incidents, of which they were the privileged spectators, and the general sense of well-ordered power and popular contentment, of good governance on the one hand and identity of interest on the other, which marked the whole proceedings, will continue to produce their effect on all who were there present long after the Delhi Durbar has passed away, save as the treasured memory of a splendid and ennobling scene.

21. There is still another sense in which, as His Excellency anticipated, the Durbar has achieved a most beneficial result, and has had a far-reaching effect. The growing power of the railway, of the press, and other means of communication, has done much to bring the different parts of India into contact with one another, and to obliterate their divergences; but on no previous occasion have so many of the Chiefs and nobles and representative persons of India of all races and religions had an opportunity of meeting together, not for an hour or a day, but for a period of weeks. Much was done by the friendly exchange of ideas at social gatherings and official functions to break down the barriers of ignorance or distrust which have tended to keep different classes and individuals apart, and have proved a serious obstacle to the cohesion of the body politic. That the

Chiefs themselves thoroughly appreciated the opportunities afforded is clearly shown by the remarks of His Highness the Nizam already quoted, and by messages of a similar character which have reached the Viceroy from many other quarters. Nor is it the Chiefs alone who benefited in this way. Advantage was taken of the occasion by our civil and military officers of different Provinces who were assembled for the Durbar, and who are precluded by their duties at ordinary times from meeting, to discuss together many matters of the highest administrative importance, and to compare ideas on points of policy or practice in a way which, within the narrow limits of their own Provinces, would have been impossible. We are confident that there was not an officer present, British or Indian, who did not feel a sense of pride at serving the Government of an Empire so vast and beneficent, or who did not carry away with him the stimulus of an added zeal to give of his best to the service of his Sovereign and country.

22. But the Durbar did not produce its effect only on those who were able to attend. We have reason to believe that the great mass of the people of India, whether in British territory or in the States under His Majesty's protection, were profoundly impressed by the report of the ceremonies that took place, and that their imaginations were not untouched by the great idea of which these were but the outward form. Local celebrations were held everywhere throughout the country on the same day; and even the humblest participant can hardly have failed to entertain some conception of a national unity achieved under the firm but kindly sway of the British sceptre, and carrying with it the privileges of common citizenship in a world-wide Empire. In other ways too, the event was brought home to the minds of the populace. By an act of grace 16,188 prisoners were released from British Indian jails, and similar clemency was shown in the majority of the Native States. Nor must we omit to mention in this connection the impetus which was given to internal trade, more especially in the Native States, by the requirements of an assembly on so vast a scale as that recently held, and for those of the very numerous local celebrations.

23. Upon the effect of the Durbar beyond the limits of India, we are not in a position to pronounce with authority, but from the references to it contained in the newspapers of all countries, we are entitled to believe that it was very great, and that the outside world has thereby been enabled to form a more correct idea of the scale and polity of our Indian Empire, to judge of the difficulties that have been met and surmounted in its creation, and to realise the power and prestige which must attach to the State, that for the first time in history has not only succeeded in moulding into a single whole the scattered and often warring atoms, which hitherto formed the congeries of countries and peoples included within the Indian continent, but has also by the justice and high purpose of its administration infused the entire mass with a spirit of devotion to a common Sovereign.

24. Of the honours, favours, and concessions, by which the occasion was marked, a complete list will be found in the Gazette Extraordinary of the 1st January. We have already alluded to the promotions in, and appointments to, the Orders of the Bath, the Star of India and the Indian Empire, and to the honours of Knighthood conferred by His Majesty. His Majesty was graciously pleased also to award 15 Kaisar-i-Hind Medals of the 1st class, and 18 of the 2nd class. Further honours, reserved for Chiefs only, consisted of the addition of 2 guns to the permanent salute of the Nawab of Janjira, the grant of

permanent salutes of 9 guns to the Sawbwas of Keng Tung, Möng Nai and Hsi Paw, who are the three principal Shan Chiefs, and the grant of personal salutes of 9 guns each to the Chiefs of Bhor and Danta and to Nawab Sir Amir-ud-din Ahmad Khan Bahadur K.C.I.E., of Loharu.

The British officers of the Indian Army were intensely gratified by the grant to them of that designation, while the Native officers equally appreciated the announcement that six of their number would be annually appointed as orderly officers in attendance upon His Majesty. Other favours to the Army included the addition of 20 appointments to the first class and 60 to the second class of the Order of British India, the grant of honorary rank, on retirement, to Native officers in possession of that decoration, the grant of extra meritorious service medals and extra long service and good conduct medals, with gratuities in each case, money grants to all British and Native Corps, the grant of special privileges to the Native Mountain Artillery, and the release or mitigation of punishment of various classes of military offenders. His Highness the Raja of Nabha received the honorary rank of Colonel of the 14th (Ferozepore) Sikh Infantry, and His Highness the Maharao of Kota the honorary rank of Major in the Deoli Irregular Force, whose head-quarters adjoin his State.

Various civil titles were conferred by His Excellency the Viceroy on distinguished Native gentlemen, and in six very special cases grants of land or *inams* were bestowed. We have already alluded to the release of prisoners in British India. In the Viceroy's speech in addition to certain measures of financial relief to those Native States which had suffered from famine, was foreshadowed the very considerable reduction of taxation that was definitely announced in the Budget three months later, and that will always be associated by the people with the year of His Majesty's Coronation.

25. We should be guilty of an inexcusable omission if we did not acknowledge the devotion and ability with which the many duties connected with the Durbar were discharged. From first to last the preparations proceeded rapidly and harmoniously, every programme for the Durbar fortnight was carried out without a hitch, and the difficult task of winding up the Camp was expeditiously and satisfactorily performed, the final meeting of the Committees being held on the 10th April.

Where all did so well, it is difficult to particularise; but the following names appear to call for particular notice. Our cordial thanks are due to the Central and Executive Committees. Of the former, we must specially mention Sir Hugh Barnes, the President, and Major-General G. Henry; and of the latter, Captain A. D. Bannerman, the Secretary, and Major H. Hudson. Mr. Gordon Walker and Major M. W. Douglas combined their membership of these committees with other arduous duties as Commissioner and Deputy Commissioner of Delhi: similarly Colonel H. F. Lyons-Montgomery of the Executive Committee was also the Officer of the Supply and Transport Corps, who was responsible for the very complete Commissariat arrangements.

To Lieutenant-Colonel C. J. Bamber, as Sanitary Commissioner, and Lieutenant Colonel H. B. Thornhill, as Executive Sanitary Officer, is chiefly due, under Providence, the immunity of the Camp from any serious outbreak of disease, though plague was rife over the greater part of the Continent, and, but for the precautions taken, there would certainly have been danger of cholera. From the time the Camp was started in July 1902, there were altogether ten cases of plague, of which nine were imported, but the arrangements effectually prevented the disease from taking hold.

Rai Bahadur Ganga Ram was in executive charge of the numerous public works, including the building of the Amphitheatre, the structural additions in the Fort, the construction of roads, and the provision of the water-supply. The electric installation for the Fort was undertaken by Messrs. Osler and Co., and that for the Central Camp by Messrs. Kilburn and Co. The latter included 100 arc lights, and more than 8000 incandescent lamps disposed among the various tents. We can pay no higher compliment to the efficiency of the work done by the firm under the supervision of Major A. M. Stuart and Captain C. O. Halliday, R.E., than to say that during the month for which the light was employed there was not a single failure.

The postal arrangements included 16 special offices and numerous pillar boxes, and were satisfactorily carried out by Rai Bahadur Daulat Ram, C.I.E., under the supervision of the Postmaster-General of the Punjab. The Telegraph Department, under Mr. O. Lees, opened 11 telegraph offices, and a telephone exchange with 25 branches to the more important camps; it gave general satisfaction, the facilities afforded to the Press being, we understand, particularly appreciated.

The Punjab Police under the orders of Mr. C. Brown, the Inspector-General, added to their well-earned reputation by the excellence of their arrangements for the regulation of traffic and the prevention of disorder and crime. Their powers of suppression were never called into action, as disorder and crime were non-existent.

The light railway constructed and managed by Captain H. A. L. Hepper, R.E., proved of the greatest service. The efforts of the main lines to meet the very heavy traffic incidental to the Durbar also deserve recognition. Crowding and some delay were inevitable, and the difficulty of preventing these was enhanced by the awkward and confined situation of the Delhi main station, into which most of the traffic had perforce to be brought. The experience gained will doubtless lead to improved arrangements on any future occasion of the kind, while the remodelling of the station on the present occasion has been a great advantage to what has now become the centre of the Indian Railway system.

We have already alluded to the striking success with which the programmes of the various ceremonies were carried out. Sir Hugh Barnes was in immediate charge of all matters of ceremonial. Of the staff which ably assisted him, he has specially brought to our notice the name of Mr. R. Hughes-Buller of the Indian Civil Service. The ticket arrangements were successfully undertaken by Mr. W. E. Jardine, also of the Civil Service.

Of the amusements provided for visitors, the Club and the Polo Tournament, organised by Colonel the Hon. E. Baring, Military Secretary to the Viceroy, were deservedly popular.

Interesting notes by the officers in charge of the various branches of the arrangements are included among the enclosures with this despatch.

26. As regards the expenditure from public revenues on the Durbar, we are not yet in a position to give final figures for certain of the heads included in the actual cost. Our

most recent calculations were stated in paragraphs 138 to 140 of Part II. of the Financial Statement for 1903-04, where it was shown that the aggregate net charge to Imperial Revenues seemed unlikely to exceed Rs. 12,61,000, while the net charge against Provincial Revenues was estimated at Rs. 14,83,000: or a total under the two headings of about £180,000. It is possible that the credit side of the account may be increased by further recoveries, and a close scrutiny of the charges debited to the Durbar, which has been taken in hand, may show that some items ought properly to be debited to ordinary heads of expenditure. On the other hand, some difficulty has been experienced in distributing the total military expenditure, which has shown a considerable excess over the original forecast, between the Durbar and the manœuvres that preceded it; and we have not yet completed the enquiries which will enable us to apply a fair and reasonable principle of division.

27. In accordance with His Majesty's command special gold and silver medals were struck in honour of the occasion, the head of His Majesty being depicted on the one side and a suitable inscription in the Persian character on the other. We are now engaged in distributing these medals to the principal official participators in the Durbar, and to selected officers and men of the British and Indian armies who were present. The gold medals are for presentation to the Ruling Chiefs and a few high officers of Government. The total of the silver medals is about 2500.

28. In a supplementary despatch we propose to send, for Your Lordship's information, copies of reports which we have called for from the various Local Governments and administrations as to the local celebrations of the Coronation that were held throughout India on the same day as the Delhi Durbar, *viz.*, 1st January, 1903.

We have the honour to be,

MY LORD,

Your Lordship's most obedient humble servants,

(Signed) CURZON.
" KITCHENER.
" T. RALEIGH.
" E. F.-G. LAW.
" E. R. ELLES.
" A. T. ARUNDEL.
" DENZIL IBBETSON.

APPENDIX IV

[No. 161 of 1903]

GOVERNMENT OF INDIA

FOREIGN DEPARTMENT

INTERNAL

To

The Right Hon. W. St. J. F. BRODRICK,

His Majesty's Secretary of State for India.

Simla, *the 22nd October, 1903.*

Sir,

In our letter No. 58, dated the 7th May, 1903, we had the honour to furnish Lord George Hamilton with a report of the proceedings at Delhi in December and January last in honour of the Coronation of His Majesty the King, Emperor of India. We then promised to submit, for His Lordship's information, a further communication descriptive of the celebrations held throughout India on the 1st January, 1903, the same day as the Delhi Durbar.

2. We now enclose copies of the reports of local celebrations that have been received from the Local Governments and Administrations.

3. From these papers it will be seen that not only in the districts and cities of British India, including even such remote portions of His Majesty's dominions as the Andaman and Nicobar Islands, but also in the Native States, the occasion was regarded by all classes of the people as one of peculiar importance, and that the general rejoicings which everywhere took place were accompanied by remarkable manifestations of loyalty to the Imperial Crown.

4. In addition to the usual parades, *feux de joie* and salutes, local Durbars were held at most district head-quarters and at the capital of almost every State, at which honours granted to Chiefs or to the leading notables were announced, Kaisar-i-Hind medals and honorary certificates were conferred on those who had won these distinctions by services to the public, and loyal congratulatory addresses were received. The public buildings were illuminated, and in the majority of places there was a display of fireworks; while the public offices and schools were closed for several days, and prisoners were released. But over and above these formal and *quasi*-official celebrations, the fervent loyalty of the public

broke out into further rejoicings, the marked spontaneity of which was specially striking. Not only at capitals and head-quarters, but throughout the districts, attempts were made to celebrate His Majesty's Coronation in a befitting way, and these attempts were attended with uniform success. As one of our officers in the Deccan reports it: "If I were asked what struck me as the most significant feature, I should say it was the complete accord and co-operation of officials and non-officials, and of men of every different race, caste, and creed." Another writes: "In fact, it would be no exaggeration to say that the day was observed everywhere as a great national or religious holiday is observed in India, with this addition, that all communities took part in observing it." Varied as were the celebrations throughout the diverse countries and nations included in the Indian Empire, the religious note dominated everywhere, and prayers for Their Majesties were offered up by all classes and creeds with the public solemnity of great religious festivals. The next most striking feature of the celebrations was one which indicates clearly the devotion of India to a personal Sovereign. Pictures of Their Majesties were unveiled or carried in procession through the towns, on richly caparisoned elephants where these were available, and elsewhere in litters or cars. Photographs, prints, and commemorative medals were freely distributed; and in Burma the people, with the assistance of a portrait, celebrated according to the full traditions of the old Court the actual coronation of an Emperor of the country. The poor and school-children were feasted. The Native Chiefs and great land-owners remitted arrears of revenue and rent, and native bankers cancelled debts. Bonfires blazed on a thousand hills. The frontier and wild forest and hill tribes celebrated the occasion by their national dances.

5. Nor were the celebrations confined to merely temporary rejoicings. Memorial schools, hospitals, lying-in-wards, and charitable dispensaries were started; beds and scholarships endowed; Town Halls and Libraries founded; Coronation wells sunk and tanks dug, and groves planted. In short, the loyalty and devotion of the Indian Chiefs and peoples to their common Sovereign were expressed in every way that modern enlightenment or ancient tradition could suggest; and the political effect and sense of the unity of the Empire produced by these local celebrations and rejoicings will, we believe, be, if possible, hardly less profound, while they were, from the nature of the circumstances, necessarily more widespread even than the memory of the Great Coronation Durbar at Delhi itself.

6. These celebrations, however spontaneous, were not successfully carried out without imposing a considerable strain upon the energy and responsibility of our local officers—civil, political, and military; and we desire to express our high appreciation of the manner in which they performed their task.

We have the honour to be,

SIR,

Your most obedient, humble servants,

(Signed) CURZON.
" T. RALEIGH.
" E. F.-G. LAW.
" E. R. ELLES.
" A. T. ARUNDEL.
" DENZIL IBBETSON.

APPENDIX V

The Gazette of India

EXTRAORDINARY

SIMLA: FRIDAY, JUNE 26, 1903

STAR OF INDIA

NOTIFICATION

Simla; the 26th June, 1903.

His Excellency the Grand Master of the Most Exalted Order of the Star of India is pleased to announce that His Majesty the KING, EMPEROR OF INDIA, has been graciously pleased to make the following appointments to the said Order:

TO BE COMPANIONS.

THOMAS GORDON WALKER, Esquire, Indian Civil Service, Commissioner and Superintendent, Delhi Division, and a Member of the Central Committee, Coronation Durbar, Delhi.

Colonel JAMES WHITE THURBURN, Royal Engineers, Chief Engineer and Secretary to the Government of the Punjab in the Public Works Department, Buildings and Roads Branch, and a Member of the Central Committee, Coronation Durbar, Delhi.

By Order of the Grand Master,

L. W. DANE,

Secretary to the Most Exalted Order of the Star of India.

INDIAN EMPIRE

NOTIFICATION

Simla; the 26th June, 1903.

His Excellency the Grand Master of the Most Eminent Order of the Indian Empire is pleased to announce that His Majesty the KING, EMPEROR OF INDIA, has been graciously pleased to make the following appointments to the said Order:

TO BE COMPANIONS.

JOHN POLLEN, Esquire, Indian Civil Service, Commissioner of Customs, Salt, Opium, and Akbari, and Reporter-General of External Commerce for the Presidency of Bombay.

CHARLES BROWN, Esquire, Inspector-General of Police to the Government of the Punjab. In charge of the Police arrangements, Coronation Durbar, Delhi.

Lieutenant-Colonel HENRY BEAUFOY THORNHILL, Indian Army, Cantonment Magistrate of Bareilly.

GEORGE HUDDLESTON, Esquire, Officiating General Traffic Manager, East Indian Railway.

Major MONTAGU WILLIAM DOUGLAS, Indian Army, lately Deputy Commissioner of the Delhi District, and a Member of the Executive Committee, Coronation Durbar, Delhi.

CHARLES JAMES KEENE, Esquire, Deputy Traffic Superintendent, North-Western Railway.

Major HAVELOCK HUDSON, Indian Army, lately Assistant Quarter-Master-General and a Member of the Executive Committee, Coronation Durbar, Delhi.

Captain ARTHUR D'ARCY GORDON BANNERMAN, Indian Army, Political Assistant, 1st Class, and Secretary of the Executive Committee, Coronation Durbar, Delhi.

Rai Bahadur GUNGA RAM, Executive Engineer, 1st Grade, Public Works Department, Punjab, and Superintendent of Works, Coronation Durbar, Delhi.

By Order of the Grand Master,

L. W. DANE,

Secretary to the Most Eminent Order of the Indian Empire.

APPENDIX VI

OFFICERS ON SPECIAL DUTY IN CONNECTION WITH THE DELHI DURBAR

1.—Central Committee.

Sir Hugh Barnes, K.C.S.I., K.C.V.O., Indian Civil Service	Secretary to the Government of India in the Foreign Department, *President.*
Major-General G. Henry, R.E., C.B.	Quartermaster-General in India.
Mr. T. G. Walker, C.S.I., Indian Civil Service	Commissioner of the Delhi Division.
Lieut.-Colonel the Hon. E. Baring, C.V.O.	Military Secretary to the Viceroy.
Colonel J. W. Thurburn, R.E., C.S.I.	Chief Engineer of the Punjab.
Lieut.-Colonel C. J. Bamber, I.M.S.	Sanitary Commissioner in the Punjab.
Mr. F. S. Cowie, Indian Civil Service	Assistant Secretary to the Government of India in the Foreign Department, *Secretary.*

2.—Executive Committee.

Major M. W. Douglas, C.I.E.	Deputy Commissioner of Delhi.
Lieut.-Colonel H. F. Lyons Montgomery	Director of Supply and Transport, Delhi Durbar.
Major H. Hudson, C.I.E.	Deputy Assistant Quartermaster-General.
Captain A. d'A. G. Bannerman, C.I.E.	Indian Political Department, *Secretary.*

3.—Attachés of the Foreign Department, and other Officers on duty in connection with the organisation of the Durbar.

Captain R. B. Berkeley	Rajputana Attaché.
Mr. B. S. Carey, C.I.E.	Burma Attaché.
Major P. Z. Cox, C.I.E.	With the Maskat Deputation.
Lieutenant Crawshay Williams, R.A. . .	With the Siamese Representative.
Mr. L. M. Crump, Indian Civil Service .	Hyderabad Attaché.
Mr. T. C. Edwards, Indian Civil Service .	Assistant Secretary to the Government of India in the Foreign Department.
Mr. E. V. Gabriel, Indian Civil Service .	Central India Attaché.

Captain C. O. Halliday, R.E.	Inspecting Officer, Electrical Installation.
Captain E. F. Hood	With the Japanese Deputation.
Mr. R. Hughes-Buller, Indian Civil Service .	Special Assistant to Sir H. Barnes.
Mr. W. E. Jardine, Indian Civil Service .	In charge of ticket arrangements.
Mr. A. R. Knapp, Indian Civil Service . .	Madras Attaché.
Captain S. G. Knox	Baluchistan Attaché.
Major E. F. Marriott	Baroda Attaché.
Captain F. McConaghey	Kashmir Attaché.
Captain E. W. McK. Ballantyne . . .	With the Governor of the French Settlements.
Mr. H. T. Morgan, Indian Civil Service .	United Provinces Attaché.
Mr. H. A. Playfair	Central Provinces Attaché.
Mr. C. L. S. Russell, Indian Civil Service .	Mysore Attaché.
Major T. E. Scott, C.I.E., D.S.O.. . . .	With the Japanese Deputation.
Major A. M. Stuart, R.E.	In charge of Electrical Installation.
Mr. E. A. C. Walsh, Indian Civil Service .	Bengal Attaché.
Captain B. C. Waterfield	North-West Frontier Province Attaché.
Captain F. W. Wodehouse	Bombay Attaché.
Major A. E. Woods	Assam Attaché.
Mr. R. E. Younghusband, Indian Civil Service	Punjab Attaché.

Aides-de-Camp to Sir H. Barnes.

Lieutenant D. Lorimer.	Captain R. W. R. Barnes, D.S.O.
Captain H. Stewart.	Captain H. F. Bateman-Champain.

Lieutenant T. Keyes.

Special Railway Officers.

Captain H. A. L. Hepper, R.E.	Lieutenant J. B. Corry, D.S.O., R.E.
Lieutenant C. L. Magniac, R.E.	Lieutenant M. R. Elles, R.E.
Captain H. R. Stockley, R.E.	Lieutenant F. S. Garwood, R.E.

Mr. H. L. Kemball	In charge of the Durbar Detective Agency.
Mr. C. Brown	Inspector-General of Police, Punjab.
Mr. A. G. Hammond	Deputy Inspector-General of Police, Punjab.
Mr. S. Smith	Ditto. ditto.
Mr. S. E. Wallace	Assistant to Inspector-General of Police, Punjab.
Mr. E. H. G. Rotten	Assistant Inspector-General, Railway Police, Punjab.
Lieut.-Colonel H. B. Thornhill, C.I.E. .	Sanitary Officer and Special Camp Magistrate.
Major J. R. Dunlop Smith, C.I.E. . .	In charge of Native Chiefs' Retainers' Review.
Rai Bahadur Gunga Ram, C.I.E. . .	Superintendent of Works.
Mr. F. G. Maclean, C.I.E.	Director-General of Telegraphs.

Mr. H. M. Kisch, Indian Civil Service . . Director-General of Post Office.
Mr. C. Stewart-Wilson, Indian Civil Service . Postmaster-General, Punjab.
Mr. C. C. Sheridan . . . . . . Superintendent, Durbar Posts.

Officers of the Guard of Honour.

Major G. Staunton.
Lieutenant F. L. Makgill-Crichton-Maitland.
Lieutenant J. K. Dick-Cunyngham, D.S.O.

On duty connected with Musical Arrangements.

Captain G. B. Sanford . . . . . . Director of Music.
Captain J. Chrystie, R.G.A.
Lieutenant J. S. Crosthwaite.
Captain C. Hodgkinson.

Mr. P. Bramley . . . . Marshal of the State Entry.
Major A. G. Maxwell, 6th Bengal Cavalry . Chief Herald.*
Mr. F. T. Bates . . . . Executive Engineer, Irrigation Department, Delhi.
Major D. M. Davidson, I.M.S. . . . Civil Surgeon, Delhi.

Assistant Commissioners of Delhi.

Mr. H. D. Craik, Indian Civil Service.
Mr. L. B. Fyfe, Indian Civil Service.

District Superintendents of Police, Punjab.

Mr. W. F. L. Bean.
Mr. R. E. Blewitt.
Mr. A. H. Close.
Mr. H. S. Dunsford.
Mr. E. L. French.
Mr. G. S. Halliday.
Mr. W. A. E. Lake.
Mr. S. C. Mitchell.
Mr. G. T. C. Plowden.
Mr. G. A. Rundall.
Mr. A. C. Stewart.
Mr. T. W. Temple.
Mr. A. H. Wilkin.

Assistant District Superintendents of Police, Punjab.

Mr. H. J. C. Baskett.
Mr. F. B. Clough.
Mr. G. A. Cocks.
Mr. L. C. Glascock.
Mr. D. S. Hadow.
Mr. E. C. Handyside.
Mr. W. L. Hyde.
Mr. G. G. B. Isaacs.
Mr. D. Petrie.
Mr. C. Stead.
Mr. E. W. Tomkins.
Mr. G. A. Weston.

* The following were the trumpeters who accompanied the Herald at the Proclamation:

Trumpeter Desylva	2nd Madras Lancers.
„ Donovan	4th Dragoon Guards.
Trumpet Major Gore	5th Dragoon Guards.
Trumpeter Hari Singh	6th Bengal Cavalry.
„ Hill	R. H. Artillery, E Battery.
„ Innes	2nd Bombay Lancers.
„ Kala Singh	9th Bengal Lancers.
„ Minton	9th Lancers.
Trumpeter Muhammad Khan.	1st Central India Horse.
Trumpeter Muhammad Yar Khan.	6th Bengal Cavalry.
Trumpeter Lance-Corporal Nutall.	5th Dragoon Guards.
Trumpeter Pay	4th Lancers.
„ Prem Singh	3rd Punjab Cavalry.
„ Smith	15th Hussars.
„ Stevens	5th Dragoon Guards.

Police Officers, Viceroy's Camp.

Mr. F. J. Cassera. Captain H. T. Dennys. Mr. F. C. Isemonger.

3.—OFFICERS IN EXECUTIVE CHARGE OF CAMPS.

Captain F. G. Smallwood, R.A.	Viceroy's Camp.
Mr. O. V. Bosanquet, Indian Civil Service	Foreign and Press Camp.
Mr. J. N. Gupta, Indian Civil Service	Native Press Camp.
Captain J. C. D. Pinney, D.A.Q.M.G.	Maskat Camp.
Captain J. H. Hugo, I.M.S.	Nepal Camp.
Captain E. B. Peacock	Government of India Secretariat Camp.
Major M. Cowper, D.A.Q.M.G.	Commander-in-Chief's Camp, and the Camps of the Lieutenants-General, Bengal, Bombay, Madras, and Punjab.
Captain L. A. G. Hanmer	Visitors' Camp No. I.
Captain H. L. Tomkins	Visitors' Camp No. II.
Captain T. B. Sellar	Visitors' Camp No. III. and European Mutiny Veterans' Camp.
Captain E. K. Molesworth, R.E.	Madras Central Camp.
Major R. F. R. Formby	Madras Provincial Camp.
Captain F. W. Wodehouse	Bombay Central Camp.
Captain J. R. B. G. Carter	Bombay Chiefs' and Provincial Camps.
Major J. Strachey	Bengal Central Camp.
Mr. E. C. Ryland	Bengal Provincial Camp.
Mr. H. G. S. Tyler	United Provinces Central Camp.
Mr. P. Bramley	United Provinces Provincial Camp.
Major G. A. Robertson	Punjab Central Camp.
Captain C. H. Buck	Punjab Provincial Camp.
Captain J. S. Dunlop	Burma Central Camp.
Mr. B. S. Carey, Indian Civil Service, C.I.E.	Burma Provincial Camp.
Lieut. H. de L. Pollard Lowsley, R.E.	Central Provinces Central Camp.
Mr. A. S. Womack	Central Provinces Provincial Camp.
Captain H. W. G. Cole	Assam Central Camp.
Major A. E. Woods	Assam Provincial Camp.
Mr. L. M. Crump, Indian Civil Service	Hyderabad Central Camp. Berar Provincial Camp.
Lieutenant D. E. Robertson	Mysore Central Camp.
Mr. C. L. S. Russell, Indian Civil Service	Mysore Chiefs' Camp.
Mr. E. V. Gabriel, Indian Civil Service	Central India Central Camp.
Lieut.-Colonel C. Herbert	Central India Chiefs' Camp.
Mr. F. St. G. Manners Smith, C.E.	Rajputana Central Camp.
Captain R. B. Berkeley	Rajputana Chiefs' Camp.

Captain S. G. Knox	Baluchistan Central and Chiefs' Camps.
Captain B. C. Waterfield	North-West Frontier Province Central Camp.
Muhammad Abdul Karim Khan	North-West Frontier Province Provincial Camp.
Major E. F. Marriott	Baroda Camp.
Captain F. McConaghey	Kashmir Camp.

4.—Officers in Medical Charge of Camps and other Medical Officers on duty.

Lieut.-Colonel C. J. Bamber, I.M.S.	Administrative Medical Officer.
Major F. Wyville Thomson, I.M.S.	Special Health Officer.
Captain C. H. James, I.M.S.	Special Plague Medical Officer.
Captain W. E. A. Armstrong, I.M.S.	Viceroy's Camp.
Major F. J. Drury, I.M.S.	Foreign and Press Camp.
Major W. M. Molesworth, I.M.S.	Madras Central and Provincial Camp.
Lieut.-Colonel A. E. J. Croly, R.A.M.C.	Bombay Central Camp.
Lieut.-Colonel A. V. Anderson	Bombay Provincial Camp.
Lieut.-Colonel F. Peck	Bengal Central Camp.
Captain W. W. Clemesha	Bengal Provincial Camp.
Captain J. M. Crawford, I.M.S.	United Provinces Central Camp.
Major J. Chaytor White, I.M.S.	United Provinces Provincial Camp.
Lieut.-Colonel J. A. Cunningham, I.M.S.	Punjab Central and Provincial Camps.
Lieut.-Colonel R. E. G. Davis	Burma Central and Provincial Camps.
Colonel Moriarty, I.M.S.	Central Provinces Camp.
Captain A. Leventon, I.M.S.	Assam Camp.
Lieut.-Colonel G. H. D. Gimlette, C.I.E., I.M.S.	Hyderabad Central and Berar Camps.
Captain R. F. Standage, I.M.S.	Mysore Camp.
Lieut.-Colonel P. A. Weir, I.M.S.	Central India Central Camp.
Captain R. W. Knox, I.M.S.	Central India Chiefs' Camp.
Lieut.-Colonel D. ffrench-Mullen, I.M.S.	Rajputana Central Camp.
Major R. C. McWatt	Rajputana Chiefs' Camp.
Lieut.-Colonel J. C. Fullerton, I.M.S.	Baluchistan Central and Provincial Camps.
Lieut.-Colonel W. A. Sykes, I.M.S.	North-West Frontier Province Central and Provincial Camps.
Shaikh Lal Muhammad Khan Sahib	Baroda Camp.
Major W. R. Edwards	Kashmir Camp.

5.—Camp Magistrates.

Lieut.-Colonel H. B. Thornhill, C.I.E.	Special Camp Magistrate.
Major R. F. R. Formby	Madras Provincial Camp.
Sardar Khan Bahadur Muhammad Yakub, C.I.E.	Bombay Provincial Camp.
Mr. A. N. Moberly, Indian Civil Service	Bengal Provincial Camp.

Mr. L. C. Porter, Indian Civil Service	United Provinces Provincial Camp.
Mr. C. E. Browne	Burma Provincial Camp.
Mr. C. G. Chenevix-Trench, Indian Civil Service	Central Provinces Provincial Camp.
Mr. Abdul Majid	Assam Provincial Camp.
Captain E. Barnes	Central India Camp.
Captain C. T. Ducat	Rajputana Camp.
Captain C. B. Winter	Baluchistan Camp.
Major S. H. Godfrey	North-West Frontier Province Camp.
Major A. F. Bruce	Kashmir.

6.—SUPPLY AND TRANSPORT OFFICERS, AND OTHER MILITARY OFFICERS EMPLOYED ON DUTIES CONNECTED WITH THE ORGANISATION OF THE DURBAR.

Lieut.-Colonel F. Lyons Montgomery	Director of Supply and Transport.
Lieutenant W. Alves	Personal Assistant to Director of Supply and Transport.
Lieutenant A. H. Babington	Supply and Transport Corps (Base Depôt).
Major G. de S. Barrow	Deputy Assistant Quartermaster-General for Mobilization.
Major A. H. Bingley	Deputy Assistant Quartermaster-General.
Major L. T. Bowles	Station Staff Officer.
Captain E. P. Carter	In charge of Ordnance Depôt.
Lieutenant H. F. Collingridge	Asssistant Railway Staff Officer.
Lieutenant H. W. Davies	Supply and Transport Corps (Central Supply Depôt).
Major R. H. Ewart, D.S.O.	Supply and Transport Corps, Assistant Director for Forage.
Major J. P. C. Hennessy	Supply and Transport Corps (Base Depôt).
Captain J. H. Lloyd	Staff Captain for Mobilization.
Lieutenant J. A. Longridge	Supply and Transport Corps (Central Supply Depôt).
Major D. J. Meagher	Military Dairy Farm.
Captain C. H. G. Moore	Supply and Transport Corps (Central Camp).
Major C. F. Murray	Supply and Transport Officer, Viceroy's Camp.
Major A. L. Phillips	Supply and Transport Corps, Deputy Director of Supply.
Lieutenant T. Thorne	Ordnance Department.
Lieutenant W. L. O. Twiss	Assistant to Assistant Quartermaster-General.
Captain W. de L. Williams, D.S.O.	Assistant Director for Transport.

7.—ARTS EXHIBITION.

Sir George Watt, Kt., C.I.E.	Director.
Mr. Percy Brown	Assistant Director.
Colonel Sir Swinton Jacob, K.C.I.E.	President, Judging Committee.

Members, Judging Committee.

General S. Beatson, C.B.	Mr. R. D. Mackenzie.
Mr. C. L. Burns.	Munshi Madho Lal.
Chevalier O. Ghilardi.	Bhai Ram Singh.
Colonel T. H. Hendley, C.I.E., I.M.S.	Mr. E. Thurston.
Mr. R. E. V. Arbuthnot, I. C. S.	Secretary, Judging Committee.

8.—Bishops and Chaplains on duty at the State Service.

The Right Rev. Bishop Copleston, D.D.	Metropolitan of India and Ceylon.
The Right Rev. H. Whitehead, D.D.	Bishop of Madras.
The Right Rev. G. A. Lefroy	Bishop of Lahore.
The Right Rev. A. Clifford, D.D.	Bishop of Lucknow.
The Rev. T. E. F. Cole	Bengal.
The Rev. C. E. C. de Coetlogon	Bombay.
The Rev. K. G. Foster	Bengal.
The Ven. H. W. Griffith	Archdeacon of Lahore.
The Rev. R. M. Kirwan	Bengal.
The Rev. H. O. Moore	Bengal.
The Ven. W. E. Scott	Archdeacon of Bombay.

9.—Officers of the Staff and Body-Guard of His Excellency the Viceroy.

Risaldar Abdul Karim Khan, Bahadur	Body-Guard.
Captain F. L. Adam	A.-D.-C.
Lieutenant G. A. Akers-Douglas	A.-D.-C.
Khan Bahadur Amir Bakhsh	Hospital Assistant.
Captain R. G. T. Baker-Carr	A.-D.-C.
Lieut.-Colonel the Hon. E. Baring, C.V.O.	Military Secretary.
Major E. L. C. Berger	A.-D.-C.
Lieutenant R. H. S. Dashwood	A.-D.-C.
Risaldar-Major Debi Dyal Singh, Sardar Bahadur	A.-D.-C.
Lieut.-Colonel E. H. Fenn, C.I.E.	Surgeon.
Colonel H. Goad	A.-D.-C.
Captain W. S. Goodridge, R.N.	Honorary A.-D.-C.
Major Grimston, R.E.	Comdt., Body-Guard.
Inspector Hanson	Bengal Police.
Lieut.-Colonel the Hon. C. Harbord, C.B.	A.-D.-C.
Jemadar Himmat Khan	Body-Guard.
Captain H. N. Holden	Adjutant, Body-Guard.
Risaldar-Major Sardar Bahadur Hukam Singh	A.-D.-C.

Lieutenant L. A. Jones-Mortimer	A.-D.-C.
Ressaidar Kamal-ud-din	Body-Guard.
Lieutenant V. A. S. Keighly	A.-D.-C.
Captain A. W. F. Knox	A.-D.-C.
Mr. F. W. Latimer, C.I.E.	Assistant Private Secretary.
Sir W. R. Lawrence, K.C.I.E., Indian Civil Service	Private Secretary,
Major F. Lee	A.-D.-C.
Captain the Hon. R. H. Lindsay	A.-D.-C.
The Hon. Mr. D. C. Masson, C.I.E., V.D.	A.-D.-C.
Veterinary-Lieutenant Palin	Viceroy's Escort.
Commander Petley, R.N.	Honorary A.-D.-C.
Captain A. V. Poynter	A.-D.-C.
Major Rice, 31st Punjab Infantry	Viceroy's Escort.
Lieutenant the Hon. F. W. Stanley	A.-D.-C.
Captain the Earl of Suffolk	A.-D.-C.
Subadar-Major (Honorary Captain) Tara Singh, Sardar Bahadur.	A.-D.-C.
Risaldar-Major (Honorary Captain) Wali Muhammad, Sardar Bahadur.	A.-D.-C.
Captain C. Wigram	A.-D.-C.
Lieutenant K. Wigram	A.-D.-C.
Captain the Hon. J. R. L. Yarde-Buller	A.-D.-C.

10.—Officers of the Staffs of Their Royal Highnesses the Duke of Connaught and the Grand Duke of Hesse.

Major Beevor, R.A.M.C. Lieut.-Colonel the Hon. C. E. Bingham	On H.R.H. the Duke of Connaught's Staff.
Major A. R. Dick	On H.R.H. the Grand Duke of Hesse's Staff.
Sir M. FitzGerald, Bart.	On H.R.H. the Duke of Connaught's Staff.
Risaldar-Major Ghulam Raza, 13th Bengal Lancers	Orderly Officer on H.R.H. the Duke of Connaught's Staff.
Colonel L. Herbert, C.V.O. Lieut.-Colonel A. W. Jarvis, C.M.G., M.V.O.	On H.R.H. the Duke of Connaught's Staff.
Captain Kraemer	On H.R.H. the Grand Duke of Hesse's Staff.
Lieut.-Colonel J. Leslie	On H.R.H. the Duke of Connaught's Staff.
Baron Massenbach	On H.R.H. the Grand Duke of Hesse's Staff.
Mirza Umrao Beg, Risaldar, 1st Bombay Lancers	Orderly Officer on H.R.H. the Duke of Connaught's Staff.
Major-General Von Wachter	On H.R.H. the Grand Duke of Hesse's Staff.
Inspector Willayat Ullah Khan, Thugi and Dakaiti Department	On H.R.H. the Duke of Connaught's Staff.

11.—Imperial Cadet Corps.

Major-General H.H. Maharaja Sir Pratap Singh, G.C.S.I., K.C.B., A.D.C., of Idar (Honorary Commandant).
Major W. A. Watson (Commandant).
Captain D. H. Cameron (Adjutant).
Thakur Dip Singh (Native Adjutant), Bikaner.
Agha Kasim Shah.
Muhammad Akbar Khan.
Maharaj Akhe Singh.
Sahibzada Amanatulla Khan.
Amar Singh.
Sardar Basant Singh.
Kunwar Bharat Singh.
Kunwar Deo Singh.
H.H. Maharaj Rana Ram Singh Bahadur, of Dholpur.
Thakur Gopal Singh.
H.H. Nawab Muhammad Iftikhar Ali Khan Bahadur, of Jaora.
H.H. Maharaja Sardar Singh Bahadur, of Jodhpur.
H.H. Maharaja Madan Singh Bahadur, of Kishangarh.
Kunwar Khuman Singh.
Sardar Muhammad Khan.
Kunwar Kama Pratap Singh.
Kunwar Rai Singhji.
Kunwar Ram Singhji.
H.H. Raja Sajjan Singh, of Rutlam.
Raja Samandar Singh.
Sahibzada Taley Muhammad Khan.
Nawab Wali-ud-din Khan.
Kunwar Zorawar Singhji.

12.—Pages at the Grand Chapter.

Sahibzada Hamidulla Khan, of Bhopal . Mian Hari Singh, of Kashmir	His Excellency the Viceroy's pages.
Raj Rana Man Singh, of Dilwara . . . . Sri Rao Raja Udai Bhau Singh, Sipah Salar Jang Bahadur, of Dholpur . . .	H.R.H. the Duke of Connaught's pages.

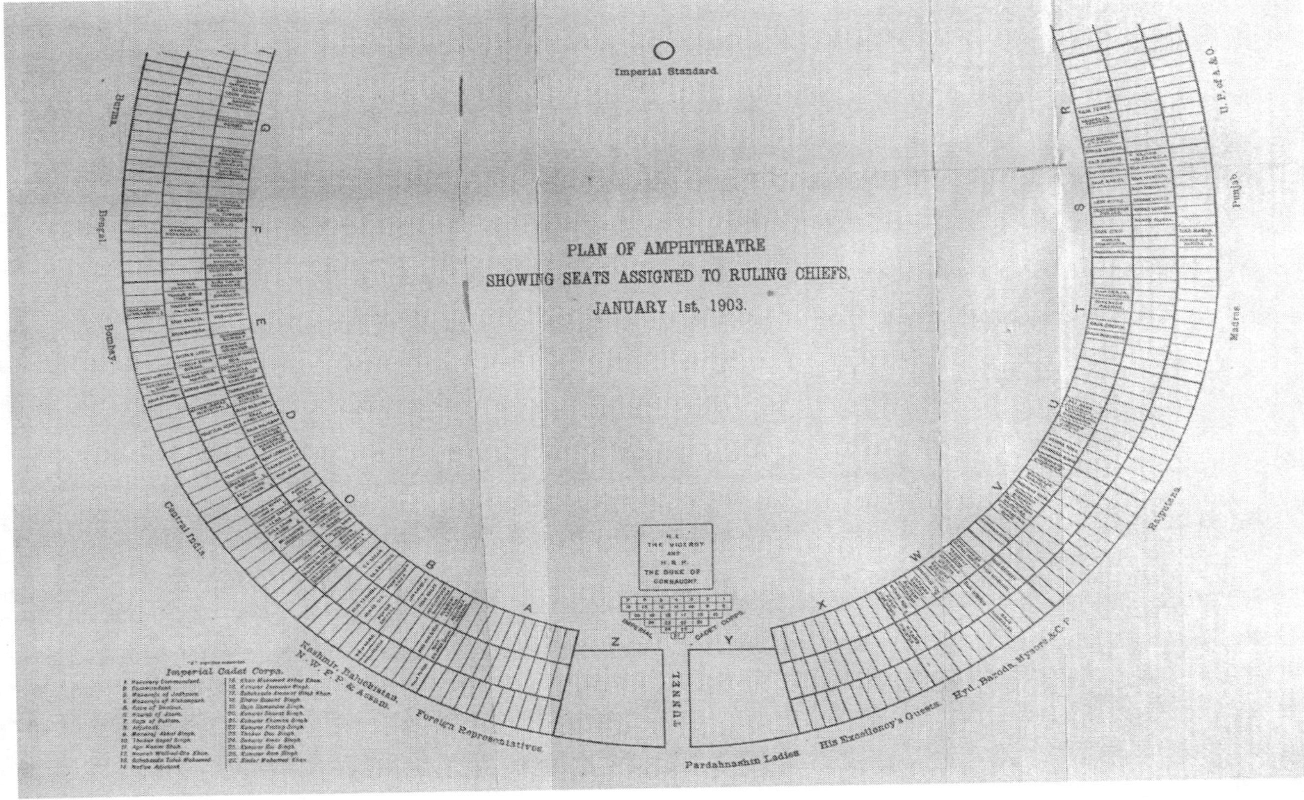
PLAN OF AMPHITHEATRE
SHOWING SEATS ASSIGNED TO RULING CHIEFS,
JANUARY 1st, 1903.
Imperial Standard.
H.E. THE VICEROY AND H.R.H. THE DUKE OF CONNAUGHT
IMPERIAL CADET CORPS
TUNNEL
Pardahnashin Ladies
His Excellency's Guests.
Hyd. Baroda Mysore & C.P.
Rajputana.
Madras
Punjab
U.P. of A.&O.
Foreign Representatives.
Kashmir, Baluchistan, N.W.F.P. & Assam.
Central India.
Bombay.
Bengal.
Burma.
A
B
C
D
E
F
G
R
S
T
U
V
W
X
Y
Z
Imperial Cadet Corps.

APPENDIX VII

OFFICIAL GUESTS AT THE DELHI DURBAR

THEIR ROYAL HIGHNESSES THE DUKE AND DUCHESS OF CONNAUGHT.

HIS ROYAL HIGHNESS THE GRAND DUKE OF HESSE.

HIS EXCELLENCY VISCOUNT KITCHENER OF KHARTOUM, Commander-in-Chief of His Majesty's Forces in India.

RULING CHIEFS.

HYDERABAD.

Hyderabad, H.H. the Nizam of, G.C.B., G.C.S.I.	Accompanied by his son, Osman Ali Khan, his Minister, Maharaja Peshkar Sir Kishen Pershad, K.C.I.E., and followers.

BARODA.

Baroda, H.H. the Gaekwar of, G.C.S.I. .	Accompanied by his son, Shrimant Yuvraj Fateh Singh Rao Gaekwar, and 500 persons.

MYSORE.

Mysore, H.H. the Maharaja of	Accompanied by his brother, Maharaj Kumar Shri Kantviava Yuvraj Narasaraja Wudjar, and 500 persons.

KASHMIR.

Kashmir, Major-General H.H. the Maharaja of, G.C.S.I.	Accompanied by his brother, Raja Sir Amar Singh, K.C.S.I., and 500 persons.

RAJPUTANA.

Alwar, H.H. the Maharaja of	Accompanied by 400 persons.
Bharatpur, the Maharaja of	Accompanied by 500 persons.
Bikaner, Major H.H. the Maharaja of, K.C.I.E.	Accompanied by 500 persons.

Bundi, H.H. the Maharao Raja of, G.C.I.E., K.C.S.I.	Accompanied by 500 persons.
Dholpur, H.H. the Maharaj Rana of . .	Accompanied by 400 persons.
Dungarpur H.H. the Maharawal of . .	Accompanied by 400 persons.
Jaipur, H.H. the Maharaja of, G.C.S.I., G.C.I.E., G.C.V.O.	Accompanied by 500 persons.
Jaisalmer, H.H. the Maharawal of . .	Accompanied by 400 persons.
Jhalawar, H.H. the Raj Rana of . . .	Accompanied by 300 persons.
Jodhpur, H.H. the Maharaja of . . .	Accompanied by 500 persons.
Karauli, H.H. the Maharaja of, G.C.I.E. .	Accompanied by 500 persons.
Kishangarh, H.H. the Maharaja of . .	Accompanied by 400 persons.
Kota, Major H.H. the Maharao of, K.C.S.I. .	Accompanied by 500 persons.
Lawa, the Thakur of	Accompanied by 100 persons.
Shahpura, the Raja Dhiraj of . . .	Accompanied by 100 persons.
Sirohi, H.H. the Maharao of, G.C.I.E., K.C.S.I.	Accompanied by 400 persons.
Tonk, H.H. the Nawab of, G.C.I.E. . .	Accompanied by 500 persons.
Udaipur, H.H. the Maharana of, G.C.S.I. .	Accompanied by 500 persons.

Central India.

Alipura, the Raja of, C.S.I.	Accompanied by 100 persons.
Barwani, the Rana of	Accompanied by 200 persons.
Bhopal, H.H. the Begum of . . .	Accompanied by her sons, Nawab Nasrulla Khan and Sahibzada Ubaidulla Khan, and 500 persons.
Charkhari, H.H. the Maharaja of, K.C.I.E. .	Accompanied by 300 persons.
Datia, H.H. the Maharaja of, K.C.S.I. . .	Accompanied by his son, the Maharaj Kunwar, and his Minister, Rao Bahadur Janki Parsad, and 400 persons.
Dewas (Senior Branch), H.H. the Raja of .	Accompanied by 400 persons.
Dewas (Junior Branch), H.H. the Raja of .	Accompanied by his brother, the Khase Sahib, and 400 persons.
Dhar, H.H. the Raja of	Accompanied by his half-brothers, Satya Sahib and Sitaram Sahib, and 400 persons.
Gwalior, Colonel H.H. the Maharaja of, G.C.S.I., G.C.V.O., A.-D.-C.	Accompanied by 500 persons.
Indore, H.H. the Maharaja of, G.C.S.I. .	Accompanied by his son, Bala Sahib Tukaji Rao, and 500 persons.
Jaora, H.H. the Nawab of	Accompanied by his Minister, Khan Bahadur Yar Muhammad Khan, C.S.I., and 300 persons.
Narsingarh, H.H. the Raja of . . .	Accompanied by 300 persons.
Orchha, H.H. the Maharaja of, G.C.I.E. .	Accompanied by his son, Raja Bahadur Bhagwant Singh, and 500 persons.

Piploda, the Thakur of	Accompanied by 100 persons.
Rajgarh, H.H. the Raja of	Accompanied by 300 persons.
Rewa, H.H. the Maharaja of, G.C.S.I. . .	Accompanied by his Sardar, Lal Jagganandhan Singh, and 500 persons.
Rutlam, H.H. the Raja of	Accompanied by 300 persons.
Samthar, H.H. the Maharaja of . . .	Accompanied by 300 persons.

BALUCHISTAN.

Kalat, H.H. the Khan of, G.C.I.E. . .	Accompanied by 500 persons.
Las Bela, the Jam of	Accompanied by 100 persons.

BOMBAY.

Bansda, the Raja of	Accompanied by 200 persons.
Bariya, the Raja of	Accompanied by 200 persons.
Bhavnagar, H.H. the Thakur Sahib of .	Accompanied by 300 persons.
Bhor, the Pant Sachiv of	Accompanied by 200 persons.
Cambay, H.H. the Nawab of . . .	Accompanied by 300 persons.
Cutch, H.H. the Rao of, G.C.I.E. . .	Accompanied by his heir, Kumar Shri Vijarajji, and 500 persons.
D'thali, the Amir of	Accompanied by 100 persons.
Gondal, H.H. the Thakur Sahib of, G.C.I.E.	Accompanied by 300 persons.
Idar, Major-General H.H. the Maharaja of, G.C.S.I., K.C.B., A.-D.-C.	Accompanied by 400 persons.
Janjira, the Nawab of, K.C.I.E. . . .	Accompanied by 300 persons.
Junagadh, H.H. the Nawab of, K.C.S.I. .	Accompanied by 300 persons.
Khairpur, H.H. the Mir of, G.C.I.E. . .	Accompanied by his Wazir, Khan Bahadur Kadirdad Khan *valad* Gul Khan, and 400 persons.
Kolhapur, H.H. the Maharaja of, G.C.S.I., G.C.V.O.	Accompanied by his brother, Pirajirao Ghatge Sarjirao Vazarat Maab, Meherban, Chief of Kagal, senior, and 500 persons.
Lahej, the Sultan of, K.C.S.I. . . .	Accompanied by 200 persons.
Limri, the Thakur Sahib of, K.C.I.E. .	Accompanied by 200 persons.
Miraj (Senior), the Chief of	Accompanied by 100 persons.
Morvi, H.H. the Thakur Sahib of, G.C.I.E. .	Accompanied by 300 persons.
Palitana, the Thakur Sahib of, K.C.S.I. .	Accompanied by 200 persons.
Porbandar, H.H. the Rana of . . .	Accompanied by 300 persons.
Shehr and Mokalla, H.H. the Sultan of .	Accompanied by his son, Sultan Omar-bin-Awadth, and 300 persons.

PUNJAB.

Bahawalpur, H.H. the Nawab of . . .	Accompanied by 500 persons.
Dujana, the Nawab of	Accompanied by 100 persons.

Faridkot, H.H. the Raja of	Accompanied by 300 persons.
Jind, H.H. the Raja of	Accompanied by 300 persons.
Kalsia, the Sardar of	Accompanied by 100 persons.
Kapurthala, H.H. the Raja of, K.C.S.I. .	Accompanied by 300 persons.
Keonthal, the Raja of	Accompanied by 100 persons.
Loharu, the Nawab of, K.C.I.E.	Accompanied by 200 persons.
Maler Kotla, Sahibzada Ahmad Ali Khan, son of H.H. the Nawab of.	Accompanied by 300 persons.
Nabha, Colonel H.H. the Raja of, G.C.S.I., G.C.I.E.	Accompanied by his son, Tikka Ripu Daman Singh, and 400 persons.
Nalagarh (Hindur), the Raja of	Accompanied by 100 persons.
Patiala, H.H. the Maharaja of . . .	Accompanied by his uncle, Kunwar Ranbir Singh, and 500 persons.
Sirmur (Nahan), H.H. the Raja of, K.C.S.I.	Accompanied by 100 persons.

MADRAS.

Cochin, H.H. the Raja of, G.C.S.I. . .	Accompanied by 500 persons.
Pudukota, H.H. the Raja of	Accompanied by 300 persons.
Travancore, H.H. the Maharaja of, G.C.S.I., G.C.I.E.	Accompanied by 500 persons.

BENGAL.

Kuch Behar, Colonel H.H. the Maharaja of, G.C.I.E., C.B., A.-D.-C.	Accompanied by his eldest son, Maharaj Kumar Rajendra Narain, and 300 persons.
Moharbhanj, the Maharaja of . . .	Accompanied by 100 persons.
Sikkim, Kumar Sidkyong Tulku, son of the Maharaja of	Accompanied by 400 persons.
Tippera (Hill), H.H. the Raja of . . .	Accompanied by his eldest son, Jubraj Birendra Kishore Deb Burman, and 300 persons.

UNITED PROVINCES.

Rampur, Major H.H. the Nawab of . .	Accompanied by his Minister, Shaikh Abdul Ghafur, and 300 persons.
Tehri (Garhwal), H.H. the Raja of, K.C.S.I.	Accompanied by 300 persons.

BURMA.

Gantarawadi, the Sawbwa of . . .	Accompanied by 100 persons.
Hsenwi (South), the Sawbwa of . . .	Accompanied by 100 persons.
Keng Tung, the Sawbwa of	Accompanied by 200 persons.
Mõng Nai, the Sawbwa of	Accompanied by 200 persons.
Mõng Pawn, the Sawbwa of . . .	Accompanied by 100 persons.
Yawng Hwe, the Sawbwa of . . .	Accompanied by 100 persons.

NORTH-WEST FRONTIER PROVINCE.

Chitral, the Mehtar of	Accompanied by 100 persons.
Dir, the Nawab of	Accompanied by 100 persons.
Nawagai, the Khan (now Nawab) of . .	Accompanied by 100 persons.

CENTRAL PROVINCES.

Khairagarh, the Raja of	Accompanied by 100 persons.
Raigarh, the Raja of	Accompanied by 100 persons.
Rehrakhol, the Raja of	Accompanied by 100 persons.
Sonpur, the Raja of	Accompanied by 100 persons.

ASSAM.

Manipur, H.H. the Raja of	Accompanied by 200 persons.

MEMBERS OF THE GOVERNOR-GENERAL'S COUNCIL.

The Hon. Mr. A. T. Arundel, C.S.I., Indian Civil Service	Public Works Member.
The Hon. Major-General Sir E. R. Elles, K.C.B.	Military Member.
The Hon. Sir D. C. J. Ibbetson, K.C.S.I., Indian Civil Service	Home, and Revenue and Agriculture Member.
The Hon. Sir E. FitzG. Law, K.C.M.G., C.S.I.	Finance Member.
The Hon. Mr. T. Raleigh, C.S.I.	Law Member.

HEADS OF LOCAL GOVERNMENTS AND ADMINISTRATIONS.

H.E. the Right Hon. Baron Ampthill, G.C.I.E.	Governor of Madras.
H.E. the Right Hon. Baron Northcote, G.C.I.E.	Governor of Bombay.
The Hon. Mr. J. A. Bourdillon, C.S.I., Indian Civil Service	Acting Lieutenant-Governor of Bengal.
The Hon. Sir J. D. La Touche, K.C.S.I., Indian Civil Service	Lieutenant-Governor of the United Provinces of Agra and Oudh.
The Hon. Sir C. M. Rivaz, K.C.S.I., Indian Civil Service	Lieutenant-Governor of the Punjab.
The Hon. Sir F. W. R. Fryer, K.C.S.I., Indian Civil Service	Lieutenant-Governor of Burma.
The Hon. Mr. J. P. Hewett, C.S.I., C.I.E., Indian Civil Service	Officiating Chief Commissioner of the Central Provinces.

The Hon. Mr. J. B. Fuller, C.S.I., C.I.E., Indian Civil Service	Chief Commissioner of Assam.
The Hon. Lieut.-Colonel Sir D. W. K. Barr, K.C.S.I.	Resident at Hyderabad.
The Hon. Lieut.-Colonel Sir D. Robertson, K.C.S.I.	Resident in Mysore.
The Hon. Mr. C. S. Bayley, C.S.I., Indian Civil Service	Agent to the Governor-General in Central India.
The Hon. Mr. A. H. T. Martindale, C.S.I., Indian Civil Service	Agent to the Governor-General in Rajputana.
The Hon. Colonel C. E. Yate, C.S.I., C.M.G.	Agent to the Governor-General in Baluchistan.
The Hon. Lieut.-Colonel H. A. Deane, C.S.I.	Chief Commissioner and Agent to the Governor-General in the North-West Frontier Province.
Lieut.-Colonel M. J. Meade, C.I.E. . .	Resident at Baroda.
Mr. E. G. Colvin, Indian Civil Service . .	Resident in Kashmir.
Lieut.-Colonel C. W. Ravenshaw . . .	Resident in Nepal.

SPECIAL GUESTS OF GOVERNMENT.

The Hon. Sir R. C. Baker, K.C.M.G. . .	Delegate of the Commonwealth of Australia.
Sir H. S. Barnes, K.C.S.I., K.C.V.O., Indian Civil Service	President of the Durbar Central Committee.
Rana Bahadur H.E. Maharaja Chandra Shamsher Jang	Prime Minister of Nepal.
General Chow Phya Surawongse . . .	Representative of H.M. the King of Siam.
The Right Rev. Bishop Copleston, D.D. .	Metropolitan of India and Ceylon.
H.E. Sir E. A. R. Galhardo, K.C.I.E. . .	Governor-General of Portuguese India.
H.E. Mons. V. Lanrezac	Governor of the French Settlements in India.
The Hon. Sir F. Maclean, K.C.I.E. . .	Chief Justice of Bengal.
Sardar Muhammad Ismail Khan . . .	Envoy of H.H. the Amir of Afghanistan.
Lieut.-General Baron Yasukata Oku . .	Representative of His Imperial Majesty the Emperor of Japan.
THE RIGHT HON. THE EARL OF PEMBROKE, G.C.V.O.	Lord Steward of His Majesty's Household.
HIS GRACE THE DUKE OF PORTLAND, K.G., G.C.V.O.	Master of the Horse to His Majesty the King.
The Hon. Sir R. Solomon, K.C.M.G. . .	Delegate of the Colonies of South Africa.
Timur bin Fasal, Saiyyid	Son of H.H. the Sultan of Maskat.
THE RIGHT HON. BARON WOLVERTON .	Vice-Chamberlain of His Majesty's Household.

Members of the Consular Body.

Don Rafael Acquaroni y de Solis . . .	Consul for Spain at Bombay.
Mofakhames Sultan Mirza Ali Mahmud Khan	Consul-General for Persia at Bombay.
Mr. A. A. Apcar	Consul for Siam at Calcutta.
Mons. A. de Koster	Consul for the Netherlands at Calcutta.
Viscount de Wrem	Consul-General for Portugal at Bombay.
Mons. M. Gerard	Consul-General for Belgium at Bombay.
Mr. S. Hayashi	Consul for Japan at Bombay.
Mr. C. C. Kilburn	Consul-General for Denmark at Calcutta.
Count A. R. Massiglia	Consul-General for Italy at Calcutta.
Emin Bey Mehemed	Consul-General for Turkey at Bombay.
Mr. F. C. Pallachi	Consul for Greece at Calcutta.
Mr. R. F. Patterson	Consul-General for the United States of America at Calcutta.
Herr E. R. Maurig von Sarnfeld . . .	Consul-General for the Austro-Hungarian Empire at Calcutta.
Mr. E. Voigt	Consul-General for Sweden and Norway at Calcutta.
Dr. E. A. Voretzsch	Acting Consul-General for Germany at Calcutta.

Officers of the Royal Navy.

Rear Admiral H.E. Sir C. C. Drury, K.C.S.I.	Commander-in-Chief of His Majesty's Naval Forces in the East Indies.
Commander Gilpin Brown	H.M.S. *Renown.*
Captain A. M. Farquhar	H.M.S. *Renown.*
Captain A. Christian	H.M.S. *Highflyer.*
Flag Lieutenant N. H. Carter . .	Attached to His Excellency the Commander-in-Chief of His Majesty's Naval Forces in the East Indies.

Railway Officials.

Mr. W. A. Dring	Agent, East Indian Railway.
Colonel H. D. Olivier, R.E.	Agent, Bombay, Baroda and Central India Railway.
Mr. H. Wenden, C.I.E.	Agent, Great Indian Peninsula Railway Company.
Mr. C. T. Beckett	Agent, Bengal Nagpur Railway Company.
Mr. R. S. Strachey	Agent, Assam Bengal Railway.

Mr. S. Finney	Manager, North-Western Railway.
Mr. G. Huddleston	Traffic Manager, East Indian Railway.
Mr. E. F. Jacob, C.I.E.	Traffic Manager, North-Western Railway.
Mr. E. H. Stone	Chief Engineer, East Indian Railway.

Official Guests of His Excellency the Viceroy.

Mr. E. N. Baker, C.S.I., Indian Civil Service	Officiating Secretary to the Government of India, Finance Department.
Major-General Sir E. G. Barrow, K.C.B. .	Secretary to the Government of India, Military Department.
Mr. L. W. Dane, Indian Civil Service . .	Officiating Secretary to the Government of India, Foreign Department.
Surgeon-General Sir B. Franklin, K.C.I.E. .	Director-General, Indian Medical Service.
The Hon. Sir A. H. L. Fraser, K.C.S.I., Indian Civil Service	President of the Police Commission.
Sir T. Higham, K.C.I.E.	Member of the Irrigation Commission.
Mr. J. M. Macpherson, C.S.I.	Secretary to the Government of India, Legislative Department.
Colonel R. C. G. Mayne, C.B.	A.-D.-C. to His Majesty the King.
Mr. J. O. Miller, C.S.I., Indian Civil Service .	Secretary to the Government of India, Revenue and Agricultural Department.
Mr. S. Preston, C.I.E.	Secretary to the Government of India, Public Works Department.
Mr. H. H. Risley, C.I.E., Indian Civil Service	Officiating Secretary to the Government of India, Home Department.
Colonel Sir C. C. Scott-Moncrieff, K.C.S.I., K.C.M.G.	President of the Irrigation Commission.

Official Guests of Local Governments.

Madras.

The Hon. Sir G. Arbuthnot, Indian Civil Service	Member of Council.
The Hon. Mr. J. N. Atkinson, Indian Civil Service	Member, Board of Revenue.
The Hon. Mr. Justice R. S. Benson, Indian Civil Service	Judge of the High Court.
Major W. M. Campbell	Military Secretary to His Excellency the Governor.
The Hon. Mr. G. S. Forbes, Indian Civil Service	Secretary, Revenue Department.

Mr. H. P. Hodgson	Planter.
Mr. G. T. Mackenzie, Indian Civil Service	Political Resident in Travancore and Cochin.
The Hon. Nawab Muhammad Sahib, Saiyid Bahadur	Member of the Legislative Council.
Lieut.-Colonel Sir G. M. J. Moore, Kt., C.I.E.	Member of Council.
Sir J. F. Price, K.C.S.I.	Honorary Magistrate.
Major A. D. G. Shelly	Chairman, South Indian Railway.
The Hon. Mr. H. A. Sim, C.I.E., Indian Civil Service	Member, Board of Revenue.
Surgeon-General D. Sinclair, C.S.I.	Surgeon-General with the Government.
The Hon. Mr. F. J. E. Spring, C.I.E.	Secretary, Public Works Department.
The Hon. Mr. G. H. Stuart	Director of Public Instruction.
Mr. H. A. Stuart, Indian Civil Service	Secretary of the Police Commission.
The Hon. Mr. J. Thomson, C.S.I., Indian Civil Service	Member of Council.
The Hon. Sir C. A. White	Chief Justice of Madras.
The Hon. Sir Henry Winterbotham, K.C.S.I., Indian Civil Service	Senior Member of Council.
The Right Rev. H. Whitehead, D.D.	Bishop of Madras.
Mr. L. M. Wynch, I.C.S.	Private Secretary to His Excellency the Governor.
Captain R. H. Dick-Cunyngham	Aide-de-Camp.
Captain R. D'A. Fife	Aide-de-Camp.
Captain the Hon. R. Lygon	Aide-de-Camp.
Captain H. M. Martin	Extra Aide-de-Camp.
Captain R. L. Mathews	Aide-de-Camp.
Sardar Bahadur Shaikh Farid, Risaldar-Major	Aide-de-Camp.
Captain N. B. G. Strong	Aide-de-Camp.
Major F. C. Logan-Home	Commandant, Body-guard.
Captain H. C. Oakes	Adjutant, Body-guard.
Raì Bahadur Hon. P. Ananda Charlu, C.I.E.	Member of the Viceroy's Legislative Council.
The Zamindar of Ettiyapuram	Tinnevelly District.
Rao Bahadur C. Jambulingam Mudaliyar, C.I.E.	Judge of the City Civil Court.
The Zamindar of Mandasa	Ganjam District.
Khan Bahadur Sir Muhammad Munawar, K.C.I.E.	Prince of Arcot.
Raja of Parlakimedi	Zamindar in the Ganjam District.
The Hon. K. Perraju Pantulu	Member of the Legislative Council.

Diwan Bahadur P. Rajaratna Mudaliyar, C.I.E.	Member of the Irrigation Commission.
Rao Sahib Diwan Bahadur C. Rama Chandra	Vakil, High Court.
Maharaja Bahadur Ranga Rao, K.C.I.E.	Raja of Bobbili, Zamindar in the Vizagapatam District.
M. R. Ry. C. Sankaram Nayar Avargal	Vakil, High Court.
Diwan Bahadur S. Srinivasa Raghava Aiyangar, C.I.E.	Inspector-General of Registration. Member of the Police Commission.
The Hon. G. Srinivasa Rao	Member of the Legislative Council.
Mr. N. Subrahmanyan, B.L.	Administrator-General.
The Raja of Venkatagiri, K.C.I.E.	Zamindar, Nellore District.
Maharaja Vikarama Deo of Jeypore	Zamindar in the Vizagapatam District.

Bombay.

Mr. G. A. Anderson	Secretary, Public Works Department (Railways).
Mr. H. W. J. Bagnell, Indian Civil Service	Political Officer with the Nawab of Janjira.
Mr. Baig	Oriental Translator to the Government of Bombay.
The Hon. Mr. Justice E. T. Candy, C.S.I., Indian Civil Service	Puisne Judge, High Court.
Mr. G. Carmichael, Indian Civil Service	Political Officer with the Raja of Bariya.
Mr. J. E. Down	Inspector-General of Police.
The Hon. Mr. S. W. Edgerley, C.I.E., Indian Civil Service	Acting Chief Secretary.
Lieut.-Colonel W. B. Ferris	Political Officer with His Highness the Maharaja of Kolhapur.
The Hon. Mr. E. M. H. Fulton, Indian Civil Service	Member of Council.
Captain F. de B. Hancock	Political Officer with the Chiefs of Kathiawar.
Mr. C. H. A. Hill, Indian Civil Service	Private Secretary to His Excellency the Governor.
The Hon. Mr. W. C. Hughes, C.I.E., M.Inst.C.E.	Chairman, Bombay Port Trust.
Mr. A. M. T. Jackson, Indian Civil Service	Secretary to Government.
The Hon. Sir Lawrence H. Jenkins	Chief Justice.
Mr. R. M. Kennedy	Commissioner, Southern Division.
The Hon. Mr. F. S. P. Lely, C.S.I.	Commissioner, Northern Division.
Brigadier-General P. J. Maitland, C.B.	Political Resident, Aden.
Surgeon-General W. McConaghey, M.D., I.M.S.	Surgeon-General.
The Hon. Mr. D. McIver	Additional Member of Council.

The Hon. Sir James Monteath, K.C.S.I., Indian Civil Service	Member of Council.
The Hon. Mr. S. M. Moses	Additional Member of Council.
Mr. John W. P. Muir-Mackenzie, Indian Civil Service	Chief Secretary, Member, Irrigation Commission.
Colonel Ferrers Nicholson.	Government Solicitor, Commanding Bombay Volunteer Rifles.
Lieut.-Colonel G. B. O'Donnell . . .	Political Officer with His Highness the Maharaja of Idar.
Lieut.-Colonel R. Owen	Military Secretary to His Excellency the Governor.
Captain C. U. Price	30th Baluch Infantry, Political Officer with His Highness the Mir of Khairpur.
Mr. H. O. Quin, Indian Civil Service . .	Agent to the Governor, Kathiawar.
The Hon. Mr. Samuel Rebsch . . .	Chairman, Bombay Improvement Trust.
The Hon. Mr. Basil Scott	Advocate-General.
Mr. J Sladen, Indian Civil Service . .	Political Officer with the Raja of Bansda.
Lieut.-Colonel F. W. Snell	Political Officer with His Highness the Rao of Cutch.
The Hon. Mr. J. Tate	Secretary, Public Works Department.
Mr. C. W. Waddington	Principal of the Rajkumar College, Rajkot.
Captain G. Warneford	Assistant Political Resident, Aden.
Mr. C. C. Watson, Indian Civil Service .	Political Officer with the Kathiawar Chiefs.
Mr. A. D. Younghusband, Indian Civil Service	Commissioner, Central Division.
Sheikh Abdul Hamid	Risaldar (5th Sindh Horse), Native Aide-de-Camp.
Captain J. A. S. Balmain	15th Hussars, Aide-de-Camp.
Captain G. H. Boileau, R.E. . . .	Aide-de-Camp.
Captain G. N. Cartwright, R.A. . . .	Aide-de-Camp.
Captain J. H. M. Davie	Royal Scots, Aide-de-Camp.
Captain the Hon. C. F. Greville . . .	7th Hussars, Aide-de-Camp.
Captain J. T. Weatherby	Oxfordshire Light Infantry, Aide-de-Camp.
Captain M. D. Wood	West Yorkshire Regiment, Aide-de-Camp.
Major J. C. Pollard	Commandant, His Excellency the Governor's Body-guard.
Captain J. H. Crawford	Adjutant, His Excellency the Governor's Body-guard.

The Hon. Rao Bahadur Achyut Bhaskar Desai.

Adamji Pirbhai.

The Hon. Mir Allah Baksh Khan.

Meherban Anandao Khanderao *alias* Balasahib Raste.

Sardar Bahadur Becherdas Veharidas Desai.

The Hon. Sir Bhalchandra Krishna Bhatavadekar, Kt.
Mr. Bomanji Dinshaw Petit.
The Hon. Mr. Justice N. G. Chandavarkar.
The Hon. Rao Bahadur Chunilal Venilal, C.I.E.
Khan Sahib Dadamiya Anwarkha.
The Hon. Mr. Daji Abaji Khare, B.A., LL.B.
Sir Dinshaw Manockji Petit, Bart.
Fardunji Kuvarji-Tarapurwala, C.I.E.
Fazalbhai Vishram, C.I.E.
Gangadhar Lakshman Swami.
The Hon. Mr. G. K. Gokhale, B.A.
The Hon. Mr. Gokuldas Kahandas Parekh, B.A., LL.B.
Gordhandas Khattan Makanji.
Goverdhandas Gokuldas Tejpal.
Sir Harkisandas Narottamdas, K.C.I.E.
Rao Bahadur Himatlal Dhirajram.
Jam Bambho Khan.
Sir Jamsetji Jijibhai, Bart.
Jamsetji Nasarwanji Tata.
Meherban Lakhamganda Basav Prabhu, Barrister-at-Law.
Meherban Lingapa Jayappa *alias* Appasehab Desai.
Rao Bahadur Makandrai Mani Rai.
Sardar Khan Bahadur Muhammad Yakub Sheikh Ismail, C.I.E.
Mulji Bhowanidas Barbhaya.
Mir Muzaffer Husein Khan.
Nagojirao Ramchandrarao Patankar.
Khan Bahadur Navroji Pestanji Vakil, C.I.E.
Rao Bahadur Ramchandra Trimbak Acharya.
Ramkrishna Gopal Bhandarkar, M.A., Ph.D., C.I.E.
H.H. the Hon. Sir Sultan Muhammad Shah, the Aga Khan, G.C.I.E.
Dr. Temalji Bhikaji Nariman.
Thakur of Utelia.
Vinayak Dhundiraj Biwalkar.
Vihaldas Damodher Thackersey.
Virchand Dipchand, C.I.E.
Wadero Ali Murad.
Wadero Allah Baksh Khan.

Bengal.

Mr. R. A. D'O. Bignell	Commissioner of Calcutta Police.
The Hon. Mr. C. W. Bolton, C.S.I., Indian Civil Service	Member of the Board of Revenue and Additional Member of His Excellency the Viceroy's Council.
Major W. J. Buchanan	Inspector-General of Jails.
The Hon. Mr. C. E. Buckland, C.I.E., Indian Civil Service	Member of the Board of Revenue.
Mr. E. Cable.	
Mr. R. W. Carlyle, C.I.E., Indian Civil Service	Inspector-General of Police.
The Hon. Mr. E. W. Collin, Indian Civil Service	Secretary to Government.
Major J. Colvin	Superintendent of the Kuch Behar State.
Mr. W. D. Cruickshank	Secretary of the Bank of Bengal.
The Hon. Mr. H. Elworthy	Bengal Council.
Mr. M. Finucane, C.S.I., Indian Civil Service	Commissioner of the Burdwan Division.
Major G. Grant-Gordon	Northern Bengal Mounted Rifles.
The Hon. Mr. R. T. Greer, Indian Civil Service	Chairman of the Corporation of Calcutta.
The Hon. Mr. B. L. Gupta, Indian Civil Service	Legal Remembrancer.

Mr. F. L. Halliday	Bengal Police, Officer in charge of the Central Camp.
Mr. E. L. L. Hammond, Indian Civil Service	Assistant Private Secretary.
The Hon. Mr. Justice R. Harington . .	Puisne Judge of the High Court.
Colonel Hendley, C.I.E.	Inspector-General of Civil Hospitals.
Mr. H. Holmwood, Indian Civil Service .	District and Sessions Judge of Patna.
Mr. R. Hudson.	
Mr. W. A. Inglis, Indian Civil Service . .	Secretary to Government.
The Rev. Father Lafont.	
The Hon. Mr. W. C. Macpherson, Indian Civil Service	Secretary to Government.
Mr. W. H. Michael, Indian Civil Service .	Accountant-General, Bengal.
Mr. A. Pedler, C.I.E.	Director of Public Instruction.
Sir Patrick Playfair, C.I.E.	
The Hon. Sir H. T. Prinsep, Indian Civil Service	Puisne Judge of the High Court.
The Hon. Mr. Justice R. F. Rampini, Indian Civil Service	Puisne Judge of the High Court and Additional Member of His Excellency the Viceroy's Council.
Mr. H. L. Stephenson, Indian Civil Service .	Officiating Chief Secretary.
Mr. H. B. St. Leger	Officer in charge of Police, Bengal Provincial Camp.
The Hon. Mr. C. Turner	President of the Bengal Chamber of Commerce and Additional Member of His Excellency the Viceroy's Council.
Mr. J. C. White	Political Officer, Sikkim.
Lieut.-Colonel R. R. H. Whitwell, I.M.S. .	Civil Surgeon of Patna.
The Hon. Mr. J. T. Woodroffe	Advocate General.
Captain C. J. Allanson, 42nd Gurkha Rifles .	Extra Aide-de-Camp.
Commander E. J. Beaumont, Royal Indian Marine	Honorary Aide-de-Camp.
Captain B. H. Bignell, 17th Bombay Infantry	Aide-de-Camp.
Lieutenant R. L. Bignell, 41st Dogra Infantry	Extra Aide-de-Camp.
Lieutenant G. Chatterton	Extra Aide-de-Camp, Royal Garrison Artillery.
Captain H. T. Fulton, D.S.O.	Aide-de-Camp.
Captain E. Harding-Newman, Royal Artillery	Extra Aide-de-Camp.
Lieut.-Colonel J. Hodding, C.I.E. . . .	Honorary Aide-de-Camp.
Mr. A. F. M. Abdur Rahman, Khan Bahadur	Judge, Small Cause Court, Calcutta.
Nawab Bahadur Saiyid Amir Husain, C.I.E.	Calcutta.
Syed Ashgar Husain Khan, *alias* Khurshed Nawab	Patna.
Khan Bahadur Badruddin Haidar . . .	Calcutta.

Sahibzada Muhammad Bakhtiyar Shah, C.I.E.	Calcutta.
Rai Krishna Chandra Bandopadhyaya Bahadur	Executive Engineer.
Maharaja Dhiraj Bijay Chand Mahtab Bahadur	Burdwan.
Dr. Kailash Chandar Bose, Rai Bahadur, C.I.E.	Municipal Commissioner, Calcutta.
Babu Rajendra Coomar Bose . . .	Assistant Sessions Judge.
Babu Damoodur Dass Burman . . .	Calcutta.
Nawab Saiyid Abdus Sobhan Chaudhuri .	Bogra.
Rai Madhu Sudan Chowdhury Bahadur .	District Superintendent of Police.
Raja Bahadur Ram Ranjan Chuckerbutty .	Hitampur, Birbhum.
Rai Badri Das Bahadur	Calcutta.
Raja Binaya Krishna Deb	Calcutta.
Kumar Gopendra Krishna Deb . . .	District Judge.
Raja Bahadur Baikuntha Nath Dey . .	Balasore.
Babu Ramanath Ghosh	Calcutta.
The Hon. Mr. Tarini Kumar Ghosh . .	Member, Bengal Legislative Council.
Rai Hari Ram Goenka Bahadur . . .	Municipal Commissioner, Calcutta.
Mr. Syed Nurul Huda	District Judge.
Khan Bahadur Jannat Hosain Khan . .	District Superintendent of Police.
Raja Ban Bihari Kapur, C.S.I. . . .	Burdwan.
The Hon. Khan Bahadur Syed Mahomed .	Member, Bengal Legislative Council.
Syed Muhammad Mehdi Hossain Khan, *alias* Badshah Nawab	Patna.
Babu Priya Nath Mukerjee	Deputy Magistrate.
Babu Narayan Chunder Naik . . .	Deputy Magistrate.
The Hon. Maharaja Monindra Chandra Nandy	Member, Bengal Legislative Council.
Dr. Prasanna Kumar Ray	Officiating Principal, Presidency College.
Raja Ashutosh Nath Roy	Cossimbazar, Murshidabad.
Maharaja Girija Nath Roy	Dinajpur.
Raja Bahadur Shashi Shakhareswar Roy .	Tahirpur, Rajshahi.
Rai Bahadur Sita Nath Roy	Calcutta.
Kumar Ranendra Narayan Roy Chowdry .	Joydebpur, Dacca.
Mr. H. M. Rustomji	Sheriff, Calcutta.
The Hon. Babu Chaturbhooj Sahai . .	Member, Bengal Legislative Council.
Nawab Bahadur Khwaja Salimulla . .	Dacca.
Babu Annoda Prasad Sarkar . . .	Executive Engineer.
Babu Lalit Mohan Sen	Extra Assistant Conservator of Forests.
The Hon. Maulvi Seraj-ul-Islam, Khan Bahadur	Member, Bengal Legislative Council.

Maharaja Bahadur Sir Harballabh Narayan Sing, K.C.I.E.	Sonbursa, Bhagalpur.
Raja Bahadur Ram Narain Singh . .	Khaira, Monghyr.
The Hon. Maharaja Bahadur Sir Rameshwar Singh, K.C.I.E., of Darbhanga	
The Hon. Maharaja Bahadur Sir Ravaneshwar Prasad Singh, K.C.I.E., of Gidhaur	Member, Bengal Legislative Council.
Babu Sarat Chandra Singh	Paikpara, Calcutta.
Raja Thukurai Bhagabat Dayal Singh . .	Chainpur, Palamau.
Raja Bahadur Ranajit Sinha . . .	Nashipur, Murshidabad.
Babu Nalin Bihari Sircar, C.I.E. . .	Calcutta.
Syud Maulvi Wajid Hosain	Deputy Magistrate.
The Hon. Asif Kadr Saiyid Wasif Ali Mirza .	Member, Bengal Legislative Council.

United Provinces of Agra and Oudh.

The Hon. Mr. R. S. Aikman, Indian Civil Service	Puisne Judge, High Court.
Mr. E. B. Alexander, Indian Civil Service .	Commissioner, Meerut Division.
The Hon. Mr. P. C. Banerji	Puisne Judge, High Court.
The Hon. Mr. H. F. Blair, Indian Civil Service	Puisne Judge, High Court.
Mr. R. H. Brereton	Inspector-General of Police.
The Hon. Mr. W. R. Burkitt, Indian Civil Service	Puisne Judge, High Court.
Mr. W. M. Colvin	Member of the Police Commission.
The Hon. Mr. T. Conlan, C.I.E. . . .	Member of the Legislative Council.
The Hon. Mr. A. W. Cruickshank . .	Additional Member of the Legislative Council.
Mr. J. S. C. Davis, Indian Civil Service .	Agent for Tehri.
Mr. I. L. Ferrier	Assistant District Superintendent of Police.
The Most Rev. Charles Gentile, D.D., O.C. .	Archbishop of Agra.
The Hon. Mr. J. E. Gill, Indian Civil Service	Member of the Legislative Council.
Mr. W. B. Gordon	Secretary, Irrigation Commission.
Mr. H. D. Griffin, Indian Civil Service . .	Judicial Secretary.
The Hon. Mr. J. Hooper, Indian Civil Service	Officiating Member, Board of Revenue.
The Hon. Mr. W. H. L. Impey, C.S.I. .	Chief Secretary.
Colonel C. H. Joubert, I.M.S. . . .	Inspector-General of Civil Hospitals.
The Hon. Mr. Justice G. E. Knox, I.C.S. .	Vice-Chancellor of the Allahabad University.
Mr. T. C. Lewis	Director of Public Instruction.
Major C. Mactaggart, I.M.S. . . .	Inspector-General of Prisons.
Mr. E. J. Mardon, Indian Civil Service .	Magistrate and Collector.
Mr. H. Marsh, C.I.E.	Secretary, Public Works Department, Irrigation Branch, and Chief Engineer.

The Hon. Mr. A. McRobert	President of the Upper India Chamber of Commerce and Member of the Legislative Council.
The Hon. Mr. J. S. Meston, Indian Civil Service	Financial Secretary.
The Hon. Mr. W. H. Nightingale . . .	Secretary, Public Works Department, Buildings and Roads, and Chief Engineer.
Mr. J. W. Oliver	Conservator of Forests.
Mr. E. R. Parsons	Deputy Inspector-General of Police, Railway Branch (in Provincial Camp).
Mr. L. C. Porter, Indian Civil Service . .	Magistrate and Collector.
The Hon. Mr. D. T. Roberts, C.S.I., Indian Civil Service	Member, Board of Revenue.
Mr. Ross Scott, I.C.S.	Judicial Commissioner of Oudh.
Mr. A. M. W. Shakespear, Indian Civil Service	Agent for Benares.
The Hon. Sir John K. C. Stanley, Kt., J.P. .	Chief Justice of the High Court.
Mr. R. C. Strachey	Personal Assistant to the Inspector-General of Police in the Provincial Camp.
Mr. J. B. Thomson, Indian Civil Service .	Member, Board of Revenue.
Mr. P. F. N. Toulmin	Assistant Inspector-General of Police, Special Branch (in Provincial Camp).
Mr. A. T. Webster	District Superintendent of Police.
Mr. G. P. Boys	Honorary Aide-de-Camp.
Captain E. H. D. Stracey	Aide-de-Camp.
Mr. T. B. Traill	Extra Aide-de-Camp.
Mr. A. R. Withers	Extra Aide-de-Camp.

H.H. the Maharaja of Benares, G.C.I.E. .	Accompanied by 300 followers.
Khan Bahadur Maulvi Abdul Hamid . .	Deputy Collector.
Khan Bahadur Ahmad Nur Khan, *alias* Mangal Khan	Pilibhit
Nawab Saiyid Ahmad Shah	Sardhana, District Meerut.
Sahibzada Ali Muhammad Khan, of Mahmudabad	District Sitapur.
Nawab Asad-ulla Khan, Khan Bahadur .	Vice-Chairman, Municipal Board, Meerut.
Lala Baij Nath, Rai Bahadur . . .	Judge, Small Cause Court, Agra.
Pandit Bakht Narayan	Subordinate Judge, Oudh.
Balwant Singh, C.I.E.	Raja of Awa, District Etah.
Rai Bepin Behari Chakravarti Bahadur, B.A.	Executive Engineer, Buildings and Roads Branch.
Bhagwati Prasad Singh	Maharaj of Bulrampur, District Gonda.
Kunwar Bharat Singh	District and Sessions Judge.

Bhup Indra Bahadur Singh	Raja of Kantit, District Mirzapur.
Bhup Indra Bikram Singh, C.I.E. . .	Raja of Piyagpur, District Bahraich.
Lala Bisheshar Prasad	Mauranwan, District Unao.
Chandra Chur Singh	Kunwar, of Atra Chandapur, District Rae Bareli.
Datt Prasad Singh	Raja of Mursan, District Aligarh.
Lala Durga Prasad	Sarwan Baragaon, District Hardoi.
Fateh Singh	Raja of Pawayan, District Shahjehanpur.
Pandit Girraj Kishor Datt	Munsif, Agra.
Babu Gunga Bakhsh Singh	Tikari, District Rae Bareli.
Babu Gyanendra Nath Chakravarti, M.A., LL.B.	Officiating Inspector of Schools.
Hafiz Abdul Karim, C.I.E., C.V.O. . .	Munshi, Agra.
Sheikh Hafiz Abdul Karim, C.I.E., Khan Bahadur	Meerut.
Thakur Harihar Bakhsh	Saraura, District Sitapur.
Saiyid Hasan Shah	Honorary Magistrate, Bulandshahr.
Pandit Het Ram, C.I.E.	Ex-Diwan of the Rewa State, Bareilly.
Sheikh Inayat Ullah	Saidanpur, District Bara Banki.
Kunwar Itmad Ali Khan	Sadabad, District Muttra.
Jai Krishna Das, Bahadur, C.S.I. . . .	Raja of Moradabad.
Raja Bahadur Koshal Kishor Prasad Mal .	Majhauli, District Gorakhpur.
Krishna Kunwar	Raja of Sahespur, District Moradabad.
Raî Krishna Sah Bahadur	Honorary Magistrate and Member, Municipal Board, Naini Tal.
Lal Ram Pratap Singh	Raja of Manda, District Allahabad.
Lal Ratan Sen Singh	Bansi, District Basti.
The Hon. Pandit Madan Mohan Malaviya .	Member of the Lieutenant-Governor's Legislative Council.
Rai Mahabir Prasad Narayan Singh Bahadur, Thakur	District Allahabad.
Rai Mahendra Nath Ohdedar Bahadur .	Assistant Surgeon.
Babu Manohar Lal	Chairman, Municipal Council, Fyzabad.
Maulvi Mehdi Ali Khan	Honorary Secretary, Muhammadan Anglo-Oriental College, Aligarh.
Nawab Bahadur Mehdi Hasan Khan (Abu Sahib)	Lucknow.
Mirza Bahadur Muhammad Abbas . .	Lucknow.
Nawab Mumtaz-ud-Daula Muhammad Faiyaz Ali Khan, C.S.I.	Pahasu, District Bulandshahr.
Muhammad Kazim Husain Khan . .	Raja of Paintipur, District Sitapur.
Mr. Muhammad Rafiq, B.L. . . .	Judge, Small Cause Court, Oudh.
Muhammad Siddiq Khan	Raja of Nanpura, District Bahraich.

Munshi Muhammad Siraj-ud-din, B.L.	Subordinate Judge, Agra.
Muhammad Naim Khan	Kailaspur, Saharanpur, Honorary Magistrate.
Sardar Narayan Singh	Honorary Magistrate, Rae Bareli.
Pandit Maharaj Narayan Sivapuri, Rai Bahadur	Deputy Collector.
Narpati Singh	Raja of Asothar, District Fatehpur.
Khan Bahadur Nasrat Ali Chaudhri	Honorary Magistrate, Lucknow, and Secretary, British Indian Association.
Shaikh Naushad Ali Khan	Mailariganj, District Bara Banki.
The Hon. Rai Bahadur Nihal Chand	Member of the Lieutenant-Governor's Legislative Council.
Pratab Bahadur Singh	Raja of Kila Partabgarh, District Partabgarh.
Maharaja Sir Pratab Narayan Singh, K.C.I.E.	Ajudhya, District Fyzabad.
Raghubar Dayal Seth	Muizzuddinpur, District Sitapur.
Raghuraj Singh	Raja of Mankapur, District Gonda.
Rampal Singh	Raja of Kalakankar, District Partabgarh.
Rampal Singh	Raja of Kori Sadauli, District Rae Bareli.
Babu Ram Prasad	Munsiff, Oudh.
Ram Pratab Singh	Raja of Mainpur, District Mainpuri.
Pandit Rama Shankar Misra	Magistrate and Collector.
Ram Singh	Raja of Rampura, District Jalaun.
Ranbir Singh	Raja, Dehra Dun.
Maulvi Muhammad Sami-ullah Khan, C.M.G.	Retired Judge, Aligarh.
Raja Sardar Singh Bahadur	Katehra, District Jhansi.
Rana Sheoraj Singh	Thalrai (Khajurgaon), District Rae Bareli.
The Hon. Shyam Sinha	Raja of Tajpur, District Bijnor, Member of the Lieutenant-Governor's Legislative Council.
Rai Sri Ram Bahadur	Assistant Engineer, Irrigation Branch.
The Hon. Rai Sri Ram Bahadur	Member of the Lieutenant-Governor's Legislative Council.
Mahamahopadhyaya Pandit Sudhakar Dube	Benares.
The Hon. Tasadduq Rasul Khan, C.S.I.	Raja of Jehangirabad, District Bara Banki, Member of the Lieutenant-Governor's Legislative Council.
Uday Raj Singh	Raja of Kashipur, District Naini Tal.
Nawab Yusuf Ali Khan	Aligarh.

Punjab.

The Hon. Mr. A. Anderson, C.I.E., Indian Civil Service	Commissioner, Lahore, and Member of the Punjab Legislative Council.
Mr. H. A. Anderson, C.S.I., Indian Civil Service	Commissioner, Jullundur.

Lieut.-Colonel T. E. L. Bate, C.I.E., I.M.S. .	Inspector-General of Jails.
Mr. W. Bell	Director of Public Instruction.
Mr. J. Benton	Chief Engineer, Public Works Department.
The Hon. Mr. W. O. Clark	Judge, Chief Court.
Mr. J. F. Connolly, Indian Civil Service .	Revenue and Financial Secretary.
Mr. A. H. Diack, Indian Civil Service . .	Officiating Chief Secretary.
Mr. R. A. Gamble, Indian Civil Service .	Accountant-General.
Mr. C. J. Hallifax, Indian Civil Service .	Judicial and General Secretary.
The Hon. Colonel J. B. Hutchinson . .	Member of the Punjab Legislative Council.
Mr. D. C. Johnstone, Indian Civil Service .	Divisional Judge, Sialkot.
Mr. A. Kensington, Indian Civil Service .	Divisional Judge, Lahore.
Mr. L. W. King, C.S.I., Indian Civil Service .	Commissioner, Multan.
Colonel J. McConaghey, M.D., I.M.S. . .	Inspector-General of Civil Hospitals.
The Hon. Mr. A. H. Reid	Judge, Chief Court.
The Hon. Mr. F. A. Robertson, Indian Civil Service	Judge, Chief Court
Mr. J. G. Silcock, Indian Civil Service . .	Commissioner, Rawalpindi.
The Hon. Mr. C. L. Tupper, C.S.I., Indian Civil Service	Financial Commissioner.
The Hon. Mr. J. Wilson, C.S.I., Indian Civil Service	Member of the Punjab Legislative Council.
Lieutenant Alexander	Extra Aide-de-Camp.
Lieutenant O. W. E. Bannerman . . .	Extra Aide-de-Camp.
Captain E. G. Drummond	Aide-de-Camp.
Maulvi Abu Saiyid Muhammad Hussain .	Batala, District Gurdaspur.
Saiyid Ahmad	Imam of Jama Mosque, District Delhi.
Raja Ali Bahadur Khan	District Gujrat.
Mian Anrodh Singh	Ramgarh, District Amballa.
Bhai Arjan Singh	Begrian, District Ludhiana.
Sardar Bahadur Arjan Singh . . .	Chabal, District Amritsar.
Sardar Arur Singh	Naushera Nangal, District Amritsar.
Ashiq Muhammad Khan	District Multan.
Aslam Hayat Khan	Khan of Wali, District Rawalpindi.
Nawab Bahadur Azmat Ali Khan . . .	Mandal, District Karnal.
Sardar Badam Singh	Malandh, District Ludhiana.
Sardar Khan Bahadur Khan	Tumandar of the Khosa tribe of Batil, District Dera Ghazi Khan.
Sardar Bahram Khan	Son of the Hon. Nawab Sir Imam Bakhsh Khan, K.C.I.E.
Sardar Bakhshish Singh	Sindhanwalia, District Amritsar.
Raja Balbir Singh	Kutlehr, District Kangra.
Sardar Balwant Singh	Ber, District Ludhiana.
Sardar Balwant Singh	Butala, District Gujranwala.

Bedi Sujan Singh	Una, District Hoshiarpur.
Sardar Bhagwant Singh	Bhadaur, District Ludhiana.
Sardar Charanjit Singh	Ahluwalia, District Jullundur.
Sardar Daljit Singh	Ahluwalia, District Jullundur.
Sardar Deo Indar Singh	Ghanauli, District Amballa.
Khan Bahadur Dhanjibhai Fakirji Commodore, C.I.E.	District Rawalpindi.
Sardar Dial Singh	Kunjahia of Butala, District Sialkot.
Sardar Dost Muhammad Khan . . .	Mazari, District Dera Ghazi Khan.
Sardar Drihan Khan	Drishak, Tumandar of the Drishak tribe, District Dera Ghazi Khan.
Nawab Fateh Ali Khan	Kazilbash, District Lahore.
Sardar Fazl Ali Khan	Kasrani, Tumandar of the Kasrani tribe of Kot Kasrani, District Dera Ghazi Khan.
Rai Bahadur Gagar Mal	District Amritsar.
Tika Gajindar Singh	Son of Jai Singh, Raja of Siba, District Kangra.
Khan Bahadur Mian Ghulam Farid Khan .	Retired Extra Assistant Commissioner, District Gurdaspur.
Mian Ghulam Mohi-ud-din	Baghbanpura, District Lahore.
Malik Ghulam Muhammad Khan . . .	Jodhra, District Rawalpindi.
Sheikh Ghulam Sadiq	District Amritsar.
Bhai Gulbakhsh Singh	District Amritsar.
Bhai Gurdit Singh	District Lahore.
Sardar Gurdit Singh	Shamgarh, District Karnal.
Khan Bahadur Malik Hakim Khan . .	Nun of Kot Hakim Khan, District Shahpur.
Rai Bahadur Hardhian Singh . . .	District Delhi.
Subadar Hari Singh, Sardar	Sardar of Lodhram, District Ludhiana.
The Hon. Kunwar Sir Harnam Singh, K.C.I.E.	
Sardar Bahadur Harnam Singh . . .	Kharrar, District Amballa.
Sardar Muhammad Husain Khan . .	Bozdar Chief, District Dera Ghazi Khan.
Nawab Ibrahim Ali Khan	Kunjpura, District Karnal.
Mirza Ikram-ullah Khan	Wazirabad, District Gujranwala.
Ilahi Bakhsh Khan Bahadur . . .	Delhi.
The Hon. Nawab Sir Imam Bakhsh Khan, K.C.I.E.	Member of the Legislative Council.
Lala Ishri Parshad	Government Treasurer, District Delhi.
Mir Jafar Ali Khan	Kotaha, District Amballa.
Honorary Major Raja Jai Chand . . .	Lambagraon, District Kangra.
Sardar Jallab Khan	Guranani, Tumandar of the Gurchani tribe, District Dera Ghazi Khan.
Sardar Jasmer Singh	Thol Thango, District Karnal.

Sardar Sahib Jiwan Singh, C.S.I. . . .	Shahzadpur, District Amballa.
Sardar Bahadur Jowala Singh . . .	Jharauli, District Karnal.
Raja Karmdad Khan	Gakkhar of Pharwala, District Rawalpindi.
Khawaja Muhammad Ghulam Sadiq . .	District Amritsar.
Khawaja Tasadduq Hussain, B.A. . .	Extra Assistant Commissioner and Mir Munshi to Punjab Government.
Baba Sir Khem Singh, Bedi, K.C.I.E. . .	District Rawalpindi.
Malik Kuda Bakhsh	Tiwana of Khawajabad, District Shahpur.
Kirthi Singh	Raja of Shekhpura.
Sardar Kishen Singh	Thal Thangor, District Karnal.
Sardar Bahadur Lachmi Sahai . . .	District Amritsar.
Rada Lehna Singh	Manaswal, District Hoshiarpur.
Lutt Husain Khan *alias* Mian Shah Nawaz Khan	Sirai, District Dera Ghazi Khan.
The Hon. Rai Madan Gopal Bahadur . .	Member of the Punjab Legislative Council.
Thakur Mahan Chand	District Gurdaspur.
Sardar Massu Khan	Chief of the Tibbi Lund tribe, of Tibbi Lund, District Dera Ghazi Khan.
Malik Mubariz Khan	Jehanabad, District Shahpur.
Malik Muhammad Amin Khan . . .	Shamsabad, District Rawalpindi.
Khan Sahib Muhammad Alam Khan . .	Kotla Nihang, District Amballa.
Khan Bahadur Muhammad Barkat Ali Khan	Retired Extra Assistant Commissioner, District Lahore.
Muhammad Hayat Khan	Khokhar, of Ahmedabad, District Jhelum.
Muhammad Khan Malik Khan . . .	Mitha Tiwana, District Shahpur.
Muhammad Tahir	District Ludhiana.
Mukhdum Hussain Bakhsh	District Multan.
Sardar Narain Singh	Manakmajra, District Amballa.
Raja Narindar Chand	Nadaun, District Kangra.
Sardar Bahadur Narindar Singh . . .	District Lahore.
Diwan Narindra Nath, M.A. . . .	District Lahore.
Guru Naunihal Singh	Kartarpur, District Jullundur.
Sardar Naurang Khan	Chief of the Sari Lund tribe, of Sari Lund, District Dera Ghazi Khan.
Sardar Partap Singh	Ahluwalia, District Jullundur.
Sardar Bahadur Partab Singh . . .	Mianpur, District Amballa.
Sardar Partab Singh	Ghanauli, District Amballa.
Raja Rampal of Kutlehr	District Kangra.
Lala Ram Saran Dass	Lahore.
Sardar Richpal Singh	Siranwali, District Sialkot.
Raja Rugnath Sing	Jaswan, District Hoshiarpur.
Rustam Ali Khan	Mandal, District Karnal.
Saadat Ali Khan	Kamalia, District Montgomery.

Said-ud-din Ahmad Mirza	Delhi.
Khan Bahadur Saifulla Khan . . .	Khangarh, District Muzaffargarh.
Sardar Sarup Singh	Malari, District Lahore.
Lala Sheo Parshad	District Delhi.
Diwan Bahadur Sodhi Hukam Singh, Rai Bahadur	Retired Extra Assistant Commissioner, District Lahore.
Sodhi Ram Narain Singh	Anandpur, District Hoshiarpur.
Sodhi Sher Singh	Haranpur, District Jhelum.
Rai Sri Kishen Das Bahadur . . .	Delhi.
Mian Sukhdarshan Singh	Ramgarh Kathauli, District Amballa.
Sardar Taggia Khan	Representing the minor Chief of the Langhari tribe, District Dera Ghazi Khan.
Sardar Tek Singh	Chhachi, District Rawalpindi.
Umar Daraz Ali Khan	Mandal, District Karnal.
Malik Umar Hayat Khan	Tiwana, District Shahpur.
Sardar Umrao Singh	Majithia, District Amritsar.
Baba Uttam Singh	Basirpur, District Montgomery.
Malik Yar Muhammad Khan . . .	Kalabagh, District Mianwali.
Khan Bahadur Yusuf Shah	District Amritsar.
Khan Bahadur Shams-ul-ulma Maulvi Saiyid Muhammad Zia-ud-Din Khan, LL.D.	District Delhi.

Burma.

The Hon. Mr. C. G. Bayne, C.S.I., Indian Civil Service	Member of Legislative Council, and Chief Secretary.
Mr. C. E. Browne	Officer in charge of the Shan Chiefs.
Mr. G. C. Buchanan	Chairman, Port Trust.
Lieut.-Colonel R. E. S. Davis, I.M.S. . .	Civil Surgeon, Rangoon.
The Hon. Mr. J. G. Findlay	Member of the Legislative Council.
The Hon. Mr. H. Groves	Member of the Legislative Council and Chief Engineer.
The Hon. Mr. W. T. Hall, Indian Civil Service	Member of the Legislative Council and Commissioner of Pegu.
Commander G. E. Holland, R.I.M., D.S.O., C.I.E.	Honorary Aide-de-Camp, Port Officer.
Mr. W. H. A. St. J. Leeds	President of the Rangoon Municipality.
The Hon. Mr. J. Lowis, B.L. . . .	Member of the Legislative Council and Government Advocate.
Colonel S. C. F. Peile, C.I.E. . . .	Inspector-General of Police.
Sir J. G. Scott, K.C.I.E.	Superintendent, Southern Shan States.
Mr. H. P. Todd-Naylor, C.I.E., M.A., Indian Civil Service	Commissioner.

The Hon. Sir H. T. White, C.I.E., Indian Civil Service	Chief Judge.
Mr. J. B. Wingate, Indian Civil Service	Secretary to Government.
Lieutenant Pickering	West Riding Regiment, A.-D.-C.
Gopal Singh	Naib Commandant.
Leong Chye, K.I.H.	Merchant.
Maung Aung Zan, K.S.M.	Extra Assistant Commissioner.
Maung Hlwa, T.D.M.	Myoôk.
Maung Hkun Môn, K.S.M.	Myoôk in charge of the sub-State of Hsum Hsai.
Maung Ket, K.S.M.	Extra Assistant Commissioner.
Maung Ni, A.T.M.	Assistant District Superintendent of Police.
Maung On Gaing, C.I.E., A.T.M.	Municipal Commissioner, Rangoon.
Maung Po, K.S.M., the Hon.	Member, Burma Legislative Council.
Maung Po, A.T.M.	Myoza of Hsa Mong Hkam.
Maung Po Ni, A.T.M.	Inspector of Police.
Maung Pule, A.T.M.	Myoôk.
Maung San Pè, T.D.M.	Extra Assistant Commissioner.
Maung Shwe Po, A.T.M.	Retired Extra Assistant Commissioner.
Maung Shwe Tha, A.T.M.	Assistant District Superintendent of Police.
Maung Tha Do We, A.T.M.	Retired Extra Assistant Commissioner.
Maung Thu Taw U., T.D.M.	Assistant District Superintendent of Police.
Maung Tin Gyaw, T.D.M.	Extra Assistant Commissioner.
Maung Tun, K.S.M.	Myoôk.
Maung Tun Gywe, A.T.M.	Myoôk.
Maung Tun Hal, T.D.M.	Inspector of Police.
Maung Tun Min, T.D.M.	Assistant District Superintendent of Police.
Muhammad Suleman	Inspector of Police.
U Rê Gyaw Thu, K.S.M.	Merchant.
Zawar Hussain	Hospital Assistant.

Central Provinces.

Mr. D. J. A. Campbell, Indian Civil Service	Divisional Judge.
Mr. L. S. Carey, Indian Civil Service	Commissioner, Hoshangabad.
Mr. C. R. Cleveland, Indian Civil Service	Inspector-General of Police.
Mr. M. W. Fox-Strangways, Indian Civil Service	Commissioner of Jubbulpore.
Mr. S. Ismay, C.S.I., Indian Civil Service	Judicial Commissioner.
Brigadier-General P. D. Jeffreys, C.B.	Commanding the Jubbulpore District.
Mr. H. M. Laurie, Indian Civil Service	Second Secretary.
Mr. J. B. Leventhrope	Secretary, Public Works Department.
Lieut.-Colonel H. K. McKay, C.I.E., I.M.S.	Civil Surgeon.
Colonel M. D. Moriarty, I.M.S.	Administrative Medical Officer.

Mr. A. Munro	Director of Public Instruction.
Mr. A. B. Napier, Indian Civil Service	Commissioner of Excise.
Mr. B. Robertson, Indian Civil Service, C.I.E.	Chief Secretary.
Mr. F. G. Sly, Indian Civil Service	Commissioner of Settlements.
Lieut.-Colonel C. M. Sumner	Commanding South Lancashire Regiment at Jubbulpur.
Mr. J. Walker, Indian Civil Service	Deputy Commissioner, Nagpur.
Lieutenant L. L. Wheatley, D.S.O.	45th Sikhs.

Raja Ajit Singh.
Raja Azam Shah.
Rao Sahib Balwant Rao Bhuskute.
Rao Bahadur Bihari Lal.
Brijraj Singh Deo.
Rai Bahadur Chandi Pershad Dixit.
Mr. Gangadhar Rao Madho Chitnavis, C.I.E.
Rai Bahadur Gansha Bapu.
Raja Gokul Dass Seth.
Raja Kamransha.
Thakur Kashinath Kesheo, Rao Bahadur.
Rai Kasturchand Daga Bahadur.
Rai Lal Nripraj Singh Deo Bahadur.
Rao Bahadur Lataria Bhan.
Mr. Mahdi Hasan.
Mr. Madho Rao Bhau.
Thakur Maharaj Singh, Rai Bahadur.
Thakur Mardan Singh.
Mr. R. Mitra.
Khan Sahib Muhammad Ahfazal Rahim.
Diwan Muhammad Ali Khan.
Rao Sahib Nirbhe Singh Mandloi.
Porshotam, B.
Rao Bahadur Raghoba Mahadik.
Raja Bahadur Raghuji Rao.
Aba Sahib Raghunath Rao.
Thakur Raghuraj Singh.
Rao Sahib Rang Rao Hari.
Mr. Shridhar Ganesh Paranjpe.
Rao Sahib Venkat Rao.
Raja Vishwanath Singh.
Maulvi Zahur-ul-Islam.

Assam.

Mr. B. C. Allen, Indian Civil Service	Personal Assistant to the Chief Commissioner.
Dr. W. Booth	Director of Public Instruction.
Mr. J. Buckingham, C.I.E.	Honorary Magistrate, Sibsagar.
Colonel C. W. Carr-Calthrop, I.M.S.	Principal Medical Officer and Sanitary Commissioner.
Lieut.-Colonel J. W. Cowley	Staff Officer to the General Officer Commanding the Assam District.
Mr. A. W. Davis	Inspector-General of Police and Jails, etc.
Mr. R. H. Henderson, C.I.E.	Honorary Paymaster, Surma Valley Light Horse.
Mr. F. C. Henniker, Indian Civil Service	Director, Department of Land Records and Agriculture.
Mr. C. H. Holder	Assam Valley Light Horse.
Colonel D. M. Lumsden, C.B.	Colonel (unattached list), Assam Valley Light Horse.

Mr. P. G. Melitus, C.I.E., Indian Civil Service	Commissioner, Assam Valley Districts.
Mr. F. J. Monahan, Indian Civil Service	Secretary to the Chief Commissioner.
Mr. G. J. Perram, M.I.C.E.	Secretary, Public Works Department.
Brigadier-General Sir A. J. F. Reid, K.C.B.	General Officer Commanding Assam District.
Mr. J. Taylor	Honorary Captain, Assam Valley Light Horse. Representative of the Steamer Companies in Assam.
Mr. Abdul Majid	Assistant Commissioner.
Maulvi Ali Amjad Khan	Zamindar, Sylhet.
Babu Baikuntha Nath Sarma	Zamindar, Sylhet.
Srijut Bhowani Charan Sarma	Honorary Magistrate, Tezpur.
Rai Sahib Bhuban Ram Das	Vice-Chairman, Gauhati Municipality.
Srijut Chandra Narayan Sing	Jorhat.
Srijut Chandra Narayan Singh	Mauzadar of Beltola, Kamrup.
Rai Dulal Chandra Deb Bahadur	Government Pleader, Sylhet.
Babu Durga Charan Sen	Sub-Judge, Sylhet.
Raja Giris Chandra Rai	Sylhet.
Raja Jagannath Barua Bahadur	Honorary Magistrate, Jorhat.
Srijut Kaliprasad Chaliha	Pleader and Vice-Chairman, Sibsagar Local Board.
Babu Kamini Kumar Chandra, M.A., B.L.	Pleader, Silchar.
Raja Kine Singh	Seim of Nongkhlaw, Khasi and Jaintia Hills.
Srijut Lakeswar Burua Gohain	Jorhat.
Rai Madhab Chandra Bardalai Bahadur	Extra Assistant Commissioner, Gauhati.
Khan Bahadur Majid Bakht Mazumdar	Zamindar, Sylhet.
Srijut Malbhog Barua	Honorary Magistrate, Dibrugarh.
Srijut Manik Chandra Barua	Gauhati.
Maulvi Muhammad Ahia	Zamindar, Sylhet.
Srijut Nandi Nath Barua	Nowgong.
Raja Prabhat Chandra Barua	Gauripur.

Hyderabad.

Captain H. K. Barr	Personal Assistant to the Resident.
Mr. A. Elliott, C.I.E.	Officiating Commissioner, Hyderabad Assigned Districts.
Lieut.-Colonel R. Vernon Garrett	Deputy Commissioner, Hyderabad Assigned Districts.
Mr. H. Godwin-Austen	Deputy Commissioner, Hyderabad Assigned Districts.
Mr. A. C. Hankin, C.I.E.	Inspector-General of Police, His Highness the Nizam's Dominions, and Member of the Police Commission.

Lieut.-Colonel W. Hastings	Inspector-General of Police, Jails, etc., Hyderabad Assigned Districts.
Lieut.-Colonel E. C. M. Lushington . .	Military Secretary to the Resident.
Colonel Afsar-ud-Daula, C.I.E.	
Bhagwant Rao Shankar Rao . . .	Special (Honorary) Magistrate, Daryapur, Ellichpur District.
Kumar Shri Harbhamji Raoji . . .	Deputy Commissioner, Akola.
Mr. G. S. Khaparde	Member, Amraoti City Municipality.
Khan Bahadur Khwaja Abdul Baki . .	Member of the District Board, Buldana.
Khan Bahadur Muhammad Salam-ulla .	Nawab Jagirdar of Deulghat, Buldana.
Shams-ud-din Khan	Hospital Assistant.

Mysore.

Mr. L. Davidson	Commissioner of Coorg.
Major J. Logan	Commanding Coorg and Mysore Rifle Volunteers.
Mr. R. C. H. Moss-King, Indian Civil Service	First Assistant to the Resident in Mysore.
Mr. W. H. Sprott.	
Rai Annasami Moodaliar Bahadur, B.P. .	Bangalore.
Rai Bahadur A. Mandanna	Coorg.
Rai Bahadur C. Somiah	Coorg.

Central India.

Lieutenant L. Bayley	6th Bengal Cavalry, Personal Assistant to the Agent to the Governor-General in Central India.
Major S. F. Bayley	Political Agent, Baghelkhand.
Captain F. G. Beville	Political Agent in Bundelkhand.
Mr. R. H. Gunion	Principal of the Daly College, Indore.
Lieut.-Colonel C. Herbert	Resident at Gwalior.
Major L. Impey	Political Agent in Bhopal.
Captain C. E. Luard	Superintendent of Gazetteer, Central India.
Mr. L. W. Reynolds	Assistant to the Agent to the Governor-General.
Major M. A. Tighe	Political Agent in Malwa. Ticket Officer in the Chiefs' Camp.
Mr. H. G. Waterfield	Assistant to the General Superintendent, Thagi and Dakaiti Department.
Captain C. J. Windham	First Assistant to the Agent to the Governor-General.
Major F. E. Younghusband, C.I.E. . .	Resident at Indore.

Nawab Bahadur of Banda.	Rai Radhe Lal Bahadur.

Rai Sahib Dwarkanath Sivapuri.	Pandit Ram Kishan Pant, Rao Bahadur.
Sardar Bahadur Dyal Singh Gyani.	Seth Chand Mal of Rutlam.
Khan Bahadur Ghulam Kadir Khan.	Seth Ram Chandar, Rai Bahadur.

Rajputana.

Maharaj Balbhadra Singh	Attaché to the Agent to the Governor-General.
Mr. E. H. Blakesley, Indian Civil Service .	Settlement Officer, Dholpur.
Mr. H. V. Cobb, Indian Civil Service . .	Resident, Jaipur.
Major K. D. Erskine	Resident, Western Rajputana States.
Lieut.-Colonel C. G. F. Fagan . . .	Political Agent, Alwar.
Colonel Sir Swinton Jacob, K.C.I.E. . .	Consulting Engineer for Irrigation, Government of India.
Captain S. H. Jacob	Assistant Resident, Jodhpur, and Officer in charge of Enquiry Office, Rajputana Chiefs' Camp.
Colonel W. Loch, A.-D.-C., I.A. . . .	Principal, Mayo College.
Captain A. B. Minchin, C.I.E. . . .	First Assistant to the Agent to the Governor-General.
Mr. Darashaw N. Modi	Attaché to the Agent to the Governor-General.
Captain S. B. Patterson	Assistant to the Agent to the Governor-General.
Major A. F. Pinhey, C.I.E.	Resident, Mewar.
Major C. H. Pritchard	Political Agent, Haraoti and Tonk.
Mr. H. Sherring	Headmaster of the Mayo College, Ajmer.
Major W. C. R. Stratton	Political Agent, Eastern Rajputana States.
Mr. A. L. P. Tucker, C.I.E., Indian Civil Service	Commissioner, Ajmer-Merwara.
Mr. G. G. White	Secretary in the Public Works Department to the Agent to the Governor-General in Rajputana and Central India.
Rai Champa Lal Seth Bahadur . . .	Ajmer Government Treasurer, Ajmer.
Nemi Chand Seth	Banker, Ajmer.
Rai Umed Mal Seth Bahadur . . .	Banker of Ajmer.
Rao Bahadur Singh, C.I.E.	Istimrardar of Ajmer.
Pandit Sukhdeo Prasad, Rao Bahadur, C.I.E.	Diwan, Jodhpur State.

Baluchistan.

Mr. W. S. Davis	First Assistant to the Agent to the Governor-General in Baluchistan.
General Sir A. Gaselee, G.C.I.E., K.C.B. .	General Officer Commanding the Quetta District.
Captain A. L. Jacob	Second Assistant to the Agent to the Governor-General in Baluchistan.

Major C. W. Jacob	Commandant, Zhob Levy Corps.
Lieut.-Colonel Kelly	Assistant Adjutant-General, Quetta District.
Major A. McConaghey	Deputy Commissioner, Thal-Chotiali.
Major A. H. McMahon, C.S.I., C.I.E. . .	British Commissioner, Afghan Boundary Commission.
Major J. Ramsay, C.I.E.	Officiating Revenue Commissioner.
Major H. L. Showers	Political Agent, Kalat.
Sardar Abdul Rashid	Shahwani.
Abdul Wahid Khan	Durani.
Malik Akhtar Khan	Mando Khel.
Alam Khan, Abdullazai	Mina Bazzar.
Mir Alam Khan	Badini Rakhshani.
Mir Malik Alam Khan	Mehtarzai.
Ali Muhammad	Haruni.
Sardar Alu Khan	Musa Khel.
Khan Bahadur Arbab Khudadad Khan .	Kansi.
Ata Khan	Shirani.
Malik Azam Khan	Kudezai.
Mir Azim Khan	Shahwani.
Saiyid Bahar Shah.	
Khan Sahib Baha-ud-din	Bozai.
Sardar Bahadur Bangal Khan	Jogizai.
Bangal Khan	Tarin.
Mir Bahawal Khan	Satakzai.
Sardar Bakhtiyar Khan	Rustamzai.
Baluch Khan	Mandai.
Rai Bhik Chand Seth Bahadur . . .	Municipal Commissioner, Quetta.
Chandan Khan	Tarasezai.
Saiyid Chiragh Shah.	
Dada Khan	Zarkun.
Malik Dewa Khan	Hamzazai.
Mulla Dilbar	Fakirzai.
Sardar Dost Muhammad	Lehri.
Mir Fakir Muhammad	Bazinjo.
Sardar Ghaus Bakhsh	Raisani.
Ghulam Ali Khan	Wadera Baledi.
Khan Bahadur Ghulam Haidar Khan . .	Achakzai.
Khan Sahib Haji Harun	Panezai.
Halim Khan	Sarangzai.
Hassan Khan	Dumar.
Khan Sahib Iskan Khan	Tarin.
Khan Sahib Jamal Khan	Musa Khel.

Mir Jan Beg	Jamaldini Rakhshani.
Kaisar Khan	Wadera Magassi.
Khan Bahadur Sardar Khair Bakhsh Khan	Marri.
Khoidad Malik	Mirzai.
Sardar Mehrab Khan	Domki.
Sardar Mehrab Khan	Khetran.
Saiyid Mehr Shah	Kharsin.
Khan Sahib Mian Khan	Kibzai.
Mir Mohim Khan	Gurgnari.
Sardar Bahadur Muhammad Akbar Khan	Jogizai.
Mir Muhammad Ali Khan	Zagar Mengal.
Sardar Muhammad Azim Khan	Muhammadshahi.
Mir Muhammad Baka Khan	Kaheri.
Saiyid Muhammad Hassan	Shinghari.
Sardar Muhammad Khan	Barozai.
Khan Bahadur Nawab Khan	Luni.
Nawab Khan	Wanechi.
Nur Muhammad	Wadera, Bangalzai.
Sardar Pasand Khan	Zarakzai.
Payo Khan	Dumar.
Mir Pahar Khan	Sasoli.
Mir Rahim Khan	Kurd.
Khan Bahadur, Mir Rasul Bakhsh	Raisani.
Sardar Rasul Bakhsh	Lango.
Mulla Saleh Muhammad.	
Khan Bahadur Samandar Khan	Lehri.
Mir Sarbuland Khan	Barozai.
Sardar Khan	Wadera Rind.
Nawab Sir Shahbaz Khan, K.C.I.E.	Bugti.
Sardar Shakar Khan	Mengal.
Mir Sher Muhammad Khan	Urerani.
Khan Bahadur Sohbat Khan	Gola.
Malik Sultan Muhammad Khan	Sargari.
Wahab Khan	Panezai.
Mir Walhari Khan	Marghzani.
Sardar Yar Muhammad	Kurd.
Khan Bahadur Yusuf Khan	Kurd.
Sardar Zarghun Khan	Jogizai.
Mir Zehri Khan	Musiani.

North-West Frontier Province.

Mr. C. E. F. Bunbury	Judicial Commissioner.
Mr. R. I. R. Glancy, Indian Civil Service	Assistant Secretary to the Chief Commissioner.
Captain S. H. Godfrey	Political Agent, Dir, Swat and Chitral, in charge of the Malakand Chiefs.
Mr. A. H. Grant, Indian Civil Service	Secretary to the Agent to the Governor-General.
Pandit Harnam Dass	Assistant Surgeon in subordinate charge of the Central and Provincial Camps.
Mr. C. G. Hastings, C.I.E.	Inspector-General of Police.
Risaldar Kaushi Nand, Sardar	Personal Assistant.
Mr. M. O'Dwyer	Revenue Commissioner.
Lieut.-Colonel Scott-Moncrieff, C.I.E.	Secretary to the Chief Commissioner of the Public Works Department.
Captain H. B. St. John	Personal Assistant to the Chief Commissioner.
Khan Bahadur Abdul Ghafur Khan	Khan of Teri.
Khan Bahadur Abdul Ghafur Khan	Khan of Zaida.
Nawab Hafiz Abdulla Khan	Alizai. Dera Ismail Khan.
Nawab Allahdad Khan	Saddozai. Dera Ismail Khan.
Aminulla Khan	Orakzai. Peshawar.
Barakat Khan	Sultan of Boi. Hazara.
Khan Bahadur Dost Muhammad Khan, Arbab	Khalil. Peshawar.
Mirza Ghulam Ahmad, C.I.E.	Peshawar.
Ghulam Kasim Khan	Nawab of Tonk. Dera Ismail Khan.
Khan Bahadur Haq Nawaz Khan, C.I.E.	Dera Ismail Khan.
Khan Bahadur Ibrahim Khan	Mardan.
Raja Jehandad Khan	Hazara.
Khushdil Khan	Bangash. Kohat.
Khan Bahadur Khwaja Muhammad Khan	Hoti Mardan, Peshawar.
Khan Bahadur Mohabbat Khan	Toru. Peshawar.
Nawab Muhammad Afzal Khan, Khan Bahadur	Dera Ismail Khan.
Colonel Nawab Muhammad Aslam Khan, C.I.E., A.-D.-C.	Peshawar.
Khan Bahadur Muhammad Azam Khan	Arbab Mohmand. Peshawar.
Khan Bahadur Muhammad Hussain Khan	Arbab Mohmand. Peshawar.
Raja Sher Ahmad Khan	Hazara.
Sardar Sultan Jan, C.I.E.	Kohat.

Kashmir.

Baldeo Singh	Raja of Poonch.
Muhammad Nazim Khan, C.I.E.	Mir of Hunza.
Sikandar Khan, C.I.E.	Raja of Nagar.
Mr. Stainton	In charge of the Gilgit Agency Chiefs.
Major G. H. Bretherton, D.S.O.	

IMPERIAL SERVICE TROOPS.

Brigadier-General Stuart Beatson, C.B.	Inspector-General, with 230 officers and 6000 men of the Imperial Service Troops.

PRESS REPRESENTATIVES.

Representatives of the "Times," "Manchester Guardian," "Daily Telegraph," "Sphere," "Punch," "Pall Mall Magazine," "Graphic," and "Daily Graphic," "Daily Mail," the Press Association, "Illustrated London News," "Black and White," "Reuter," "Indian Daily Telegraph," "Madras Mail," "Pioneer," "Central News Agency," "Times of India," "Advocate of India," "Bombay Gazette," "Voice of India," "Rangoon Gazette," "Statesman," "Englishman," "Civil and Military Gazette," and "Indian Daily News;" and the following native papers—the "Hindoo Patriot," "Indian Mirror," "Amrita Bazar Patrika," "Bengalee," "Bangabasi," "Hindi Bangabasi," "Hitabadi," "Sanjivani," "Basumati," and "Moslem Chronicle," Calcutta; "Muslim Herald," "Rust Goftar," "Bombay Samachar," "Indu Prakash," "Jam-i-Jamshed," and "Kaisar-i-Hind," Bombay; "Swades Mitram," "Muhammadan Madras," and "Hindu Madras," Madras; "Tribune," "Observer," and "Paisa Akbar," Lahore; "Burma Herald," Rangoon; "Kayasth Samachar," Allahabad; "Advocate" and "Oudh Akbar," Lucknow; "Agra Akbar," Agra; "Bharat Jiwan," Benares; "Civil and Military News," Ludhiana; "Victoria Paper," Sialkot; "Baluchistan Gazette," Quetta; "Proja Bandhu," Ahmednagar; "Dnyan Prakash" and "Jagadhitechhu," Poona; "Al Haq," "Sukkar," and "Behar Times," Bankipur.

APPENDIX VIII

THE MUTINY VETERANS

Colonel A. R. D. Mackenzie, C.B.
Sergeant Adams.
Ensign Bailey.
Sergeant Boileau.
Captain C. Briscoe.
Mr. Browne.
Private Caldera.
Captain Courtenay, I.S.M.D.
Sergeant Cross.
Captain Crummy.
Mr. W. H. Des Brosses (Apothecary).
Mr. R. J. Dennett.
Conductor T. O. Donnell.
Major Dunn, V.D.
The Reverend W. Fergusson.
Drum-Major Freegrade.
Sub-Conductor Gateley.
Lieutenant Hardaker.
Sergeant Johnson.
Conductor William Mathews.
Sergeant Owen.
Captain Price.
Mr. Quilter.
Captain Rautliff.
Mr. Rance.
Captain Rogers.
Mr. Sausman (Apothecary).
Mr. Young.

Havildar Peeroomull	Queen's Own Sappers and Miners.
Havildar Mahomed Khassam	8th Madras Infantry.
Subadar Govind Rai	4th P. W. O. L. Cavalry.
Subadar Amir Husain, Bahadur	1st Madras Lancers.
Colour-Havildar Veeraswami	Queen's Own Sappers and Miners.
Havildar Sheikh Farid	Queen's Own Sappers and Miners.
Havildar Yacoob Khan	36th Native Infantry.
Dafadar Mahomed Ayab	13th Bengal Cavalry.
Risaldar Mahomed Akbar Khan	1st Punjab Cavalry.
Jemadar Gholam Khan	2nd Punjab Cavalry.
Jemadar Shah Pasand Khan	Guides Cavalry.
Kot-Dafadar Yunas Khan	Guides Cavalry.
Dafadar Mihar Ali	Guides Cavalry.
Kot-Dafadar Shamsuddin	2nd Punjab Cavalry.
Risaldar-Major Sardar Bahadur Mir Alam Khan	6th Bengal Cavalry.

Subadar Amir Khan	19th Bengal Infantry.
Subadar Shah Pasand	10th Bengal Infantry.
Dafadar Mahomed Islam	Guides Cavalry.
Jemadar Mir Afzal	6th Punjab Infantry.
Subadar Daim Khan Naick Sher Zaman	1st Punjab Infantry.
Havildar Karab Ali Subadar Kadar Khan	21st Punjab Infantry.
Jemadar Mahomed Ismail Jemadar Nawab Khan Resaldar Pardhan Bhagwant Sahai	Cavalry No. 3 (*sic*).
Dafadar Ganga Ram	14th Bengal Lancers.
Havildar Budhi Ballabh Pant	
Naick Nar Har Singh Joshi	
Havildar Bishen Singh	3rd Gurkhas.
Naick Kallian Singh	C 16th Brigade, R.A.
Risaldar Mahomed Nur Khan	7th Bengal Cavalry.
Subadar-Major Sheodas Singh	7th Native Infantry.
Havildar Janki Pershad	Barabanki Police.
Dafadar Amir Khan	Guides.
Dafadar Sher Mahomed	17th Bengal Cavalry.
Subadar Ram Gholam	Bengal Sappers and Miners.
Dafadar Jawahir Singh	18th Bengal Cavalry.
Havildar Jagannath Pandy	1st Oudh Irregular Infantry.
Havildar Taja Tiwari	16th Native Infantry.
Naick Goordeen Singh	4th Native Infantry.
Jemadar Bhowam Singh Subadar-Major Baldeo Patak	16th Native Infantry.
Naick Umrao Singh	Sappers and Miners.
Dafadar Baldeo Singh	1st Bengal Lancers.
Dafadar Asafdaula Khan	3rd Bengal Cavalry.
Risaldar-Major Mathura Singh, Sardar Bahadur	6th Bengal Cavalry.
Subadar Ajudhiya Patak Naick Pancham	Bengal Sappers and Miners.
Subadar Yacoob Khan	4th P. W. O. Cavalry.
Subadar Syed Ali	19th Madras Infantry.
Havildar Jamal Khan	34th Madras Infantry.
Havildar Lutchmiah	22nd Madras Infantry.
Havildar Syed Cawder	24th Madras Infantry.
Havildar Azeemoddin Subadar Morad Khan	26th Madras Infantry.

Subadar Sheikh Hosen	27th Madras Infantry.
Havildar Usman Khan	
Havildar Jalal Sharif	16th Madras Infantry.
Subadar Ally Beg	12th Madras Infantry.
Havildar Sheikh Abdullah	17th Madras Infantry.
Risaldar Lilladhur Singh.	
Subadar-Major Baloo Khan Kechai Khan	27th Bombay Infantry.
Hospital Assistant Khan Bahadur Elahi Bux.	
Naick Heyt Ram	1st Bengal Infantry.
Dafadar Tej Singh	2nd Punjab Cavalry.
Woordie-Major Sheikh Shabrati.	
Risaldar-Major Muhammad Abdul Kadir, K.B.	7th Irregular Cavalry.
Dafadar Muhammad Nazir Shah	17th Bengal Cavalry.
Subadar Muhammad Ali Shah	Late Nawab Jan Fishan Khan Cavalry.
Risaldar Muhammad Amin	2nd Bengal Cavalry.
Subadar Bhim Singh	2-1 Gurkha Rifles.
Jemadar Tejbir	1-1 Gurkha Rifles.
Subadar Bahadur	
Jemadar Sobha Singh	32nd Punjab Infantry.
Subadar Duni Chand, Bahadur	Guides Cavalry.
Dafadar Bakhsh Khan	
Dafadar Allah Bakhsh Khan.	
Jemadar Kishan Sahai	1st Troop State Regiment (*sic*).
Havildar Jeewa Singh	14th Bengal Infantry.
Risaldar-Major Wajid Ali, Sardar Bahadur	4th Regiment Cavalry.
Dafadar Umed Husein	
Havildar Munawar	Guides Infantry.
Havildar Gujar	1st Punjab Infantry.
Havildar Sarwar Shah	17th Bengal Infantry.
Havildar Said Khan	1st Punjab Infantry.
Havildar Dewa Singh	2nd Punjab Infantry.
Risaldar Rahmat Khan	7th Bengal Cavalry.
Dafadar Harnam Singh	70th Cavalry (*sic*).
Hospital Assistant Muhammad Usman Ghani	
Dafadar Sipahdar Beg	8th Bengal Cavalry.
Honorary Captain Muhammad Hussain, Risaldar-Major, Sardar Bahadur	7th Bengal Lancers.
Honorary Captain Juthia Khatri, Subadar-Major, Sardar Bahadur	13th Bengal Infantry.
Subadar Kashi Ram	Ordnance Department.
Subadar Said Abbas, Bahadur	5th Light Cavalry.
Subadar Said Mohiuddin, Bahadur	36th Madras Rifles.
Jemadar Said Hosein	

Havildar Goman Singh	5th Gurkhas.
Havildar Mohan Singh	5th Gurkhas.
Havildar Golab Singh Bora	5th Gurkhas.
Havildar Kalloo	5th Gurkhas.
Havildar Moti	34th Native Infantry.
Havildar Jagat Ram	3rd Gurkhas.
Havildar Luchman	3rd Gurkhas.
Havildar Dasoudha Singh	Guides.
Subadar Chogatta Singh	1st Sikhs.
Subadar-Major Nandu Misra	3rd Bengal Infantry.
Havildar Punjab Singh	Mazbi Regiment.
Jemadar Aminuddowla Khan	3rd Bengal Cavalry.
Honorary Captain Subadar-Major Moti Negri, Sardar Bahadur	2nd Gurkhas.
Subadar Mohan Singh Mohur	2nd Gurkhas.
Subadar Mani Ram Ghallay	2nd Gurkhas.
Subadar Dhanbeer	2nd Gurkhas.
Subadar Mahabir Jhanski	2nd Gurkhas.
Havildar Sissoo Thapa	2nd Gurkhas.
Havildar Naick Parbat Rana	2nd Gurkhas.
Havildar Harakbir Nagarkoti	2nd Gurkhas.
Havildar Ticca Ram Rana	2nd Gurkhas.
Havildar Nathu Bhist	2nd Gurkhas.
Havildar Dhanbir Lohar	2nd Gurkhas.
Havildar Raghobar Rana	2nd Gurkhas.
Havildar Dhanbir Groon	2nd Gurkhas.
Bugle-Major Naddu Dami	2nd Gurkhas.
Havildar Umar Singh Routh	2nd Gurkhas.
Havildar Perbeer Thapa	2nd Gurkhas.
Havildar Singhbir Ally	2nd Gurkhas.
Havildar Mookti Ram	2nd Gurkhas.
Havildar Jahi Singh	3rd Gurkhas.
Naick Chander Singh	5th Gurkhas.
Risaldar Abdullah Khan	5th Punjab Cavalry.
Subadar-Major Jai Singh	Guides.
Havildar Amar Singh.	
Havildar Jawahir Singh	21st Punjab Infantry.
Kot-Dafadar Sham Singh.	
Kot-Havildar Mahna Singh	5th Punjab Infantry.
Dafadar Jahangir Khan	3rd Bengal Cavalry.
Subadar Sher Singh	1st Punjab Infantry.
Subadar Maya Dass	28th Punjab Infantry.
Subadar Jawahir Singh	5th Madras (Burma).

Subadar Jawahir Singh	16th Bengal Infantry.
Risaldar Waryam Singh	2nd Central India Horse.
Subadar Gurdit Singh	19th Regiment.
Subadar-Major Budh Singh	
Havildar Ali Bakhsh	4th Punjab Infantry.
Havildar Golab Singh	
Havildar Wasawa Singh	25th Bengal Infantry.
Naick Kesar Singh	31st Bengal Infantry.
Naick Punjab Singh	7th Regiment.
Havildar Dewa Singh	25th Regiment.
Dafadar Buta Singh	10th Bengal Lancers.
Lance Dafadar Shadi	
Lance Dafadar Waryam Singh	1st Bengal Cavalry.
Subadar Ratan Singh (Sub-Inspector) . .	5th Punjab Infantry.
Sardar Ganda Singh, Risaldar.	
Jemadar Ganda Singh	4th Punjab Infantry.
Subadar Jawahir Shah	31st Bengal Infantry.
Jemadar Amir Singh	1st Bailey Guard.
Havildar Jawahir Singh	4th Punjab Infantry.
Havildar Gurdit Singh	5th Punjab Infantry.
Havildar Rahmat Bakhsh	1st Punjab Infantry.
Dafadar Jai Singh	1st Cavalry.
Naick Chattar Singh	4th Punjab Infantry.
Havildar Jehar Singh	4th Sikhs.
Trumpet-Major Ellabu Bakhsh . . .	7th and 8th Regiments, 15th Bengal Cavalry.
Subadar Kala Singh	25th Bengal Infantry.
Naick Roshan Khan	Bengal Sappers and Miners.
Dafadar Natha Singh	10th Bengal Infantry.
Subadar Ganesh Dass	31st Punjab Infantry.
Jemadar Mokham Din	25th Punjab Infantry.
Kot-Dafadar Bishen Singh	19th Bengal Lancers.
Risaldar Sardar Chet Singh	9th Bengal Lancers.
Subadar Jwala Singh	5th Punjab Infantry.
Havildar Chattar Singh	14th Bengal Native Infantry.
Risaldar Golab Singh	19th Bengal Lancers.
Jemadar Sher Baz Khan	2nd Punjab Cavalry.
Naick Khuda Bakhsh.	
Subadar Karam Khan	2nd Punjab Infantry.
Subadar Nabi Bakhsh	3rd Punjab Infantry.
Subadar Ghasita Khan	Guides.
Naick Ganga Singh	19th Punjab Infantry.
Dafadar Jamal Singh	2nd Punjab Cavalry.
Dafadar Prem Singh	3rd Bengal Cavalry.

Dafadar Amar Singh	1st Punjab Cavalry.
Dafadar Mir Muazam Ali	3rd Light Cavalry.
Subadar-Major Mohesa Singh	10th Bengal Infantry.
Subadar Nagina Singh	
Havildar Sham Singh	25th Punjab Infantry.
Havildar Ganga Singh	
Havildar Bikarma Singh	30th Punjab Infantry.
Dafadar Ishar Singh	12th Bengal Infantry.
Naik Sheru	3rd Punjab Infantry.
Havildar Bhola Singh	15th Sikhs.
Risaldar Gurdit Singh	4th Bengal Cavalry.
Havildar Bhagtia	66th Regiment.
Havildar Yacoob Khan	27th Madras Infantry.
Subadar Mitha Khan.	
Subadar Mauladad Khan.	
Havildar Sabrati.	
Risaldar Juma Khan	9th Bengal Cavalry.
Subadar Kaher Din	4th Regiment.
Subadar Pertab Singh	20th Punjab Infantry.
Jemadar Kishen Singh	28th Punjab Infantry.
Subadar-Major Bhola Singh, Sardar Bahadur	32nd Pioneers.
Subadar Jwala Singh	
Subadar Asa Singh	
Subadar Hari Singh	
Subadar Fateh Singh	
Havildar Buta Singh	
Subadar Jhanda Singh	
Subadar Sawan Singh	
Jemadar Jiwan Singh	34th Punjab Infantry.
Dafadar Sultan Khan.	
Subadar Jita Singh.	
Jemadar Kahu Singh	14th Sikhs.
Jemadar Rahim Bakhsh	11th Bengal Lancers.
Dafadar Roda	11th Bengal Lancers.
Subadar Raja Singh, Bahadur.	
Jemadar Thakur Bijodh Singh	13th Native Infantry.
Dafadar Ladha Singh.	
Jemadar Kahan Singh.	
Havildar Ratan Singh.	
Dafadar Amir Khan.	
Havildar Gobind Singh.	
Risaldar-Major Sardar Hazara Singh.	
Sergeant Nahar Singh.	

Havildar Chanda Singh	32nd Punjab Infantry.
Subadar-Major Ali Bakhsh, Bahadur	Sappers and Miners.
Subadar Daya Singh.	
Dafadar Bootai Khan.	
Subadar-Major Miran Bakhsh, Sardar Bahadur	2nd Punjab Infantry.
Jemadar Kutab Din Khan	2nd Central India Horse.
Dafadar Harjas	16th Bengal Cavalry.
Havildar Jetha Singh	2nd Punjab Infantry.
Dafadar Mir Sadik Ali	4th Cavalry.
Dafadar Abbas Ali	4th Cavalry.
Dafadar Imdad Ali	4th Cavalry.
Dafadar Dhiraj Singh	4th Cavalry.
Dafadar Ditta Khan	4th Cavalry.
Woordie-Major Asadula Khan	Guides.
Havildar Prem Singh.	
Colour-Havildar Hayamji Israel.	
Risaldar Wali Muhammad.	
Risaldar Allah Bakhsh	2nd Bombay Lancers.
Dafadar Sarfaraz Khan.	
Dafadar Sunt Singh.	
Dafadar Daulat Singh	
Jemadar Shah Sowar	Guides.
Havildar Mahomed Umar	
Havildar Khajan Singh	14th Sikhs.
Havildar Ahmad Khan	
Retired Tehsildar Ajab Singh	
Naick Jodh Singh	14th Native Infantry.
Naick Ghazi Khan	15th Infantry.
Havildar Imam Bakhsh	4th Punjab Infantry.
Havildar Hardhan Singh.	
Colour-Havildar Rurai Khan	25th Punjab Infantry.
Dafadar Ganda Singh	2nd Punjab Cavalry.
Jemadar Jodh Singh	Royal Artillery.
Havildar Bullah	25th Punjab Infantry.
Havildar Jiwan Singh	15th Sikhs.
Dafadar Bahadur Khan	3rd Bengal Cavalry.
Dafadar Abdulla Khan	3rd Bengal Cavalry.
Havildar Baz Khan	24th Bengal Infantry.
Subadar Prem Singh	31st Punjab Infantry.
Subadar Bhup Singh	39th Punjab Infantry.
Jemadar Dilmir Khan	30th Punjab Infantry.
Subadar Sahba	4th Punjab Infantry.

Jemadar Zaman Khan	4th Punjab Infantry.
Risaldar Amir Chand	Guides.
Dafadar Hari Singh	
Naick Nigahya	4th Punjab Infantry.
Naick Umar Bakhsh	
Subadar Kahan Singh	2nd Punjab Infantry.
Havildar Fazl	
Naick Ala Singh	
Dafadar Jawahir Singh	19th Bengal Lancers.
Risaldar Jawahir Singh	
Risaldar Kishen Singh	
Risaldar Mahomed Shariar	
Risaldar Bhooroo Singh	2nd Punjab Cavalry.
Havildar Samund Singh	31st Punjab Infantry.
Naick Sobha	Royal Artillery.
Subadar Nur Ahmad	26th Punjab Infantry.
Havildar Wazir Singh	
Subadar Rahmatullah Beg	3rd Sikhs.
Havildar Nand Singh	15th Sikhs.
Subadar Ahmad Khan	1st Punjab Infantry.
Dafadar Hukam Singh	1st Punjab Cavalry.
Havildar Ishar Singh	4th Punjab Infantry.
Bugle-Major Piram Ditta	
Havildar Sahib Singh	
Subadar Hira Singh	36th Regiment.
Risaldar Amir Khan	3rd Bengal Cavalry.
Dafadar Pertab Singh	19th Bengal Lancers.
Subadar Waryam Singh	28th Punjab Infantry.
Jemadar Mehtab Singh	
Havildar Khuda Bakhsh	5th Gurkhas.
Dafadar Indar Singh	9th Bengal Lancers.
Dafadar Jawahir Singh (2)	19th Bengal Lancers.
Dafadar Kishen Singh	9th Bengal Lancers.
Risaldar Kapur Singh	17th Bengal Lancers.
Subadar Sher Khan	21st Punjab Infantry.
Jemadar Bhagwan Singh	4th Sikhs.
Havildar Rasul Khan	19th Punjab Infantry.
Lance-Dafadar Mana Singh	2nd Punjab Cavalry.
Subadar Gholam Hosein	2nd Punjab Infantry.
Naick Jit Singh	3rd Gurkhas.
Naick Arjun Khatri	
Havildar Sewa Singh	Guides.
Havildar Hira Singh	71st Native Infantry.

Naick Wazir Ali.	
Jemadar Malak Kutab Din.	
Jemadar Kali Charan	Commander-in-Chief's Camp.
Subadar Jwala Singh	32nd Pioneers.
Havildar Bur Singh	32nd Pioneers.
Havildar Kishen Singh	32nd Pioneers.
Havildar Wasawa Singh	32nd Pioneers.
Havildar Gurdit Singh	32nd Pioneers.
Havildar Dewa Singh	32nd Pioneers.
Havildar Tahal Singh	32nd Pioneers.
Havildar Amar Singh	32nd Pioneers.
Havildar Jwala Singh	32nd Pioneers.
Havildar Buta Singh	32nd Pioneers.
Naick Sher Singh	32nd Pioneers.
Naick Mihan Singh	32nd Pioneers.
Naick Lehna Singh	32nd Pioneers.
Naick Lehna Singh	32nd Pioneers.
Lance-Naick Hukam Singh	32nd Pioneers.
Lance-Naick Budha Singh	32nd Pioneers.
Havildar Ala Singh	32nd Pioneers.
Sardar Nihal Singh, Deputy Inspector . .	23rd Punjab Infantry.
Naick Atar Singh	31st Bengal Infantry.
Naick Dewa Singh	1st Punjab Infantry.
Naick Sham Singh	23rd Pioneers.
Risaldar Sardul Singh	11th Bengal Lancers.
Dafadar Gurdit Singh	11th Bengal Lancers.
Dafadar Ganga Singh	11th Bengal Lancers.
Farrier-Major Miran Bakhsh . . .	11th Bengal Lancers.
Havildar Khan Singh	4th Sikhs.
Dafadar Mirzullah Khan	
Honorary Captain Risaldar-Major Ganda Singh, Sardar Bahadur	19th Bengal Lancers.
Jemadar Sher Singh	45th Sikhs.
Subadar-Major Bhagwan Singh, Khan Bahadur	30th Burma.
Dafadar Mahomed Khan	Central India Horse.
Sepoy Atar Singh	Agra Mounted Police.
Sepoy Bhagwan Singh	Agra Mounted Police.
Sowar Chet Singh.	
Sowar Sikandar Khan.	
Havildar Nihal Singh	26th Punjab Infantry.
Havildar Bagga Singh	2nd Sikhs.
Havildar Ramzani	25th Punjab Infantry.

Havildar Azim Bakhsh	14th Sikhs.
Dafadar Aman Khan	3rd Punjab Cavalry.
Dafadar Ramjas	7th Bengal Cavalry.
Havildar Umar Bakhsh.	
Subadar Baldeo	33rd Regiment.
Havildar Daman Singh	14th Sikhs.
Havildar Sahib Singh	9th Police.
Sepoy Ram Singh.	
Naick Hira Singh	14th Sikhs.
Risaldar Mehtab Singh	10th Bengal Lancers.
Risaldar Gulab Singh	
Jemadar Asa Singh	
Jemadar Bhag Khan	
Kot-Dafadar Hakim Rai	
Dafadar Jawand Singh	
Dafadar Uttam Singh	
Dafadar Tahal Singh	
Dafadar Hazara Singh	
Sowar Badhawa Singh (1)	
Sowar Badhawa Singh (2)	
Sowar Jiwan Khan	
Sowar Dewa Singh	
Sowar Karam Singh	
Sepoy Man Singh	Kumaon Battalion.
Sepoy Guman Singh	5th Gurkhas and Guides.
Sepoy Jhanda Singh	2nd Punjab Infantry.
Sowar Chanda Singh	32nd Pioneers.
Sepoy Nihal Singh	
Sepoy Gurdit Singh	
Sepoy Nihal Singh	32nd Pioneers.
Sepoy Sher Singh	
Sepoy Amar Singh	
Sepoy Chet Singh	
Risaldar Rahamatullah.	
Subadar Fazaldad Khan.	

APPENDIX IX

MILITARY OFFICERS

General Sir R. C. Low, G.C.B., Bengal Cavalry.
Lieut.-General Sir G. B. Wolseley, K.C.B., British Service.
Lieut.-General Sir B. Blood, K.C.B., R.E.
Major-General H. L. Smith-Dorrien, D.S.O., British Service.
Major-General Sir E. L. Elliot, K.C.B., D.S.O., Indian Army.
Major-General T. B. Tyler, C.S.I., Royal Artillery.
Major-General W. Hill, C.B., Indian Army.
Major-General D. J. S. McLeod, C.B., D.S.O., Madras General List Cavalry.
Major-General B. A. Combe, C.B., British Service.
Major-General W. T. Shone, C.B., D.S.O., R.E.
Major-General H. A. Bushman, C.B., British Service.
Brigadier-General B. Duff, C.B., C.I.E., Indian Army.
Brigadier-General J. S. Collins, British Service.
Brigadier-General J. Leach, Royal Artillery.
Brigadier-General Sir J. W. Murray, K.C.B., British Service.
Brigadier-General F. H. Plowden, British Service.
Brigadier-General Sir J. Willcocks, K.C.M.G., D.S.O., British Service.
Brigadier-General G. L. R. Richardson, C.B., C.S.I., C.I.E., Indian Army.
Brigadier-General G. H. More-Molyneux, C.B., D.S.O., C.I.E., Indian Army.
Brigadier-General H. P. Leach, C.B., D.S.O., R.E.
Brigadier-General H. A. Abbott, C.B., Indian Army.
Brigadier-General A. R. Martin, C.B., Indian Army.
Colonel J. E. Nixon, C.B., Indian Army.
Colonel E. Balfe, Indian Army.
Colonel W. B. Capper, British Service.
Colonel H. I. W. Hamilton, D.S.O., A.-D.-C., British Service.
Colonel C. H. Des Voeux, Indian Army.
Colonel A. H. Hewat, Royal Horse Artillery.
Colonel J. A. Coxhead, C.B., Royal Artillery.
Colonel H. N. McRae, C.B., A.-D.-C., Indian Army.

Colonel F. J. Aylmer, V.C., Royal Engineers.
Colonel J. C. F. Gordon, C.I.E., Indian Army.
Brevet-Colonel G. F. Francis, Indian Army.
Brevet-Colonel A. A. Pearson, Indian Army.
Brevet-Colonel C. W. Muir, C.B., C.I.E., Indian Army.
Lieut.-Colonel C. de C. Hamilton, Royal Artillery.
Lieut.-Colonel E. C. Hill, British Service.
Lieut.-Colonel W. R. Birdwood, Indian Army.
Lieut.-Colonel J. M. S. Brunker, Royal Horse Artillery.
Lieut.-Colonel S. D. Rainsford, Royal Artillery.
Lieut.-Colonel D. C. Carter, Royal Artillery.
Lieut.-Colonel H. S. Dawkins, Royal Artillery.
Lieut.-Colonel E. Gunner, Royal Artillery.
Lieut.-Colonel A. Keene, D.S.O., Royal Artillery.
Lieut.-Colonel R. A. G. Harrison, C.M.G., Royal Artillery.
Lieut.-Colonel J. W. Hawkins, Royal Horse Artillery.
Lieut.-Colonel M. O. Little, 9th Lancers.
Lieut.-Colonel F. C. Beatson, C.B., British Service.
Lieut.-Colonel C. M. T. Western, Royal Artillery.
Lieut.-Colonel R. C. Onslow, Indian Army.
Lieut.-Colonel G. C. P. Onslow, Royal Engineers.
Lieut.-Colonel G. F. N. Tinley, Indian Army.
Lieut.-Colonel J. A. Bell, Indian Army.
Lieut.-Colonel R. W. Sherard, Indian Army.
Lieut.-Colonel A. W. L. Bayly, C.B., D.S.O., Indian Army.
Lieut.-Colonel W. E. Phillips, Indian Army.
Lieut.-Colonel A. B. Dunsterville, 1st Battalion, East Surrey Regiment.
Lieut.-Colonel S. D. Gordon, 13th Bengal Lancers.
Lieut.-Colonel H. C. T. Littledale, 4th Dragoon Guards.
Lieut.-Colonel M. C. Barton, D.S.O., Royal Engineers.
Lieut.-Colonel F. Hawkins, 1st Brahmans.
Major-General C. J. Burnett, C.B., British Service.
Major-General Sir C. C. Egerton, K.C.B., D.S.O., Indian Army.
Major-General J. H. Wodehouse, C.B., C.M.G., R.A.
Major-General Sir R. Westmacott, K.C.B., D.S.O., Indian Army.
Major-General F. W. Kitchener, C.B., British Service.
Major-General A. G. Creagh, C.B., British Service.
Brigadier-General J. H. S. Craigie, British Service.
Brigadier-General F. H. Whitby, British Service.
Brigadier-General E. G. H. Bingham, R.A.
Brigadier-General R. G. W. Hepburne, British Service.
Brigadier-General J. P. C. Neville, Indian Army.
Major A. G. Peyton, 9th Bengal Lancers, Deputy Assistant Adjutant-General.

Major J. B. Edwards, D.S.O., 1st Central India Horse, Deputy Assistant Adjutant-General.

Major J. M. Stewart, 2nd Battalion, 5th Gurkha Rifles, Deputy Assistant Adjutant-General, 3rd Infantry Brigade.

Major W. G. Ley, 1st Battalion, North Staffordshire Regiment, Deputy Assistant Adjutant-General, 4th Infantry Brigade.

Captain H. R. Palmer, R.A.

Major-General L. W. Christopher, C.B., Director-General, Supply and Transport.

Lieut.-Colonel W. R. Yielding, C.I.E., D.S.O.	Supply and Transport Corps.
Major C. G. R. Thackwell, D.S.O.	
Major F. C. W. Rideout	
Major D. M. Thompson	
Major H. M. C. A. Johnston	
Captain F. W. Hawks	
Captain T. E. Madden	
Captain H. H. Roddy	
Captain A. S. R. Annesley	

Major-General C. H. Scott, C.B., R.A. Director-General of Ordnance.

Lieutenant J. Sesson, Assistant Commissary, Ordnance Department, Northern Circle.

Surgeon-General Sir T. J. Gallwey, K.C.M.G., C.B., R.A.M.C., Principal Medical Officer, His Majesty's Forces in India.

Colonel J. F. Supple, C.B., R.A.M.C.
Colonel J. M. Beamish, R.A.M.C.
Colonel T. S. Weir, I.M.S.
Lieut.-Colonel W. T. Johnston, R.A.M.C.
Lieut.-Colonel H. S. McGill, R.A.M.C.
Lieut.-Colonel Z. A. Ahmed, I.M.S.
Lieut.-Colonel L. A. Waddell, C.I.E., I.M.S.
Lieut.-Colonel M. S. Eyre, I.M.S.
Lieut.-Colonel J. Shearer, D.S.O., I.M.S.
Lieut.-Colonel C. C. Manifold, I.M.S.
Major G. B. Russell, R.A.M.C.
Major H. M. Adamson, R.A.M.C.
Major D. Hennessy, R.A.M.C.
Major P. Hehir, I.M.S.
Major H. M. Morris, I.M.S.
Major M. A. Kerr, I.M.S.
Major G. T. Mould, I.M.S.
Major H. N. Thompson, D.S.O.

Veterinary Lieut.-Colonel B. L. Glover, C.B., Army Veterinary Department.

Veterinary-Major A. F. Appleton, Army Veterinary Department.

Captain H. H. F. Turner, 2nd Bengal Lancers (Football and Hockey Tournament).

Major C. E. Salveson, R.E., Bengal Sappers and Miners.

Brevet-Major J. M. C. Colvin, V.C., R.E., Bengal Sappers and Miners.

Subadar-Major Hira Singh, Bengal Sappers and Miners.

Subadar Ram Chandar Sawant, Bahadur, Bombay Sappers and Miners.

4TH DRAGOON GUARDS.

Major F. B. L. Woodwright, Commandant.

Major the Hon. R. Leigh, Second-in-Command.

15TH HUSSARS.

Lieut.-Colonel T. Ch. de Crespigny, Commandant.

Brevet-Lieut.-Colonel W. E. Peyton, D.S.O., Second-in-Command.

9TH LANCERS.

Lieut.-Colonel S. W. Follett, Commandant.
Lieut.-Colonel E. T. Lund, Second-in-Command.

ROYAL HORSE ARTILLERY.

Major A. H. Short, D Battery.
Major V. F. W. A. Paget, I Battery.

ROYAL FIELD ARTILLERY.

Major E. M. Lachlan, 13th Battery, 1st Brigade Division.
Major W. K. McLeod, 67th Battery, ditto.
Major R. J. G. Elkington, 24th Battery, 38th Brigade Division.
Major G. F. White, 72nd Battery, ditto.
Major L. Forde, 51st Battery, 39th Brigade Division.
Major J. E. Harvey, 54th Battery, ditto.

ROYAL GARRISON ARTILLERY.

Major F. R. Thackeray, 71st Company, 30-Pounder Brigade Division.
Major A. H. Block, 72nd Company, ditto.
Major F. T. Graeme, 91st Company, 5-inch guns, ditto.
Major S. V. Thornton, 94th Company, 6-inch guns, ditto.
Major M. F. Fegen, No. 6 Mountain Battery, ditto.
Captain J. E. L. Bruce, Peshawar Mountain Battery, ditto.

1ST BATTALION, NORTHAMPTONSHIRE REGIMENT.

Lieut.-Colonel W. C. Fawcett, Commandant.
Major W. Weallens, Second-in-Command.

1ST BATTALION, SOUTH WALES BORDERERS.

Lieut.-Colonel C. V. Trower, Commandant.
Major C. E. Curll, Second-in-Command.

2ND BATTALION, WELSH REGIMENT.

Lieut.-Colonel W. V. Dickinson, Commandant.
Major A. R. Reade, Second-in-Command.

2ND BATTALION, GORDON HIGHLANDERS.

Lieut.-Colonel W. A. Scott, C.B., Commandant.
Major H. Wright, D.S.O., Second-in-Command.

2ND BATTALION, ARGYLL AND SUTHERLAND HIGHLANDERS.

Lieut.-Colonel J. H. Campbell, Commandant.
Captain D. Darroch, Second-in-Command.

1st Battalion, Royal Irish Rifles.

Lieut.-Colonel A. T. Swaine, Commandant.
Major F. J. Tobin, D.S.O., Second-in-Command.

1st Battalion, Bedfordshire Regiment.

Lieut.-Colonel H. Lysons, V.C., Commandant.
Major G. J. N. Logan Home, Second-in-Command.

1st Battalion, Norfolk Regiment.

Lieut.-Colonel A. C. Becher, Commandant.
Captain C. B. Close, Second-in-Command.

3rd Battalion, Rifle Brigade.

Lieut.-Colonel G. Cockburn, D.S.O., Commandant.
Major V. A. Couper, Second-in-Command.

2nd Battalion, King's Royal Rifles.

Lieut.-Colonel H. Gore Browne, Commandant.
Captain J. H. G. Feilden, Second-in-Command.

2nd Battalion, Yorkshire Regiment.

Lieut.-Colonel J. A. Fearon, Commandant.
Major J. A. S. Thomson, Second-in-Command.

1st Battalion, North Staffordshire Regiment.

Lieut.-Colonel H. S. B. Hodgkinson, Commandant.
Major A. W. Prior, Second-in-Command.

1st Battalion, Royal Munster Fusiliers Detachment.

Brevet-Major G. D. Crocker.

20th Punjab Infantry, commanded by Brevet-Colonel J. B. Woon.
38th Dogras, commanded by Major H. P. Burne.
1-2nd Gurkhas, commanded by Major D. C. F. Macintyre.
1-39th Garhwal Rifles, commanded by Lieut.-Colonel A. C. O'Donnell.
4th Hyderabad Infantry, commanded by Lieut.-Colonel M. T. Shewen.
18th Madras Infantry, commanded by Lieut.-Colonel W. H. Lowry.
28th Punjab Infantry, commanded by Major G. R. Crawford.
2nd Punjab Infantry, commanded by Brevet-Colonel A. A. Barret.
15th Sikhs, commanded by Lieut.-Colonel G. F. Rowcroft, D.S.O.
4th Rajputs, commanded by Lieut.-Colonel H. Read.
32nd Pioneers, commanded by Lieut.-Colonel H. R. Brander.

23rd Pioneers, commanded by Brevet-Lieut.-Colonel A. F. Hogge.
27th Baluch Infantry, commanded by Lieut.-Colonel G. E. Even.
1-3rd Gurkhas, commanded by Lieut.-Colonel H. Rose.
6th Jats, commanded by Lieut.-Colonel C. H. Westmorland.
33th Rajputs, commanded by Lieut.-Colonel W. T. Fairbrother.
4th Pioneers, commanded by Lieut.-Colonel H. B. Borradaile, D.S.O.
9th Bengal Lancers, commanded by Lieut.-Colonel F. W. P. Angelo.
4th Bombay Cavalry, commanded by Major F. Wadeson.
11th Bengal Lancers, commanded by Lieut.-Colonel F. G. Delamain.
8th Bengal Lancers, commanded by Lieut.-Colonel E. H. Rivett-Carnac.
19th Bengal Lancers, commanded by Lieut.-Colonel H. S. Massey.
18th Bengal Lancers, commanded by Lieut.-Colonel G. A. Money.
3rd Bengal Cavalry, commanded by Lieut.-Colonel H. J. Middleton.
Guides, commanded by Brevet-Lieut.-Colonel G. T. Younghusband, C.B.
5th Punjab Cavalry, commanded by Major H. Templer.
1st Central India Horse, commanded by Lieut.-Colonel F. H. R. Drummond, C.I.E.
14th Bengal Lancers, commanded by Major G. H. Weller.
Royal Scots Fusiliers, commanded by Major H. S. McC. Stannell.

VOLUNTEERS.

Detachments from the following Volunteer Corps:

Behar Light Horse.
Cawnpur Light Horse.
Surma Valley Light Horse.
Calcutta Light Horse.
Bombay Light Horse.
Oudh Light Horse.
Punjab Light Horse.
Assam Valley Light Horse.
Bombay Artillery Volunteers.
Bombay Volunteer Rifles.
Northern Bengal Mounted Rifles.
Dera Dun Mounted Rifles.
Chota Nagpur Mounted Rifles.
Bangalore Rifle Volunteers.
East Indian Railway Volunteer Rifles.
Eastern Bengal State Railway Volunteer Rifles.
1st Great Indian Peninsula Railway Volunteer Rifle Corps.
1st Bombay, Baroda and Central India Railway Volunteers.
Nilgiri Volunteer Rifles.
Berar Volunteer Rifles.
Baluchistan Volunteer Rifles.
Madras Railway Volunteers.
Madras Artillery Volunteers.
Madras Volunteer Guards.
Sind Volunteer Rifles.
Cossipore Railway Volunteers.
Coorg and Mysore Rifle Volunteers.

Printed by BALLANTYNE, HANSON & Co.
London & Edinburgh

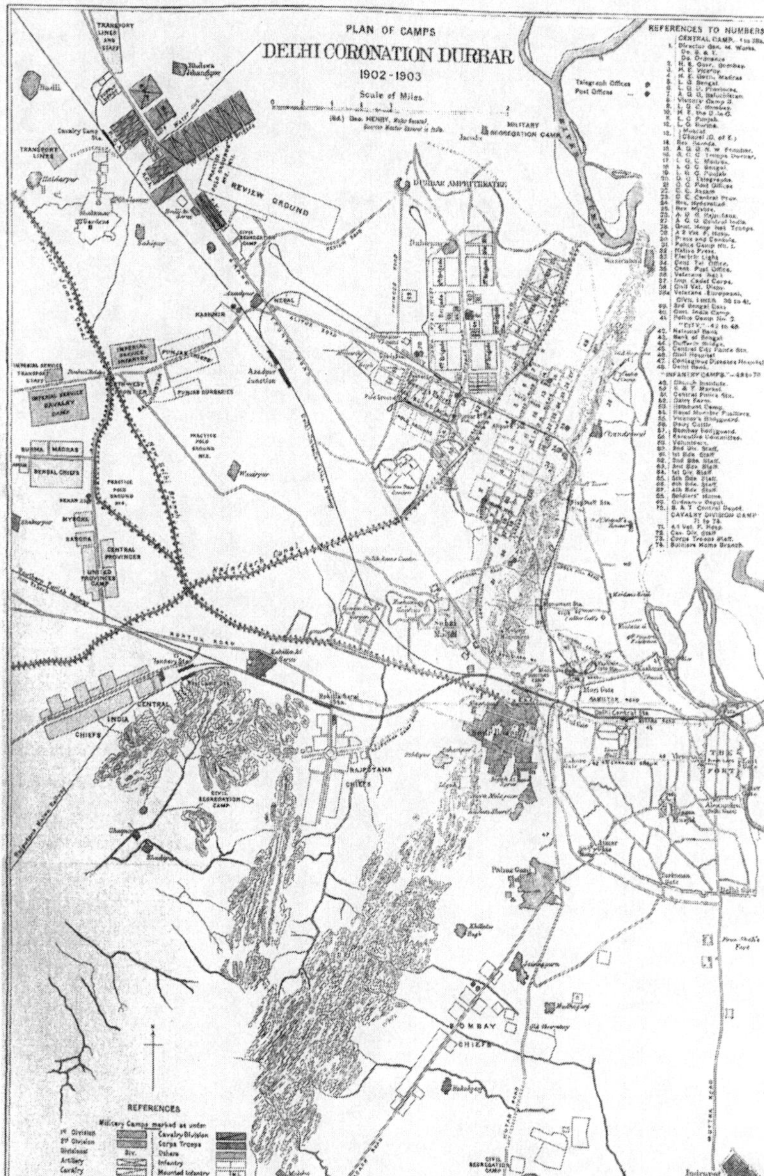
PLAN OF CAMPS
DELHI CORONATION DURBAR
1902-1903
Scale of Miles.
MILITARY SEGREGATION CAMP
DURBAR AMPHITHEATRE
REVIEW GROUND
TRANSPORT LINES
REFERENCES TO NUMBERS.
Telegraph Offices
Post Offices
IMPERIAL SERVICE CAVALRY CAMP
IMPERIAL SERVICE INFANTRY
PUNJAB
PUNJAB DURBARIES
BURMA
MADRAS
BENGAL CHIEFS
MYSORE
BARODA
CENTRAL PROVINCES
UNITED PROVINCES CAMP
CENTRAL INDIA CHIEFS
RAJPUTANA CHIEFS
CIVIL SEGREGATION CAMP
BOMBAY CHIEFS
THE FORT
REFERENCES